Cultural Interface of India with South Asia

CULTURAL INTERFACE OF INDIA WITH SOUTH ASIA

Dr Prem Shankar Choudhary

MD PUBLICATIONS PVT LTD
NEW DELHI
www.mdppl.com

Published by :

MD Publications Pvt Ltd
'MD House', 11, Darya Ganj
New Delhi - 110 002
Phone : +91-11-41563325 (Customer Service)
+91-11-41562846 (Editorial)
E-mail (orders): contact@mdppl.com
Website: www.mdppl.com

ISBN : 978-81-7533-168-6

Published and Printed by Mrs. Rajni Gupta on behalf of **MD Publications Pvt Ltd** at Times Press, New Delhi.

CONTENTS

PREFACE

South Asia, also known as Southern Asia, is a southern region of the Asian continent, which comprises the sub-Himalayan countries and, for some authorities, also includes the adjoining countries on the west and the east. It is surrounded by Western Asia, Central Asia, Eastern Asia, and Southeastern Asia.

Geophysically, the term *Indian subcontinent* is used to describe those regions which lie on the Indian plate, bordered on the north by the Eurasian Plate. However, a good proportion of the Pakistani land mass is not on the Indian plate, but on the fringes of the Iranian plateau. As in the case of the Hindukush mountains, everything to the south-east of the Iranian Plateau is considered South Asia. But, geopolitically, *Southern Asia* subsumes the Indian subcontinent and includes both, the territories found internal to the Indian plate and those in proximity to it. Afghanistan, for instance, is sometimes grouped in this region due to socio-political, historical, and ethnic (Pashtun) ties to neighbouring Pakistan.

The boundaries of South Asia vary based on how South Asia is defined. South Asia's north, east, and west boundaries vary based on definitions used. South Asia's southern border is the Indian Ocean. The UN subregion of Southern Asia's northern boundary would be the Himalayas, its western boundary would be made up of the Iraq-Iran border, Turkey-Iran border, Georgia-Iran border, and the Azerbaijan-Iran border. Its eastern boundary would be the India-Myanmar border and the Bangladesh-Myanmar border.

South Asia, which consists of the nations of Bangladesh, Bhutan, India, Maldives, Nepal, Pakistan, and Sri Lanka, is ethnically diverse, with more than 2,000 ethnic entities with populations ranging from hundreds of millions to small tribal groups. India is the largest country of South Asia. This book analyses history of South Asian countries and political and historical relation between India and other South Asian countries.

I am very grateful to Mr. Pranav Gupta, Director, MD Publications Pvt Ltd for his cooperation and support for this book.

Dr Prem Shankar Choudhary

Chapter 1

India

INDIAN HISTORY

The history of India begins with the Indus Valley Civilization, which spread and flourished in the north-western part of the Indian subcontinent, from c. 3300 to 1300 BCE. Its Mature Harappan period lasted from 2600-1900 BCE. This Bronze Age civilization collapsed at the beginning of the second millennium BCE and was followed by the Iron Age Vedic period, which extended over much of the Indo-Gangetic plains and which witnessed the rise of major kingdoms known as the Mahajanapadas. In one of these kingdoms Magadha, Mahavira and Gautama Buddha were born in the 6th century BCE, who propagated their Shramanic philosophies among the masses.

Later, successive empires and kingdoms ruled the region and enriched its culture from the Achaemenid Persian empire around 543 BCE, to Alexander the Great in 326 BCE. The Indo-Greek Kingdom, founded by Demetrius of Bactria, included Gandhara and Punjab from 184 BCE; it reached its greatest extent under Menander, establishing the Greco-Buddhist period with advances in trade and culture.

The subcontinent was united under the Maurya Empire during the 4th and 3rd centuries BCE. It subsequently became fragmented, with various parts ruled by numerous Middle kingdoms for the next ten centuries. Its northern regions were united once again in the 4th century CE, and remained so for two centuries thereafter, under the Gupta Empire. This period, of Hindu religious and intellectual resurgence, is known among its admirers as the "Golden Age of India." During the same time, and for several centuries afterwards, Southern India, under the rule of the Chalukyas, Cholas, Pallavas and Pandyas, experienced its own golden age, during which Indian civilization, administration, culture, and religion (Hinduism and Buddhism) spread to much of south-east Asia.

Islam arrived on the subcontinent in 712 CE, when the Arab general Muhammad bin Qasim conquered Sindh and Multan in southern Punjab, setting the stage for several successive Islamic invasions between the 10th and 15th centuries CE from Central Asia, leading to the formation of Muslim empires in the Indian subcontinent, including the Ghaznavid, the Ghorid, the Delhi Sultanate and the Mughal Empire. Mughal rule came to cover most of the northern parts of the subcontinent. Mughal rulers introduced middle-eastern art and architecture to India. In addition to the Mughals, several independent Hindu kingdoms, such as the Maratha Empire, the Vijayanagara Empire and various Rajput kingdoms, flourished contemporaneously, in Western and Southern India respectively. The Mughal Empire suffered a gradual decline in the early eighteenth century, which provided opportunities for the Afghans, Balochis and Sikhs to exercise control over large areas in the northwest of the subcontinent until the British East India Company gained ascendancy over South Asia.

Beginning in the mid-18th century and over the next century, India was gradually annexed by the British East India Company. Dissatisfaction with Company rule led to the First War of Indian Independence, after which India was directly administered by the British Crown and witnessed a period of both rapid development of infrastructure and economic decline.

During the first half of the 20th century, a nationwide struggle for independence was launched by the Indian National Congress, and later joined by the Muslim League. The subcontinent gained independence from Great Britain in 1947, after being partitioned into the dominions of India and Pakistan. Pakistan's eastern wing became the nation of Bangladesh in 1971.

STONE AGE

Isolated remains of *Homo erectus* in Hathnora in the Narmada Valley in Central India indicate that India might have been inhabited since at least the Middle Pleistocene era, somewhere between 200,000 to 500,000 years ago. The Mesolithic period in the Indian subcontinent covered a timespan of around 25,000 years, starting around 30,000 years ago. Modern humans seem to have settled the subcontinent towards the end of the last Ice Age, or approximately 12,000 years ago. The first confirmed permanent settlements appeared 9,000 years ago in the Rock Shelters of Bhimbetka in modern Madhya Pradesh. Early Neolithic culture in South Asia is represented by the Mehrgarh findings (7000 BCE onwards) in present day Balochistan, Pakistan. Traces of a Neolithic culture have been found submerged in the Gulf of Khambat, radiocarbon dated to 7500 BCE. Late Neolithic cultures sprang up in the Indus Valley region between 6000 and 2000 BCE and in southern India between 2800 and 1200 BCE.

The region of the subcontinent that is now the country of Pakistan has been inhabited continuously for at least two million years. The ancient history of the region includes some of South Asia's oldest settlements and some of its major civilizations.

The earliest archaeological site in Pakistan is the palaeolithic hominid site in the Soan River valley. Village life began with the Neolithic site of Mehrgarh, while the first urban civilization of the region was the Indus Valley Civilization, with major sites at Mohenjo-daro and Harappa.

BRONZE AGE

The Bronze Age on the Indian subcontinent began around 3300 BCE with the beginning of the Indus Valley Civilization. Inhabitants of the ancient Indus river valley, the Harappans, developed new techniques in metallurgy and produced copper, bronze, lead and tin.

The Indus Valley Civilization which flourished from about 2600 BCE to 1900 BCE marked the beginning of the urban civilization on the subcontinent. The ancient civilization included urban centers such as Harappa and Mohenjo-daro (in modern day Pakistan), Dholavira and Lothal (in modern day India). It was centred on the Indus River and its tributaries, and extended into the Ghaggar-Hakra River valley, the Ganges-Yamuna Doab, Gujarat, and northern Afghanistan.

The civilization is noted for its cities built of brick, road-side drainage system and multi-storied houses. Among the settlements were the major urban centres of Harappa and Mohenjo-daro, as well as Dholavira, Ganweriwala, Lothal, Kalibangan and Rakhigarhi. It is thought by some that geological disturbances and climate change, leading to a gradual deforestation may ultimately have contributed to the civilization's downfall. The decline of the Indus Valley Civilization also included a break down of urban society and of the use of distinctively urban traits such as the use of writing and seals.

INDUS VALLEY CIVILIZATION

The Indus Valley Civilization (c. 3000–1500 BCE, Mature period 2600–1900 BCE), abbreviated **IVC**, was an ancient civilization that flourished in the Indus River basin. Primarily centred in the Sindh and Punjab provinces of Pakistan, and Gujarat and Rajasthan in India, it extends westward into the Balochistan province of Pakistan as well. Remains have been excavated from Afghanistan, Turkmenistan and Iran, as well. The mature phase of this civilization is technically known as the **Harappan Civilization**, after the first of its cities to be unearthed; Harappa in Pakistan. Excavation of IVC sites has been ongoing since 1920, with important breakthroughs occurring as recently as 1999.

The civilization is sometimes referred to as the **Indus Ghaggar-Hakra civilization** or the **Indus-Sarasvati civilization**. The appellation *Indus-Sarasvati* is based on the possible identification of the Ghaggar-Hakra River with the Sarasvati River mentioned in the Rigveda, but this usage is disputed on linguistic and geographical grounds.

The IVC has been tentatively identified with the toponym Meluhha known from Sumerian records. It has been compared in particular with the civilizations of Elam (also in the context of the Elamo-Dravidian hypothesis) and with Minoan Crete (because of isolated cultural parallels such as the ubiquitous goddess worship and depictions of bull-leaping). The mature (Harappan) phase of the IVC is contemporary to the Early to Middle Bronze Age in the Ancient Near East, in particular the Old Elamite period, Early Dynastic to Ur III Mesopotamia, Prepalatial Minoan Crete and Old Kingdom to First Intermediate Period Egypt.

The language of the IVC has not yet been determined. Proto-Dravidian, Proto-Indo-Iranian, Proto-Munda, the prefixing Para-Munda and a "Language X" or "lost phylum" perhaps related or ancestral to the Nihali language have been proposed as the language.

DISCOVERY AND EXCAVATION

The ruins of Harrappa were first described in 1842 by Charles Masson in his *Narrative of Various Journeys in Baluchistan, Afghanistan and the Panjab,* where locals talked of an ancient city extending "thirteen cosses" (about 25 miles), but no archaeological interest would attach to this for nearly a century.

In 1856, British engineers John and William Brunton were laying the East Indian Railway Company line connecting the cities of Karachi and Lahore. John wrote: "I was much exercised in my mind how we were to get ballast for the line of the railway." They were told of an ancient ruined city near the lines, called Brahminabad. Visiting the city, he found it full of hard well-burnt bricks, and "convinced that there was a grand quarry for the ballast I wanted", the city of Brahminabad was reduced to ballast. A few months later, further north, John's brother William Brunton's "section of the line ran near another ruined city, bricks from which had already been used by villagers in the nearby village of Harappa at the same site. These bricks now provided ballast along 93 miles (150 km) of the railroad track running from Karachi to Lahore."

In 1872–75 Alexander Cunningham published the first Harappan seal (with an erroneous identification as Brahmi letters). It was half a century later, in 1912, that more Harappan seals were discovered by J. Fleet, prompting an excavation campaign under Sir John Hubert Marshall in 1921–22 and resulting in the discovery of the hitherto unknown civilization at Harappa by Sir John Marshall, Rai Bahadur Daya Ram Sahni and Madho Sarup Vats, and at Mohenjo-daro by Rakhal Das Banerjee, E. J. H. MacKay, and Sir John Marshall. By 1931, much of Mohenjo-Daro had been excavated, but excavations continued, such as that led by Sir Mortimer Wheeler, director of the Archaeological Survey of India in 1944. Among other archaeologists who worked on IVC sites before the partition of the subcontinent in 1947 were Ahmad Hasan Dani, Brij Basi Lal, Nani Gopal Majumdar, and Sir Marc Aurel Stein.

Following the partition of British India, the bulk of the archaeological finds were inherited by Pakistan where most of the IVC was based, and excavations from this time include those led by Sir Mortimer Wheeler in 1949, archaeological adviser to the Government of Pakistan. Outposts of the Indus Valley civilization were excavated as far west as Sutkagan Dor in Baluchistan, as far north as at Shortugai on the Amudarya or Oxus River in current Afghanistan.

PERIODISATION

The mature phase of the Harappan civilization lasted from c. 2600 to 1900 BCE. With the inclusion of the predecessor and successor cultures—Early Harappan and Late Harappan, respectively—the entire Indus Valley Civilization may be taken to have lasted from the 33rd to the 14th centuries BCE. Two terms are employed for the periodization of the IVC: *Phases* and *Eras*. The Early Harappan, Mature Harappan, and Late Harappan phases are also called the Regionalisation, Integration, and Localisation eras, respectively, with the Regionalization era reaching back to the Neolithic Mehrgarh II period. "Discoveries at Mehrgarh changed the entire concept of the Indus civilization," according to Ahmad Hasan Dani, professor emeritus at Quaid-e-Azam University, Islamabad. "There we have the whole sequence, right from the beginning of settled village life."

GEOGRAPHY

The Indus Valley Civilization encompassed most of Pakistan, extending from Balochistan to Sindh, with an upward reach to Punjab from east of the Jhelum River to Rupar on the upper Sutlej; recently, Indus sites have been discovered in Pakistan's northwestern Frontier Province as well. Other IVC colonies can be found in Afghanistan while smaller isolated colonies can be found as far away as Turkmenistan and in Gujurat. Coastal settlements extended from Sutkagan Dor in Western Baluchistan to Lothal in Gujarat. An Indus Valley site has been found on the Oxus River at Shortughai in northern Afghanistan, in the Gomal River valley in northwestern Pakistan, at Manda on the Beas River near Jammu, India, and at Alamgirpur on the Hindon River, only 28 km from Delhi. Indus Valley sites have been found most often on rivers, but also on the ancient seacoast, for example, Balakot, and on islands, for example, Dholavira.

There is evidence of dry river beds overlapping with the Hakra channel in Pakistan and the seasonal Ghaggar River in India. Many Indus Valley (or *Harappan*) sites have been discovered along the Ghaggar-Hakra beds. Among them are: Rupar, Rakhigarhi, Sothi, Kalibangan, and Ganwariwala. According to J. G. Shaffer and D. A. Lichtenstein, the Harappan Civilization "is a fusion of the Bagor, Hakra, and Koti Dij traditions or 'ethnic groups' in the Ghaggar-Hakra valley on the borders of India and Pakistan."

According to some archaeologists, over 500 Harappan sites have been discovered along the dried up river beds of the Ghaggar-Hakra River and its tributaries, in contrast to only about 100 along the Indus and its tributaries; consequently, in their opinion, the appellation *Indus Ghaggar-Hakra civilisation* or *Indus-Saraswati civilisation* is justified. However, these politically inspired arguments are disputed by other archaeologists who state that the Ghaggar-Hakra desert area has been left untouched by settlements and agriculture since the end of the Indus period and hence shows more sites than found in the alluvium of the Indus valley; second, that the number of Harappan sites along the Ghaggar-Hakra river beds have been exaggerated and that the Ghaggar-Hakra, when it existed, was a tributary of the Indus, so the new nomenclature is redundant. "Harappan

Civilization" remains the correct one, according to the common archaeological usage of naming a civilization after its first findspot.

ORIGINS

There are several theories as to the origin of the Indus Valley civilization. The earliest hypothesis was that it was an early form of a Vedic and early Sanskrit civilization which would come to dominate most of South Asia, which was presumed to have been characterized by influence from Indo-European migrations. However, this theory began to be rejected when no signs of the traditional culture associated with the Vedas was uncovered in that of the Indus Valley. The absence of horses amongst the many realistic representations of animals was also considered significant, considering the importance of horses and chariots to the culture described in the Vedas. Detailed bone analysis has revealed that the horse itself was introduced to the subcontinent only at the beginning of the second millennium B.C., which contributes to the chronological problem with this theory. Finally, the concept of urban life which dominates the Indus Valley civilization is foreign to the more rural lifestyle which is described in the Vedas.

The next theory put forward was that the civilization was of proto-Dravidian origin. This theory was first proposed by researchers from Russia and Finland who attempted to show that Indus valley symbols could be derived from the Dravidian language group. Today, the Dravidian language family is concentrated mostly in southern India and northern Sri Lanka, but pockets of it still remain throughout the rest of India and Pakistan (the Brahui language), which lends credence to the theory. Finnish Indologist Asko Parpola concludes that the uniformity of the Indus inscriptions precludes any possibility of widely different languages being used, and that an early form of Dravidian language must have been the language of the Indus people. However, the proto-Dravidian origin theory is far from being confirmed due to an emphasis on linguistic connection while evidence of a broader cultural connection remains to be found.

EARLY HARAPPAN

The Early Harappan Ravi Phase, named after the nearby Ravi River, lasted from circa 3300 BCE until 2800 BCE. It is related to the Hakra Phase, identified in the Ghaggar-Hakra River Valley to the west, and predates the Kot Diji Phase (2800-2600 BCE, Harappan 2), named after a site in northern Sindh, Pakistan, near Mohenjo Daro. The earliest examples of the Indus script date from around 3000 BCE.

The mature phase of earlier village cultures is represented by Rehman Dheri and Amri in Pakistan. Kot Diji (Harappan 2) represents the phase leading up to Mature Harappan, with the citadel representing centralised authority and an increasingly urban quality of life. Another town of this stage was found at Kalibangan in India on the Hakra River.

Trade networks linked this culture with related regional cultures and distant sources of raw materials, including lapis lazuli and other materials for bead-making. Villagers had, by this time, domesticated numerous crops, including peas, sesame seeds, dates and cotton, as well as various animals, including the water buffalo. Early Harappan communities turned to large urban centres by 2600 BCE, from where the mature Harappan phase started.

MATURE HARAPPAN

By 2600 BCE, the Early Harappan communities had been turned into large urban centers. Such urban centers include Harappa and Mohenjo-daro in Pakistan and Lothal in India. In total, over 1,052 cities and settlements have been found, mainly in the general region of the Indus Rivers and their tributaries.

CITIES

A sophisticated and technologically advanced urban culture is evident in the Indus Valley Civilization making them the first urban centers in the region. The quality of municipal town planning suggests the knowledge of urban planning and efficient municipal governments which placed a high priority on hygiene, or, alternately, accessibility to the means of religious ritual.

As seen in Harappa, Mohenjo-daro and the recently partially excavated Rakhigarhi, this urban plan included the world's first urban sanitation systems. Within the city, individual homes or groups of homes obtained water from wells. From a room that appears to have been set aside for bathing, waste water was directed to covered drains, which lined the major streets. Houses opened only to inner courtyards and smaller lanes. The house-building in some villages in the region still resembles in some respects the house-building of the Harappans.

The ancient Indus systems of sewerage and drainage that were developed and used in cities throughout the Indus region were far more advanced than any found in contemporary urban sites in the Middle East and even more efficient than those in many areas of Pakistan and India today. The advanced architecture of the Harappans is shown by their impressive dockyards, granaries, warehouses, brick platforms and protective walls. The massive walls of Indus cities most likely protected the Harappans from floods and may have dissuaded military conflicts.

The purpose of the citadel remains debated. In sharp contrast to this civilization's contemporaries, Mesopotamia and Ancient Egypt, no large monumental structures were built. There is no conclusive evidence of palaces or temples—or of kings, armies, or priests. Some structures are thought to have been granaries. Found at one city is an enormous well-built bath, which may have been a public bath. Although the citadels were walled, it is far from clear that these structures were defensive. They may have been built to divert flood waters.

Most city dwellers appear to have been traders or artisans, who lived with others pursuing the same occupation in well-defined neighborhoods. Materials from distant regions were used in the cities for constructing seals, beads and other objects. Among the artifacts discovered were beautiful glazed faïence beads. Steatite seals have images of animals, people (perhaps gods) and other types of inscriptions, including the yet undeciphered writing system of the Indus Valley Civilization. Some of the seals were used to stamp clay on trade goods and most probably had other uses as well.

Although some houses were larger than others, Indus Civilization cities were remarkable for their apparent, if relative, egalitarianism. All the houses had access to water and drainage facilities. This gives the impression of a society with relatively low wealth concentration, though clear social leveling is seen in personal adornments.

SCIENCE

The people of the Indus Civilization achieved great accuracy in measuring length, mass, and time. They were among the first to develop a system of uniform weights and measures. Their measurements are said to be extremely precise; however, a comparison of available objects indicates large scale variation across the Indus territories. Their smallest division, which is marked on an ivory scale found in Lothal, was approximately 1.704 mm, the smallest division ever recorded on a scale of the Bronze Age. Harappan engineers followed the decimal division of measurement for all practical purposes, including the measurement of mass as revealed by their hexahedron weights.

These chert weights were in a perfect ratio of 4:2:1 with weights of 0.05, 0.1, 0.2, 0.5, 1, 2, 5, 10, 20, 50, 100, 200, and 500 units, with each unit weighing approximately 28 grams, similar to the English Imperial ounce or Greek uncia, and smaller objects were weighed in similar ratios with the units of 0.871. However, as in other cultures, actual weights were not uniform throughout the area. The weights and measures later used in Kautilya's *Arthashastra* (4th century BCE) are the same as those used in Lothal.

Unique Harappan inventions include an instrument which was used to measure whole sections of the horizon and the tidal lock. In addition, Harappans evolved some new techniques in metallurgy and produced copper, bronze, lead and tin. The engineering skill of the Harappans was remarkable, especially in building docks after a careful study of tides, waves and currents. The function of the so-called "dock" at Lothal, however, is disputed.

In 2001, archaeologists studying the remains of two men from Mehrgarh, Pakistan, made the discovery that the people of the Indus Valley Civilisation, from the early Harappan periods, had knowledge of proto-dentistry. Later, in April 2006, it was announced in the scientific journal *Nature* that the oldest (and first early Neolithic) evidence for the drilling of human teeth *in vivo* (i.e., in a living person) was found in Mehrgarh. Eleven drilled molar crowns from nine adults were discovered in a Neolithic graveyard in Mehrgarh that dates from 7,500-9,000 years ago. According to the authors, their discoveries point to a tradition of proto-dentistry in the early farming cultures of that region.

A touchstone bearing gold streaks was found in Banawali, which was probably used for testing the purity of gold (such a technique is still used in some parts of India).

ARTS AND CULTURE

Various sculptures, seals, pottery, gold jewelry and anatomically detailed figurines in terracotta, bronze and steatite have been found at the excavation sites.

A number of gold, terra-cotta and stone figurines of girls in dancing poses reveal the presence of some dance form. Also, these terra-cotta figurines included cows, bears, monkeys, and dogs. Sir John Marshall is known to have reacted with surprise when he saw the famous Indus bronze statuette of a slender-limbed dancing girl in Mohenjo-daro:

... When I first saw them I found it difficult to believe that they were prehistoric; they seemed to completely upset all established ideas about early art, and culture. Modeling such as this was unknown in the ancient world up to the Hellenistic age of Greece, and I thought, therefore, that some mistake must surely have been made; that these figures had found their way into levels some 3000 years older than those to which they properly belonged. ... Now, in these statuettes, it is just this anatomical truth which is so startling; that makes us wonder whether, in this all-important matter, Greek artistry could possibly have been anticipated by the sculptors of a far-off age on the banks of the Indus.

Many crafts "such as shell working, ceramics, and agate and glazed steatite bead making" were used in the making of necklaces, bangles, and other ornaments from all phases of Harappan sites and some of these crafts are still practiced in the subcontinent today. Some make-up and toiletry items (a special kind of combs (kakai), the use of collyrium and a special three-in-one toiletry gadget) that were found in Harappan contexts still have similar counterparts in modern India. Terracotta female figurines were found (ca. 2800-2600 BCE) which had red color applied to the "manga" (line of partition of the hair).

Seals have been found at Mohenjo-daro depicting a figure standing on its head, and another sitting cross-legged in what some call a yoga-like pose.

A harp-like instrument depicted on an Indus seal and two shell objects found at Lothal indicate the use of stringed musical instruments. The Harappans also made various toys and games, among them cubical dice (with one to six holes on the faces), which were found in sites like Mohenjo-daro.

TRADE AND TRANSPORTATION

The Indus civilization's economy appears to have depended significantly on trade, which was facilitated by major advances in transport technology. These advances included bullock carts that are identical to those seen throughout South Asia today, as well as boats. Most of these boats were probably small, flat-bottomed craft, perhaps driven by sailer, similar to those one can see on the Indus River today; however, there is secondary evidence of sea-going craft. Archaeologists have discovered a massive, dredged canal and what they regard as a docking facility at the coastal city of Lothal in western India (Gujarat state). An extensive canal network, used for irrigation, has however also been discovered by H.P. Francfort.

During 4300–3200 BCE of the chalcolithic period (copper age), the Indus Valley Civilization area shows ceramic similarities with southern Turkmenistan and northern Iran which suggest considerable mobility and trade. During the Early Harappan period (about 3200–2600 BCE), similarities in pottery, seals, figurines, ornaments, etc., document intensive caravan trade with Central Asia and the Iranian plateau.

Judging from the dispersal of Indus civilisation artifacts, the trade networks, economically, integrated a huge area, including portions of Afghanistan, the coastal regions of Persia, northern and western India, and Mesopotamia.

There was an extensive maritime trade network operating between the Harappan and Mesopotamian civilizations as early as the middle Harappan Phase, with much commerce being handled by "middlemen merchants from Dilmun" (modern Bahrain and Failaka located in the Persian Gulf). Such long-distance sea trade became feasible with the innovative development of plank-built watercraft, equipped with a single central mast supporting a sail of woven rushes or cloth.

Several coastal settlements like Sotkagen-dor (astride Dasht River, north of Jiwani), Sokhta Koh (astride Shadi River, north of Pasni) and Balakot (near Sonmiani) in Pakistan along with Lothal in India testify to their role as Harappan trading outposts. Shallow harbors located at the estuary of rivers opening into the sea allowed brisk maritime trade with Mesopotamian cities.

AGRICULTURE

Some post-1980 studies indicate that food production was largely indigenous to the Indus Valley. It is known that the people of Mehrgarh used domesticated wheats and barley, and the major cultivated cereal crop was naked six-row barley, a crop derived from two-row barley. Archaeologist Jim G. Shaffer (1999: 245) writes that the Mehrgarh site "demonstrates that food production was an indigenous South Asian phenomenon" and that the data support interpretation of "the prehistoric urbanization and complex social organization in South Asia as based on indigenous, but not isolated, cultural developments." Others, such as Dorian Fuller, however, indicate that it took some 2000 years before Middle Eastern wheat was acclimatised to South Asian conditions.

WRITING OR SYMBOL SYSTEM

Well over 400 distinct Indus symbols (some say 600) have been found on seals, small tablets, or ceramic pots and over a dozen other materials, including a "signboard" that apparently once hung over the gate of the inner citadel of the Indus city of Dholavira.

Typical Indus inscriptions are no more than four or five characters in length, most of which (aside from the Dholavira "signboard") are exquisitely tiny; the longest on a single surface, which is less than 1 inch (2.54 cm) square, is 17 signs long; the longest on any object (found on three different faces of a mass-produced object) has a length of 26 symbols.

While the Indus Valley Civilization is often characterized as a literate society on the evidence of these inscriptions, this description has been challenged on linguistic and archaeological grounds: it has been pointed out that the brevity of the inscriptions is unparalleled in any known premodern literate society. Based partly on this evidence, a controversial paper by Farmer, Sproat, and Witzel (2004) argues that the Indus system did not encode language, but was instead similar to a variety of non-linguistic sign systems used extensively in the Near East and other societies. Others have claimed on occasion that the symbols were exclusively used for economic transactions, but this claim leaves unexplained the appearance of Indus symbols on many ritual objects, many of which were mass-produced in molds. No parallels to these mass-produced inscriptions are known in any other early ancient civilizations.

Photos of many of the thousands of extant inscriptions are published in the *Corpus of Indus Seals and Inscriptions* (1987, 1991), edited by A. Parpola and his colleagues. Publication of a final third volume, which will reportedly republish photos taken in the 1920s and 1930s of hundreds of lost or stolen inscriptions, along with many discovered in the last few decades, has been announced for several years, but has not yet found its way into print. For now, researchers must supplement the materials in the *Corpus* by study of the tiny photos in the excavation reports of Marshall (1931), Mackay (1938, 1943), Wheeler (1947), or reproductions in more recent scattered sources.

RELIGION

In view of the large number of figurines found in the Indus valley, it has been widely suggested that the Harappan people worshipped a Mother goddess symbolizing fertility. However, this view has been disputed by S. Clark. Some Indus valley seals show swastikas which are found in later religions and mythologies, especially in Indian religions such as Hinduism. The earliest evidence for elements of Hinduism are present before and during the early Harappan period. Phallic symbols resembling the Hindu Siva lingam have been found in the Harappan remains.

Many Indus valley seals show animals. One famous seal shows a figure seated in a posture reminiscent of the Lotus position and surrounded by animals was named after Pashupati (lord of cattle), an epithet of Shiva and Rudra.

In the earlier phases of their culture, the Harappans buried their dead; however, later, especially in the Cemetery H culture of the late Harrapan period, they also cremated their dead and buried the ashes in burial urns, a transition notably also alluded to in the Rigveda, where the forefathers "both cremated (*agnidagdhá-*) and uncremated (*ánagnidagdha-*)" are invoked (RV 10.15.14).

LATE HARAPPAN

Around 1800 BCE, signs of a gradual decline began to emerge, and by around 1700 BCE, most of the cities were abandoned. However, the Indus Valley Civilization did not disappear suddenly, and many elements of the Indus Civilization can be found in later cultures. Current archaeological data suggests that material culture classified as Late Harappan may have persisted until at least c. 1000-900 BCE and was partially contemporaneous with the Painted Grey Ware culture. Archaeologists have emphasised that, just as in most areas of the world, there was a continuous series of cultural developments. These link "the so-called two major phases of urbanisation in South Asia".

A possible natural reason for the IVC's decline is connected with climate change that is also signaled for the neighboring areas of the Middle East: The Indus valley climate grew significantly cooler and drier from about 1800 BCE, linked to a general weakening of the monsoon at that time. Alternatively, a crucial factor may have been the disappearance of substantial portions of the Ghaggar-Hakra river system. A tectonic event may have diverted the system's sources toward the Ganges Plain, though there is complete uncertainty about the date of this event as most settlements inside Ghaggar-Hakra river beds have not yet been dated. Although this particular factor is speculative, and not generally accepted, the decline of the IVC, as with any other civilization, will have been due to a combination of various reasons. New geological research is now being conducted by a group led by Peter Clift, from the University of Aberdeen, to investigate how the courses of rivers have changed in this region since 8000 years ago in order to test whether climate or river reorganizations are responsible for the decline of the Harappan. A 2004 paper indicated that the isotopes of the Ghaggar-Hakra system do not come from the Himalayan glaciers, and were rain-fed instead, contradicting a Harappan time mighty "Sarasvati' river.

LEGACY

In the aftermath of the Indus Civilization's collapse, regional cultures emerged, to varying degrees showing the influence of the Indus Civilization. In the formerly great city of Harappa, burials have been found that correspond to a regional culture called the Cemetery H culture. At the same time, the Ochre Coloured Pottery culture expanded from Rajasthan into the Gangetic Plain. The Cemetery H culture has the earliest evidence for cremation, a practice dominant in Hinduism until today.

IRON AGE

The **Iron Age** in the **Indian subcontinent** succeeds the Late Harappan (Cemetery H) culture, also known as the last phase of the Indus Valley Tradition. The cultures of the Punjab and Rajasthan in this phase spread eastward across the Gangetic plain. For this reason, the succession of Iron Age cultures of northern India and Pakistan are also known as the **Indo-Gangetic Tradition**.

The Painted Gray Ware culture (ca 1200-800 BCE) and the Northern Black Polished Ware culture (ca 700-300 BCE) belong to the "Regionalization Era" of the Indo-Gangetic Tradition. This corresponds to the later phase of the Vedic period and Mahajanapadas and the rise of the Maurya Empire. Chandragupta Maurya and Ashoka the Great belong to this period.

The earliest Iron Age site in South India is Hallur.

India enters the classical period from the 6th century BC with the births of Mahavira and Gautama Buddha, followed by the Sanskrit grammar of Panini, the Edicts of Ashoka, and the emerging Middle kingdoms of India.

VEDIC PERIOD

The **Vedic Period** (or **Vedic Age**) is the period in the history of India during which the Vedas, the oldest sacred texts of Hinduism, were being composed. Scholars place the Vedic period in the second and first millennia BCE continuing up to the 6th century BCE based on literary evidence.

The associated culture, sometimes referred to as **Vedic civilization**, was centered in northern and northwestern part of the Indian subcontinent. Its early phase saw the formation of various kingdoms of ancient India. In its late phase (from ca. 600 BCE), it saw the rise of the Mahajanapadas, and was succeeded by the Maurya Empire (from ca. 320 BCE), the golden age, classical age of Sanskrit literature, and the Middle kingdoms of India.

The reconstruction of the history of Vedic India is based on text-internal details. Linguistically, the Vedic texts could be classified in five chronological strata:

1. **Rigvedic**: The Rigveda is by far the most archaic of the Vedic texts preserved, and it retains many common Indo-Iranian elements, both in language and in content, that are not present in any other Vedic texts. Its creation must have taken place over several centuries, and apart from that of the youngest books (first part of 1 and all of 10), would have been complete by 1000 BCE. Archaeologically, this period may correspond with the Gandhara Grave Culture, the *Cemetery H* culture of the Punjab and the *Ochre Coloured Pottery culture* (OCP) further east. It is undisputed that there is a strong component in certain traits of cultural continuity of the indigenous IVC.

2. **Mantra language**: This period includes both the mantra and prose language of the Atharvaveda (Paippalada and Shaunakiya), the Rigveda Khilani, the Samaveda Samhita (containing some 75 mantras not in the Rigveda), and the mantras of the Yajurveda. Many of these texts are largely derived from the Rigveda, but have undergone certain changes, both by linguistic change and by reinterpretation. Conspicuous changes include change of *vishva* "all" by *sarva,* and the spread of the *kuru-* verbal stem (for Rigvedic *krno-*). This is the time of the early Iron Age in north-western India, corresponding to the *Black and Red Ware* (BRW) culture, and the kingdom of the Kurus, dating from ca. the 10th century BCE.

3. **Samhita prose**: This period marks the beginning of the collection and codification of a Vedic canon. An important linguistic change is the complete loss of the injunctive. The Brahmana part ('commentary' on mantras and ritual) of the Black Yajurveda (MS, KS, TS) belongs to this period. Archaeologically, the *Painted Grey Ware* (PGW) culture from ca. 900 BCE corresponds, and the shift of the political center from the Kurus to the Pancalas on the Ganges.

4. **Brahmana prose**: The Brahmanas proper of the four Vedas belong to this period, as well as the Aranyakas, the oldest of the Upanishads (BAU, ChU, JUB) and the oldest Shrautasutras (BSS, VadhSS).

5. **Sutra language**: This is the last stratum of Vedic Sanskrit leading up to c. 500 BCE, comprising the bulk of the Œrauta and Grhya Sutras, and some Upanishads (e.g. KathU, MaitrU). All but the five prose Upanishads are post-Buddhist). Videha (N. Bihar) as a third political center is established.

6. **Epic and Paninian Sanskrit**: The language of the Mahabharata and Ramayana epics, and the Classical Sanskrit described by Panini is considered post-Vedic, and belongs to the time after 500 BCE. Archaeologically, the rapid spread of *Northern Black Polished Ware* (NBP) over all of northern India corresponds to this period. The earliest Vedanta, the Buddha, and the Pali Prakrit dialect of Buddhist scripture belong to this period.

Historical records set in only after the end of the Vedic period, and remain scarce throughout the Indian Middle Ages. The end of Vedic India is marked by linguistic, cultural and political changes. The grammar of Panini marks a final apex in the codification of Sutra texts, and at the same time the beginning of Classical Sanskrit. The invasion of Darius I of the Indus valley in the early 6th century BCE marks the beginning of outside influence, continued in the kingdoms of the Indo Greeks, new waves of immigration from 150 BCE (Abhira, Shaka), Kushan and ultimately the Islamic Sultans. The most important historical source of the geography of post-Vedic India is the 2nd century Greek historian Arrian whose report is based on the Mauryan time ambassador to Patna, Megasthenes.

RIGVEDIC PERIOD

The origin of the Vedic civilization and its relation to the Indus Valley civilization, Indo-Aryan migration and Gandhara Grave culture related cultures remains controversial and politically charged in Indian society, often leading to disputes on the history of Vedic culture. The Rigveda is primarily a collection of religious hymns, and allusions to, but not explanation of, various myths and stories, mainly in the younger books 1 and 10. The oldest hymns, probably in books 2–7, although some hold book 9, the Soma Mandala, to be even more ancient, contain many elements inherited from pre-Vedic, common Indo-Iranian society. Therefore, it is difficult to define the precise beginning of the "Rigvedic period", as it emerges seamlessly from the era preceding it. Also, due to the semi-nomadic nature of the society described, it cannot be easily localized, and in its earliest phase describes tribes that were essentially on the move.

Rigvedic Aryans have a lot in common with the Andronovo culture and the Mittanni kingdoms as well as with early Iranians. The Andronovo culture is believed to be the site of the first horse-drawn chariots.

POLITICAL ORGANIZATION

The *grama* (wagon train), *vis* and *jana* were political units of the early Vedic Aryans. A *vish* was a subdivision of a *jana* or "krishti", and a *grama* was a smaller unit than the other two. The leader of a *grama* was called *gramani* and that of a *vish* was called *vishpati*.

The *rashtra* (polity) was governed by a *rajan* (chieftain, 'king'). The king is often referred to as *gopa* (protector) and occasionally as *samrat* (supreme ruler). He governed the people with their consent and approval. He was elected from a restricted class of 'royals' (rajanya). There were various types of meetings such as the *vidhata* or "Sabha". Gana was the non-monarchial assembly that is a parallel one to the monarchial assemblies of that period headed by Jyestha the same was referred in Buddhist text named Jettaka.The Sabha, situated outside of settlement, was restricted to the Vratyas, bands of roving Brahmins and Kshatriyas in search of cattle, with a common woman (pumscali) while the vidhata was the potlatch-like ritual distribution of bounty .

The main duty of the king was to protect the tribe. He was aided by several functionaries, including the *purohita* (chaplain) and the *senani* (army chief; *sena*: army). The former not only gave advice to the ruler but also was his chariot driver and practiced spells and charms for success in war. Soldiers on foot (*pattis*) and on chariots (*rathins*), armed with bow and arrow, were common. The king employed *spaœ* (spies) and *dutas* (messengers). He collected taxes (originally ceremonial gifts, *bali*), from the people which he had to redistribute.

SOCIETY AND ECONOMY

The concept of *varna* (class) and the rules of marriage were rigid as is evident from Vedic verses (RV 10.90, W. Rau 1957). The status of the Brahmins and Kshatriyas was higher than that of the Vaishyas and Shudras. The Brahmins were specialized in creating poetry, preserving the sacred texts, and carrying out various types of rituals. Functioning as intellectual leadership, they also restricted social mobility between the varnas, as in the fields of science, war, literature, religion and the environment. The proper enunciation of verses in ritual was considered essential for prosperity and success in war and harvests. Kshatriyas amassed wealth (cattle), and many commissioned the performance of sacrifices. Kshatriyas helped in administering the polity, maintained the structure of society and the economy of a tribe, and helped in maintaining law and order.

In the Early Vedic Period all the three upper classes Brahmins, Kshatriyas, and Vaishyas were considered as —relatively— equal Arya, but in the Later Vedic Age the Brahmins and Kshatriyas became upper class. The Vaishyas were pastoralists and farmers; the Shudras were the lower class; they included artisans and were meant to serve the upper three classes . As the caste system became deep-rooted there were many restrictions and rules which were to be followed.

Cattle were held in high esteem and frequently appear in Rigvedic hymns; goddesses were often compared to cows, and gods to bulls. Agriculture grew more prominent with time as the community gradually began to settle down in post-Rigvedic times. The economy was based on bartering with cattle and other valuables such as salt or metals.

Families were patrilineal, and people prayed for the abundance of sons. The Society was strictly organized in a system of four varna (classes, to be distinguished from caste, jati)

VEDIC RELIGIOUS PRACTICES

The Vedic forms of belief are the precursor to modern Hinduism. Texts considered to date to the Vedic period are mainly the four Vedas, but the Brahmanas, Aranyakas and the older Upanishads as well as the oldest Shrautasutras are also considered to be Vedic. The Vedas record the liturgy connected with the rituals and sacrifices performed by the 16 or 17 Shrauta priests and the purohitas.

The rishis, the composers of the hymns of the Rigveda, were considered inspired poets and seers (in post-Vedic times understood as "hearers" of an eternally existing Veda, *Œrauta* means "what is heard").

The mode of worship was performance of sacrifices which included the chanting of Rigvedic verses, singing of Samans and 'mumbling' of offering mantras (Yajus) . The priests executed rituals for the three upper classes (varna) of Vedic society, strictly excluding the Sudras. People offered for abundance of rain, cattle, sons, long life and gaining 'heaven'.

The main deities of the Vedic pantheon were Indra, Agni (the sacrificial fire), and Soma and some deities of social order such as Mitra-Varuna, Aryaman, Bhaga and Amsa, further nature deities such as Surya (the Sun), Vayu (the wind), Prithivi (the earth). Goddesses included Ushas (the dawn), Prithvi and Aditi (the mother of the Aditya gods or sometimes the cow). Rivers, especially Saraswati, were also considered goddesses. Deities were not viewed as all-powerful. The relationship between humans and the deity was one of transaction, with Agni (the sacrificial fire) taking the role of messenger between the two. Strong traces of a common Indo-Iranian religion remain visible, especially in the Soma cult and the fire worship, both of which are preserved in Zoroastrianism. The Ashvamedha (horse sacrifice) has parallels in the 2nd millennium BC Andronovo culture, in Rome and old Ireland, was continued in India until at least the 4th century AD and revived under Jay Singh in 1740 AD.

Vedic religion evolved into the Hindu paths of Yoga and Vedanta, a religious path considering itself the 'essence' of the Vedas, interpreting the Vedic pantheon as a unitary view of the universe with 'God' (Brahman) seen as immanent and transcendent in the forms of Ishvara and Brahman. These post-Vedic systems of thought, along with later texts like Upanishads, epics (namely Gita of Mahabharat), have been fully preserved and form the basis of modern Hinduism. The ritualistic traditions of Vedic religion are preserved in the conservative Œrauta tradition, in part with the exception of animal sacrifice, which was mostly abandoned by the higher castes by the end of the Vedic period, partly under the influence of the Buddhist and Jain religions, and their criticism of such practices.

THE LATER VEDIC PERIOD

The transition from the early to the later Vedic period was marked by the emergence of agriculture as the dominant economic activity and a corresponding decline in the significance of cattle rearing. Several changes went hand in hand with this. For instance, several large kingdoms arose because of the increasing importance of land and long distance trade. The late Vedic period, from ca. 500 BCE onward, more or less seamlessly blends into the period of the Middle kingdoms of India known from historical sources.

KINGDOMS

The late Vedic period was marked by the rise of the sixteen *Mahajanapadas* referred to in some of the literature. The power of the king and the Kshatriyas greatly increased. Rulers gave themselves titles like *ekarat* (the one ruler), *sarvabhauma* (ruler of all the earth) and *chakravartin* ('who moves the wheel'). The kings performed sacrifices like *rajasuya*, (royal consecration) *vajapeya* (including a chariot race) and, for supreme dominance over other kings, the ashvamedha (horse sacrifice). The coronation ceremony was a major social occasion. Several functionaries, in addition to the purohita and the senani, took part. The role of the people in political decision making and the status of the Vaishyas as such was greatly decreased.

PERSIAN AND GREEK INVASIONS

Much of the northwestern Indian Subcontinent (present day Eastern Afghanistan and Pakistan) came under the rule of the Persian Achaemenid Empire in c. 520 BCE during the reign of Darius the Great, and remained so for two centuries thereafter. In 334 BCE, Alexander the Great conquered Asia Minor and the Achaemenid Empire, reaching the north-west frontiers of the Indian subcontinent. There, he defeated King Puru in the Battle of the Hydaspes (near modern-day Jhelum, Pakistan) and conquered much of the Punjab; however, Alexander's troops refused to go beyond the Hyphases (Beas) River near modern day Jalandhar, Punjab. Alexander left many Macedonian veterans in the conquered regions; he himself turned back and marched his army southwest.

The Persian and Greek invasions had important repercussions on Indian civilization. The political systems of the Persians was to influence future forms of governance on the subcontinent, including the administration of the Mauryan dynasty. In addition, the region of Gandhara, or present-day eastern Afghanistan and north-west Pakistan, became a melting pot of Indian, Persian, Central Asian and Greek cultures and gave rise to a hybrid culture, Greco-Buddhism, which lasted until the 5th century CE and influenced the artistic development of Mahayana Buddhism.

THE MAGADHA EMPIRE

Magadha formed one of the sixteen Mahâjanapadas (Sanskrit, "great countries") or regions in ancient India. The core of the kingdom was the area of Bihar south of the Ganges; its capital was Rajagaha (modern Rajgir). Magadha expanded to include Eastern Uttar Pradesh, most of Bihar, and Bengal with the conquest of Licchavi and Anga respectively. The ancient kingdom of Magadha is mentioned in the Ramayana, Mahabharata, Puranas. It is also heavily mentioned in Buddhist and Jain texts. The earliest reference to the Magadha people occurs in the Atharva-Veda where they are found listed along with the Angas, Gandharis, and Mujavats as despised peoples. Two of India's major religions started from Magadha; two of India's greatest empires, the Maurya Empire and Gupta Empire, originated from Magadha. These empires saw advancments in ancient India's science, mathematics, astronomy, religion, and philosophy and were considered the Indian "Golden Age". The Magadha kingdom included republican communities such as the community of Rajakumara. Villages had their own assemblies under their local chiefs called Gramakas. Their administrations were divided into executive, judicial, and military functions.

The kingdom of the Magadha roughly corresponds to the modern districts of Patna and Gaya in southern Bihar, and parts of Bengal in the east. It was bounded on the north by the river Ganga, on the east by the river Champa, on the south by the Vindhya mountains and on the west by the river Sona. During the Buddha's time and onward, its boundaries included Anga. Dr. Ranajit Pal, however, maintains that modern Bihar in Esatern India became Magadha only after the Ashokan period. The earliest epigraphic record that mentions Magadha is Ashoka's Bairat edict far from Bihar. Magan in western Baluchistan must have been the ancient Magadha. The Sumerian records mention Dilmun, Magan, and Melukhkha which shows that Magan was nearer to Sumer than Melukhkha. The fact that the name Mogadham is common among Iranians show that Magadha was once in western Baluchistan area which was India. The Sisunaks of Magan were the Sishunagas. The Kak-kings like Kak-Siwe-Tempti were the Kakavarnas. Dr. Pal also maintains that Patali(28°19'58" La., 57°52'16" Lo.) near Kohnouj and Konarak in the Gulf area was the Palibothra of Megasthenes.

HISTORY

There is little certain information available on the early rulers of Magadha. The most important sources are the Puranas, the Buddhist Chronicles of Sri Lanka, and other Jain and Buddhist texts, such as the Pali Canon. Based on these sources, it appears that Magadha was ruled by the Úiúunâga dynasty for some 200 years, c. 684 BC - 424 BC.

Siddhartha Gautama himself was born a prince of Kapilavastu in Kosala around 563 BC, during the Siúunâga Dynasty. As the scene of many incidents in his life, including his enlightenment, Magadha is often considered a blessed land. King Bimbisara of the Siúunâga Dynasty led an active and expansive policy, conquering Anga in what is now West Bengal.

The death of King Bimbisara was at the hands of his son, Prince Ajatashatru. King Pasenadi, king of neighboring Kosala and father-in-law of King Bimbisara, revoked the gift of the Kashi province and a war was triggered between Kosala and Magadha. Ajatashatru was trapped by an ambush and captured with his army. However, King Pasenadi allowed him and his army return to Magadha, and restored the province of Kashi. King Pasendi also gave his daughter in marriage to the new young king.

Accounts differ slightly as to the cause of King Ajatashatru's war with the Licchavi republic, an area north of the river Ganges. It appears that Ajatashatru sent a minister to the area who for three years worked to undermine the unity of the Licchavis. To launch his attack across the Ganga River (Ganges), Ajatashatru built a fort at the town of Pataliputra. Torn by disagreements the Licchavis were easily defeated once the fort was constructed. Jain texts tell how Ajatashatru used two new weapons: a catapult, and a covered chariot with swinging mace that has been compared to a modern tank. Pataliputra began to grow as a center of commerce and became the capitol of Magadha after Ajatashatru's death.

The Siúunâga dynasty was overthrown in 424 BC by Mahâpadma Nanda, the first of the so-called Nine Nandas (Mahapadma and his eight sons). The Nanda Dynasty ruled for about 100 years.

In 326 BC, the army of Alexander the Great approached the boundaries of the Magadha. The army, exhausted and frightened at the prospect of facing another giant Indian army at the Ganges, mutinied at the Hyphasis (modern Beas) and refused to march further East. Alexander, after the meeting with his officer, Coenus, was persuaded that it was better to return and turned south, conquering his way down the Indus to the Ocean.

Around 321 BC, the Nanda Dynasty ended and Chandragupta became the first king of the great Mauryan Dynasty and Mauryan Empire. The Empire later extended over most of Southern Asia under King Asoka, who was at first known as 'Asoka the Cruel' but later became a disciple of Buddhism and became known as 'Dhamma Asoka'. Later, the Mauryan Empire ended and the Gupta Empire began. The capital of the Gupta Empire remained Pataliputra, in Magadha.

MAGADHA DYNASTIES

Dynasties: Brihadratha Dynasty, Pradyota Dynasty, Siúunâga Dynasty (c. 684 - 424 BC), Nanda Dynasty, Maurya Dynasty, Sunga Dynasty, Kanva Dynasty, Gupta Dynasty.

Amongst the sixteen Mahajanapadas, Magadha rose to prominence under a number of dynasties that peaked with the reign of Asoka Maurya, one of India's most legendary and famous emperors.

BRIHADRATHA DYNASTY

According to the Puranas,the Magadha Empire was established by the Brihadratha Dynasty, who was the sixth in line from Emperor Kuru of the Bharata dynasty through his eldest son Sudhanush. The first prominent Emperor of the Magadhan branch of Bharathas was Emperor Brihadratha. His son Jarasandha appears in popular legend and is slain by Bhima in the Mahabharata. Vayu Purana mentions that the Brihadrathas ruled for 1000 years.

PRADYOTA DYNASTY

The Brihadrathas were succeeded by the Pradyotas who according to the Vayu Purana ruled for 138 years. One of the Pradyota traditions was for the prince to kill his father to become king. During this time, it is reported that there was high crimes in Magadha. The people rose up and elected Shishunaga to become the new king, which destroyed the power of the Pradyotas and created the Shishunaga dynasty.

SHISHUNAGA DYNASTY

According to tradition, the Shishunaga dynasty founded the Magadha Empire in 684 BC, whose capital was Rajagriha, later Pataliputra, near the present day Patna. This dynasty lasted till 424 BC, when it was overthrown by the Nanda dynasty. This period saw the development of two of India's major religions that started from Magadha. Gautama Buddha in the 6th or 5th century BC was the founder of Buddhism, which later spread to East Asia and South-East Asia, while Mahavira revived and propagated the ancient sramanic religion of Jainism.

NANDA DYNASTY

The Nanda dynasty was established by an illegitimate son of the king Mahanandin of the previous Shishunaga dynasty. Mahapadma Nanda died at the age of 88, ruling the bulk of this 100-year dynasty. The Nandas were followed by the Maurya dynasty.

MAURYA DYNASTY

In 321 BC, exiled general Chandragupta Maurya founded the Maurya dynasty after overthrowing the reigning Nanda king Dhana Nanda to establish the Maurya Empire. During this time, most of the subcontinent was united under a single government for the first time. Capitalising on the destabilization of northern India by the Persian and Greek incursions, the Mauryan empire under Chandragupta would not only conquer most of the Indian subcontinent, but also push its boundaries into Persia and Central Asia, conquering the Gandhara region. Chandragupta was succeeded by his son Bindusara, who expanded the kingdom over most of present day India, barring the extreme south and east.

The only region that was not under the Mauryan's were present day Tamil Nadu and Kerala (which was a Tamil kingdom then). There are references in one of the oldest

Tamil Sangam literature, *Purananuru*, that a Mauryan army was driven out by a unified Tamil army under the leadership of Ilanchetchenni, a Chola King. This unified Tamil force is supposed to be broken by King Kharavela, a Kalinga ruler, as per one of his inscriptions.

The kingdom was inherited by his son Ashoka The Great who initially sought to expand his kingdom. In the aftermath of the carnage caused in the invasion of Kalinga, he renounced bloodshed and pursued a policy of non-violence or ahimsa after converting to Buddhism. The Edicts of Ashoka are the oldest preserved historical documents of India, and from Ashoka's time, approximate dating of dynasties becomes possible. The Mauryan dynasty under Ashoka was responsible for the proliferation of Buddhist ideals across the whole of East Asia and South-East Asia, fundamentally altering the history and development of Asia as a whole. Ashoka the Great has been described as one of the greatest rulers the world has seen.

MAURYA EMPIRE

The **Maurya Empire** (322–185 BCE), ruled by the Mauryan dynasty, was a geographically extensive and powerful political and military empire in ancient India.

Originating from the kingdom of Magadha in the Indo-Gangetic plains (modern Bihar, Eastern Uttar Pradesh and Bengal) in the eastern side of the sub-continent, the empire had its capital city at Pataliputra (near modern Patna). The Empire was founded in 322 BCE by Chandragupta Maurya, who had overthrown the Nanda Dynasty and began rapidly expanding his power westwards across central and western India taking advantage of the disruptions of local powers in the wake of the withdrawal westward by Alexander the Great's Macedonian and Persian armies. By 316 BCE the empire had fully occupied Northwestern India, defeating and conquering the satraps left by Alexander.

At its greatest extent, the Empire stretched to the north along the natural boundaries of the Himalayas, and to the east stretching into what is now Assam. To the west, it reached beyond modern Pakistan and significant portions of what is now Afghanistan, including the modern Herat and Kandahar provinces and Balochistan. The Empire was expanded into India's central and southern regions by Emperor Bindusara, but it excluded a small portion of unexplored tribal and forested regions near Kalinga.

The Mauryan Empire was perhaps the largest empire to rule the Indian subcontinent. Its decline began fifty years after Ashoka's rule ended, and it dissolved in 185 BCE with the foundation of the Sunga Dynasty in Magadha.

Under Chandragupta, the Mauryan Empire conquered the trans-Indus region, which was under Macedonian rule. Chandragupta then defeated the invasion led by Seleucus I, a Greek general from Alexander's army. Under Chandragupta and his successors, both internal and external trade, and agriculture and economic activities, all thrived and expanded across India thanks to the creation of a single and efficient system of finance, administration and security. After the Kalinga War, the Empire experienced half a century of peace and security under Ashoka: India was a prosperous and stable empire of great economic and military power whose political influence and trade extended across Western and Central Asia and Europe. Mauryan India also enjoyed an era of social harmony, religious transformation, and expansion of the sciences and of knowledge. Chandragupta Maurya's embrace of Jainism increased social and religious renewal and reform across his society, while Ashoka's embrace of Buddhism was the foundation of the reign of social and political peace and non-violence across all of India. Ashoka sponsored the spreading of Buddhist ideals into Sri Lanka, Southeast Asia, West Asia and Mediterranean Europe.

Chandragupta's minister Kautilya Chanakya wrote the *Arthashastra,* one of the greatest treatises on economics, politics, foreign affairs, administration, military arts, war, and religion ever produced in the East. Archaeologically, the period of Mauryan rule in South Asia falls into the era of Northern Black Polished Ware (NBPW). The *Arthashastra* and the Edicts of Ashoka are primary sources of written records of the Mauryan times. The Mauryan empire is considered one of the most significant periods in Indian history. The *Lion Capital of Asoka* at Sarnath, is the emblem of India.

CHANAKYA AND CHANDRAGUPTA MAURYA

Following Alexander's advance into the Punjab, a brahmin named Chanakya (real name Vishnugupt, also known as Kautilya) traveled to Magadha, a kingdom that was large and militarily-powerful and feared by its neighbors, but was dismissed by its king Dhana, of the Nanda Dynasty. However, the prospect of battling Magadha deterred Alexander's troops from going further east: he returned to Babylon, and re-deployed most of his troops west of the Indus river. When Alexander died in Babylon, soon after in 323 BCE, his empire fragmented, and local kings declared their independence, leaving several smaller satraps in a disunited state. Chandragupta Maurya deposed Dhana. The Greek generals Eudemus, and Peithon, ruled until around 316 BCE, when Chandragupta Maurya (with the help of Chanakya, who was now his advisor) surprised and defeated the Macedonians and consolidated the region under the control of his new seat of power in Magadha.

Chandragupta Maurya's rise to power is shrouded in mystery and controversy. On the one hand, a number of ancient Indian accounts, such as the drama *Mudrarakshasa* (*Poem of Rakshasa - Rakshasa* was the prime minister of Magadha) by Visakhadatta, describe his royal ancestry and even link him with the Nanda family. A kshatriya tribe known as the Maurya's are referred to in the earliest Buddhist texts, Mahaparinibbana Sutta. However, any conclusions are hard to make without further historical evidence. Chandragupta first emerges in Greek accounts as "Sandrokottos". As a young man he is said to have met Alexander. He is also said to have met the Nanda king, angered him, and made a narrow escape. Chanakya's original intentions were to train a guerilla army under Chandragupta's command. The Mudrarakshasa of Visakhadutta as well as the

Jaina work Parisishtaparvan talk of Chandragupta's alliance with the Himalayan king Parvatka, sometimes identified with Porus (John Marshall "Taxila", p18, and al.) This Himalayan alliance gave Chandragupta a composite and powerful army made up of Yavanas (Greeks), Kambojas, Shakas (Scythians), Kiratas (Nepalese), Parasikas (Persians) and Bahlikas (Bactrians) .

With the help of these frontier martial tribes from Central Asia, Chandragupta was able to defeat the Nanda/Nandin rulers of Magadha and found the powerful Maurya empire in northern India.

CONQUEST OF MAGADHA

Chanakya encouraged Chandragupta and his army to take over the throne of Magadha. Using his intelligence network, Chandragupta gathered many young men from across Magadha and other provinces, men upset over the corrupt and oppressive rule of king Dhana, plus resources necessary for his army to fight a long series of battles. These men included the former general of Taxila, other accomplished students of Chanakya, the representative of King Porus of Kakayee, his son Malayketu, and the rulers of small states.

Preparing to invade Pataliputra, Maurya hatched a plan. A battle was announced and the Magadhan army was drawn from the city to a distant battlefield to engage Maurya's forces. Maurya's general and spies meanwhile bribed the corrupt general of Nanda. He also managed to create an atmosphere of civil war in the kingdom, which culminated in the death of the heir to the throne. Chanakya managed to win over popular sentiment. Ultimately Nanda resigned, handing power to Chandragupta, and went into exile and was never heard of again. Chanakya contacted the prime minister, Rakshasas, and made him understand that his loyalty was to Magadha, not to the Magadha dynasty, insisting that he continue in office. Chanakya also reiterated that choosing to resist would start a war that would severely affect Magadha and destroy the city. Rakshasa accepted Chanakya's reasoning, and Chandragupta Maurya was legitimately installed as the new King of Magadha. Rakshasa became Chandragupta's chief advisor, and Chanakya assumed the position of an elder statesman.

BUILDING INDIA'S FIRST EMPIRE

Having become the king of one of India's most powerful states, Chandragupta invaded the Punjab. One of Alexander's richest satraps, Peithon, satrap of Media, had tried to raise a coalition against him. Chandragupta managed to conquer the Punjab capital of Taxila, an important centre of trade and Hellenistic culture, increasing his power and consolidating his control.

CHANDRAGUPTA MAURYA

Chandragupta was again in conflict with the Greeks when Seleucus I, ruler of the Seleucid Empire, tried to reconquer the northwestern parts of India, during a campaign in 305 BCE, but failed. The two rulers finally concluded a peace treaty: a marital treaty (Epigamia) was concluded, implying either a marital alliance between the two dynastic lines or a recognition of marriage between Greeks and Indians, Chandragupta received the satrapies of Paropamisadae (Kamboja and Gandhara), Arachosia (Kandhahar) and Gedrosia (Balochistan), and Seleucus I received 500 war elephants that were to have a decisive role in his victory against western Hellenistic kings at the Battle of Ipsus in 301 BCE. Diplomatic relations were established and several Greeks, such as the historian Megasthenes, Deimakos and Dionysius resided at the Mauryan court.

Chandragupta established a strong centralized state with a complex administration at Pataliputra, which, according to Megasthenes, was *"surrounded by a wooden wall pierced by 64 gates and 570 towers— (and) rivaled the splendors of contemporaneous Persian sites such as Susa and Ecbatana."* Chandragupta's son Bindusara extended the rule of the Mauryan empire towards southern India. He also had a Greek ambassador at his court, named Deimachus (Strabo 1–70).

Megasthenes describes a disciplined multitude under Chandragupta, who live simply, honestly, and do not know writing:

> " The Indians all live frugally, especially when in camp. They dislike a great undisciplined multitude, and consequently they observe good order. Theft is of very rare occurrence. Megasthenes says that those who were in the camp of Sandrakottos, wherein lay 400,000 men, found that the thefts reported on any one day did not exceed the value of two hundred drachmae, and this among a people who have no written laws, but are ignorant of writing, and must therefore in all the business of life trust to memory. They live, nevertheless, happily enough, being simple in their manners and frugal. They never drink wine except at sacrifices. Their beverage is a liquor composed from rice instead of barley, and their food is principally a rice-pottage." Strabo XV. i. 53-56, quoting Megasthenes.

BINDUSARA

Chandragupta died after a reign for 24 years and was succeeded by his son, Bindusara, also known as Amitrochates (destroyer of foes) in Greek accounts, around 298 BCE. Details are scarce regarding Bindusara; however, the incorporation of southern peninsular India is sometimes credited to him. According to Jain tradition, his mother was a woman by the name of Durdhara. The Puranas assign him a reign of 25 years. He has been identified with the Indian title Amitraghata (slayer of Enemies), found in Greek texts as Amitrochates.

ASHOKA THE GREAT

Chandragupta's grandson **Ashokavardhan Maurya**, better known as Ashoka the Great (ruled 273- 232 BCE), is considered by contemporary historians to be perhaps the greatest of Indian monarchs, and perhaps the world. H.G. Wells calls him the "greatest of kings".

As a young prince, Ashoka was a brilliant commander who crushed revolts in Ujjain and Taxila. As monarch he was ambitious and aggressive, re-asserting the Empire's superiority in southern and western India. But it was his conquest of Kalinga which proved to be the pivotal event of his life. Although Ashoka's army succeeded in overwhelming Kalinga forces of royal soldiers and civilian units, an estimated 100,000 soldiers and civilians were killed in the furious warfare, including over 10,000 of Ashoka's own men. Hundreds of thousands of people were adversely affected by the destruction and fallout of war. When he personally witnessed the devastation, Ashoka began feeling remorse, and he cried 'what have I done?'. Although the annexation of Kalinga was completed, Ashoka embraced the teachings of Gautama Buddha, and renounced war and violence. For a monarch in ancient times, this was an historic feat.

Ashoka implemented principles of *ahimsa* by banning hunting and violent sports activity and ending indentured and forced labor (many thousands of people in war-ravaged Kalinga had been forced into hard labor and servitude). While he maintained a large and powerful army, to keep the peace and maintain authority, Ashoka expanded friendly relations with states across Asia and Europe, and he sponsored Buddhist missions. He undertook a massive public works building campaign across the country. Over 40 years of peace, harmony and prosperity made Ashoka one of the most successful and famous monarchs in Indian history. He remains an idealized figure of inspiration in modern India.

The Edicts of Ashoka, set in stone, are found throughout the Subcontinent. Ranging from as far west as Afghanistan and as far south as Andhra (Nellore District), Ashoka's edicts state his policies and accomplishments. Although predominantly written in Prakrit, two of them were written in Greek, and one in both Greek and Aramaic. Ashoka's edicts refer to the Greeks, Kambojas, and Gandharas as peoples forming a frontier region of his empire. They also attest to Ashoka's having sent envoys to the Greek rulers in the West as far as the Mediterranean. The edicts precisely name each of the rulers of the Hellenic world at the time such as *Amtiyoko* (Antiochus), *Tulamaya* (Ptolemy), *Amtikini* (Antigonos), *Maka* (Magas) and *Alikasudaro* (Alexander) as recipients of Ashoka's proselytism. The Edicts also accurately locate their territory "600 yojanas away" (a yojanas being about 7 miles), corresponding to the distance between the center of India and Greece (roughly 4,000 miles).

ADMINISTRATION

The Empire was divided into four provinces, with the imperial capital at Pataliputra. From Ashokan edicts, the names of the four provincial capitals are Tosali (in the east), Ujjain in the west, Suvarnagiri (in the south), and Taxila (in the north). The head of the provincial administration was the *Kumara* (royal prince), who governed the provinces as king's representative. The *kumara* was assisted by Mahamatyas and council of ministers. This organizational structure was reflected at the imperial level with the Emperor and his *Mantriparishad* (Council of Ministers).

Historians theorize that the organization of the Empire was in line with the extensive bureaucracy described by Kautilya in the Arthashastra: a sophisticated civil service governed everything from municipal hygiene to international trade. The expansion and defense of the empire was made possible by what appears to have been the largest standing army of its time. According to Megasthenes, the empire wielded a military of 600,000 infantry, 30,000 cavalry, and 9,000 war elephants. A vast espionage system collected intelligence for both internal and external security purposes. Having renounced offensive warfare and expansionism, Ashoka nevertheless continued to maintain this large army, to protect the Empire and instill stability and peace across West and South Asia.

ECONOMY

For the first time in South Asia, political unity and military security allowed for a common economic system and enhanced trade and commerce, with increased agricultural productivity. The previous situation involving hundreds of kingdoms, many small armies, powerful regional chieftains, and internecine warfare, gave way to a disciplined central authority. Farmers were freed of tax and crop collection burdens from regional kings, paying instead to a nationally-administered and strict-but-fair system of taxation as advised by the principles in the *Arthashastra*. Chandragupta Maurya established a single currency across India, and a network of regional governors and administrators and a civil service provided justice and security for merchants, farmers and traders. The Mauryan army wiped out many gangs of bandits, regional private armies, and powerful chieftains who sought to impose their own supremacy in small areas. Although regimental in revenue collection, Maurya also sponsored many public works and waterways to enhance productivity, while internal trade in India expanded greatly due to newfound political unity and internal peace.

Under the Indo-Greek friendship treaty, and during Ashoka's reign, an international network of trade expanded. The Khyber Pass, on the modern boundary of Pakistan and Afghanistan, became a strategically-important port of trade and intercourse with the outside world. Greek states and Hellenic kingdoms in West Asia became important trade partners of India. Trade also extended through the Malay peninsula into Southeast Asia. India's exports included silk goods and textiles, spices and exotic foods. The Empire was enriched further with an exchange of scientific knowledge and technology with Europe and West Asia. Ashoka also sponsored the construction of thousands of roads, waterways, canals, hospitals, rest-houses and other public works. The easing of many overly-rigorous administrative practices, including those regarding taxation and crop collection, helped increase productivity and economic activity across the Empire.

In many ways, the economic situation in the Maurya Empire is comparable to the Roman Empire several centuries later, which both had extensive trade connections and both had organizations similar to corporations. While Rome had organizational entities which were largely used for public state-driven projects, Mauryan India had numerous private commercial entities which existed purely for private commerce. This was due to the Mauryas having to contend with pre-existing private commercial entities hence they were more concerned about keeping the support of these pre-existing organizations, while the Romans did not have such pre-existing entities to contend with hence they were able to prevent such entities from developing.

RELIGION

Jainism

Emperor Chandragupta Maurya became the first major Indian monarch to initiate a religious transformation at the highest level when he embraced Jainism, a religious movement resented by orthodox Hindu priests who usually attended the imperial court. At an older age, Chandragupta renounced his throne and material possessions to join a wandering group of Jain monks. Chandragupta was a disciple of Acharya Bhadrabahu. It is said that in his last days, he observed the rigorous but self purifying Jain ritual of santhara i.e. fast unto death, at Shravan Belagola in Karnatka. However, his successor, Emperor Bindusara, preserved Hindu traditions and distanced himself from Jain and Buddhist movements. Samprati, the grandson of Ashoka also embraced Jainism. Samrat Samprati was influenced by the teachings of Jain monk Arya Suhasti Suri and he is known to have built 1,25,000 Jain Temples across India. Some of them are still found in towns of Ahmedabad, Viramgam, Ujjain & Palitana. It is also said that just like Ashoka, Samprati sent messengers & preachers to Greece, Persia & middle-east for the spread of Jainism. But till date no research has been done in this area. Thus, Jainism became a vital force under the Mauryan Rule. Chandragupta & Samprati, are credited for spread of Jainism in Southern India. Lakhs of Jain Temples & Jain Stupas were erected during their reign. But due to lack of royal patronage & its strict principles, along with rise of Shankaracharya & Ramanujacharya, Jainism,once the major religion of southern India, declined.

Buddhism

But when Ashoka embraced Buddhism, following the Kalinga War, he renounced expansionism and aggression, and the harsher injunctions of the *Arthashastra* on the use of force, intensive policing, and ruthless measures for tax collection and against rebels. Ashoka sent a mission led by his son and daughter to Sri Lanka, whose king Tissa was so charmed with Buddhist ideals that he adopted them himself and made Buddhism the state religion. Ashoka sent many Buddhist missions to West Asia, Greece and South East Asia, and commissioned the construction of monasteries, schools and publication of Buddhist literature across the empire. He is believed to have built as many as 84,000 stupas across India, and he increased the popularity of Buddhism in Afghanistan. Ashoka helped convene the Third Buddhist Council of India and South Asia's Buddhist orders, near his capital, a council that undertook much work of reform and expansion of the Buddhist religion.

Hinduism

While himself a Buddhist, Ashoka retained the membership of Hindu priests and ministers in his court, and he maintained religious freedom and tolerance although the Buddhist faith grew in popularity with his patronage. Indian society began embracing the philosophy of *ahimsa*, and given the increased prosperity and improved law enforcement, crime and internal conflicts reduced dramatically. Also greatly discouraged was the caste system and orthodox discrimination, as Hinduism began to absorb the ideals and values of Jain and Buddhist teachings. Social freedom began expanding in an age of peace and prosperity.

ARCHITECTURAL REMAINS

Architectural remains of the Maurya period are rather few. Remains of a hypostyle building with about 80 columns of a height of about 10 meters have been found in Kumrahâr near Patna, and is one of the very few site that has been connected to the rule of the Mauryas in that city. The style is rather reminiscent of Persian Achaemenid architecture. The grottoes of Barâbar are another example of Mauryan architecture, especially the decorated front of the Lomas Rishi grotto. These were offered by the Mauryas to the Buddhist sect of the Ajivikas.

The most widespread example of Maurya architecture are the Pillars of Ashoka, often exquisitely decorated, with more than 40 spread throughout the sub-continent.

NATURAL HISTORY IN THE TIMES OF THE MAURYAS

The protection of animals in India became serious business by the time of the Maurya dynasty; being the first empire to provide a unified political entity in India, the attitude of the Mauryas towards forests, its denizens and fauna in general is of interest.

The Mauryas firstly looked at forests as a resource. For them, the most important forest product was the elephant. Military might in those times depended not only upon horses and men but also battle-elephants; these played a role in the defeat of Seleucus, Alexander's governor of the Punjab. The Mauryas sought to preserve supplies of elephants since it was cheaper and took less time to catch, tame and train wild elephants than to raise them. Kautilya's *Arthashastra* contains not only maxims on ancient statecraft, but also unambiguously specifies the responsibilities of officials such as the *Protector of the Elephant Forests*.

On the border of the forest, he should establish a forest for elephants guarded by foresters. The Superintendent should with the help of guards...protect the elephants whether along on the mountain, along a river, along lakes or in marshy tracts...They should kill anyone slaying an elephant.—*Arthashastra*

The Mauryas also designated separate forests to protect supplies of timber, as well as lions and tigers, for skins. Elsewhere the *Protector of Animals* also worked to eliminate thieves, tigers and other predators to render the woods safe for grazing cattle.

The Mauryas valued certain forest tracts in strategic or economic terms and instituted curbs and control measures over them. They regarded all forest tribes with distrust and controlled them with bribery and political subjugation. They employed some of them, the food-gatherers or *aranyaca* to guard borders and trap animals. The sometimes tense and conflict-ridden relationship nevertheless enabled the Mauryas to guard their vast empire.

When Ashoka embraced Buddhism in the latter part of his reign, he brought about significant changes in his style of governance, which included providing protection to fauna, and even relinquished the royal hunt. He was perhaps the first ruler in history to advocate conservation measures for wildlife and even had rules inscribed in stone edicts. The edicts proclaim that many followed the king's example in giving up the slaughter of animals; one of them proudly states:

> Our king killed very few animals.
>
> *—Edict on Fifth Pillar*

However, the edicts of Ashoka reflect more the desire of rulers than actual events; the mention of a 100 'panas' (coins) fine for poaching deer in royal hunting preserves shows that rule-breakers did exist. The legal restrictions conflicted with the practices freely exercised by the common people in hunting, felling, fishing and setting fires in forests.

CONTACTS WITH THE HELLENISTIC WORLD

Foundation of the Empire

Relations with the Hellenistic world may have started from the very beginning of the Maurya Empire. Plutarch reports that Chandragupta Maurya met with Alexander the Great, probably around Taxila in the northwest:

> "Sandrocottus, when he was a stripling, saw Alexander himself, and we are told that he often said in later times that Alexander narrowly missed making himself master of the country, since its king was hated and despised on account of his baseness and low birth." Plutarch 62-3

Reconquest of the Northwest (c. 310 BCE)

Chandragupta ultimately occupied Northwestern India, in the territories formerly ruled by the Greeks, where he fought the satraps (described as "Prefects" in Western sources) left in place after Alexander (Justin), among whom may have been Eudemus, ruler in the western Punjab until his departure in 317 BCE or Peithon, son of Agenor, ruler of the Greek colonies along the Indus until his departure for Babylon in 316 BCE.

> "India, after the death of Alexander, had assassinated his prefects, as if shaking the burden of servitude. The author of this liberation was Sandracottos, but he had transformed liberation in servitude after victory, since, after taking the

throne, he himself oppressed the very people he has liberated from foreign domination" Justin XV.4.12-13

"Later, as he was preparing war against the prefects of Alexander, a huge wild elephant went to him and took him on his back as if tame, and he became a remarkable fighter and war leader. Having thus acquired royal power, Sandracottos possessed India at the time Seleucos was preparing future glory." Justin XV.4.19

Conflict and alliance with Seleucus (305 BCE)

Seleucus I Nicator, the Macedonian satrap of the Asian portion of Alexander's former empire, conquered and put under his own authority eastern territories as far as Bactria and the Indus (Appian, History of Rome, The Syrian Wars 55), until in 305 BCE he entered in a confrontation with Chandragupta:

"Always lying in wait for the neighboring nations, strong in arms and persuasive in council, he [Seleucus] acquired Mesopotamia, Armenia, 'Seleucid' Cappadocia, Persis, Parthia, Bactria, Arabia, Tapouria, Sogdia, Arachosia, Hyrcania, and other adjacent peoples that had been subdued by Alexander, as far as the river Indus, so that the boundaries of his empire were the most extensive in Asia after that of Alexander. The whole region from Phrygia to the Indus was subject to Seleucus." Appian, History of Rome, The Syrian Wars 55

Though no accounts of the conflict remain, it is clear that Seleucus fared poorly against the Indian Emperor as he failed in conquering any territory, and in fact, was forced to surrender much that was already his. Regardless, Seleucus and Chandragupta ultimately reached a settlement and through a treaty sealed in 305 BCE, Seleucus, according to Strabo, ceded a number of territories to Chandragupta, including southern Afghanistan and parts of Persia.

Accordingly, Seleucus obtained five hundred war elephants, a military asset which would play a decisive role at the Battle of Ipsus in 301 BCE.

MARITAL ALLIANCE

A matrimonial alliance was also agreed upon (called Epigamia in ancient sources, meaning either the recognition of marriage between trans-indus inhabitants and Greeks, or a dynastic alliance):

"He (Seleucus) crossed the Indus and waged war with Sandrocottus [Maurya], king of the Indians, who dwelt on the banks of that stream, until they came to an understanding with each other and contracted a marriage relationship." Appian, History of Rome, The Syrian Wars 55

It is generally thought that there was an marital alliance made between a Seleucid princess and Chandragupta, and that the Seleucid princess may have been bethrothed to the Mauryan Dynasty. This practice in itself was quite common in the Hellenistic world to formalize alliances. There is thus a possibility that some of the descendants of Chandragupta were partly of Hellenic descent, whether Chandragupta married the Seleucid princess, or his son Bindusara, and that the Maurya dynasty was considered as closely connected to the Seleucid one. Bindusara himself, born earlier around 320 BCE, could not have been the result of such a union, but he may have been the one who married the Seleucid princess, just before his rise as Emperor in 298 BCE.

Although Indian sources mention him as the son of brahmin woman, the marriage arrangement has led some to suggest that Ashoka may have been a product of this union with a Seleucid princess although the general view is that Ashoka was born from a Brahmin mother who was a minor queen of Bindusara, based on the account of the 2nd century CE Ashokavardhana ("Legend of Ashoka"). The practice of Mauryan rulers to have harems is repeatedly mentioned in sources such as the Ashokavardhana however, which would suggest a multiplicity of bloodlines and a numerous descent for each king.

At the very least, this treaty on "Epigamia" implies lawful marriage between Greeks and Indians was recognized at the State level, although it is unclear whether it occurred among dynastic rulers or common people, or both.

Exchange of ambassadors

Seleucus dispatched an ambassador, Megasthenes, to Chandragupta, and later Deimakos to his son Bindusara, at the Mauryan court at Pataliputra (Modern Patna in Bihar state). Later Ptolemy II Philadelphus, the ruler of Ptolemaic Egypt and contemporary of Ashoka, is also recorded by Pliny the Elder as having sent an ambassador named Dionysius to the Mauryan court.

Exchange of presents

Classical sources have also recorded that following their treaty, Chandragupta and Seleucus exchanged presents, such as when Chandragupta sent various aphrodisiacs to Seleucus:

> "And Theophrastus says that some contrivances are of wondrous efficacy in such matters [as to make people more amorous]. And Phylarchus confirms him, by reference to some of the presents which Sandrakottus, the king of the Indians, sent to Seleucus; which were to act like charms in producing a wonderful degree of affection, while some, on the contrary, were to banish love" Athenaeus of Naucratis, "

His son Bindusara 'Amitraghata' (Slayer of Enemies) also is recorded in Classical sources as having exchanged present with Antiochus I:

> "But dried figs were so very much sought after by all men (for really, as Aristophanes says, "There's really nothing nicer than dried figs"), that even Amitrochates, the king of the Indians, wrote to Antiochus, entreating him (it is

Hegesander who tells this story) to buy and send him some sweet wine, and some dried figs, and a sophist; and that Antiochus wrote to him in answer, "The dry figs and the sweet wine we will send you; but it is not lawful for a sophist to be sold in Greece" Athenaeus, "Deipnosophistae" XIV.67

Greek populations in India

Greek populations apparently remained in the northwest of the Indian subcontinent under Ashoka's rule. In his Edicts of Ashoka, set in stone, some of them written in Greek, Ashoka describes that Greek populations within his realm converted to Buddhism:

"Here in the king's domain among the Greeks, the Kambojas, the Nabhakas, the Nabhapamkits, the Bhojas, the Pitinikas, the Andhras and the Palidas, everywhere people are following Beloved-of-the-Gods' instructions in Dharma." Rock Edict Nb13 (S. Dhammika).

Fragments of Edict 13 have been found in Greek, and a full Edict, written in both Greek and Aramaic has been discovered in Kandahar. It is said to be written in excellent Classical Greek, using sophisticated philosophical terms. In this Edict, Ashoka uses the word Eusebeia ("Piety") as the Greek translation for the ubiquitous "Dharma" of his other Edicts written in Prakrit:

"Ten years (of reign) having been completed, King Piodasses (Ashoka) made known (the doctrine of) Piety (Eusebeia) to men; and from this moment he has made men more pious, and everything thrives throughout the whole world. And the king abstains from (killing) living beings, and other men and those who (are) huntsmen and fishermen of the king have desisted from hunting. And if some (were) intemperate, they have ceased from their intemperance as was in their power; and obedient to their father and mother and to the elders, in opposition to the past also in the future, by so acting on every occasion, they will live better and more happily."

Buddhist missions to the West (c.250 BCE)

Also, in the Edicts of Ashoka, Ashoka mentions the Hellenistic kings of the period as a recipient of his Buddhist proselytism, although no Western historical record of this event remain:

"The conquest by Dharma has been won here, on the borders, and even six hundred yojanas (5,400-9,600 km) away, where the Greek king Antiochos rules, beyond there where the four kings named Ptolemy, Antigonos, Magas and Alexander rule, likewise in the south among the Cholas, the Pandyas, and as far as Tamraparni (Sri Lanka)." (Edicts of Ashoka, 13th Rock Edict, S. Dhammika).

Ashoka also claims that he encouraged the development of herbal medicine, for men and animals, in their territories:

"Everywhere within Beloved-of-the-Gods, King Piyadasi's [Ashoka's] domain, and among the people beyond the borders, the Cholas, the Pandyas, the

> Satiyaputras, the Keralaputras, as far as Tamraparni and where the Greek king Antiochos rules, and among the kings who are neighbors of Antiochos, everywhere has Beloved-of-the-Gods, King Piyadasi, made provision for two types of medical treatment: medical treatment for humans and medical treatment for animals. Wherever medical herbs suitable for humans or animals are not available, I have had them imported and grown. Wherever medical roots or fruits are not available I have had them imported and grown. Along roads I have had wells dug and trees planted for the benefit of humans and animals." 2nd Rock Edict

The Greeks in India even seem to have played an active role in the propagation of Buddhism, as some of the emissaries of Ashoka, such as Dharmaraksita, are described in Pali sources as leading Greek ("Yona") Buddhist monks, active in Buddhist proselytism (the Mahavamsa, XII).

Subhagsena and Antiochos III (206 BCE)

Sophagasenus was an Indian Mauryan ruler of the 3rd century BCE, described in ancient Greek sources, and named Subhagsena or Subhashsena in Prakrit. His name is mentionned in the list of Mauryan princes, and also in the list of the Yadava dynasty, as a descendant of Pradyumana. He may have been a grandson of Ashoka, or Kunala, the son of Ashoka. He ruled an area south of the Hindu Kush, possibly in Gandhara. Antiochos III, the Seleucid king, after having made peace with Euthydemus in Bactria, went to India in 206 BC and is said to have renewed his friendship with the Indian king there:

> "He (Antiochus) crossed the Caucasus and descended into India; renewed his friendship with Sophagasenus the king of the Indians; received more elephants, until he had a hundred and fifty altogether; and having once more provisioned his troops, set out again personally with his army: leaving Androsthenes of Cyzicus the duty of taking home the treasure which this king had agreed to hand over to him." Polybius 11.39

Decline

Ashoka was followed for 50 years by a succession of weaker kings. Brhadrata, the last ruler of the Mauryan dynasty, held territories that had shrunk considerably from the time of emperor Ashoka, although he still upheld the Buddhist faith.

Sunga coup (185 BCE)

He was assassinated in 185 BCE during a military parade, by the commander-in-chief of his guard, the Brahmin general Pusyamitra Sunga, who then took over the throne and established the Sunga dynasty. Buddhist records such as the Ashokavardhana write that the assassination of Brhadrata and the rise of the Sunga empire led to a wave of persecution for Buddhists, and a resurgence of Hinduism. According to John Marshall, Pusyamitra may have been the main author of the persecutions, although later Sunga kings seem to have been more supportive of Buddhism. Other historians, such as Etienne

Lamotte and Romila Thapar, among others, have argued that archaeological evidence in favor of the allegations of persecution of Buddhists are lacking, and that the extent and magnitude of the atrocities have been exaggerated.

Establishment of the Indo-Greek Kingdom (180 BCE)

The fall of the Mauryas left the Khyber Pass unguarded, and a wave of foreign invasion followed. The Greco-Bactrian king, Demetrius, capitalized on the break-up, and he conquered southern Afghanistan and Pakistan around 180 BC, forming the Indo-Greek Kingdom. The Indo-Greeks would maintain holdings on the trans-Indus region, and make forays into central India, for about a century. Under them, Buddhism flourished, and one of their kings Menander became a famous figure of Buddhism, he was to establish a new capital of Sagala, the modern city of Sialkot. However, the extent of their domains and the lengths of their rule are subject to much debate. Numismatic evidence indicates that they retained holdings in the subcontinent right up to the birth of Christ. Although the extent of their successes against indigenous powers such as the Sungas, Satavahanas, and Kalingas are unclear, what is clear is that Scythian tribes, renamed Indo-Scythians, brought about the demise of the Indo-Greeks from around 70 BCE and retained lands in the trans-Indus, the region of Mathura, and Gujarat.

SUNGA DYNASTY

The Sunga dynasty was established in 185 BC, about fifty years after Ashoka's death, when the king Brihadratha, the last of the Mauryan rulers, was assassinated by the then commander-in-chief of the Mauryan armed forces, Pusyamitra Sunga, while he was taking the Guard of Honour of his forces. Pusyamitra Sunga then ascended the throne.

KANVA DYNASTY

The Kanva dynasty replaced the Sunga dynasty, and ruled in the eastern part of India from 71 BC to 26 BC. The last ruler of the Sunga dynasty was overthrown by Vasudeva of the Kanva dynasty in 75 BC. The Kanva ruler allowed the kings of the Sunga dynasty to continue to rule in obscurity in a corner of their former dominions. Magadha was ruled by four Kanva rulers. In 30 BC, the southern power swept away both the Kanvas and Sungas and the province of Eastern Malwa was absorbed within the dominions of the conqueror. Following the collapse of the Kanva dynasty, the Satavahana dynasty of the Andhra kindgom replaced the Magandhan kingdom as the most powerful Indian state.

GUPTA DYNASTY

Gupta dynasty ruled from around 240 to 550 AD. The Gupta Empire was one of the largest political and military empires in ancient India. The Gupta age is referred to as the Classical age of India by most historians. The time of the Gupta Empire was an Indian "Golden Age" in science, mathematics, astronomy, religion and philosophy. They had their capital at Pataliputra. The difference between Gupta and Mauryan administration was that the in the Mauryan administration power was centralised but in the Gupta administration power was more decentralised. The king occupied a powerful and important position and often took titles to assert his supremacy. A council of ministers and some officials helped him. The empire was divided into provinces and provinces were further divided into districts.

Villages were the smallest units. The kingdom covered Gujarat, North-east India, south-eastern Pakistan, Orissa, northern Madhya Pradesh and eastern India. Art and architecture flourished during the Gupta age. People were mostly Vaishnavas. Temples devoted to Shiva and Vishnu were built during this period. Early temples had a large room where the idol of god was kept. Today these can be found in Deogarh in Jhansi. Temples were mostly made of brick or stone. The doorways were very decorative. Wall murals flourished during this age.These can be seen in Ajanta caves which are about 100 km from Aurangabad. These murals depict the life of Buddha.Yajnas were performed by Brahmins. All forms of worship were carried out in Sanskrit. Astronomy made rapid strides. Aryabhatta and Varahamihira were two great Astronomers and Mathematicians.

Aryabhatta stated that the earth moved round the sun and rotated on its own Axis. Metallurgy too made rapid strides. Proof is the Iron Pillar near Mehrauli on the outskirts of Delhi. Ayurveda was known to the people of Gupta age. People livedin a happy and prosperous life. Most people lived in villages and led a simple life. Rest houses and hospitals were set up. Laws were simple and punishments were not very harsh. However there was a serious flaw. The bad, inhuman treatment of the Chandalas or Untouchables. They were made to live outside the city and even their shadows were considered capable of polluting. The material sources of this age were Kalidasa's works i.e Raghuvamsa, Meghdoot, Malavikagnimitram and Abhinjnana Shakuntalam, works of Fa-hein,the Chinese buddhist scholar, Allahàbad pillar inscription called Prayag Prashsti, Books by Harisena and others.

GUPTA EMPIRE

The **Gupta Empire** was ruled by members of the Gupta dynasty from around 320 to 550 AD and covered most of Northern India, parts of eastern Pakistan and what is now western India and Bangladesh. The time of the Gupta Empire is referred to as Golden Age of India in science, mathematics, astronomy, religion and Indian philosophy. The peace and prosperity created under leadership of Guptas enabled the pursuit of scientific and artistic endeavors. Historians place the Gupta dynasty alongside with the Han Dynasty, Tang Dynasty and Roman Empire as a model of a classical civilization. The capital, of the Guptas, was Pataliputra, present day Patna, in the Indian state of Bihar.

The origins of the Guptas are shrouded in obscurity. The Chinese traveler I-tsing(Hieun-Tsang) provides the first evidence of the Gupta kingdom in Magadha. He came to India in 672 AD and heard of 'Maharaja Sri-Gupta' who built a temple for Chinese pilgrims near Mrigasikhavana. I-tsing gives the date for this event merely as

'500 years before'. This does not match with other sources and hence we can assume that I-tsing's computation was a mere guess. Very recently a few scholars have linked Guptas with rulers mentioned in *Bhagwatam*; however, these things are largely disputed and the idea seems politically motivated and to promote the sale of books written and promoted by some entities.

The most likely date for the reign of Sri-Gupta is c. 240-280 AD. His successor Ghatotkacha ruled probably from c. 280-319 AD. In contrast to his successor, he is also referred to in inscriptions as 'Maharaja'.

At the beginning of the 5th century the Guptas established and ruled a few small Hindu kingdoms in Magadha and around modern-day Uttar Pradesh.

CHANDRA GUPTA

Ghatotkacha (c. 280–319) AD, had a son named Chandra Gupta. (Not to be confused with Chandragupta Maurya (340-293 BC), founder of the Mauryan Empire.) In a breakthrough deal, Chandra Gupta was married to a Lichchhavi—the main power in Magadha. With a dowry of the kingdom of Magadha (capital Pataliputra) i, conquering much of jp maghada¾, Prayaga and Saketa. He established a realm stretching from the Ganga River (Ganges River) to Prayaga (modern-day Allahabad) by 321.

SAMUDRAGUPTA

Samudragupta succeeded his father in A.D. 335, and ruled for about 45 years, till his death in A.D. 380. He took the kingdoms of Shichchhatra and Padmavati early in his reign. He then attacked the Malwas, the Yaudheyas, the Arjunayanas, the Maduras and the Abhiras, all of which were tribes in the area. By his death in 380, he had incorporated over twenty kingdoms into his realm, his rule extended from the Himalayas to the river Narmada and from the Brahmaputra to the Yamuna. He gave himself the titles *King of Kings* and *World Monarch*. He is considered the *Napoleon of India*. He performed *Ashwamedha yajna* (horse sacrifice) to underline the importance of his conquest.

Samudragupta was not only a talented military leader but also a great patron of art and literature. The important scholars present in his court were Harishena, Vasubandhu and Asanga. He was a poet and musician himself. He was a firm believer in Hinduism and is known to have worshipped Lord Vishnu. He was considerate of other religions and allowed Sri Lanka's buddhist king to build a monastery at Bodh Gaya.

CHANDRA GUPTA II

Chandra Gupta II, the Sun of Power (*Vikramaditya*), ruled from 380 till 413. His daughter Prabhavatigupta was married to Rudrasena II, the Vakataka king of Deccan (this daughter was forced to be married by the father). Only marginally less successful than his father, Chandra Gupta II expanded his realm westwards, defeating the Saka Western Kshatrapas of Malwa, Gujarat and Saurashtra in a campaign lasting until 409, but with his main opponent Rudrasimha III defeated by 395, and crushing the Bengal

(Vanga) chiefdoms. This extended his control from coast-to-coast, established a second (trading) capital at Ujjain and was the high point of the empire.

Despite the creation of the empire through war, the reign is remembered for its very influential style of Hindu art, literature, culture and science, especially during the reign of Chandra Gupta II. Some excellent works of Hindu art such as the panels at the Dashavatara Temple in Deogarh serve to illustrate the magnificence of Gupta art. Above all it was the synthesis of the sacred and sexual elements that gave Gupta art its distinctive flavour. During this period, the Guptas were supportive of thriving Buddhist and Jain cultures as well, and for this reason there is also a long history of non-Hindu Gupta period art. In particular, Gupta period Buddhist art was to be influential in most of East and Southeast Asia. Much of advances was recorded by the Chinese scholar and traveller Faxian (Fa-hien) in his diary and published afterwords.

The court of Chandragupta was made even more illustrious by the fact that it was graced by the *Navaratna* (Nine Jewels), a group of nine who excelled in the literary arts. Amongst these men was the immortal Kalidasa whose works dwarfed the works of many other literary geniuses, not only in his own age but in the ages to come. Kalidasa was particularly known for his fine exploitation of the *sringara* (erotic) element in his verse.

CHANDRA GUPTA II'S CAMPAIGNS AGAINST FOREIGN TRIBES

- Fourth century AD Sanskrit poet Kalidasa, credits Chandragupta Vikramaditya with having conquered about twenty one kingdoms, both in and outside India. After finishing his campaign in the East, South and West India, Vikramaditya (Chandra Gupta II) proceeded northwards, subjugated the Parasikas (Persians), then the Hunas and the Kambojas tribes located in the west and east Oxus valleys respectively. Thereafter, the glorious king proceeds across the Himalaya and reduced the Kinnaras, Kiratas etc and lands into India proper .
- According to the *Brihat-Katha-Manjari* of the Kashmiri Pandit Kshmendra, king Vikramaditya (Chandra Gupta II) had *"unburdened the sacred earth of the Barbarians like the Shakas, Mlecchas, Kambojas, Yavanas, Tusharas, Parasikas, Hunas, etc. by annihilating these sinful Mlecchas completely".*

KUMARAGUPTA I

Chandragupta II was succeeded by his son Kumaragupta I. Known as the *Mahendraditya,* he ruled until 455. Towards the end of his reign a tribe in the Narmada valley, the Pushyamitras, rose in power to threaten the empire.

SKANDAGUPTA

Skandagupta is generally considered the last of the great rulers. He defeated the Pushyamitra threat, but then was faced with invading Hephthalites or "White Huns", known in India as the Huna, from the northwest. He repulsed a *Huna* attack c. 477, But the expense of the wars drained the empire's resources and contributed to its decline. Skandagupta died in 487 and was succeeded by his son Narasimhagupta *Baladitya*.

MILITARY ORGANIZATION

The Imperial Guptas could not have achieved their successes through force of arms without an efficient martial system. Historically, the best accounts of this comes not from the Hindus themselves but from Chinese and Western observers. However, a contemporary Indian document, regarded as a military classic of the time, the *Siva-Dhanur-veda,* offers some insight into the military system of the Guptas. Like Indian kings before them, and The Guptas seem to have relied heavily on infantry archers, and the bow was one of the dominant weapons of their army. The Hindu version of the longbow was composed of metal, or more typically bamboo, and fired a long bamboo cane arrow with a metal head.

Unlike the composite bows of Western and Central Asian foes, bows of this design would be less prone to warping in the damp and moist conditions often prevalent to the region. The Indian longbow was reputedly a powerful weapon capable of great range and penetration and provided an effective counter to invading horse archers. Iron shafts were used against armored elephants, and fire arrows were also part of the bowmen's arsenal. India historically has had a prominent reputation for its steel weapons. One of these was the steel bow. Due to its high tensility, the steel bow was capable of long range and penetration of exceptionally thick armor. These were less common weapons than the bamboo design and found in the hands of noblemen rather than in the ranks. Archers were frequently protected by infantry equipped with shields, javelins, and longswords.

The Guptas also had knowledge of siegecraft, catapults, and other sophisticated war machines.

The Guptas apparently showed little predilection for using horse archers, despite the fact these warriors were a main component in the ranks of their Scythian, Parthian, and Hepthalite (*Huna*) enemies. However, the Gupta armies were probably better disciplined. Able commanders like Samudragupta and Chandragupta II would have likely understood the need for combined armed tactics and proper logistical organization. Gupta military success likely stemmed from the concerted use elephants, armored cavalry, and foot archers in tandem against both Hindu kingdoms and foreign armies invading from the Northwest. The Guptas also maintained a navy, allowing them to control regional waters.

The collapse of the Gupta Empire in the face of the *Huna* onslaught was due not directly to the inherent defects of the Gupta army, which after all had initially defeated these people under Skandagupta. More likely, internal dissolution sapped the ability of the Guptas to resist foreign invasion, as was simultaneously occurring in Western Europe and China.

HUNA INVASIONS AND THE END OF EMPIRE

Narasimhagupta (467-473) was followed by Kumaragupta II (473-476) and Buddhagupta (476-495). In the 480's the Hephthalite king Toramana broke through the Gupta defenses in the northwest, and much of the empire was overrun by the *Huna* by 500. The empire disintegrated under the attacks of Toramana and his successor, Mihirakula; the *Huna* conquered several provinces of the empire, including Malwa, Gujarat, and Thanesar, broke away under the rule of local dynasties. It appears from inscriptions that the Guptas, although their power was much diminished, continued to resist the *Huna*, and allied with the independent kingdoms to drive the *Huna* from most of northern India by the 530's. The succession of the sixth-century Guptas is not entirely clear, but the last recognized ruler of the dynasty's main line was Vishnugupta, reigning from 540 to 550.

LEGACY OF THE GUPTA EMPIRE

The Gupta Empire is considered by many scholars to be the "classical age" of Hindu and Buddhist art and literature. The Rulers of the Gupta Empire were strong supporters of developments in the arts, architecture, science, and literature. The Guptas circulated a large number of gold coins, called dinars, with their inscriptions. This period is also very rich in Sanskrit literature. Several important works were composed by well-known writers, such as *Mrichchakatika* or *The Little Clay Cart* by Shudraka, along with ones like *Shakuntala, Kumarasambhava* and *Meghduta* by Kalidasa and others. *Panchatantra,* the animal fables by Vishnu Sharma, and 13 plays by Bhasa, were also written in this period. Some of the best works of Sanskrit Literature , and thus of Indian Literature , were written down during this period. The Gupta Dynasty also left behind an effective administrative system. During times of peace, the Gupta system was decentralized, with only taxation flowing to the capital at Pataliputra. During times of war however, the government realigned and fought its invaders. The system was soon extinguished in fighting off the Hunnic Invasions.

The most significant achievements of this period, however, were in religion, education, mathematics, art, Sanskrit literature and drama, and Kama Sutra, the principles of pleasure . Hinduism witnessed a crystallization of its components: major sectarian deities, image worship, devotionalism, and the importance of the temple. Education included grammar, composition, logic, metaphysics, mathematics, medicine, and astronomy. These subjects became highly specialized and reached an advanced level. The Indian numeral system, i.e the decimal system which is currently in use;sometimes erroneously attributed to the Arabs, who took it from India to Europe where it replaced the Roman system—and the decimal system are Indian inventions of this period. Aryabhatta's expositions on astronomy in 499, moreover, gave calculations of the solar year and the shape and movement of astral bodies with remarkable accuracy.

In medicine, the Guptas were notable for their establishment and patronage of free hospitals. And although progress in physiology and biology was hindered by religious injunctions against contact with dead bodies, which discouraged dissection and anatomy, Indian physicians excelled in pharmacopoeia, cesarean section, bone setting, and skin grafting. Indeed Hindu medical advances were soon adopted in the Arab and Western worlds.

The great universities in central and eastern India received an influx of students from many parts of the world. Most notable were the universities of Nalanda and Vikramasila.

CONTRIBUTIONS TO THE WORLD AND ACHIEVEMENT

Gupta astronomers also made many advances in astronomy by using their mathematical breakthroughs. It was during this empire that philosophers in India first proposed that the earth was not flat but was instead round and rotated on an axis by viewing a lunar eclipses. They also made discoveries about gravity and the planets of the solar system, which they used to tell the horoscopes. Doctors also invented several medical instruments, and even performed operations. These ideas spread throughout the world through trade. The Gupta reign was certainly the "Golden Age" of India.

GUPTA DYNASTY

The **Gupta dynasty** ruled the **Gupta Empire** of India, from around 320 to 550.

Some of its main rulers were:

- Samudragupta
- Ramagupta
- Chandragupta II
- Kumaragupta I
- Skandagupta
- Narasimhagupta
- Buddhagupta
- Purugupta
- Vishnugupta

MEDIEVAL INDIAN KINGDOMS

EARLY MIDDLE KINGDOMS — THE GOLDEN AGE

The middle period was a time of notable cultural development. The Satavahanas, also known as the Andhras, were a dynasty which ruled in Southern and Central India starting from around 230 BCE. Satakarni, the sixth ruler of the Satvahana dynasty, defeated the Sunga dynasty of North India. Gautamiputra Satakarni was another notable ruler of the dynasty. Kuninda Kingdom was a small Himalayan state that survived from around the 2nd century BCE to roughly the 3rd century CE. The Kushanas invaded north-western India about the middle of the 1st century CE, from Central Asia, and founded an empire that eventually stretched from Peshawar to the middle Ganges and, perhaps, as far as the Bay of Bengal. It also included ancient Bactria (in the north of modern Afghanistan) and southern Tajikistan. The Western Satraps (35-405 CE) were Saka rulers of the western and central part of India. They were the successors of the Indo-Scythians and contemporaneous with the Kushans who ruled the northern part of the Indian subcontinent, and the Satavahana (Andhra) who ruled in Central India.

Different empires such as the Pandyan Kingdom, Early Cholas, Chera dynasty, Kadamba Dynasty, Western Ganga Dynasty, Pallavas and Chalukya dynasty dominated the southern part of the Indian peninsula, at different periods of time. Several southern kingdoms formed overseas empires that stretched across South East Asia. The kingdoms warred with each other and Deccan states, for domination of the south. Kalabhras, a Buddhist kingdom, briefly interrupted the usual domination of the Cholas, Cheras and Pandyas in the South.

SÂTAVÂHANAS

The Sâtavâhanas, were a dynasty which ruled from Junnar (Pune), Prathisthan (Paithan) in Maharashtra and Amaravati (Dharanikota) in Andhra Pradesh over Southern and Central India from around 230 BCE onward. Although there is some controversy about when the dynasty came to an end, the most liberal estimates suggest that it lasted about 450 years, until around 220 CE. The Satavahanas are credited for establishing peace in the country, resisting the onslaught of foreigners after the decline of Mauryan empire.

EARLY RULERS

The Satavahanas/ Andhras initially ruled in the area of *Andhradesa*, the Telugu name for the people country between the rivers Krishna and Godavari, which was always their heartland. The Pûrânas list 30 Andhra rulers. Many are known from their coins and inscriptions as well.

SIMUKA (C.230-207 BCE)

After becoming independent around 230 BCE, Simuka, the founder of the dynasty, conquered Maharashtra, Andhra Pradesh, Malwa and part of Madhya Pradesh. He was succeeded by his brother Kanha (or Krishna) (r. 207-189 BCE), who further extended his kingdom to the west and the south.

SATAKARNI (C.180-124 BCE)

His successor Sâtakarnî I was the sixth ruler of the Satavahana. He is said in the Puranas to have ruled for 56 years.

Satakarni defeated the Sunga dynasty of North India by wrestling Western Malwa from them, and performed several Vedic sacrifices at huge cost, including the Horse Sacrifice. He also was in conflict with the Kalinga ruler Kharavela, who mentions him in the Hathigumpha inscription. According to the Yuga Purana he conquered Kalinga following the death of Kharavela. He extended Satavahana rule over Madhya Pradesh and pushed back the Sakas from Pataliputra (he is thought to be the Yuga Purana's "Shata", an abbreviation of the full name "Shri Sata" that occurs on coins from Ujjain), where he subsequently ruled for 10 years.

By this time the dynasty was well established, with its capital at Pratishthânapura (Paithan) in Maharashtra, and its power spreading into all of South India.

KANVA SUZERAINTY (75-35 BCE)

Many small rulers succeeded Satakarni, such as Lambodara, Apilaka, Meghasvati and Kuntala Satakarni, who are thought to have been under the suzerainty of the Kanva dynasty. The Puranas (the Matsya Purana, the Vayu Purana, the Brahmanda Purana, the Vishnu Purana) all state that the first of the Andhra kings rose to power in the 1st century BCE, by slaying Susarman, the last ruler of the Kanvas. This feat is usually thought to have been accomplished by Pulomavi (c. 30-6 BCE), who then ruled over Pataliputra.

VICTORY OVER THE SHAKAS, YAVANAS AND PAHLAVAS

The first century CE saw another incursion of the Sakas of Central Asia into India, where they formed the dynasty of the Western Kshatrapas. The four immediate successors of Hâla (r. 20-24 CE) had short reigns totalling about a dozen years. During the reign of the Western Satrap Nahapana, the Satavahanas lost a considerable territory to the satraps, including eastern Malwa, Southern Gujarat, and Northern Konkan, from Broach to Sopara and the Nasik and Poona districts.

GAUTAMIPUTRA SATAKARNI (78-106 CE)

Eventually Gautamiputra (Sri Yagna) Sâtakarni (also known as Shalivahan) (r. 78-106 CE) defeated the Western Satrap ruler Nahapana, restoring the prestige of his dynasty by reconquering a large part of the former dominions of the Sâtavâhanas. He was an ardent supporter of Hinduism.

According to the Nasik inscription made by his mother Gautami Balasri, he is the one...

...who crushed down the pride and conceit of the Kshatriyas (the native Indian princes, the Rajputs of Rajputana, Gujarat and Central India); who destroyed the Shakas (Western Kshatrapas), Yavanas (Indo-Greeks) and Pahlavas (Indo-Parthians),... who rooted the Khakharata familly (The Kshaharata familly of Nahapana); who restored the glory of the Satavahana race.

Gautamiputra Satakarni may also have defeated Shaka king Vikramaditya in 78 AD and started the calendar known as Shalivahana era or Shaka era, which is followed by the Marathi and Telugu people even to this day.

Gautamiputra Sâtakarni's son, Vashishtiputra Pulumâyi (r. 106-130 CE), succeeded him. Gautamiputra was the first Sâtavâhana king to issue the portrait-type coinage, in a style derived from the Western Satraps.

SUCCESSORS

Gautamiputra's brother, Vashishtiputra Sâtakarni, married the daughter of Rudradaman I of the Western Satraps dynasty. Around 150 CE, Rudradaman I, now his father-in-law, waged war against the Satavahanas, who were defeated twice in these conflicts. Vashishtiputra Satakarni was only spared his life because of his familly links with Rudradaman:

"Rudradaman (...) who obtained good report because he, in spite of having twice in fair fight completely defeated Satakarni, the lord of Dakshinapatha, on account of the nearness of their connection did not destroy him."

—*Junagadh rock inscription*

As a result of his victories, Rudradaman regained all the former territories previously held by Nahapana, except for the extreme south territories of Poona and Nasik. Satavahana dominions were limited to their original base in the Deccan and eastern central India around Amaravati.

However, the last great king of this dynasty, Yajna Satakarni, defeated the Western Satraps and reconquered their southern regions in western and central India. During the reign of Sri Yajna Sâtakarni (170-199 CE) the Sâtavâhanas regained some prosperity, and some of his coins have been found in Surashtra but around the middle of the third century, the dynasty came to an end.

DECLINE OF THE SATAVAHANAS

Four or five kings of Yajna Satakarni's line succeeded him, and continued to rule till about the mid 200s CE. However, the dynasty was soon extinguished following the rise of its feudatories, perhaps on account of a decline in central power.

Several dynasties divided the lands of the kingdom among themselves. Among them were:

- Western Satraps in the northwestern part of the kingdom.
- Abhiras in the western part of the kingdom. They were ultimately to succeed the Sâtavâhanas in their capital Pratishthânapura.
- Chutus of Banavasi in North Karnataka.

- Kadambas of Banavasi in North Karnataka.
- Ikshvaku dynasty (or Srîparvatiyas) in the Krishna-Guntur region.
- Pallavas of Kanchipuram, of whom the first ruler was Simhavarman I (r. 275-300 CE).

COINAGE

The Satavahanas are the first native Indian rulers to issue their own coins with portraits of their rulers, starting with king Gautamiputra Satakarni, a practice derived from that of the Western Satraps he defeated, itself originating with the Indo-Greek kings to the northwest.

Satavahana coins give unique indications as to their chronology, language, and even facial features (curly hair, long ears and strong lips). They issued mainly lead and copper coins; their portrait-style silver coins were usually struck over coins of the Western Kshatrapa kings.

The coin legends of the Satavahanas, in all areas and all periods, used a Prakrit dialect without exception. Some reverse coin legends are in a Dravidian language/Proto-Telugu, which seems to have been in use in their heartland abutting the Kistna, probably Amaravati, Guntur district, Andhra Pradesh.

Their coins also display various traditional symbols, such as elephants, lions, horses and chaityas (stupas), as well as the "Ujjain symbol", a cross with four circles at the end. The legendary Ujjayini emperor Vikramaditya on whose name the Vikram Samvat is initiated might be Satakarni II a Satavahana emperor as the Ujjayini symbol also appeared on the Satavahana coins.

CULTURAL ACHIEVEMENTS

Of the Sâtavâhana kings, Hâla (r. 20-24 CE) is famous for compiling the collection of Maharashtri poems known as the *Gaha Sattasai* (Sanskrit: Gâthâ Saptashatî), although from linguistic evidence it seems that the work now extant must have been re-edited in the succeeding century or two. The Lilavati describes his marriage with a Ceylonese Princess.

The Satavahanas influenced South-East Asia to a great extent, spreading Hindu culture, language and religion into that part of the world. Their coins had images of ships.

ART OF AMARAVATI

The Sâtavâhana kings are also remarkable for their contributions to Buddhist art and architecture. They built great stupas in the Krishna River Valley, including the stupa at Amaravati in Andhra Pradesh. The stupas were decorated in marble slabs and sculpted with scenes from the life of the Buddha, portrayed in a characteristic slim and elegant style. The Satavahana empire colonized southeast Asia and spread Indian culture to those parts.

Mahayana Buddhism, which may have originated in Andhra (northwestern India being the alternative candidate), was carried to many parts of Asia by the rich maritime culture of the Satavahanas. The Amaravati style of sculpture spread to Southeast Asia at this time.

ART OF SANCHI

The Satavahanas contributed greatly to the embellishment of the Buddhist stupa of Sanchi. The gateways and the balustrade were built after 70 BCE, and appear to have been commissioned by them. An inscription records the gift of one of the top architraves of the Southern Gateway by the artisans of the Satavahana king Satakarni:

Gift of Ananda, the son of Vasithi, the foreman of the artisans of rajan Siri Satakarni.

Throughout, the Buddhist art of the Satavahanas remained aniconic, denying any human representation of the Buddha, even in highly descriptive scenes. This remained true until the end of the Satavahana rule, in the 2nd century CE.

PANDYAN KINGDOM

The Pandyan kingdom was an ancient Tamil state in South India of unknown antiquity. The Pandyas were one of the three ancient Tamil kingdoms (Chola and Chera being the other two) who ruled the Tamil country until end of the 15th century. They initially ruled from Korkai, a sea port on the southern most tip of the Indian peninsula, and in later times moved to Madurai.

The early Pandyan dynasty of the Sangam literature went into obscurity during the invasion of the Kalabhras. The dynasty revived under Kadungon in the early 6th century, pushed the Kalabhras out of the Tamil country and ruled from Madurai. They again went into decline with the rise of the Cholas in the 9th century and were in constant conflict with them. The Pandyas allied themselves with the Sinhalese and the Cheras in harassing the Chola empire until they found an opportunity for reviving their fortunes during the late 13th century.

The Pandyas entered their golden age under Jatavarman Sundara Pandyan (c. 1251) who expanded the empire into Telugu country and invaded and conquered the northern half of Sri Lanka. They also had extensive trade links with the Southeast Asian maritime empires of Srivijaya and their successors. During their history, the Pandyas were repeatedly in conflict with the Pallavas, Cholas, Hoysalas and finally the Muslim invaders from the Delhi Sultanate. The Pandyan Kingdom finally became extinct after the establishment of the Madurai Sultanate in the 16th century.

The Pandyas excelled in both trade and literature. They controlled the pearl fisheries along the south Indian coast, between Sri Lanka and India, which produced one of the finest pearls known in the ancient world. Tradition holds that the legendary Sangams were held in Madurai under their patronage, and that some of the Pandya kings were poets themselves.

The origin of the word "Pandya" has been a subject of much speculation. Some scholars believe that it descended from the "Pandavas" of Mahabharata, while others argue that the name could be derived from the word "Pandi" the original name of the Tamil country.

Historians have used several sources to identify the origins of the early Pandyan dynasty with the pre-Christian Era and also to piece together the names of the Pandyan kings. Unfortunately, the exact genealogy of these kings have not been authoritatively established yet.

SANGAM LITERATURE

Various Pandya kings find mention in a number of poems in the Sangam Literature. Among them Nedunjeliyan, 'the victor of Talaiyalanganam', and Mudukudimi Peruvaludi 'of several sacrifices' deserve special mention. Besides several short poems found in the *Akananuru* and the *Purananuru* collections, there are two major works - *Mathuraikkanci* and the *Netunalvatai* (in the collection of *Pattupattu*) give a glimpse into the society and commercial activities in the Pandyan kingdom during the Sangam age.

It is difficult to estimate the exact date of these Sangam age Pandyas. The period covered by the extant literature of the Sangam is unfortunately not easy to determine with any measure of certainty. Except the longer epics *Silapathikaram* and *Manimekalai*, which by common consent belong to the age later than the Sangam age, the poems have reached us in the forms of systematic anthologies. Each individual poem has generally attached to it a colophon on the authorship and subject matter of the poem, the name of the king or chieftain to whom the poem relates and the occasion which called forth the eulogy are also found.

It is from these colophons and rarely from the texts of the poems themselves, that we gather the names of many kings and chieftains and the poets and poetesses patronized by them. The task of reducing these names to an ordered scheme in which the different generations of contemporaries can be marked off one another has not been easy. To add to the confusions, some historians have even denounced these colophons as later additions and untrustworthy as historical documents.

Any attempt at extracting a systematic chronology from these poems should take into consideration the casual nature of these poems and the wide differences between the purposes of the anthologist who collected these poems and the historian's attempts to arrive at a continuous history.

EPIGRAPHY

The earliest Pandya to be found in epigraph, is Nedunjeliyan figuring in the *Minakshipuram* record assigned from the second to the first centuries BCE. The record documents a gift of rock-cut beds, to a Jain ascetic. Punch marked coins in the Pandya country dating from around the same time have also been found.

Pandyas are also mentioned in the Pillars of Ashoka (inscribed 273 - 232 BCE). Asoka in his inscriptions refers to the peoples of south India as the Cholas, Cheras, Pandyas and Satiyaputras as recipients of his Buddhist proselytism. These kingdoms, although not part of the Mauryan Empire, were in friendly terms with Asoka:

> "The conquest by Dharma has been won here, on the borders, and even six hundred yojanas (5,400–9,600 km) away, where the Greek king Antiochos rules, beyond there where the four kings named Ptolemy, Antigonos, Magas and Alexander rule, likewise in the south among the Cholas, the Pandyas, and as far as Tamraparni (Sri Lanka)."

Kharavela, the Kalinga king who ruled during the second century BCE, in his Hathigumpha inscription, claims to have destroyed a confederacy of Tamil states ("Tamiradesasanghatam") which had lasted 132 years, and to have acquired a large quantity of Pearls from the Pandyas.

ZENITH FOLLOWED BY THE END OF PANDYAS

The Pandyan kingdom was replaced by the Chola princes who assumed the title as Chola Pandyas in the 11th century. After being overshadowed by the Pallavas and Cholas for centuries, Pandyan glory was briefly revived by Maravaramban Sundara Pandyan and (probably his younger brother or son) the much celebrated Jatavarman Sundara Pandyan in 1251 and the Pandya power extended from the Telugu countries on banks of the Godavari river to the northern half of Sri Lanka. The revival of the Pandyan dynasty was to coincide with the gradual but steady decline of the Chola empire, with the last two or three Chola kings who followed Kulothunga III were either very weak or incompetent.

The Cholas of course did not lack valour but had been unable to stop the revival of the Pandiyan empire from the times of Maravaramban Sundara Pandyan, the revival of the Kadava Pallavas at Kanchi under Kopperinchunga I and indeed the growing in power and status of the Telugu Cholas, the Renanti and the Irungola Cholas of the Telugu country for the last three-named had been very trusted allies of the Cholas up to Kulothunga III, having helped him in conquering Kalinga. In fact the marital alliance of Kulothunga III and one of his successors Raja Raja III with the Hoysalas did not prove to be of any advantage, though initially at least Kulothunga III took the help of the Hoysalas in countering the Pandiyan resurgence.

Kulothunga III had even conquered Karur, Cheranadu in addition to Madurai, Ilam and Kalinga. However, it ultimately proved that his strength was because of the support from Hoysalas whose king Veera Ballala II was his son-in-law. However, Veera Ballala II himself had lost quite a bit of his territories between 1208-1212 to his local adversaries in Kannada country, like the Kalachuris, Seunas etc. The resurgent Pandiyans under Maravarman Sundara Pandiyan went to war against Kulothunga and first at Kandai and then near Manaparai on the outskirts of modern Tiruchirappalli, the Pandiyans routed the Chola army and entered Tiruchy, Srirangam and Thanjavur victorious in war. But it appears that in the Tiruchy and Srirangam areas, there was renewed control of the Cholas, presumably with the help of the Hoysalas under Vira Someswara with the Hoysalas later shifting their allegience to the Pandyans either during the last years of Maravarman Sundara Pandyan or the early years of his successor Jatavarman Sundara Pandyan.

Jatavarman Sundara Pandiyan was a very brave, ambitious warrior king, who it appears wanted to completely subjugate the Cholas. It appears while he initially tolerated the presence of the Hoysalas under Vira Someshwara with his son Visvanatha or Ramanatha ruling from Kuppam near Samayapuram on the outskirts of Srirangam. This was because other feudatories of the Hoysalas were also growing in power and threatening the Hoysala kingdom itself. Besides, the Muslim invasion of the Deccan had started under Malik Kafur. The challenged Hoysalas did have foothold in and around Tiruchy and Srirangam for a few years and seemed to have indulged in some temple building activity at Srirangam also. But Jatavarman Sundara Pandiyan, who challenged Rajendra III in 1276-79, seems to have first concentrated on strengthening himself with the help of the Hoysalas. He first vanquished the Kadava Pallavas under Kopperinchungan-II, who had challenged the Hoysala army stationed in and around Kanchi and killed a few of their commanders. This alliance of the Hoysalas and the Pandiyans seems to have antagonized Rajendra Chola III who veered away from the Hoysalas. For a while the Kadava Pallavas and the Cholas came together, despite an earlier Chola, Raja Raja III having been held in captivity by Kopperinchunga II and his release being secured by the Hoysalas.

Jatavarman Sundara Pandiyan seized the opportunity with the Hoysalas being in Tiruchy and not having any ally, the rapidly weakening Cholas seeking alliance with the Kadava Pallavas who were themselves being threatened by the Telugu Cholas. In 1254 (or 1260) Jatavarman first dragged the Hoysalas into war by routing his son Ramanatha out of Tiruchy. Vira Someshwara Hoysala who had given the control of the empire to his sons had to come out of his slumber and tried to challenge Jatavarman and between Samayapuram and Tiruchy, the armies of Vira Someshwara were routed with Vira Someshwara losing his life in this battle. This ended the presence of the Hoysalas in Tamil country. Jatavarman did not stop here, he went inside Kannada country after conquering Tiruchy and occupied parts of Hoysala territory up to the Konkana coast and established his son Vira Pandiyan as ruler of those territories. Temporarily at least the Hoysalas were in disarray in Kannada country itself.

Next the Pandiyan prince Jatavarman concentrated on completely wiping out the Chola empire. Rajadhiraja III had interfered in an earlier Pandiyan war of succession and defeated a confederation of Pandiyan princes. The predecessors of Jatavarman Sundara Pandiyan had suffered at the time of the Chola invasion and he wanted to take revenge. This was his opportunity. Rajendra III had been counting on Hoysala assistance in case he was challenged by the Pandiyans keeping in mind the earlier marital alliance of the Cholas with the Hoysalas. Unfortunately for Rajendra III, the Hoysalas had lost all pretensions of trying to pose as a major regional power in Kannada and Tamil countries as they had been wiped out of Tamizhagam and indeed lost territories inside Kannada country itself to Jatavarman Sundara Pandiyan.

Initially, Jatavarman consodlidated the Pandiyan hold on Tiruchy and Srirangam and marched towards Tanjore and Kumbakonam. The Chola capital of Gangaikondacholapuram too was not far from reach. During the years 1270-1276 it appeared that Rajendra III ruled mainly in and around Gangaikondacholapuram and Tanjore. Tiruchy and Srirangam had been lost to the Cholas for ever at least from 1254 AD. Though Rajendra III had been opposed to the Hoysalas due to their alliance with the Pandiyans, with new hostilities emerging between Hoysalas and the Pandiyans, Rajendra III had hoped for renewed friendship and military alliance with the Hoysalas. When challenged by Jatavarman Sundara Pandiyan, the brave but tactically naive Rajendra III marched against the Pandiyans between Tanjore and Tiruchy, hoping for assistance and participation in war from the Hoysalas. However, the already vanquished Hoysalas were more keen on preserving their own skin and did not prefer going to war and in the process, risk another defeat by the resurgent Pandiyans. Rajendra III was hopelessly isolated and was thoroughly routed and humiliated in this war, which is variously dated as between 1268-1270. The known rule of Jatavarman Sundara Pandiyan is of course, up to 1268 only. Probably Rajendra III fled the battlefield and had continued in obscurity up to 1279 but without any of the erstwhile Chola territories. By 1280 AD, the Pandiya empire was no more.

On the death of Maravarman Kulasekara Pandyan I in 1308, a conflict stemming from succession disputes arose amongst his sons. Sundara Pandya and Vira Pandya fought each other for the throne. Soon Madurai fell into the hands of the invading armies of the Delhi Sultanate who were making the most of corruption and anarchy in the subcontinent. Pandyas and their descendants were confined to a small region around Thirunelveli for a few more years and after the 17th century C.E. we hear no more of them.

After Madurai fell into the hands of the invading armies of the Delhi Sultanate, the Pandyas sought the help of Vijayanagar Empire. The Vijayanagar Empire replaced the Delhi Sultanate in Madurai and appointed Nayak governors to rule from Madurai.

GOVERNMENT AND SOCIETY

Trade

Megasthenes reported about the pearl fisheries of the Pandyas, indicating that the Pandyas derived great wealth from the pearl trade.

RELIGION

Historical Madurai was a stronghold of Saivism. Following the invasion of Kalabhras, Jainism gained foothold in Pandyan kingdom. Jainism was something not new to the land of Pandyas as references to a jainist past(and buddhist) are found in ancient Tamil literature with the advent of Bhakti movements, Saivism and Vaishnavism resurfaced. Persecutions of Jains(Samanas) were held under the patronage of Pandyan Kings. The later day Pandyas after 600 AD were Hindus who claimed to descend from Lord Shiva and Goddess Parvati. Pandyan Nedumchadayan was a staunch Vaishnavite.

EARLY CHOLAS

The **Early Cholas** of the pre and post Sangam period (300 B.C.E. – 200 C.E.) were one of the three main kingdoms of the ancient Tamil country. Their early capitals were Urayur and Kaveripattinam. Along with Pandyas and Cheras, Chola history goes back to the period where the history is covered with the mists of time.

Although we hear the exploits of a number of Cholas of this period through Sangam literature and later folklore, it is hard to elucidate exact histories with any amount of certainty.

On the history of Cholas, as in many other subjects of Indian history, we have very little authentic written evidence. Historians during past 150 years have gleaned a great treasury of knowledge on the subject from a variety of sources such as ancient Tamil Sangam literature, oral traditions, religious texts, temple and copperplate inscriptions of the imperial cholas from the tenth century CE.

The main source for the available information of the early Cholas is the early Tamil literature of the Sangam Period. There are also brief notices on the Chola country and its towns, ports and commerce furnished by the *Periplus of the Erythraean Sea* (*Periplus Maris Erythraei*). *Periplus* is a work by an anonymous Alexandrian merchant, written in the time of Domitian (81 – 96 CE) and contains precious little information of the Chola country. Writing half a century later, the geographer Ptolemy has more to tell us about the Chola country, its port and its inland cities.

Mahavamsa, a Buddhist text, also recounts a number of conflicts between the inhabitants of Ceylon and the Tamil immigrants.

Cholas also are mentioned in the Pillars of Ashoka (inscribed 273 - 232 BCE) inscriptions, where they are mentioned among the kingdoms, which, though not subject to Ashoka, were on friendly terms with him.

Kharavela, the Kalinga king who ruled during the second century BCE, in his Hathigumpha inscription, claims to have destroyed a confederacy of Tamil states ("Tamiradesasanghatam") which had lasted 132 years.

EARLY LEGENDS

The inscriptions of the Medieval Cholas are replete with legends about the mythical Early Chola kings. The Cholas were looked upon as descended from the sun. These myths speak of the Chola king *Kantaman*, supposed contemporary of the sage Agastya, whose devotion brought the river Kavery into existence. There is also the story of the king Manu who sentenced his son to death for having accidentally killed a calf. Mahavamasa portrays King Elara who was defeated by Duttha Gamini (c. second century B.C.E.) as the just king who '...had a bell with a rope attached at the head of his bed, so that all who sought redress might ring it...'. King Shibi who rescued a dove from a hawk by giving his own flesh to the hungry hawk was also part of the early Chola legends. King Shibi was also called Sembiyan, a popular title assumed by a number of Chola kings.

These legends received enormous emphasis in the later Chola period in the long mythical genealogies incorporated into the copper-plate charters of the tenth and eleventh centuries. The earliest version of this is found in the Anbil Plates which gives fifteen names before Vijayalaya Cholan including the genuinely historical ones of Karikala, Perunarkilli and Kocengannan. The Thiruvalangadu Plate swells this list to forty-four, and the Kanyakumari Plate runs up to fifty-two. There are other lists gathered from literary works such as *Kalingathuparani*. No two of these lists agree, although some names and details are common to all.

CHOLAS IN SANGAM LITERATURE

The earliest Chola kings of whom we have tangible evidence are those mentioned in the Sangam literature, written in the period 200 BCE–300 CE. Unfortunately, it has not been possible to piece together an internal chronology of the Sangam works. Due to this, we know of several rulers, but not their chronology. The early Cholas were anxious to connect themselves with the *Mahabharata* to prove their antiquity, as is evident from the Sangam works. All three kings have been portrayed as fighting the war or involved in feeding both the armies at that legendary war.

KARIKALA CHOLA

Karikala Chola (c. 120 CE) stands pre-eminent amongst all those mentioned in *Pattinappaalai*. Karikala's father was Ilamcetcenni, a brave king and a hard fighter. 'Karikala' means 'elephant feller' or 'charred leg', which is assumed to be a reference to an accident by fire which befell the prince early in his life. *Pattinappaalai* describes this accident and the enterprising way in which the prince escaped and established himself in the Chola throne. *Pattinappalai* is a long poem on the then Chola capital Kaveripattinam. This work also describes the numerous battles of Karikala fought against the other two Tamil kings in one of which the Chera king was disgraced (received a wound on his back) and committed suicide. Karikala thus broke the confederacy that was formed against him and established hegemony over Pandyas and Cheras.

In later times Karikala was the subject of many legends found in the *Cilappatikaram* and in inscriptions and literary works of the eleventh and twelfth centuries. They attribute to him the conquest of the whole of India up to the Himalayas and the construction of the flood banks, Grand Anicut, of the Kaveri River with the aid of his feudatories. These legends however are conspicuous by their absence in the works of Sangam.

NALANKILLI AND NEDUNKILLI

The poet Kovur Kilar mentions a protracted civil war between two Chola chieftains Nalankilli and Nedunkilli. Nedunkilli shut himself in a fort in Avur, which was being besieged by Mavalattan, Nalankilli's younger brother. The poet chided Nedunkilli to come out and fight like a man instead of causing untold misery to the people of the city.

In another poem, the poet begs both the princes to give up the civil was as whoever wins, the loser will be a Chola.

KOCENGANNAN

Kalavali by Poygayar mentions the Chola king Kocengannan and his battle with the Chera king Kanaikkal Irumporai. The Chera was taken prisoner and Poygayar, who was a friend of the Chera, sang Kocenganna's prince in 40 stanzas. The Chola king, pleased with the work, released the Chera. Kalavali describes the battle fought at Kalumalam, near the Chera capital.

Kocengannan became the subject of many legends in later times and is portrayed as a pious Siva devotee who built many fine temples for Siva along the banks of the river Kaveri.

SOCIAL CONDITION

Sangam literature gives an unusually complete and true picture of the social and economic conditions during the early chola period. The culture is best described as an amalgam of the Dravidian and Aryan. The stories of *Mahabharata* and *Ramayana* were well known to the Tamil people, shown by the claims of some kings to have fed both the opposing army in the Mahabharata War. The claim that Shibi, who gave his own flesh to save a dove, as a Chola is obviously influenced by northern legends.

The land of the Cholas was fertile and there was ample food. Sangam poems say that in the Chola country watered by the river Kaveri, in a space in which an elephant could lie, one can produce enough grain to feed seven.

Hereditary monarchy was the prevailing form of government. Disputed succession and civil war was not uncommon. The sphere of the state activity was limited. In a society steeped in respect for custom, even the most perverse dictator could not have done much harm.

The Chola monarchs were approachable by subjects and justice was meted out directly by the king in most occasions. This is in marked contrast to the magnificent empires of the later Cholas where the Emperor was kept much away from contact with the lay people. The kings often took the field in person in battles and if the kings was killed or wounded in battle, his army immediately gave up the fight and surrendered.

The trade that flourished between the Chola country and the ancient Roman Empire is given in much detail by *Periplus of the Erythraean Sea* (c. 75 C.E.).

CHERA DYNASTY

The **Chera Dynasty** was a Tamil dynasty that ruled in southern India from before the Sangam era (300 BCE - 200 CE) until the fourteenth century CE. The early Cheras ruled Kerala, Kongu Nadu and Salem. Their capital was Vanchi Muthur, though this may have been located either at present-day Kodungallur in Thrissur district of Kerala or else at Karur.

The other two major Tamil dynasties were the Cholas in the eastern Coromandel Coast and Pandyas in the south central peninsula. Chera rulers engaged in frequent warfare and also sought marriage alliances with neighbouring kingdoms. Throughout the reign of the Cheras, trade continued to bring prosperity to Tamil Country (part of which is modern Kerala), with spices, ivory, timber, pearls and gems being exported to Egypt, Rome, Greece, Phoenicia, Arabia, Mesopotamia and Persia. Evidence of extensive foreign trade from ancient times is available throughout the Malabar coast, from the Roman, Greek and Arabic coins unearthed from Kollam, Kodungallur, Eyyal (near Trissur) in Kerala . Muziris, has been referenced by ancient writers, such as the author of the Periplus of the Erythraean Sea to be an inland port probably near Kodungallur. Sangam Cheran coins and inscriptions are found only in Karur, Erode and Coimbatore region of modern Tamil Nadu.

While Cheras had their own religion (Hinduism), other religious traditions came to this area during the period of the Chera kings. Jainism came to Chera Kingdom by the second century BCE.

In early Tamil literature the great Chera rulers are referred to as Cheral, Kuttuvan, Irumporai, Kollipurai and Athan. Chera rulers were also called Kothai or Makothai. The nobility among the Cheras were called Cheraman in general. The word Kerala, of possible Prakrit origins, does not appear in Sangam Literature. Ashoka's edicts mention an independent dynasty known by the name *Ceraputta,* who were outside Ashoka's empire. The unknown author of *Periplus of the Erythraean Sea* mentions Chera as *Cerobothra* ("Keralaputhra") whose capital is Karur, while Pliny, the Roman historian of the first century, calls it *Caelobothras*. It is believed that religiously the Cheras were Shaivites. The kings of the dynasty referred to themselves as Vanavar.

SANGAM CHERAS

The only source available for us regarding the early Chera Kings is the anthologies of the Sangam literature. Scholars now generally agree that this literature belongs to the first few centuries CE. The internal chronology of this literature is still far from settled. The Sangam literature is full of names of the kings and the princes, and of the poets who extolled them. Despite a rich literature that depicts the life and work of these people, these are not worked into connected history so far. Their capital is stated to be modern Karur in Tamil Nadu.

Pathirruppaththu, the fourth book in the Ettuthokai anthology mentions a number of Chera Kings of the Chera dynasty. Each King is praised in ten songs sung by the Court Poet and the Kings are in the following order:

1. Nedum Cheralathan,
2. Palyane Chel Kezhu Kuttuvan,
3. Kalankai Kanni Narmudi Cheral,
4. Kadal Pirakottiya Vel Kezhu Kuttuvan,
5. Attu Kottu Pattu Cheralathan,
6. Chelva Kadunko Azhi Athan,
7. Thakadur Erintha Perum Cheral Irumporai,
8. Kudako Ilam Cheral Irumporai.

The first two kings were the sons of Uthiyan Cheralathan and Veliyan Nallini. The third, fourth and fifth kings were sons of Nedum Cheralathan, while the mother of fourth King (also known as Chenkuttuvan) was Chola Princess Manikilli. Chelva Kadunko Vazhiyathan was the son of Anthuvan Cheral Irumporai and Porayan Perumthevi. Perum Cheral Irumporai was the son of Vazhiyathan and Ilam Cheral Irumporai was the son of a Chera ruler Kuttuvan Irumporai (son of Mantharan Cheral Irumporai).

Archaeology has also found epigraphic evidence regarding these early Cheras. The most important of these is the Pugalur (Aranattarmalai) inscription. This inscription refers to three generations of Chera rulers Adam Cheral Irrumporai, his son Perum Kadungo, and his son Ilam Kadungo. The charter was issued when Perum Kadungo was the ruler monarch and Ilam Kadungo was appointed prince. Athan refers only to a crowned King of Chera dynasty who accepted this title at the time of coronation. Athan Cheral Irumporai was the son of Perum Cheral Irumporai. It therefore follows that Perum Kadungo was the son of a crowned King of the Chera Dynasty. Perum Kadunko means that he was the Senior Ko (Senior ruler) of Kadunadu, located in the Tamil Nadu side of the Sahya Mountains.

'Purananuru' refers to Udiyan Cheral, who probably ruled in the first – second centuries CE. It is said that he fed the rival armies during the war of Mahabharata. *Imayavaramban* Neduncheralathan, another Sangam age king claimed to have conquered up to the Himalayas and to have inscribed his emblem in the face of the mountains. Senguttuvan was another famous Chera, whose contemporary Gajabahu II of Lanka according to Mahavamsa visited the Chera country.

The early Cheras controlled a large territory of the Kongu region. They also ruled the kodunthamizh regions of Travancore (Venadu) and the Malabar (Kuttanadu) west coast through vassals. They were in contact with the Satavahanas in the north and with the Romans and Greeks. Trade flourished overseas and there was a considerable exchange of gold and coins, as seen by archaeological evidence and literature. The Romans brought vast amounts of gold in exchange of 'Kari' (Pepper) from Malainadu.

BHAKTI ERA CHERAS

Little is known about the Cheras between c. third century CE and the eight century CE. An obscure dynasty, the Kalabhras, invaded the Tamil country, displaced the existing kingdoms and ruled for around three centuries. They were displaced by the Pallavas and the Pandyas in the sixth century CE. A Pandya ruler, Arikesari Parankusa Maravarman (c.730 – 765CE), mentioned in a number of Pandya copper-plate inscriptions, was a prominent ruler during this period. He claims to have defeated a prominent Chera king. The name of the Chera king is not known, however from the details of the battles between the Pandya and the Chera, the Chera territory ceded seems to have included the entire Malabar and Travancore (Kuttanadu and Venadu) and the southern Pandya country from Kanyakumari to Thirunelveli the seat of the Cheras being in Karur Kongu Nadu. The Chera kings took the title of *Perumal* during this period and patronised the Vaishnavite sect. Kulasekara Alwar who ruled in the 8th century became a devotional Vaishnavite poet. Pallavas also mention in their inscriptions about their battles with the Cheras. Pulakesin II, in his Aihole inscription mentioned " *Pulikesin II, driving the Pallava behind the forts of Kanchi, reached as far south as the Kaveri river, and there caused prosperity to the Chola, Chera and Pandya*".

In the reign of Pandya Parantaka Nedumjadaiyan (765 – 790), the Cheras were still in Karur and were a close ally of the Pallavas. Pallavamalla Nadivarman defeated the Pandya Varaguna with the help of a Chera king. Cultural contacts between the Pallava court and the Chera country were common. The Saivite saint Cheraman Perumal and the other is the Vaishnavite saint Kulasekhara, were famous in the Hindu religious movements. Kulasekhara became one of the celebrated Alvars and his poems came to be called the *Perumal Thirumozhi*. Cheraman Perumal ruled around the eighth and the ninth centuries. In this Kulasekhara calls himself *Kongar Kon* (the king of the Kongu people) hailing from Kollinagar (Karur). Adi Shankara was his contemporary. **Kongumandala Satakam** also says that Cheraman Perumal went to Kayilai with Sundarar from Kongu Nadu.

LATE MIDDLE KINGDOMS – THE CLASSICAL AGE

The classical age in India began with the resurgence of the north during Harsha's conquests around the 7th century, and ended with the fall of the Vijayanagar Empire in the South, due to pressure from the invaders to the north in the 13th century. This period produced some of India's finest art, considered the epitome of classical development, and the development of the main spiritual and philosophical systems which continued to be in Hinduism, Buddhism and Jainism.

King Harsha of Kannauj succeeded in reuniting northern India during his reign in the 7th century, after the collapse of the Gupta dynasty. His kingdom collapsed after his death. From the 7th to the 9th century, three dynasties contested for control of northern India: the Pratiharas of Malwa and later Kannauj; the Palas of Bengal, and the Rashtrakutas of the Deccan. The Sena dynasty would later assume control of the Pala kingdom, and the Pratiharas fragmented into various states. These were the first of the Rajputs, a series of kingdoms which managed to survive in some form for almost a millennium until Indian independence from the British. The first recorded Rajput kingdoms emerged in Rajasthan in the 6th century, and small Rajput dynasties later ruled much of northern India. One Rajput of the Chauhan dynasty, Prithviraj Chauhan, was known for bloody conflicts against the encroaching Islamic Sultanates. The Shahi dynasty ruled portions of eastern Afghanistan, northern Pakistan, and Kashmir from the mid-seventh century to the early eleventh century. Whilst the northern concept of a pan-Indian empire had collapsed at the end of Harsha's empire, the ideal instead shifted to the south.

The Chalukya Empire ruled parts of southern and central India from 550 to 750 from Badami, Karnataka and again from 970 to 1190 from Kalyani, Karnataka. The Pallavas of Kanchi were their contemporaries further to the south. With the decline of the Chalukya empire, their feudatories, Hoysalas of Halebidu, Kakatiya of Warangal, Seuna Yadavas of Devagiri and a southern branch of the Kalachuri divided the vast Chalukya empire amongst themselves around the middle of 12th century. Later during the middle period, the Chola kingdom emerged in northern Tamil Nadu, and the Chera kingdom in Kerala. By 1343 A.D., all these kingdoms had ceased to exist giving rise to the Vijayanagar empire.

Southern Indian kingdoms of the time expanded their influence as far as Indonesia, controlling vast overseas empires in Southeast Asia. The ports of southern India were involved in the Indian Ocean trade, chiefly involving spices, with the Roman Empire to the west and Southeast Asia to the east. Literature in local vernaculars and spectacular architecture flourished till about the beginning of the 14th century when southern expeditions of the sultan of Delhi took their toll on these kingdoms. The Hindu Vijayanagar dynasty[Karnata Rajya] came into conflict with Islamic rule (the Bahmani Kingdom) and the clashing of the two systems, caused a mingling of the indigenous and foreign culture that left lasting cultural influences on each other. The Vijaynagar Empire eventually declined due to pressure from the first Delhi Sultanates who had managed to establish themselves in the north, centered around the city of Delhi by that time.

WESTERN CHALUKYA EMPIRE

The Western Chalukya Empire ruled most of the western Deccan, South India, between the 10th and 12th centuries. This dynasty is sometimes called the *Kalyani*

Chalukya after its regal capital at Kalyani, today's Basavakalyan in Karnataka and alternatively the *Later Chalukya* from its theoretical relationship to the sixth century Chalukya dynasty of Badami. The dynasty is called Western Chalukyas to differentiate from the contemporaneous Eastern Chalukyas of Vengi, a separate dynasty. Prior to the rise of these Chalukyas, the Rashtrakuta empire of Manyakheta controlled most of deccan and central India for over two centuries. In 973, seeing confusion in the Rashtrakuta empire after a successful invasion of their capital by the Paramara of Malwa, Tailapa II a feudatory of the Rashtrakuta ruling from Bijapur region defeated his overlords and made Manyakheta his capital. The dynasty quickly rose to power and grew into an empire under Somesvara I who moved the capital to Kalyani.

For over a century, the two empires of southern India, the Western Chalukyas and the Chola dynasty of Tanjore fought many fierce wars to control the fertile region of Vengi. During these conflicts, the Eastern Chalukyas of Vengi, distant cousins of the Western Chalukyas but related to the Cholas by marriage took sides with the Cholas further complicating the situation. It was only during the rule of Vikramaditya VI in the late eleventh to early twelfth century that the Western Chalukya empire convincingly eclipsed the Cholas and reached its peak with territories spreading over most of the deccan. Vast areas between the Narmada River in the north and Kaveri River in the south came under Chalukya control. During this period the other major ruling families of the Deccan, the Hoysalas, the Seuna Yadavas of Devagiri, the Kakatiya dynasty and the Southern Kalachuri, were subordinates of the Western Chalukyas and gained their independence only when the power of the Chalukya waned during the later half of the twelfth century.

The Western Chalukyas developed an architectural style known today as a transitional style, an architectural link between the style of the early Chalukya dynasty and that of the later Hoysala empire. Most of its monuments are in the districts bordering the Tungabhadra River in central Karnataka. Well known examples are the Kasivisvesvara Temple at Lakkundi, the Mallikarjuna Temple at Kuruvatii, the Kallesvara Temple at Bagali and the Mahadeva Temple at Itagi. This was an important period in the development of fine arts in Southern India, especially in literature as the Western Chalukya kings encouraged writers in the native language of Kannada, and Sanskrit.

Knowledge of the Western Chalukyas history has come through examination of the numerous excavated Kannada language inscriptions left by the kings and from the study of important contemporary literary documents in Western Chalukya literature such as *Gada Yuddha* (982) in Kannada by Ranna and *Vikramankadeva Charitam* (1120) in Sanskrit by Bilhana. The earliest inscription is dated 957, during the rule of Tailapa II when the Western Chalukyas were still a feudatory of the Rashtrakutas and Tailapa II governed from Tardavadi in present day Bijapur district, Karnataka. The genealogy of the kings of this empire is still debated. One theory, based on contemporary literary and inscriptional evidence plus the finding that the Western Chalukyas employed titles and names commonly used by the early Chalukyas, suggests that the Western Chalukya kings belonged to the same family line as the illustrious Badami Chalukya dynasty of sixth century while other Western Chalukya inscriptional evidence indicates they were a distinct line unrelated to the early Chalukyas.

Inscriptional evidence suggests a possible rebellion by a local Chalukya King, Chattigadeva of Banavasi-12000 province (967), in alliance with local Kadamba chieftains. This rebellion however was unfruitful but paved the way for his successor Tailapa II. A few years later, Tailapa II re-established Chalukya rule and defeated the Rashtrakutas during the reign of Karka II by timing his rebellion to coincide with the confusion caused in the Rashtrakuta capital of Manyakheta by the invading Paramaras of Central India in 973. After overpowering the Rashtrakutas, Tailapa II moved his capital to Manyakheta and consolidated the Chalukya empire in the western deccan by subjugating the Paramara and other aggressive rivals and extending his control over the land between the Narmada River and Tungabhadra River. However, some inscriptions indicate that Balagamve in Mysore territory may have been a power centre up to the rule of Somesvara I in 1042.

The intense competition between the kingdoms of the western deccan and those of the Tamil kingdoms came to the fore in the eleventh century over the acutely contested fertile river valleys in the doab region of the Krishna and Godavari River called Vengi (coastal Andhra Pradesh). The Western Chalukyas and the Chola Dynasty fought many bitter wars over control of this strategic resource. The imperial Cholas gained power during the time of the famous king Rajaraja Chola I and the crown prince Rajendra Chola I. The Eastern Chalukyas of Vengi were cousins of the Western Chalukyas but became increasingly influenced by the Cholas through their marital ties with the Tamil kingdom. As this was against the interests of the Western Chalukyas, they wasted no time in involving themselves politically and militarily in Vengi. When King Satyasraya succeeded Tailapa II to the throne, he was able to protect his kingdom from Chola aggression as well as his northern territories in Konkan and Gujarat although his control over Vengi was shaky. His successor, Jayasimha II, fought many battles with the Cholas in the south while both powerful kingdoms struggled to choose the Vengi king. Simultaneously, Jayasimha II subdued the Paramara of central India.

It is known from records that Jayasimha's son, Somesvara I, moved the Chalukya capital to Kalyani in 1042 as hostilities with the Cholas continued and while both sides won and lost battles, neither lost significant territory during the ongoing politics of installing a puppet on the Vengi throne. In 1068 Somesvara I, suffering from an incurable illness, drowned himself in the Tungabhadra River (*Paramayoga*). Despite many conflicts with the Cholas in the south, Somesvara I had managed to maintain control over the northern territories in Konkan, Gujarat, Malwa and Kalinga during his rule. His successor, his eldest son Somesvara II, feuded with his younger brother, Vikramaditya VI, an ambitious warrior who had initially been governor of Gangavadi in the southern deccan when Somesvara II was the king. Married to a Chola princess (a daughter of Virarajendra Chola), Vikramaditya VI maintained a friendly alliance with them. After the death of the

Chola king in 1070, Vikramaditya VI invaded the Tamil kingdom and installed his brother-in-law, Adhirajendra, on the throne creating conflict with Kulothunga Chola I, the powerful ruler of Vengi who sought the Chola throne for himself. At the same time Vikramaditya VI undermined his brother, Somesvara II, by winning the loyalty of the Chalukya feudatories: the Hoysala, the Seuna and the Kadambas of Hangal. Anticipating a civil war, Somesvara II sought help from Vikramaditya VI's enemies, Kulothunga Chola I and the Kadambas of Goa. In the ensuing conflict of 1076, Vikramaditya VI emerged victorious and proclaimed himself king of the Chalukya empire.

The fifty year reign of Vikramaditya VI, the most successful of the later Chalukya rulers, was an important period in Karnataka's history and is referred to by historians as the "Chalukya Vikrama era". Not only was he successful in controlling his powerful feudatories in the north and south, he successfully dealt with the imperial Cholas whom he defeated in the battle of Vengi in 1093 and again in 1118. He retained this territory for many years despite ongoing hostilities with the Cholas. This victory in Vengi reduced the Chola influence in the eastern deccan and made him emperor of territories stretching from the Kaveri River in the south to the Narmada River in the north, earning him the titles *Permadideva* and *Tribhuvanamalla* (lord of three worlds). The scholars of his time paid him glowing tributes for his military leadership, interest in fine arts and religious tolerance. Literature proliferated and scholars in Kannada and Sanskrit adorned his court. Poet Bilhana, who immigrated from far away Kashmir, eulogised the king in his well known work *Vikramankadeva Charita*. Vikramaditya VI was not only an able warrior but also a devout king as indicated by his numerous inscriptions that record grants made to scholars and centers of religion.

The continual warring with the Cholas exhausted both empires, giving their subordinates the opportunity to rebel. In the decades after Vikramaditya VI's death in 1126, the empire steadily decreased in size as their powerful feudatories expanded in autonomy and territorial command. The time period between 1150 and 1200 saw many hard fought battles between the Chalukyas and their feudatories who were also at war with each other. By the time of Jagadhekamalla II, the Chalukyas had lost control of Vengi and his successor, Tailapa III, was defeated by Kakatiya Prola in 1149. Tailapa III was taken captive and later released bringing down the prestige of the Western Chalukyas. Seeing decadence and uncertainty seeping into Chalukya rule, the Hoysalas and Seunas also encroached upon the empire. Hoysala Narasimha I defeated and killed Tailapa III but was unable to overcome the Kalachuris who were vying for control of the same region. In 1157 the Kalachuris under Bijjala II captured Kalyani and occupied it for the next twenty years, forcing the Chalukyas to move their capital to Annigeri in the present day Dharwad district.

The Kalachuris were originally immigrants into the southern deccan from central India and called themselves *Kalanjarapuravaradhisavaras*. Bijjala II and his ancestors had governed as Chalukya commanders (*Mahamandaleshwar*) over the Karhad-4000 and Tardavadi-1000 provinces (overlapping region in present day Karnataka and Maharashtra) with Mangalavada or Annigeri as their capital. Bijjala II's Chikkalagi record of 1157 calls him *Mahabhujabala Chakravarti* ("emperor with powerful shoulders and arms") indicating he no longer was a subordinate of the Chalukyas. However the successors of Bijjala II were unable to hold on to Kalyani and their rule ended in 1183 when the last Chalukya scion, Somesvara IV made a final bid to regain the empire by recapturing Kalyani. Kalachuri King Sankama was killed by Chalukya general Narasimha in this conflict. During this time, Hoysala Veera Ballala II was growing ambitious and clashed on several occasions with the Chalukyas and the other claimants over their empire. He defeated Chalukya Somesvara IV and Seuna Bhillama V bringing large regions in the Krishna River valley under the Hoysala domains, but was unsuccessful against Kalachuris. The Seunas under Bhillama V were on an imperialistic expansion too when the Chalukyas regained Kalyani. Their ambitions were temporarily stemmed by their defeat against Chalukya general Barma in 1183 but they later had their vengeance in 1189.

The overall effort by Somesvara IV to rebuild the Chalukya empire failed and the dynasty was ended by the Seuna rulers who drove Somesvara IV into exile in Banavasi 1189. After the fall of the Chalukyas, the Seunas and Hoysalas continued warring over the Krishna River region in 1191, each inflicting a defeat on the other at various points in time. This period saw the fall of two great empires, the Chalukyas of the western deccan and the Cholas of Tamilakam. On the ruins of these two empires were built the Kingdoms of their feudatories whose mutual antagonisms filled the annals of Deccan history for over a hundred years, the Pandyas taking control over some regions of the erstwhile Chola empire.

ADMINISTRATION

The Western Chalukya kingship was hereditary, passing to the king's brother if the king did not have a male heir. The administration was highly decentralised and feudatory clans such as the Alupas, the Hoysalas, the Kakatiya, the Seuna, the southern Kalachuri and others were allowed to rule their autonomous provinces, paying an annual tribute to the Chalukya emperor. Excavated inscriptions record titles such as *Mahapradhana* (Chief minister), *Sandhivigrahika*, and *Dharmadhikari* (chief justice). Some positions such as *Tadeyadandanayaka* (commander of reserve army) were specialised in function while all ministerial positions included the role of *Dandanayaka* (commander), showing that cabinet members were trained as army commanders as well as in general administrative skills.

The kingdom was divided into provinces such as *Banavasi-12000, Nolambavadi-32000, Gangavadi-96000*, each name including the number of villages under its jurisdiction. The large provinces were divided into smaller provinces containing a lesser number of villages, as in *Belavola-300*. The big provinces were called *Mandala* and under them were *Nadu* further divided into *Kampanas* (groups of villages) and finally a *Bada* (village). A *Mandala* was under a member of the royal family, a trusted feudatory or a senior official. Tailapa II himself was in charge of Tardavadi province during the Rashtrakuta rule. Chiefs of *Mandalas* were transferable based on political developments. For example, an official named Bammanayya administered Banavasi-12000 under King Somesvara III but was later transferred to Halasige-12000. Women from the royal family also administered *Nadus* and *Kampanas*. Army commanders were titled *Mahamandaleshwaras* and those who headed a *Nadu* were entitled *Nadugouvnda*.

The Western Chalukyas minted punch-marked gold pagodas with Kannada and Nagari legends which were large, thin gold coins with several varying punch marks on the obverse side. They usually carried multiple punches of symbols such as a stylised lion, *Sri* in Kannada, a spearhead, the king's title, a lotus and others. Jayasimha II used the legend *Sri Jaya*, Somesvara I issued coins with *Sri Tre lo ka malla*, Somesvara Iı used *Bhuvaneka malla*, Lakshmideva's coin carried *Sri Lasha*, and Jagadhekamalla II coinage had the legend *Sri Jagade*. The Alupas, a feudatory, minted coins with the Kannada and *Nagari* legend *Sri Pandya Dhanamjaya*. Lakkundi in Gadag district and Sudi in Dharwad district were the main mints (*Tankhashaley*). Their heaviest gold coin was Gadyanaka weighting 96 grains, Dramma weighted 65 grains, Kalanju 48 grains, Kasu 15 grains, Manjadi 2.5 grains, Akkam 1.25 grains and Pana 9.6 grain.

ECONOMY

Agriculture was the empire's main source of income through taxes on land and produce. The majority of the people lived in villages and worked farming the staple crops of rice, pulses, and cotton in the dry areas and sugarcane in areas having sufficient rainfall, with areca and betel being the chief cash crops. The living conditions of the labourers who farmed the land must have been bearable as there are no records of revolts by the landless against wealthy landlords. If peasants were disgruntled the common practice was to migrate in large numbers out of the jurisdiction of the ruler who was mistreating them, thereby depriving him of revenue from their labor.

Taxes were levied on mining and forest products, and additional income was raised through tolls for the use of transportation facilities. The state also collected fees from customs, professional licenses, and judicial fines. Records show horses and salt were taxed as well as commodities (gold, textiles, perfumes) and agricultural produce (black pepper, paddy, spices, betel leaves, palm leaves, coconuts and sugar). Land tax assessment was based on frequent surveys evaluating the quality of land and the type of produce. Chalukya records specifically mention black soil and red soil lands in addition to wetland, dry land and wasteland in determining taxation rates.

Key figures mentioned in inscriptions from rural areas were the Gavundas (officials) or Goudas. The Gavundas belonged to two levels of economic strata, the *Praja Gavunda* (people's Gavunda) and the *Prabhu Gavunda* (lord of Gavundas). They served the dual purpose of representing the people before the rulers as well as functioning as state appointees for tax collection and the raising of militias. They are mentioned in inscriptions related to land transactions, irrigation maintenance, village tax collection and village council duties.

The organisation of corporate enterprises became common in the 11th century. Almost all arts and crafts were organised into guilds and work was done on a corporate basis; records do not mention individual artists, sculptors and craftsman. Only in the regions ruled by the Hoysala did individual sculptors etched their names below their creations. Merchants organised themselves into powerful guilds that transcended political divisions, allowing their operations to be largely unaffected by wars and revolutions. Their only threat was the possibility of theft from brigands when their ships and caravans traveled to distant lands. Powerful South Indian merchant guilds included the *Manigramam*, the *Nagarattar* and the *Anjuvannam*. Local guilds were called *nagaram*, while the *Nanadesis* were traders from neighbouring kingdoms who perhaps mixed business with pleasure. The wealthiest and most influential and celebrated of all South Indian merchant guilds was the self styled *Ainnurruvar*, also known as the 500 *Svamis* of Ayyavolepura (Brahmins and *Mahajanas* of present day Aihole), who conducted extensive land and sea trade and thereby contributed significantly to the total foreign trade of the empire. It fiercely protected its trade obligations (*Vira Bananjudharma* or law of the noble merchants) and its members often recorded their achievements in inscriptions called *Prasasti*. Five hundred such excavated *Prasasti* inscriptions, with their own flag and the bull as their emblem, record their pride in their business.

Rich traders contributed significantly to the king's treasury through paying import and export taxes. The edicts of the Aihole *Svamis* mention trade ties with foreign kingdoms such as Chera, Pandya, Maleya (Malayasia), Magadh, Kaushal, Saurashtra, Kurumba, Kambhoja (Cambodia), Lata (Gujarat), Parasa (Persia) and Nepal. Travelling both land and sea routes, these merchants traded mostly in precious stones, spices and perfumes, and other specialty items such as camphor. Business flourished in precious stones such as diamonds, lapis lazuli, onyx, topaz, carbuncles and emeralds. Commonly traded spices were cardamom, saffron, and cloves, while perfumes included the by-products of sandalwood, bdellium, musk, civet and rose. These items were sold either in bulk or hawked on streets by local merchants in towns.

The Western Chalukyas controlled most of South India's west coast and by the 10th century they had established extensive trade ties with the Tang Empire of China, the empires of Southeast Asia and the Abbasid Caliphate in Bhagdad, and by the 12th century Chinese fleets were frequenting Indian ports. Exports to Song Dynasty China included textiles, spices, medicinal plants, jewels, ivory, rhino horn, ebony and camphor. The same products also reached ports in the west such as Dhofar and Aden. The final destinations for those trading with the west were Persia, Arabia and Egypt. The thriving trade center of Siraf, a port on the eastern coast of the Persian Gulf, served an international clientele of merchants including those from the Chalukya empire who were feasted by wealthy local merchants during business visits. An indicator of the Indian merchants' importance in Siraf comes from records describing dining plates reserved for them. In addition to this, Siraf received aloe wood, perfumes, sandalwood and condiments. The most expensive import to South India were Arabian horse shipments, this trade being monopolised by Arabs and local Brahmin merchants. Thirteenth century traveler Marco Polo recorded that the breeding of horses never succeeded in India due to differing climatic, soil and grassland conditions.

CULTURE

Religion

The fall of the Rashtrakuta empire to the Western Chalukyas in the tenth century, coinciding with the defeat of the Western Ganga Dynasty by the Cholas in Gangavadi, was a setback to Jainism. The growth of Virashaivism in the Chalukya territory and Vaishnava Hinduism in the Hoysala region paralleled a general decreased interest in Jainism, although the succeeding kingdoms continued to be religiously tolerant. Two locations of Jain worship in the Hoysala territory continued to be patronaged, Shravanabelagola and Kambadahalli. The decline of Buddhism in South India had began in the 8th century with the spread of Adi Shankara's Advaita philosophy. The only places of Buddhist worship that remained during the Western Chalukya rule were at Dambal and Balligavi. There is no mention of religious conflict in the writings and inscriptions of the time which suggest the religious transition was smooth.

Although the origin of the Virashaiva faith has been debated, the movement grew through its association with Basavanna in the twelfth century. Basavanna and other Virashaiva saints preached of a faith without a caste system. In his Vachanas (a form of poetry), Basavanna appealed to the masses in simple Kannada and wrote "work is worship" (Kayakave Kailasa). Also known as the Lingayats (worshipers of the *Linga,* the universal symbol of Shiva), these Virashaivas questioned many of the established norms of society such as the belief in rituals and the theory of rebirth and supported the remarriage of widows and the marriage of unwed older women. This gave more social freedom to women but they were not accepted into the priesthood. Ramanujacharya, the head of the Vaishnava monastery in Srirangam, traveled to the Hoysala territory and preached the way of devotion (bhakti marga). He later wrote *Sribhashya,* a commentary on Badarayana Brahmasutra, a critique on the Advaita philosophy of Adi Shankara. Ramanujacharya's stay in Melkote resulted in the Hoysala King Vishnuvardhana converting to Vaishnavism, a faith that his successors also followed.

The impact of these religious developments on the culture, literature, and architecture in South India was profound. Important works of metaphysics and poetry based on the teachings of these philosophers were written over the next centuries. Akka Mahadevi, Allama Prabhu, and a host of Basavanna's followers, including Chenna Basava, Prabhudeva, Siddharama, and Kondaguli Kesiraja wrote hundreds of poems called Vachanas in praise of Lord Shiva. The esteemed scholars in the Hoysala court, Harihara and Raghavanka, were Virashaivas. This tradition continued into the Vijayanagar empire with such well known scholars as Singiraja, Mallanarya, Lakkana Dandesa and other prolific writers of Virashaiva literature. The Saluva, Tuluva and Aravidu dynasties of the Vijayanagar empire were followers of Vaishnavism and a Vaishnava temple with an image of Ramanujacharya exists today in the Vitthalapura area of Vijayanagara. Scholars in the succeeding Mysore Kingdom wrote Vaishnavite works supporting the teachings of Ramanujacharya. King Vishnuvardhana built many temples after his conversion from Jainism to Vaishnavism.

Society

The rise of Veerashaivaism was revolutionary and challenged the prevailing Hindu caste system which retained royal support. The social role of women largely depended on their economic status and level of education in this relatively liberal period. Freedom was more available to women in the royal and affluent urban families. Records describe the participation of women in the fine arts, such as Chalukya queen Chandala Devi's and Kalachuri queen Sovala Devi's skill in dance and music. The compositions of thirty Vachana women poets included the work of the 12th century Virashaiva mystic Akka Mahadevi whose devotion to the *bhakti* movement is well known. Contemporary records indicate some royal women were involved in administrative and martial affairs such as princess Akkadevi, (sister of King Jayasimha II) who fought and defeated rebellious feudals. Inscriptions emphasise public acceptance of widowhood indicating that Sati (a custom in which a dead man's widow used to immolate herself on her husband's funeral pyre) though present was on a voluntary basis. Ritual deaths to achieve salvation were seen among the Jains who preferred to fast to death (Sallekhana), while people of some other communities chose to jump on spikes (*Shoolabrahma*) or walking into fire on an eclipse.

In a Hindu caste system that was conspicuously present, Brahmins enjoyed a privileged position as providers of knowledge and local justice. These Brahmins were normally involved in careers that revolved around religion and learning with the exception of a few who achieved success in martial affairs. They were patronised by kings, nobles and wealthy aristocrats who persuaded learned Brahmins to settle in specific towns and villages by making them grants of land and houses. The relocation of Brahmin scholars was calculated to be in the interest of the kingdom as they were viewed as persons detached from wealth and power and their knowledge was a useful tool to educate and teach ethical conduct and discipline in local communities. Brahmins were also actively involved in solving local problems by functioning as neutral arbiters (*Panchayat*).

Regarding eating habits, Brahmins, Jains, Buddhists and Shaivas were strictly vegetarian while the partaking of different kinds of meat was popular among other communities. Marketplace vendors sold meat from domesticated animals such as goats, sheep, pigs and fowl as well as exotic meat including partridge, hare, wild fowl and boar. People found indoor amusement by attending wrestling matches (*Kusti*) or watching animals fight such as cock fights and ram fights or by gambling. Horse racing was a popular outdoor past time. In addition to these leisurely activities, festivals and fairs were frequent and entertainment by traveling troupes of acrobats, dancers, dramatists and musicians was often provided.

Schools and hospitals are mentioned in records and these were built in the vicinity of temples. Marketplaces served as open air town halls where people gathered to discuss and ponder local issues. Choirs, whose main function was to sing devotional hymns, were maintained at temple expense. Young men were trained to sing in choirs in schools attached to monasteries such as Hindu *Matha,* Jain *Palli* and Buddhist *Vihara.* These institutions provided advanced education in religion and ethics and were well equipped with libraries (*Saraswati Bhandara*). Learning was imparted in the local language and in Sanskrit. Schools of higher learning were called *Brahmapuri* (or *Ghatika* or *Agrahara*). Teaching Sanskrit was a near monopoly of Brahmins who received royal endowments for their cause. Inscriptions record that the number of subjects taught varied from four to eighteen. The four most popular subjects with royal students were Economics (*Vartta*), Political Science (*Dandaniti*), Veda (*trayi*) and Philosophy (*Anvikshiki*), subjects that are mentioned as early as Kautilyas Arthasastra.

Literature

The Western Chalukya era was a time of substantial literary activity in Kannada and Sanskrit. In a golden age of Kannada literature, Jain scholars wrote about the life of Tirthankaras and Virashaiva poets expressed their closeness to God through pithy poems called Vachanas. More than two hundred contemporary *Vachanakaras* (*Vachana* poets) including thirty women poets have been recorded. Early works by Brahmin writers were on the epics, Ramayana, Mahabharata, Bhagavata, Puranas and Vedas. In the field of secular literature, subjects such as romance, erotics, medicine, lexicon, astrology, encyclopedia etc. were written for the first time.

Most notable among Kannada scholars were Ranna, grammarian Nagavarma II and Virashaiva saint Basavanna. Ranna who was patronised by king Tailapa II and Satyasraya is one among the "three gems of Kannada literature". He was bestowed the title "Emperor among poets" (*Kavi Chakravathi*) by King Tailapa II and has five major works to his credit. Of these, *Saahasabheema Vijayam* (or *Gada yuddha*) of 982 in *Champu* style is a eulogy of his patron King Satyasraya whom he compares to Bhima in valour and achievements and narrates the duel between Bhima and Duryodhana using clubs on the eighteenth day of the Mahabharata war. He wrote *Ajitha purana* in 993 describing the life of the second Tirthankara, Ajitanatha.

Nagavarma II, poet laureate (*Katakacharya*) of King Jagadhekamalla II made contributions to Kannada literature in various subjects. His works in poetry, prosody, grammar and vocabulary are standard authorities and their importance to the study of Kannada language is well acknowledged. *Kavyavalokana* in poetics, *Karnataka-Bhashabhushana* on grammar and *Vastukosa* a lexicon (with Kannada equivalents for Sanskrit words) are some of his comprehensive contributions.

A unique and native form of poetic literature in Kannada called Vachanas developed during this time. They were written by mystics, who expressed their devotion to God in simple poems that could appeal to the masses. Basavanna, Akka Mahadevi and Allama Prabhu are the best known among them.

In Sanskrit, a well known poem (*Mahakavya*) in 18 cantos called *Vikramankadeva Charita* by Kashmiri poet Bilhana recounts in epic style the life and achievements of his patron king Vikramaditya VI. The work narrates the episode of Vikramaditya VI's accession to the Chalukya throne after overthrowing his elder brother Somesvara II.

Manasollasa or *Abhilashitartha Chintamani* by king Somesvara III (1129) was a Sanskrit work intended for all sections of society. This is an example of an early encyclopedia in Sanskrit covering many subjects including medicine, magic, veterinary science, valuing of precious stones and pearls, fortifications, painting, music, games, amusements etc. While the book does not give any of dealt topics particular hierarchy of importance, it serves as a landmark in understanding the state of knowledge in those subjects at that time.

A Sanskrit scholar Vijnaneshwara became famous in the field of legal literature for his *Mitakshara,* in the court of Vikramaditya VI. Perhaps the most acknowledged work in that field, Mitakshara is a treatise on law (commentary on *Yajnavalkya*) based on earlier writings and has found acceptance in most parts of modern India. An Englishman Colebrooke later translated into English the section on inheritance giving it currency in the British Indian court system. Some important literary works of the time related to music and musical instruments were *Sangita Chudamani, Sangita Samayasara* and *Sangita Ratnakara.*

Architecture

The reign of Western Chalukya dynasty was an important period in the development of deccan architecture. The architecture designed during this time served as a conceptual link between the Badami Chalukya Architecture of the eighth century and the Hoysala architecture popularised in the thirteenth century. The art of the Western Chalukyas is sometimes called the "Gadag style" after the number of ornate temples they built in the Tungabhadra River-Krishna River doab region of present day Gadag district in Karnataka. The dynasty's temple building reached its maturity and culmination in the 12th century with over a hundred temples built across the deccan, more than half of them in present day central Karnataka. Apart from temples, the dynasty's architecture is well known for the ornate stepped wells (*Pushkarni*) which served as ritual bathing places, a few of which are well preserved in Lakkundi. These stepped well designs were later incorporated by the Hoysalas and the Vijayanagara empire in the coming centuries.

The Kasivisvesvara Temple at Lakkundi (Gadag district), the Dodda Basappa Temple at Dambal (Gadag district), the Mallikarjuna Temple at Kuruvatii (Davangere district), the Kallesvara Temple at Bagali (Davangere district), the Siddhesvara Temple at Haveri (Haveri district), the Amrtesvara Temple at Annigeri (Dharwad district) and the Mahadeva Temple at Itagi (Koppal district) are the finest examples produced by the later Chalukya architects. The twelfth century Mahadeva Temple with its well executed sculptures is an exquisite example of decorative detail. The intricate, finely crafted carvings on walls, pillars and towers speak volumes about Chalukya taste and culture. An inscription outside the temple calls it "Emperor of Temples" (*devalaya chakravarti*) and relates that it was built by Mahadeva, a commander in the army of king Vikramaditya VI. The Kedareswara Temple (1060) at Balligavi is an example of a transitional Chalukya-Hoysala architectural style. The Western Chalukyas built temples in Badami and Aihole during their early phase of temple building activity, such as Mallikarjuna Temple, the Yellamma Temple and the Bhutanatha group of Temples.

The *vimana* of their temples (tower over the shrine) is a compromise in detail between the plain stepped style of the early Chalukyas and the decorative finish of the Hoysalas. To the credit of the Western Chalukya architects is the development of the lathe turned (tuned) pillars and use of Soapstone (Chloritic Schist) as basic building and sculptural material, a very popular idiom in later Hoysala temples. They popularised the use of decorative *Kirthimukha* (demon faces) in their sculptures. Famous architects in the Hoysala kingdom included Chalukyan architects who were natives of places such as Balligavi. The artistic wall decor and the general sculptural idiom was dravidian architecture. This style is sometimes called *Karnata dravida,* one of the notable traditions in Indian architecture.

LANGUAGE

The local language Kannada was mostly used in Western (Kalyani) Chalukya inscriptions and epigraphs. Some historians assert that ninety percent of their inscriptions are in the Kannada language while the remaining are in Sanskrit language. More inscriptions in Kannada are attributed to Vikramaditya VI than any other king prior to the twelfth century, many of which have been deciphered and translated by historians of the Archaeological Survey of India. Inscriptions were generally either on stone (*Shilashasana*) or copper plates (*Tamarashasana*).

This period saw the growth of Kannada as a language of literature and poetry, impetus to which came from the devotional movement of the Virashaivas (called Lingayatism) who expressed their closeness to their deity in the form of simple lyrics called Vachanas. At an administrative level, the regional language was used to record locations and rights related to land grants. When bilingual inscriptions were written, the section stating the title, genealogy, origin myths of the king and benedictions were generally done in Sanskrit. Kannada was used to state terms of the grants, including information on the land, its boundaries, the participation of local authorities, rights and obligations of the grantee, taxes and dues, and witnesses. This ensured the content was clearly understood by the local people without any ambiguity.

In addition to inscriptions, chronicles called *Vamshavalis* were written to provide historical details of dynasties. Writings in Sanskrit included poetry, grammar, lexicon, manuals, rhetoric, commentaries on older works, prose fiction and drama. In Kannada, writings on secular subjects became popular. Some well known works are *Chandombudhi,* a prosody, and *Karnataka Kadambari,* a romance, both written by Nagavarma I, a lexicon called *Rannakanda* by Ranna (993), a book on medicine called *Karnataka-Kalyanakaraka* by Jagaddala Somanatha, the earliest writing on astrology called *Jatakatilaka* by Sridharacharya (1049), a writing on erotics called *Madanakatilaka* by Chandraraja, and an encyclopedia called *Lokapakara* by Chavundaraya II (1025).

PALLAVA

The **Pallava** kingdom was an ancient South Indian kingdom. The Pallavas, feudatories of Andhra Satavahanas, became independent after the decline of that dynasty in Amaravati. Initially they ruled southern Andhra Pradesh, also known as Palnadu, situated in the Guntur district. Later they extended their rule to Tamil regions and established their capital at Kanchipuram around the 4th century CE. They rose in power during the reign of Mahendravarman I (571 – 630 CE) and Narasimhavarman I (630 – 668 CE) and dominated the southern Telugu and northern parts of Tamil region for about six hundred years until the end of the 9th century.

Throughout their reign they were in constant conflict with both Chalukyas of Badami in the north and the Tamil kingdoms of Chola and Pandyas in the south and were finally defeated by the Chola kings in the 8th century CE.

Pallavas are most noted for their patronage of Dravidian architecture, still seen today in Mahabalipuram. The Pallavas, who left behind magnificent sculptures and temples, established the foundations of classical Dravidian architecture. Chinese traveller Hiuen Tsang visited Kanchipuram during Pallava rule and extolled their benign rule.

Some sources describe Bodhidharma, the founder of the Chan (Zen) school of Buddhism in China, as a prince of the Pallava dynasty, a contemporary of Skandavarman IV and Nandivarman I, and the son of Simhavarman II.

PALLAVA CHRONOLOGY

The rule of the Pallavas apparently starts as early as 275 CE, but their greatest epoch corresponds to the 7th and 8th century.

Early Pallavas

The history of the early Pallavas has not yet been satisfactorily settled. The earliest documentation on the Pallavas is the three copper-plate grants, belonging to Skandavarman I and written in Prakrit. Skandavarman appears to have been the first great ruler of the early Pallavas, though there are references to other early Pallavas who were probably predecessors of Skandavarman.

Skandavarman extended his dominions from the Krishna in the north to the Pennar in the south and to the Bellary district in the West. He performed the *Aswamedha* and other Vedic sacrifices and bore the title of 'Supreme King of Kings devoted to *dharma*'.

An absence of documentation about the Pallavas following Skandavarman is broken by the Allahabad pillar inscription of Samudragupta, which indicates that he defeated the Pallava Vishnugopa (350–355 CE). With Samudragupta's expedition the Pallava eclipse set in.

In the reign of Simhavarman IV, who ascended the throne in 436 CE, the fallen prestige of the Pallavas was restored. He recovered the territories lost to the Vishnukundins in the north up to the mouth of the Krishna. The early Pallava history from this period onwards is furnished by a dozen or so copper-plate grants in Sanskrit. They are all dated in the regnal years of the kings.

With the accession of Nandivarman I (480-500 CE), the decline of the early Pallava family was seen. The Kadambas had their aggressions and even the headquarters of the Pallavas was occupied by them. In coastal Andhra the Vishnukundins established their ascendency. The Pallava authority was confined to Tondaimandalam.

With the accession of Simhavishnu, father of Mahendravarman I, c. 575 CE, the Pallava revival began in the south.

Later Pallavas

The incursion of the Kalabhras and the confusion in the Tamil country was broken by the Pandya Kadungon and the Pallava Simhavishnu. The Pallava kingdom began to gain both in territory and influence over the South Indian peninsula and were a regional power by the end of the 6th century. The Pallavas exercised control over their southern neighbours of Cholas and Pandyas. But their history is marked by the continuous conflict with the Badami Chalukyas.

Narasimhavarman I and Paramesvaravarman I were the kings who stand out with glorious achievements in both military and architectural spheres. Nandivarman II built the Shore Temple.

Kadava kingdom

During the thirteenth and the fourteenth centuries CE, a small principality of the Kadava dynasty came into brief prominence. These rulers claimed descent from the Pallavas. The notable rulers of this dynasty are Kopperunchinga I (reigned c.1216 - 1242 CE), and his son and successor Kopperunchinga II (c.1243 - 1279 CE). Together they extended the influence of their kingdom and played a major part in the ultimate demise of the Chola dynasty.

RELIGION

Pallavas were followers of Hinduism and made gifts of land to gods and brahmins. In line with the prevalent customs, some of the rulers performed the *Aswamedha* and other Vedic sacrifices.

They were, however, tolerant of other faiths. The Chinese monk Xuanzang who visited Kanchipuram during the reign of Narasimhavarman I reported that there were 100 Buddhist monasteries, and 80 temples in Kanchipuram.

Mahendravarman I was initially a patron of the Jain faith. He later re-converted to Hinduism under the influence of the Saiva saint Appar with the revival of Hinduism during the Bhakti movement in South India.

PALLAVA ARCHITECTURE

The Pallavas were instrumental in the transition from rock-cut architecture to stone temples. The earliest examples of Pallava constructions are rock-cut temples dating from 610–690 CE and structural temples between 690–900 CE. A number of rock-cut cave temples bear the inscription of the Pallava king, Mahendravarman I and his successors.

The greatest accomplishments of the Pallava architecture are the rock-cut temples at Mahabalipuram. There are excavated pillared halls and monolithic shrines known as *rathas* in Mahabalipuram. Early temples were mostly dedicated to Shiva. The Kailasanatha temple in Kanchipuram and the Shore Temple built by Narasimhavarman II are fine examples of the Pallava style temples.

HOYSALA EMPIRE

The **Hoysala Empire** in Kannada was a prominent South Indian Kannadiga empire that ruled most of the modern day state of Karnataka between the 10th and the 14th centuries. The capital of the Hoysalas was initially located at Belur but was later moved to Halebidu.

The Hoysala rulers were originally hill people of Malnad Karnataka, an elevated region in the Western Ghats range. In the 12th century, taking advantage of the internecine warfare between the then ruling Western Chalukyas and Kalachuri kingdoms, they annexed areas of present day Karnataka and the fertile areas north of the Kaveri River delta in present day Tamil Nadu. By the 13th century, they governed most of present-day Karnataka, parts of Tamil Nadu and parts of western Andhra Pradesh in Deccan India.

The Hoysala era was an important period in the development of art, architecture, and religion in South India. The empire is remembered today primarily for its temple architecture. Over a hundred surviving temples are scattered across Karnataka, including the well known Chennakesava Temple at Belur, the Hoysaleswara Temple at Halebidu, and the Kesava Temple at Somanathapura. The Hoysala rulers also patronised the fine arts, encouraging literature to flourish in Kannada and Sanskrit.

Kannada folklore tells of a young man, Sala, who was instructed by his Jain guru Sudatta to strike dead a tiger he encountered near the temple of the Goddess Vasantika at Sosevur. The word "strike" literally translates to "hoy" in Hale Kannada (Old Kannada), hence the name "Hoy-sala". This legend first appeared in the Belur inscription of Vishnuvardhana (1117), but owing to several inconsistencies in the Sala story it remains in the realm of folklore. The legend may have come into existence or gained popularity after King Vishnuvardhana's victory over the Cholas at Talakad as the Hoysala emblem depicts the fight between the mythical Sala and a tiger, the emblem of the Cholas.

Early inscriptions, dated 1078 and 1090, have implied that the Hoysalas were descendants of the Yadava by referring to the Yadava *vamsa* (clan) as Hoysala *vamsa*. But there are no early records directly linking the Hoysalas to the Yadavas of North India.

Historians refer to the founders of the dynasty as natives of Malnad Karnataka, based on numerous inscriptions calling them *Maleparolganda* or "Lord of the Male (hills) chiefs" (*Malepas*). This title in the Kannada language was proudly used by the Hoysala kings as their royal signature in their inscriptions. Literary sources from that time in Kannada (*Jatakatilaka*) and Sanskrit (*Gadyakarnamrita*) have also helped confirm they were natives of the region known today as Karnataka.

The first Hoysala family record is dated 950 and names Arekalla as the chieftain, followed by Maruga and Nripa Kama I (976). The next ruler, Munda (1006–1026), was succeeded by Nripa Kama II who held such titles as *Permanadi* that show an early alliance with the Western Ganga dynasty. From these modest beginnings, the Hoysala dynasty began its transformation into a strong subordinate of the Western Chalukyas. Through Vishnuvardhana's expansive military conquests, the Hoysalas achieved the status of a real kingdom for the first time. He wrested Gangavadi from the Cholas in 1116 and moved the capital from Belur to Halebidu.

Vishnuvardhana's ambition of creating an independent empire was fulfilled by his grandson Veera Ballala II, who freed the Hoysalas from subordination in 1187. Thus the Hoysalas began as subordinates of the Western Chalukyas and gradually established their own empire in Karnataka with such strong Hoysala kings as Vishnuvardhana, Veera Ballala II and later Veera Ballala III. During this time, peninsular India saw a four way struggle for hegemony - Pandya, Kakatiya and Seuna Yadavas of Devagiri being the other kingdoms. Veera Ballala II defeated the aggressive Pandya when they invaded the Chola kingdom and assumed the title "Establisher of the Chola Kingdom" (*Cholarajyapratishtacharya*), "Emperor of the south" (*Dakshina Chakravarthi*) and "Hoysala emperor" (*Hoysala Chakravarthi*). He founded the city of Bangalore according to Kannada folklore.

The Hoysalas extended their foothold in areas known today as Tamil Nadu around 1225, making the city of Kannanur Kuppam near Srirangam a provincial capital and giving them control over South Indian politics that began a period of Hoysala hegemony in the southern Deccan. Vira Narasimha II's son Vira Someshwara earned the honorific "uncle" (*Mamadi*) from the Pandyas and Cholas. The Hoysala influence spread over Pandya kingdom also. Toward the end of 13th century, Veera Ballala III recaptured territory lost to the Pandya uprising and expanded his kingdom to encompass all areas south of the Krishna River.

Major political changes were taking place in the Deccan region in the early 14th century when significant areas of northern India were under Muslim rule. Alla-ud-din

Khilji, the Sultan of Delhi, was determined to bring isolated South India under his domain and sent his commander, Malik Kafur, on a southern expedition to plunder the Seuna capital Devagiri in 1311. The Seuna empire was subjugated by 1318 and the Hoysala capital Halebidu (also called Dorasamudra or Dwarasamudra) was sacked twice, in 1311 and 1327.

By 1336, the Sultan had conquered the Pandyas of Madurai, the Kakatiyas of Warangal and the tiny kingdom of Kampili. The Hoysalas were the only remaining Hindu empire who resisted the invading armies. Veera Ballala III stationed himself at Tiruvannamalai and offered stiff resistance to invasions from the north and the Sultanate of Madurai to the south. Then, after nearly two decades of resistance, Veera Ballala III was killed at the battle of Madurai in 1343 and the sovereign territories of the Hoysala empire were merged with the areas administered by Harihara I in the Tungabhadra region. This new Hindu kingdom resisted the northern invasions and would later prosper and come to be known as the Vijayanagara Empire.

ECONOMY

The Hoysala administration supported itself through revenues from an agrarian economy. The kings gave grants of land as rewards for service to beneficiaries who then became landlords to tenants producing agricultural goods and forest products. There were two types of landlords (*gavunda*); *gavunda* of people (*praja gavunda*) was lower in status than the wealthy lord of *gavundas* (*prabhu gavunda*). The highlands (*malnad* regions) with its temperate climate was suitable for raising cattle and the planting of orchards and spices. Paddy and corn were staple crops in the tropical plains (*Bailnad*). The Hoysalas collected taxes on irrigation systems including tanks, reservoirs with sluices, canals and wells which were built and maintained at the expense of local villagers. Irrigation tanks such as *Vishnusagara, Shantisagara, Ballalarayasagara* were created at the expense of the state.

Importing horses for use as general transportation and in army cavalries of Indian kingdoms was a flourishing business on the western seaboard. The forests were harvested for rich woods such as teak which was exported through ports located in the area of present day Kerela. Sung dynasty records from China mention the presence of Indian merchants in ports of South China, indicating active trade with overseas kingdoms. South India exported textiles, spices, medicinal plants, precious stones, pottery, salt made from salt pans, jewels, gold, ivory, rhino horn, ebony, aloe wood, perfumes, sandalwood, camphor and condiments to China, Dhofar, Aden, and Siraf (the entryport to Egypt, Arabia and Persia). Architects (*Vishwakarmas*), sculptors, quarry workers, goldsmiths and other skilled craftsmen whose trade directly or indirectly related to temple construction were also prosperous due to the vigorous temple building activities.

The village assembly was responsible for collecting government land taxes. Land revenue was called *Siddhaya* and included the original assessment (*Kula*) plus various cesses. Taxes were levied on professions, marriages, goods in transit on chariots or carriages, and domesticated animals. Taxes on commodities (gold, precious stones, perfumes, sandalwood, ropes, yarn, housing, hearths, shops, cattle pans, sugarcane presses) as well as produce (black pepper, betel leaves, ghee, paddy, spices, palm leaves, coconuts, sugar) are noted in village records. The village assembly could levy a tax for a specific purpose such as construction of a water tank.

ADMINISTRATION

In its administrative practices, the Hoysala Empire followed some of the well-established and proven methods of its predecessors covering administrative functions such as cabinet organisation and command, the structure of local governing bodies and the division of territory. Records show the names of many high ranking positions reporting directly to the king. Senior ministers were called *Pancha Pradhanas,* ministers responsible for foreign affairs were designated *Sandhivigrahi* and the chief treasurer was *Mahabhandari* or *Hiranyabhandari. Dandanayakas* were in charge of armies and the chief justice of the Hoysala court was the *Dharmadhikari.*

The kingdom was divided into provinces named *Nadu, Vishaya, Kampana* and *Desha,* listed in descending order of geographical size. Each province had a local governing body consisting of a minister (*Mahapradhana*) and a treasurer (*Bhandari*) that reported to the ruler of that province (*Dandanayaka*). Under this local ruler were officials called *Heggaddes* and *Gavundas* who hired and supervised the local farmers and labourers recruited to till the land. Subordinate ruling clans such as Alupas continued to govern their respective territories while following the policies set by the empire.

An elite and well trained force of bodyguards known as *Garudas* protected the members of the royal family at all times. These servants moved closely yet inconspicuously by the side of their master, their loyalty being so complete that they committed suicide after his death. Hero stones (*virgal*) erected in memory of these bodyguards are called Garuda pillars. The Garuda pillar at the Hoysaleswara temple in Halebidu was erected in honor of Kuvara Lakshma, a minister and bodyguard of King Veera Ballala II.

King Vishnuvardhana's coins had the legends "victor at Nolambavadi" (*Nolambavadigonda*), "victor at Talakad" (*Talakadugonda*), "chief of the Malepas" (*Maleparolganda*), "Brave of Malepa" (*malapavira*) in Hoysala style Kannada script. Their gold coin was called *Honnu* or *Gadyana* and weighed 62 grains of gold. *Pana* or *Hana* was a tenth of the *Honnu, Haga* was a fourth of the *Pana* and *Visa* was fourth of *Haga.* There were other coins called *Bele* and *Kani.*

CULTURE

Religion

The defeat of the Jain Western Ganga Dynasty by the Cholas in early 11th century and the rising numbers of followers of Vaishnava Hinduism and Virashaivism in the

12th century was mirrored by a decreased interest in Jainism. Two notable locations of Jain worship in the Hoysala territory were Shravanabelagola and Kambadahalli. The decline of Buddhism in South India began in the 8th century with the spread of Adi Shankara's Advaita philosophy. The only places of Buddhist worship during the Hoysala time were at Dambal and Balligavi. Shantala Devi, queen of Vishnuvardhana was a Jain but nevertheless commissioned the Hindu Kappe Chennigaraya temple in Belur, evidence that the royal family was tolerant of all religions. During the rule of the Hoysalas, three important religious developments took place in present day Karnataka inspired by three philosophers, Basavanna, Madhvacharya and Ramanujacharya.

While the origin of Virashaiva faith is debated, the movement grew through its association with Basavanna in the 12th century. Basavanna and other Virashaiva saints preached of a faith without a caste system. In his Vachanas he appealed to the masses in simple Kannada and wrote "work is worship" (*Kayakave Kailasa*). Madhvacharya was critical of the teachings of Shankaracharya and argued the world is real and not an illusion. His philosophy gained popularity enabling him to establish eight Mathas (monastery) in Udupi. Ramanujacharya, the head of the Vaishnava monastery in Srirangam, preached the way of devotion (*bhakti marga*) and wrote *Sribhashya*, a critique on the Advaita philosophy of Adi Shankara.

The impact of these religious developments on culture, literature, poetry and architecture in South India was profound. Important works of literature and poetry based on the teachings of these philosophers were written during the coming centuries. The Saluva, Tuluva and Aravidu dynasties of Vijayanagar empire were followers of Vaishnavism and a Vaishnava temple with an image of Ramanujacharya exists in the Vitthalapura area of Vijayanagara. Scholars in later Mysore Kingdom wrote Vaishnavite works upholding the teachings of Ramanujacharya. King Vishnuvardhana built many temples after his conversion from Jainism to Vaishnavism. The later saints of Madhvacharya's order, Jayatirtha, Vyasatirtha, Sripadaraya, Vadirajatirtha and devotees (*dasa*) such as Vijaya Dasa, Gopaladasa and others from the Karnataka region spread his teachings far and wide. His teachings inspired later day philosophers like Vallabhacharya in Gujarat and Chaitanya in Bengal. Another wave of devotion (*bhakti*) in the 17th century–18th century found inspiration in his teachings.

Society

Hoysala society in many ways reflected the emerging religious, political and cultural developments of those times. During this period, the society became increasingly sophisticated. The status of women was varied. Some royal women were involved in administrative matters as shown in contemporary records describing Queen Umadevi's administration of Halebidu in the absence of Veera Ballala II during his long military campaigns in northern territories. She also fought and defeated some antagonistic feudal rebels. Records describe the participation of women in the fine arts, such as Queen Shantala Devi's skill in dance and music, and the 12th century Vachana poet and

Virashaiva mystic Akka Mahadevi's devotion to the *bhakti* movement is well known. Temple dancers (*Devadasi*) were common and some were well educated and accomplished in the arts. These qualifications gave them more freedom than other urban and rural women who were restricted to daily mundane tasks. The practice of sati in a voluntary form was prevalent and prostitution was socially acceptable. As in most of India, the Indian caste system was conspicuously present.

Trade on the west coast brought many foreigners to India including Arabs, Jews, Persians, Chinese and people from the Malay Peninsula. Migration of people within Southern India as a result of the expansion of the empire produced an influx of new cultures and skills. In South India, towns were called *Pattana* or *Pattanam* and the marketplace, *Nagara* or *Nagaram*, the marketplace serving as the nuclei of a city. Some towns such as Shravanabelagola developed from a religious settlement in the 7th century to an important trading center by the 12th century with the arrival of rich traders, while towns like Belur attained the atmosphere of a regal city when King Vishnuvardhana built the Chennakesava Temple there. Large temples supported by royal patronage served religious, social, and judiciary purposes, elevating the king to the level of "God on earth".

Temple building served a commercial as well as a religious function and was not limited to any particular sect of Hinduism. Shaiva merchants of Halebidu financed the construction of the Hoysaleswara temple to compete with the Chennakesava temple built at Belur, elevating Halebidu to an important city as well. Hoysala temples however were secular and encouraged pilgrims of all Hindu sects, the Kesava temple at Somanathapura being an exception with strictly Vaishnava sculptural depictions. Temples built by rich landlords in rural areas fulfilled fiscal, political, cultural and religious needs of the agrarian communities. Irrespective of patronage, large temples served as establishments that provided employment to hundreds of people of various guilds and professions sustaining local communities as Hindu temples began to take on the shape of wealthy Buddhist monasteries.

Literature

Although Sanskrit literature remained popular during the Hoysala rule, royal patronage of local Kannada scholars increased. In the 12th century some works were written in the *Champu* style, but distinctive Kannada metres became more widely accepted. The *Sangatya* metre used in compositions, *Shatpadi* (seven line), *Tripadi* (three line) metres in verses and *Ragale* (lyrical poems) became fashionable. Jain works continued to extol the virtues of Tirthankaras (Jain ascetics).

The Hoysala court supported scholars such as Janna, Rudrabhatta, Harihara and his nephew Raghavanka, whose works are enduring masterpieces in Kannada. In 1209, the Jain scholar Janna wrote *Yashodharacharite*, the story of a king who intends to perform a ritual sacrifice of two young boys to a local deity, Mariamma. Taking pity on the boys, the king releases them and gives up the practice of human sacrifice. In honour of this work, Janna received the title "Emperor among poets" (*Kavichakravarthi*) from King Veera Ballala II.

Rudrabhatta, a Smartha Brahmin (believer of monistic philosophy), was the earliest well known Brahminical writer whose patron was Chandramouli, a minister of King Veera Ballala II. Based on the earlier work of *Vishnu Purana,* he wrote *Jagannatha Vijaya* in the *Champu* style relating the life of Lord Krishna leading up to his fight with the demon Banasura.

Harihara, (also known as Harisvara) a Virashaiva writer and the patron of King Narasimha I, wrote the *Girijakalyana* in the old Jain *Champu* style which describes the marriage of Lord Shiva and Parvati in ten sections. He was one of the earliest Virashaiva writers who was not part of the *Vachana* literary tradition. He came from a family of accountants (*Karanikas*) from Halebidu and spent many years in Hampi writing more than one hundred *Ragales* (poems in blank verse) in praise of Lord Virupaksha (a form of Lord Shiva). Raghavanka was the first to introduce the *Shatpadi* metre into Kannada literature in his *Harishchandra kavya* which is considered a classic even though it occasionally violates strict rules of Kannada grammar.

In Sanskrit, the philosopher Madhvacharya wrote *Rigbhshya* on Brahmasutras (a logical explanation of Hindu scriptures, the Vedas) as well as many polemical works rebutting the doctrines of other schools of Vedas. He relied more on the Puranic literature than the Vedas for logical proof of his philosophy. Another famous writing was *Rudraprshnabhashya* by Vidyatirtha.

Architecture

The modern interest in the Hoysalas is due to their patronage of art and architecture rather than their military conquests. The brisk temple building throughout the kingdom was accomplished despite constant threats from the Pandyas to the south and the Seunas Yadavas to the north. Their architectural style, an offshoot of the Western Chalukya style, shows distinct Dravidian influences. The Hoysala architecture style is described as *Karnata Dravida* as distinguished from the traditional *Dravida,* and is considered an independent architectural tradition with many unique features.

A feature of Hoysala temple architecture is its attention to exquisite detail and skilled craftsmanship. The tower over the temple shrine (*vimana*) is delicately finished with intricate carvings, showing attention to the ornate and elaborately detailed rather than to a tower form and height. The stellate design of the base of the shrine with its rhythmic projections and recesses is carried through the tower in an orderly succession of decorated tiers. Hoysala temple sculpture replicates this emphasis on delicacy and craftsmanship in its focus on depicting feminine beauty, grace and physique. The Hoysala artists achieved this with the use of Soapstone (Chloritic schist), a soft stone as basic building and sculptural material.

The Chennakesava Temple at Belur (1117), the Hoysaleswara temple at Halebidu (1121), the Chennakesava Temple at Somanathapura (1279), the temples at Arasikere (1220), Amruthapura (1196), Belavadi (1200) and Nuggehalli (1246) are all notable examples of Hoysala art. While the temples at Belur and Halebidu are the best known because of the beauty of their sculptures, the Hoysala art finds more complete expression in the smaller and lesser known temples. The outer walls of all these temples contain an intricate array of stone sculptures and horizontal friezes (decorative mouldings) that depict the Hindu epics. These depictions are generally clockwise in the traditional direction of circumambulation (*pradakshina*). The temple of Halebidu has been described as an outstanding example of Hindu architecture and an important milestone in Indian architecture. The temples of Belur and Halebidu are a proposed UNESCO world heritage sites.

Language

Use of the Kannada and Sanskrit languages was extensive in the Hoysala empire. Temples served as local schools where learned Brahmins taught in Sanskrit, while Jain and Buddhist monasteries educated novice monks. Schools of higher learning were called *Ghatikas*. The local Kannada language was widely used in the rising number of devotional movements to express the ecstatic experience of closeness to the deity (*vachanas* and *devaranama*). Literary works were written in it on palm leaves which were tied together. While in past centuries Jain works had dominated Kannada literature, Shaiva and early Brahminical works became popular during the Hoysala reign. Writings in Sanskrit included poetry, grammar, lexicon, manuals, rhetoric, commentaries on older works, prose fiction and drama. Inscriptions on stone (*Shilashasana*) and copper plates (*Tamarashasana*) were written in Kannada, Sanskrit or were bilingual. The sections of bilingual inscriptions stating the title, genealogy, origin myths of the king and benedictions were generally done in Sanskrit. Kannada was used to state terms of the grants, including information on the land, its boundaries, the participation of local authorities, rights and obligations of the grantee, taxes and dues, and witnesses. This ensured the content was clearly understood by the local people without ambiguity.

VIJAYANAGARA EMPIRE

The Vijayanagara Empire was a South Indian empire based in the Deccan Plateau. Established in 1336 by Harihara I and his brother Bukka Raya I, it lasted until 1646 although its power declined after a major military defeat in 1565 by the Deccan sultanates. The empire is named after its capital city of Vijayanagara, whose impressive ruins surround modern Hampi, now a World Heritage Site in modern Karnataka, India. The writings of medieval European travelers such as Domingo Paes, Fernao Nuniz and Niccolò Da Conti and the literature in local vernaculars provide crucial information about its history. Archaeological excavations at Vijayanagara have revealed the empire's power and wealth.

The empire's legacy includes many monuments spread over South India, the best known being the group at Hampi. The previous temple building traditions in South India came together in the Vijayanagara Architecture style. The mingling of all faiths and vernaculars inspired architectural innovation of Hindu temple construction, first in the Deccan and later in the Dravidian idioms using the local granite. Secular royal structures show the influence of the Northern Deccan Sultanate architecture. Efficient administration and vigorous overseas trade brought new technologies like water management systems for irrigation. The empire's patronage enabled fine arts and literature to reach new heights in the languages of Kannada, Telugu, Tamil and Sanskrit, while Carnatic music evolved into its current form. The Vijayanagara Empire created an epoch in South Indian history that transcended regionalism by promoting Hinduism as a unifying factor.

Differing theories have been proposed regarding the Vijayanagara empire's origins. Some claim that Harihara I and Bukka Raya I, the founders of the empire, were Telugu people first associated with the Kakatiya kingdom who took control of the northern parts of the Hoysala Empire during its decline. Other historians propose they were Kannadigas and commanders in the army of the Hoysala Empire stationed in the Tungabhadra region to ward off Muslim invasions from the Northern India. Irrespective of their origin, historians agree the founders were supported and inspired by Vidyaranya, a saint at the Sringeri monastery to fight the Muslim invasion of South India. Writings by foreign travelers during the late medieval era combined with recent excavations in the Vijayanagara principality have uncovered much-needed information about the empire's history, fortifications, scientific developments and architectural innovations.

Before the early 14th century rise of the Vijayanagara empire, the Hindu kingdoms of the Deccan, the Seuna Yadavas of Devagiri, the Kakatiya dynasty of Warangal, the Pandya Kingdom of Madurai, and the tiny kingdom of Kampili had been repeatedly invaded by Muslims from the north, and by 1336 they had all been defeated by Alla-ud-din Khilji and Muhammad bin Tughluq, the Sultans of Delhi. The Hoysala Empire was the sole remaining Hindu kingdom in the path of the Muslim invasion. After the death of Hoysala Veera Ballala III during a battle against the Sultan of Madurai in 1343, the Hoysala empire merged with the growing Vijayanagara empire.

In the first two decades after the founding of the empire, Harihara I gained control over most of the area south of the Tungabhadra river and earned the title of *Purvapaschima Samudradhishavara* ("master of the eastern and western seas"). By 1374 Bukka Raya I, successor to Harihara I, had defeated the chiefdom of Arcot, the Reddy dynasty of Kondavidu, the Sultan of Madurai and gained control over Goa in the west and the Tungabhadra-Krishna River doab in the north. The island of Lanka paid tributes and ambassadors were exchanged with the Ming Dynasty of China. The original capital was in the principality of Anegondi on the northern banks of the Tungabhadra River in today's Karnataka. It was later moved to nearby Vijayanagara on the river's southern banks during the reign of Bukka Raya I.

With the Vijayanagara Kingdom now imperial in stature, Harihara II, the second son of Bukka Raya I, further consolidated the kingdom beyond the Krishna River and brought the whole of South India under the Vijayanagara umbrella. The next ruler, Deva Raya I, emerged successful against the Gajapatis of Orissa and undertook important works of fortification and irrigation. Deva Raya II (called *Gajabetekara*) succeeded to the throne in 1424 and was possibly the most capable of the Sangama dynasty rulers. He quelled rebelling feudal lords as well as the Zamorin of Calicut and Quilon in the south. He invaded the island of Lanka and became overlord of the kings of Burma at Pegu and Tanasserim. The empire declined in the late 15th century until the serious attempts by commander Saluva Narasimha Deva Raya in 1485 and by general Tuluva Narasa Nayaka in 1491 to reconsolidate the empire. After nearly two decades of conflict with rebellious chieftains, the empire eventually came under the rule of Krishnadevaraya, the son of Tuluva Narasa Nayaka.

In the following decades the Vijayanagara empire dominated all of Southern India and fought off invasions from the five established Deccan Sultanates. The empire reached its peak during the rule of Krishnadevaraya when Vijayanagara armies were consistently victorious. The empire annexed areas formerly under the Sultanates in the northern Deccan and the territories in the eastern Deccan, including Kalinga, while simultaneously maintaining control over all its subordinates in the south. Many important monuments were either completed or commissioned during the time of Krishnadevaraya.

Krishnadevaraya was followed by Achyuta Raya in 1530 and in 1542 by Sadashiva Raya while the real power lay with Aliya Rama Raya, the son-in-law of Krishnadevaraya, whose relationship with the Deccan Sultans who allied against him has been debated.

The sudden capture and killing of Aliya Rama Raya in 1565 at the Battle of Talikota, against an alliance of the Deccan sultanates, after a seemingly easy victory for the Vijayanagara armies, created havoc and confusion in the Vijayanagara ranks, which were then completely routed. The Sultanates' army later plundered Hampi and reduced it to the ruinous state in which it remains; it was never re-occupied. Tirumala Raya, the sole surviving commander, left Vijayanagara for Penukonda with vast amounts of treasure on the back of 550 elephants.

The empire went into a slow decline regionally, although trade with the Portuguese continued, and the British were given a land grant for the establishment of Madras. Tirumala Deva Raya was succeeded by his son Sriranga I later followed by Venkata II who made Chandragiri his capital, repulsed the invasion of the Bahmani Sultanate and saved Penukonda from being captured. His successor, Ramadeva, took power and ruled till 1632 after whose death, Venkata III became king and ruled for about ten years after which Vellore was made the capital. The empire was finally conquered by the Sultanates of Bijapur and Golkonda. The largest feudatories of the Vijayanagar empire — the Mysore Kingdom, Keladi Nayaka, Nayaks of Madurai, Nayaks of Tanjore, Nayakas of Chitradurga and Nayak Kingdom of Gingee — declared independence and went on to have a significant impact on the history of South India in the coming centuries. These Nayaka kingdoms lasted into the 18th century while the Mysore Kingdom remained a princely state until

Indian Independence in 1947 although they came under the British Raj in 1799 after the death of Tipu Sultan.

GOVERNANCE

The rulers of the Vijayanagara empire maintained the well-functioning administrative methods developed by their predecessors, the Hoysala, Kakatiya and Pandya kingdoms, to govern their territories and made changes only where necessary. The King was the ultimate authority, assisted by a cabinet of ministers (*Pradhana*) headed by the prime minister (*Mahapradhana*). Other important titles recorded in inscriptions were the chief secretary (*Karyakartha* or *Rayaswami*) and the imperial officers (*Adhikari*). All high ranking ministers and officers were required to have military training. A secretariat near the king's palace employed scribes and officers to maintain records made official by using a wax seal imprinted with the ring of the king. At the lower administrative levels, wealthy feudal landlords (*Goudas*) supervised accountants (*Karanikas* or *Karnam*) and guards (*Kavalu*). The palace administration was divided into 72 departments (*Niyogas*), each having several female attendants chosen for their youth and beauty (some imported or captured in victorious battles) who were trained to handle minor administrative matters and to serve men of nobility as courtesans or concubines.

The empire was divided into five main provinces (*Rajya*), each under a commander (*Dandanayaka* or *Dandanatha*) and headed by a governor, often from the royal family, who used the native language for administrative purposes. A *Rajya* was divided into regions (*Vishaya Vente* or *Kottam*), and further divided into counties (*Sime* or *Nadu*) themselves subdivided into municipalities (*Kampana* or *Sthala*). Hereditary families ruled their respective territories and paid tribute to the empire while some areas, such as Keladi and Madurai, came under the direct supervision of a commander.

On the battlefields, the king's commanders led the troops. The empire's war strategy rarely involved massive invasions; more often it employed small scale methods such as attacking and destroying individual forts. The empire was among the first in India to use long range artillery commonly manned by foreign gunners. (Gunners from present day Turkmenistan were considered the best). Army troops were of two types: The king's personal army directly recruited by the empire and the feudal army under each feudatory. King Krishnadevaraya's personal army consisted of 100,000 infantry, 20,000 cavalrymen and over 900 elephants. This number was only a part of the army numbering over 1.1 million soldiers, a figure that varied as an army of two million has also been recorded along with the existence of a navy as evidenced by the use of the term *Navigadaprabhu* (commander of the navy). The army recruited from all classes of society (supported by the collection of additional feudal tributes from feudatory rulers), and consisted of archers and musketeers wearing quilted tunics, shieldmen with swords and poignards in their girdles, and soldiers carrying shields so larges that no armour was necessary. The horses and elephants were fully armoured and the elephants had knives fastened to their tusks to do maximum damage in battle.

The capital city was completely dependent on the water supply systems constructed to channel and store water, and ensure a consistent supply throughout the year. The remains of these hydraulic systems have given historians a picture of the prevailing surface water distribution methods in use at that time in South India's semiarid regions. Contemporary inscriptions and notes of foreign travelers describe how huge tanks were constructed by labourers. Excavations have uncovered the remains of a well-connected water distribution system existing solely within the royal enclosure and the large temple complexes (suggesting it was for the exclusive use of royalty, and for special ceremonies) with sophisticated channels using gravity and siphons to transport water through pipelines.

The only structures resembling public waterworks are the remains of large water tanks that collected the seasonal monsoon water and then dried up in summer except for the few fed by springs. In the fertile agricultural areas near the Tungabhadra River, canals were dug to guide the river water into irrigation tanks. These canals had sluices that were opened and closed to control the water flow. In other areas the administration encouraged the digging of wells monitored by administrative authorities. Large tanks in the capital city were constructed with royal patronage while smaller tanks were funded by wealthy individuals to gain social and religious merit.

ECONOMY

The empire's economy was largely dependent on agriculture. Corn (*jowar*), cotton and pulse legumes grew in semi arid regions, while sugarcane, rice and wheat thrived in rainy areas. Betel leaves, areca (for chewing), and coconut were the principal cash crops, and large scale cotton production supplied the weaving centers of the empire's vibrant textile industry. Spices such as turmeric, pepper, cardamom and ginger grew in the remote Malnad hill region and were transported to the city for trade. The empire's capital city was a thriving business centre that included a burgeoning market in large quantities of precious gems and gold. Prolific temple-building provided employment to thousands of masons, sculptors, and other skilled artisans.

Land ownership was important. Most of the growers were tenant farmers and were given the right of part ownership of the land over time. Tax policies encouraging needed produce made distinctions between land use to determine tax levies. For example, the daily market availability of rose petals was important for perfumers, so cultivation of roses received a lower tax assessment. Salt production and the manufacture of salt pans were controlled by similar means. The making of ghee (clarified butter), which was sold as an oil for human consumption and as a fuel for lighting lamps, was profitable. Exports to China intensified and included cotton, spices, jewels, semi-precious stones, ivory, rhino horn, ebony, amber, coral, and aromatic products such as perfumes. Large vessels from China made frequent visits, some captained by the Chinese Admiral Cheng Ho, and brought Chinese products to the empire's 300 ports, large and small, on the Arabian Sea and the Bay of Bengal. The ports of Mangalore, Honavar, Bhatkal, Barkur, Cochin, Cannanore, Machilipatnam and Dharmadam were the most important.

When merchant ships docked, the merchandise was taken into official custody and taxes levied on all items sold. The security of the merchandise was guaranteed by the administration officials. Traders of many nationalities (Arabs, Persians, Guzerates, Khorassanians) settled in Calicut, drawn by the thriving trade business. Ship building prospered and keeled ships of 1000–1200 *bahares* (burden) were built without decks by sewing the entire hull with ropes rather than fastening them with nails. Ships sailed to the Red Sea ports of Aden and Mecca with Vijayanagara goods sold as far away as Venice. The empire's principal exports were pepper, ginger, cinnamon, cardamom, myrobalan, tamarind timber, anafistula, precious and semi-precious stones, pearls, musk, ambergris, rhubarb, aloe, cotton cloth and porcelain. Cotton yarn was shipped to Burma and indigo to Persia. Chief imports from Palestine were copper, quicksilver (mercury), vermilion, coral, saffron, coloured velvets, rose water, knives, coloured camlets, gold and silver. Persian horses were imported to Cannanore before a two week land trip to the capital. Silk arrived from China and sugar from Bengal.

East coast trade hummed, with goods arriving from Golkonda where rice, millet, pulse and tobacco were grown on a large scale. Dye crops of indigo and chay root were produced for the weaving industry. A mineral rich region, Machilipatnam was the gateway for high quality iron and steel exports. Diamond mining was active in the Kollur region. The cotton weaving industry produced two types of cottons, plain calico and muslin (brown, bleached or dyed). Cloth printed with coloured patterns crafted by native techniques were exported to Java and the Far East. Golkonda specialised in plain cotton and Pulicat in printed. The main imports on the east coast were non-ferrous metals, camphor, porcelain, silk and luxury goods.

CULTURE

Social life

Most information on the social life in Vijayanagara empire comes from the writings of foreign visitors and evidence that research teams in the Vijayanagara area have uncovered. The Hindu caste system was prevalent and rigidly followed, with each caste represented by a local body of elders who represented the community. These elders set the rules and regulations that were implemented with the help of royal decrees. Untouchability was part of the caste system and these communities were represented by leaders (*Kaivadadavaru*). The Muslim communities were represented by their own group in coastal Karnataka. The caste system did not, however, prevent distinguished persons from all castes from being promoted to high ranking cadre in the army and administration. In civil life, by virtue of the caste system, Brahmins enjoyed a high level of respect. With the exception of a few who took to military careers, most Brahmins concentrated on religious and literary matters. Their separation from material wealth and power made them ideal arbiters in local judicial matters, and their presence in every town and village was a calculated investment made by the nobility and aristocracy to maintain order. However, the popularity of low-caste scholars (such as Molla and

Kanakadasa) and their works (including those of Vemana and Sarvajna) is an indication of the degree of social fluidity in the society.

The practice of Sati was common, though voluntary, and mostly practiced among the upper classes. Over fifty inscriptions attesting to this have been discovered in the Vijayanagara principality alone. These inscriptions are called *Satikal* (Sati stone) or *Sati-virakal* (Sati hero stone). *Satikals* commemorated the death of a woman by entering into fire after the death of her husband while *Sati-virakals* were made for a woman who performed *Sati* after her husband's heroic death. Either way, the woman was raised to the level of a demi-goddess and proclaimed by the sculpture of a Sun and crescent moon on the stone.

The socio-religious movements of the previous centuries, such as Lingayatism, provided momentum for flexible social norms to which women were expected to abide. By this time South Indian women had crossed most barriers and were actively involved in matters hitherto considered the monopoly of men, such as administration, business and trade, and involvement in the fine arts. Tirumalamba Devi who wrote *Varadambika Parinayam* and Gangadevi who wrote *Madhuravijayam* were among the notable women poets of the era. Early Telugu women poets like Tallapaka Timmakka and Atukuri Molla became popular during this period. The court of the Nayaks of Tanjore is known to have patronised several women poets. The Devadasi system existed, as well as legalised prostitution relegated to a few streets in each city. The popularity of harems amongst men of the royalty is well known from records.

Well-to-do men wore the *Petha* or *Kulavi*, a tall turban made of silk and decorated with gold. As in most Indian societies, jewellery was used by men and women and records describe the use of anklets, bracelets, finger-rings, necklaces and ear rings of various types. During celebrations, men and women adorned themselves with flower garlands and used perfumes made of rose water, civet, musk or sandalwood. In stark contrast to the commoners whose lives were modest, the lives of the empire's kings and queens were full of ceremonial pomp in the court. Queens and princesses had numerous attendants who were lavishly dressed and adorned with fine jewellery, their daily duties being light.

Physical exercises were popular with men and wrestling was an important male preoccupation for sport and entertainment. Even women wrestlers are mentioned in records. Gymnasiums have been discovered inside royal quarters and records speak of regular physical training for commanders and their armies during peace time. Royal palaces and market places had special arenas where royalty and common people alike amused themselves by watching matches such as cock fights, ram fights and wrestling between women. Excavations within the Vijayanagara city limits have revealed the existence of various types of community-based activities in the form of engravings on boulders, rock platforms and temple floors, implying these were places of casual social interaction. Some of these games are in use today and others are yet to be identified.

Religion

Although the empire was built to shield Hindu dharma from the onslaughts of the Mughal Empire and the Deccan sultanates, the Vijayanagara kings were tolerant of all religions and sects as writings by foreign visitors show. The kings used titles such as *Gobrahamana Pratipalanacharya* ("protector of cows") and *Hindurayasuratrana* ("upholder of Hindu faith") that testified to their intention of protecting Hinduism. The Empire's founders Harihara I and Bukka Raya I were devout Shaivas (worshippers of Shiva), but made grants to the Vaishnava order of Sringeri with Vidyaranya as their patron saint, and designated *Varaha* (the boar, an avatar of Vishnu) as their emblem. The later Saluva and Tuluva kings were Vaishnava by faith, but worshipped at the feet of Lord Virupaksha (Shiva) at Hampi as well as Lord Venkateshwara (Vishnu) at Tirupati. A Sanskrit work, *Jambavati Kalyanam* by King Krishnadevaraya, called Lord Virupaksha *Karnata Rajya Raksha Mani* ("protective jewel of Karnata Empire"). The kings patronised the saints of the dvaita order (philosophy of dualism) of Madhvacharya at Udupi.

The Bhakti (devotional) movement was active during this time, and involved well known Haridasas (devotee saints) of that time. Like the Virashaiva movement of the 12th century, this movement presented another strong current of devotion, pervading the lives of millions. The haridasas represented two groups, the *Vyasakuta* and *Dasakuta*, the former being required to be proficient in the Vedas, Upanishads and other Darshanas, while the *Dasakuta* merely conveyed the message of Madhvacharya through the Kannada language to the people in the form of devotional songs (*Devaranamas* and *Kirthanas*). The philosophy of Madhvacharya was spread by eminent disciples such as Naraharitirtha, Jayatirtha, Vyasatirtha, Sripadaraya, Vadirajatirtha and others. Vyasatirtha, the *guru* (teacher) of Vadirajatirtha, Purandaradasa (Father of Carnatic music) and Kanakadasa earned the devotion of King Krishnadevaraya. The king considered the saint his *Kuladevata* (family deity) and honoured him in his writings. During this time, another great composer of early carnatic music, Annamacharya composed hundreds of *Kirthanas* in Telugu at Tirupati in present day Andhra Pradesh.

The defeat of the Jain Western Ganga Dynasty by the Cholas in early 11th century and the rising numbers of followers of Vaishnava Hinduism and Virashaivism in the 12th century was mirrored by a decreased interest in Jainism. Two notable locations of Jain worship in the Vijayanagara territory were Shravanabelagola and Kambadahalli.

Islamic contact with South India began as early as the 7th century, a result of trade between the Southern kingdoms and Arab lands. Jumma Masjids existed in the Rashtrakuta empire by the 10th century and many mosques flourished on the Malabar coast by the early 14th century. Muslim settlers married local women; their children were known as Mappillas (*Moplahs*) and were actively involved in horse trading and manning shipping fleets. The interactions between the Vijayanagara empire and the Bahamani Sultanates to the north increased the presence of Muslims in the south. The introduction of Christianity began as early as the 8th century as shown by the finding of copper plates inscribed with land grants to Malabar Christians. Christian travelers wrote of the scarcity of Christians in South India in the Middle Ages, promoting its attractiveness to missionaries. The arrival of the Portuguese in the 15th century and their connections through trade with the empire, the propagation of the faith by Saint Xavier (1545) and later the presence of Dutch settlements fostered the growth of Christianity in the south.

Literature

During the rule of the Vijayanagar Empire, poets, scholars and philosophers wrote in Sanskrit and the regional languages, Kannada, Telugu and Tamil and covered such subjects as religion, biography, *Prabhanda* (fiction), music, grammar, poetry and medicine. The Telugu language became a popular literary medium, reaching its peak under the patronage of Krishnadevaraya.

Most Sanskrit works were commentaries either on the Vedas or on the Ramayana and Mahabharata epics, written by well known figures such as Sayana and Vidyaranya that extolled the superiority of the Advaita philosophy over other rival Hindu philosophies. Other writers were famous Dvaita saints of the Udupi order such as Jayatirtha (earning the title *Tikacharya* for his polemicial writings), Vyasatirtha who wrote rebuttals to the Advaita philosophy and of the conclusions of earlier logicians, and Vadirajatirtha and Sripadaraya both of whom criticised the beliefs of Adi Sankara. Apart from these saints, noted Sanskrit scholars adorned the courts of the Vijayanagara kings and their feudatory chiefdoms. Many kings of the dynasty were themselves litterateurs and authored classics such as King Krishnadevaraya's *Jambavati Kalyana*, a poetic and dramatically skillful work.

The Kannada poets and scholars of the empire produced important writings supporting the Vaishnava Bhakti movement heralded by the Haridasas (devotees of Vishnu), Brahminical and Virashaiva (Lingayatism) literature. The *Haridasa* poets celebrated their devotion through songs called *Devaranama* (lyrical poems) in the *ragale* metre. Their inspirations were the teachings of Madhvacharya and Vyasatirtha. Purandaradasa and Kanakadasa are considered the foremost among many *Dasas* (devotees) by virtue of their immense contribution. Kumara Vyasa, the most notable of Brahmin scholars wrote *Gadugina Bharata*, a translation of the epic *Mahabharata*. This work marks a transition of Kannada literature from old Kannada to modern Kannada. Chamarasa was a famous Virashaiva scholar and poet who had many debates with Vaishnava scholars in the court of Devaraya II. His *Prabhulinga Lile*, later translated into Telugu and Tamil, was a eulogy of Saint Allama Prabhu (the saint was considered an incarnation of Lord Ganapathi while Parvati took the form of a princess of Banavasi).

At this peak of Telugu literature, the most famous writing in the *Prabhanda* style was *Manucharitamu*. King Krishnadevaraya was an accomplished Telugu scholar and wrote the celebrated *Amuktamalyada*. In his court were the eight famous scholars regarded as the pillars (Ashtadiggajas) of the literary assembly, the most famous being Allasani

Peddana honoured with the title *Andhrakavitapitamaha* (father of Telugu poetry) and Tenali Ramakrishna, Krishnadevaraya's court jester who authored several acclaimed works. This was the age of Srinatha, the greatest of all Telugu poets in legend, who wrote books like *Marutratcharitamu* and *Salivahana-sapta-sati.* He was patronised by King Devaraya II and his stature was equal to the most important ministers in the court.

Though much of the Tamil literature from this period came from Tamil speaking regions ruled by the feudatory Pandya who gave particular attention on the cultivation of Tamil literature, some poets were patronised by the Vijayanagara kings. Svarupananda Desikar wrote an anthology of 2824 verses, *Sivaprakasap-perundirattu,* on the Advaita philosophy. His pupil the ascetic, Tattuvarayar, wrote a shorter anthology, *Kurundirattu,* that contained about half the number of verses. Krishnadevaraya patronised the Tamil Vaishnava poet Haridasa whose *Irusamaya Vilakkam* was an exposition of the two Hindu systems, Vaishnava and Shaiva, with a preference for the former.

Notable among secular writings on music and medicine were Vidyaranya's *Sangitsara,* Praudha Raya's *Ratiratnapradipika,* Sayana's *Ayurveda Sudhanidhi* and Lakshmana Pandita's *Vaidyarajavallabham.*

Architecture

Vijayanagara architecture is a vibrant combination of the Chalukya, Hoysala, Pandya and Chola styles, idioms that prospered in previous centuries. Its legacy of sculpture, architecture and painting influenced the development of the arts long after the empire came to an end. Its stylistic hallmark is the ornate pillared *Kalyanamantapa* (marriage hall), *Vasanthamantapa* (open pillared halls) and the *Rayagopura* (tower). Artisans used the locally available hard granite because of its durability since the kingdom was under constant threat of invasion. While the empire's monuments are spread over the whole of Southern India, nothing surpasses the vast open air theatre of monuments at its capital at Vijayanagara, a UNESCO World Heritage Site.

In the 14th century the kings continued to build Vesara or Deccan style monuments but later incorporated dravida-style gopurams to meet their ritualistic needs. The Prasanna Virupaksha temple (underground temple) of Bukka Raya I and the Hazare Rama temple of Deva Raya I are examples of Deccan architecture. The varied and intricate ornamentation of the pillars is a mark of their work. At Hampi, though the *Vitthala* temple is the best example of their pillared *Kalyanamantapa* style, the *Hazara Ramaswamy* temple is a modest but perfectly finished example. A visible aspect of their style is their return to the simplistic and serene art developed by the Chalukya dynasty. A grand specimen of Vijayanagara art, the *Vitthala* temple, took several decades to complete during the reign of the Tuluva kings.

Another element of the Vijayanagara style is the carving of large monoliths such as the *Sasivekalu* (mustard) Ganesha and *Kadalekalu* (Ground nut) Ganesha at Hampi, the

Gomateshwara statues in Karkala and Venur, and the Nandi bull in Lepakshi. The Vijayanagara temples of Bhatkal, Kanakagiri, Sringeri and other towns of coastal Karnataka, as well as Tadpatri, Lepakshi, Ahobilam, Tirupati and Srikalahasti in Andhra Pradesh, and Vellore, Kumbakonam, Kanchi and Srirangam in Tamil Nadu are examples of this style. Vijayanagara art includes wall-paintings such as *Dasavathara* (ten avatars of Vishnu) and *Girijakalyana* (marriage of Goddess Parvati) in the Virupaksha temple at Hampi, the *Shivapurana* paintings (tales of Shiva) at the Virabhadra temple at Lepakshi, and those at the Jain *basadi* (temple) and the Kamaskshi and Varadaraja temple at Kanchi. This mingling of the South Indian styles resulted in a richness not seen in earlier centuries, a focus on reliefs in addition to sculpture that surpasses that previously in India.

An aspect of Vijayanagara architecture that shows the cosmopolitanism of the great city is the presence of many secular structures bearing Islamic features. While political history concentrates on the ongoing conflict between the Vijayanagara empire and the Deccan Sultanates, the architectural record reflects a more creative interaction. There are many arches, domes and vaults that show these influences. The concentration of structures like pavilions, stables and towers suggests they were for use by royalty. The decorative details of these structures may have been absorbed into Vijayanagara architecture during the early 15th century, coinciding with the rule of Deva Raya I and Deva Raya II. These kings are known to have employed many Muslims in their army and court, some of whom may have been Muslim architects. This harmonious exchange of architectural ideas must have happened during rare periods of peace between the Hindu and Muslim kingdoms. The "Great Platform" (*Mahanavami dibba*) has relief carvings in which the figures seem to have the facial features of central Asian Turks who were known to have been employed as royal attendants.

Language

Kannada, Telugu and Tamil were used in their respective regions of the empire. Over 7000 inscriptions (*Shasana*) including 300 copper plate inscriptions (*Tamarashasana*) have been recovered, almost half of which are in Kannada, the remaining in Telugu, Tamil and Sanskrit. Bilingual inscriptions had lost favour by the 14th century. The empire minted coins at Hampi, Penugonda and Tirupati with Nagari, Kannada and Telugu legends usually carrying the name of the ruler. Gold, silver and copper were used to issue coins called *Gadyana, Varaha, Pon, Pagoda, Pratapa, Pana, Kasu* and *Jital*. The coins contained the images of various Gods including Balakrishna (infant Krishna), Venkateshwara (the presiding deity of the temple at Tirupati), Goddesses such as Bhudevi and Sridevi, divine couples, animals such as bulls and elephants and birds. The earliest coins feature Hanuman and the Garuda (divine eagle), the vehicle of Lord Vishnu. Kannada and Telugu inscriptions have been deciphered and recorded by historians of the Archaeological Survey of India.

KAKATIYA DYNASTY

The Kakatiya dynasty was a South Indian dynasty that ruled parts of what is now Andhra Pradesh, India from 1083CE to 1323CE. Staunchly Shaivite Hindu, it was one of the great Telugu kingdoms that lasted for centuries.

The Kakatiya's ascent to power can be traced to the reign of the Western Chalukyas. Kakartya Gundyana, a subordinate of the Eastern Chalukyan monarch, Amma II (945 CE-970 CE), established the Kakatiya dynasty. The dynasty's name comes either from its association with a town known as Kakatipura (since the kings bore the title "Kakatipuravallabha") or from their worship of a goddess called Kakati. A temple dedicated to goddess Kakatamma exists in Warangal so Kakatipura could be another name for Warangal itself. Kakatiyas belonged to the Durjaya family/clan.

EARLY HISTORY

Gundaya (950 CE) was the first known historical figure among the Kakatiyas. He sacrificed his life in the service of the Rashtrakuta ruler Krishna II while fighting against the Eastern Chalukyas. The grateful Krishna II placed Gundaya's son Eriya in charge of Kurravadi near Warangal. This kingdom was created as a check on the Mudigonda Chalukyas on the eastern borders of the Rashtrakuta Empire. Eriya made Kakatipura his capital. Eriya's grandson Kakartya Gundyana rendered help on behalf of his master Krishna III to Danarnava in setting aside his brother Amma II and occupying the throne of Vengi, as a result of which he got Natavadi as a token of gratitude. Gundyana's son and successor Betaraja I took advantage of the Chalukya-Chola conflict and carved out for himself a small principality. His son and successor Prola I obtained by way of grant, Hanumamakonda from Somesvara I. Beta II, son and successor of Prola, ruled between 1076 CE and 1108 CE. During his period, Hanumakonda became the capital of the Kakatiyas. Prola II the younger brother of Beta II was the most famous among the early Kakatiya rulers. When the Chalukyan power began to decline, Prola II took advantage of the confused situation and proclaimed independence. He made extensive conquests in Telangana. He also defeated and killed Gunda, the ruler of Mantrakuta (Nuzividu taluk of Krishna district) and annexed it to his kingdom. However, in his attempts to occupy the Velanati kingdom he lost his life at the hands of Rajendra Choda, the prince of the Velanati Telugu Chodas of Chandolu. This was the emergence of the Kakatiya dynasty in its own right.

RUDRA DEVA

Prola II was succeeded by Rudradeva (1158 - 1195). Rudradeva, also known as Prataparudra I, was the eldest son of Prola II. By the year 1162 CE, Rudradeva vanquished a number of his enemies and transformed his petty principality into an extensive kingdom. Rudradeva devoted the later part of his reign to the conquest of the coastal region. He consolidated and pushed the kingdom to the north up to the Godavari delta. He built a fort at Warangal to serve as a second capital. During the years 1176-82 CE the battle of

Palanadu was fought. Rudradeva rendered military assistance to Nalagama's faction. In this battle, the military strength of Velanadu had got weakened. Exploiting the situation, Rudradeva led his forces into coastal Andhra and conquered up to Srisailam and Tripurantakam in the south. In the last year of his reign (1195 CE), he came into conflict with the Seunas (Yadavas) of Devagiri. Rudra suffered defeat and death in his encounter with Jaitrapala I. After Rudradeva's death and the imprisonment of his nephew Ganapati in the hands of the Yadavas, his younger brother Mahadeva ascended the throne and ruled the kingdom for a short span of about three years (1196-1198 CE). He led an expedition against the Yadava kingdom to avenge Rudra's death and also to release his son Ganapati. He lost his life in the battle.

GANAPATI DEVA

Following the death of Mahadeva disorder broke out in the kingdom. Recherla Rudra, the commander-in-chief of the Kakatiya ruler, saved the kingdom from crumbling. Ganapatideva was set free by Jaitrapala due to political considerations like his desire to secure himself against an attack from Warangal in the event of a conflict with the aggressive Hoysalas in the south. Ganapatideva's reign lasted for 62 years. It is one of the most brilliant epochs in the history of Andhradesa. Ganapati during his long reign brought under his sway almost the whole land inhabited by the Telugu speaking people. Though Ganapatideva was alive until 1269 CE he handed over the threads of administration to his daughter Rudramadevi in 1262 A.D. itself and retired from active politics.

Ganapatideva was known as the greatest of the Kakatiyas and the first after the Satavahanas to bring the entire Telugu area under one rule. He put an end to the rule of the Cholas in the year 1210 who accepted his suzerainty. He established order in his vast dominion and encouraged trade. It is around this period that the Golconda fort was constructed, as well as beautiful temples in the Kakatiya art form such as Ramappa Temple at the tiny village of Palampet outside of Warangal.

RUDRAMADEVI

The most prominent ruler in this dynasty was Rani Rudrama Devi 1262-1295 CE, one of the few queens in Indian history. She was born as Rudramba to Ganapathideva who had no sons. She was formally designated as a son through the ancient Putrika ceremony and given the male name of Rudradeva and declared the Queen. Despite initial misgivings by some of her generals who resented a female ruler, she suppressed the internal rebellions and external incursions. An able fighter and ruler Rudramba defended the kingdom from the Cholas and the Yadavas, earning their respect. She remains one of the few female powers of the south for all time.

PRATAPARUDRA

Rudramadevi died in the month of November, 1289 CE., fighting battle against the rebel Kayastha chief Ambadeva. On the death of Rudrama, her grandson Prataparudra, who was adopted by her as son and as heir apparent on the advice of her father Ganapatideva, ascended the throne at the beginning of the year 1290 CE. Prataparudra had to fight battles throughout his reign against either the internal rebels or the external foes. Prataparudra expanded borders towards the west, whilst introducing many administrative reforms, some of which were also later adopted in the Vijayanagar empire.

THE DEMISE OF THE DYNASTY

The conquest of South India (Deccan) by the Delhi Sultanate started in 1296 when Alauddin Khilji, the son-in-Law and commander of the Sultan Jalaluddin raided and plundered Devagiri (Maharashtra). Khilji subsequently murdered the Sultan and took over the reins of the Sultanate. The glory and wealth of the Kakatiya kingdom attracted the attention of Khilji. The first foray into the Telugu kingdom was made in 1303 CE by the Sultan's armies led by Malik Fakruddin. It was a disaster because of the valiant resistance of the Kakatiya army in the battle at Upparapalli (Karimnagar District). The second attempt was made in 1309 by Malik Kafur who managed to capture Siripur and Hanumakonda forts. Warangal fort was taken after a prolonged seize. Malik Kafur indulged in murder and mayhem around the fort which prompted King Prataparudra to make a pact and offer an enormous amount of tribute. Prataparudra asserted his independence in 1320 CE when there was a change of power in Delhi. The Khilji dynasty ended and Ghiyasuddin Tughlaq ascended the Delhi throne. Tughlaq sent his son Ulugh Khan in 1323 CE to defeat the defiant Kakatiya king. Ulugh Khan's (Muhammad bin Tughluq) raid was repulsed but he returned in a month with a larger and determined army. The unprepared and battle-weary army of Warangal was finally defeated. King Prataparudra was taken prisoner. He committed suicide by drowning himself in the river Narmada while being taken to Delhi.

MUSUNI FAMILY

The Kakatiya dynasty ended and resulted in confusion and anarchy under alien rulers for sometime. Two cousins belonging to Musuni clan under the leadership of Prolayanayaka who served as army chiefs for Kakatiya kingdom later united the Telugu people and recovered Warangal from the Delhi Sultanate and ruled for half a century.

THE ISLAMIC SULTANATES

After the Arab invasion of India's ancient western neighbour Persia, expanding forces in that area were keen to invade India, which was the richest classical civilization, with a flourishing international trade and the only known diamond mines in the world. After resistance for a few centuries by various north Indian kingdoms, short lived Islamic empires (Sultanates) got established and spread across the northern subcontinent over a period of a few centuries. But, prior to Turkic invasions, Muslim trading communities had flourished throughout coastal South India, particularly in Kerala, where they arrived in small numbers, mainly from the Arabian peninsula, through trade links via the Indian Ocean. However, this had marked the introduction of an Abrahamic Middle Eastern religion in Southern India's pre-existing dharmic Hindu culture, often in puritanical form. Later, the Bahmani Sultanate and Deccan sultanates flourished in the south.

DELHI SULTANATE

In the 12th and 13th centuries, Arabs, Turks and Afghans invaded parts of northern India and established the Delhi Sultanate at the beginning of the 13th century, in the former Rajput holdings. The subsequent Slave dynasty of Delhi managed to conquer large areas of northern India, approximate to the ancient extent of the Guptas, while the Khilji Empire was also able to conquer most of central India, but were ultimately unsuccessful in conquering and uniting most of the subcontinent. The Sultanate ushered in a period of Indian cultural renaissance. The resulting "Indo-Muslim" fusion of cultures left lasting syncretic monuments in architecture, music, literature, religion, and clothing. It is surmised that the language of Urdu (literally meaning "horde" or "camp" in various Turkic dialects) was born during the Delhi Sultanate period as a result of the intermingling of the local speakers of Sanskritic prakrits with the Persian, Turkish and Arabic speaking immigrants under the Muslim rulers. The Delhi Sultanate is the only Indo-Islamic empire to stake a claim to enthroning one of the few female rulers in India, Razia Sultan (1236-1240).

A Turco-Mongol conqueror Timur began a trek starting in 1398 to invade the reigning Sultan Nasir-u-Din Mehmud of the Tughlaq Dynasty in the north Indian city of Delhi. The Sultan's army was defeated on December 17, 1398. Timur entered Delhi and the city was sacked, destroyed, and left in ruins.

THE MUGHAL ERA

In 1526, Babur, a Timurid (Turco-Persian) descendant of Timur and Genghis Khan, swept across the Khyber Pass and established the Mughal Empire, which lasted for over 200 years. The Mughal Dynasty ruled most of the Indian subcontinent by 1600; it went into a slow decline after 1707 and was finally defeated during the *1857 war of independence* also called the Indian rebellion of 1857. This period marked vast social change in the subcontinent as the Hindu majority were ruled over by the Mughal emperors, some of whom showed religious tolerance, liberally patronising Hindu culture, and some of whom destroyed historical temples and imposed taxes on non-Muslims. During the decline of the Mughal Empire, which at its peak occupied an area slightly larger than the ancient Maurya Empire, several smaller empires rose to fill the power vacuum or themselves were contributing factors to the decline. The Mughals were perhaps the richest single dynasty to have ever existed. In 1739, Nader Shah defeated the Mughal army at the huge Battle of Karnal. After this victory, Nader captured and sacked Delhi, carrying away many treasures, including the Peacock Throne.

During the Mughal era, the dominant political forces consisted of the Mughal Empire and its tributaries and, later on, the rising successor states - including the Maratha confederacy - who fought an increasingly weak and disfavoured Mughal dynasty. The Mughals, while often employing brutal tactics to subjugate their empire, had a policy of integration with Indian culture, which is what made them successful where the short-lived Sultanates of Delhi had failed. Akbar the Great was particularly famed for this. Akbar declared "Amari" or non-killing of animals in the holy days of Jainism. He rolled back the *Jazia Tax* for non-Muslims. The Mughal Emperors married local royalty, allied themselves with local Maharajas, and attempted to fuse their Turko-Persian culture with ancient Indian styles, creating unique Indo-Saracenic architecture. It was the erosion of this tradition coupled with increased brutality and centralisation that played a large part in their downfall after Aurangzeb, who unlike previous emperors, imposed relatively non-pluralistic policies on the general population, that often inflamed the majority Hindu population.

POST-MUGHAL REGIONAL KINGDOMS

The post-Mughal era was dominated by the rise of the Maratha suzerianity as other small regional states (mostly post-Mughal tributary states) emerged, and also by the increasing activities of European powers. The Maratha Kingdom was founded and consolidated by Shivaji. By the 18th century, it had transformed itself into the Maratha Empire under the rule of the Peshwas. By 1760, the Empire had stretched across practically the entire subcontinent. This expansion was brought to an end by the defeat of the Marathas by an Afghan army led by Ahmad Shah Abdali at the Third Battle of Panipat (1761). The last Peshwa, Baji Rao II, was defeated by the British in the Third Anglo-Maratha War.

Mysore was a kingdom of southern India, which was founded around 1400 CE by the Wodeyar dynasty. The rule of the Wodeyars was interrupted by Hyder Ali and his son Tippu Sultan. Under their rule Mysore fought a series of wars sometimes against the combined forces of the British and Marathas, but mostly against the British with some aid or promise of aid from the French. Hyderabad was founded by the Qutb Shahi dynasty of Golconda in 1591. Following a brief Mughal rule, Asif Jah, a Mughal official, seized control of Hyderabad declaring himself Nizam-al-Mulk of Hyderabad in 1724. It was ruled by a hereditary Nizam from 1724 until 1948. Both Mysore and Hyderabad became princely states in British India.

The Punjabi kingdom, ruled by members of the Sikh religion, was a political entity that governed the region of modern day Punjab. This was among the last areas of the subcontinent to be conquered by the British. The Anglo-Sikh wars marked the downfall of the Sikh Empire. Around the 18th century modern Nepal was formed by Gorkha rulers, and the Shahs and the Ranas very strictly maintained their national identity and integrity.

COLONIAL ERA

Vasco da Gama's maritime success to discover for Europeans a new sea route to India in 1498 paved the way for direct Indo-European commerce. The Portuguese soon set up trading-posts in Goa, Daman, Diu and Bombay. The next to arrive were the Dutch, the British—who set up a trading-post in the west-coast port of Surat in 1619—and the French. The internal conflicts among Indian Kingdoms gave opportunities to the European traders to gradually establish political influence and appropriate lands. Although these continental European powers were to control various regions of southern and eastern India during the ensuing century, they would eventually lose all their territories in India to the British islanders, with the exception of the French outposts of Pondicherry and Chandernagore, the Dutch port of Travancore, and the Portuguese colonies of Goa, Daman, and Diu.

THE BRITISH RAJ

The British East India Company had been given permission by the Mughal emperor Jahangir in 1617 to trade in India. Gradually their increasing influence led the *de-jure* Mughal emperor Farrukh Siyar to grant them *dastaks* or permits for duty free trade in Bengal in 1717. The Nawab of Bengal Siraj Ud Daulah, the *de facto* ruler of the Bengal province, opposed British attempts to use these permits. This led to the Battle of Plassey in 1757, in which the 'army' of East India Company, led by Robert Clive, defeated the Nawab's forces. This was the first political foothold with territorial implications that the British acquired in India. Clive was appointed by the Company as its first 'Governor of Bengal' in 1757. After the Battle of Buxar in 1764, the Company acquired the civil rights of administration in Bengal from the Mughal Emperor Shah Alam II; it marked the beginning of its formal rule, which was to engulf eventually most of India and extinguish the Moghul rule and dynasty itself in a century. The East India Company monopolized the trade of Bengal. They introduced a land taxation system called the Permanent Settlement which introduced a feudal like structure in Bengal. By the 1850s, the East India Company controlled most of the Indian sub-continent, which included present-day Pakistan and Bangladesh. Their policy was sometimes summed up as Divide and Rule, taking advantage of the enmity festering between various princely states and social and religious groups.

The first major movement against the British Company's high handed rule resulted in the Indian Rebellion of 1857, also known as the "Indian Mutiny" or "Sepoy Mutiny" or the "First War of Independence". After a year of turmoil, and reinforcement of the East India Company's troops with British soldiers, the British overcame the rebellion. The nominal leader of the uprising, the last Mughal emperor Bahadur Shah Zafar, was exiled to Burma, his children were beheaded and the Moghul line abolished. In the aftermath all power was transferred from the East India Company to the British Crown, which began to administer most of India as a colony; the Company's lands were controlled directly and the rest through the rulers of what it called the Princely states.

THE INDIAN INDEPENDENCE MOVEMENT

The first step toward Indian independence and western-style democracy was taken with the appointment of Indian councillors to advise the British viceroy, and with the establishment of provincial Councils with Indian members the councillors' participation was subsequently widened in legislative councils. From 1920 leaders such as Mohandas Gandhi began mass movements to campaign against the British Raj. Revolutionary activities against the British rule also took place throughout the Indian sub-continent, these movements succeeded in bringing Independence to the Indian sub-continent in 1947.

INDEPENDENCE AND PARTITION

Along with the desire for independence, tensions between Hindus and Muslims had also been developing over the years. The Muslims had always been a minority, and the prospect of an exclusively Hindu government made them wary of independence; they were as inclined to mistrust Hindu rule as they were to resist the Raj. In 1915, Mohandas Karamchand Gandhi came onto the scene, calling for unity between the two groups in an astonishing display of leadership that would eventually lead the country to independence. The profound impact Gandhi had on India and his ability to gain independence through a totally non-violent mass movement made him one of the most remarkable leaders the world has ever known. He led by example, wearing homespun clothes to weaken the British textile industry and orchestrating a march to the sea, where demonstrators proceeded to make their own salt in protest against the British monopoly. Indians gave him the name Mahatma, or Great Soul, first suggested by the Bengali poet Rabindranath Tagore. The British promised that they would leave India by 1947.

British Indian territories gained independence in 1947, after being partitioned into the Union of India and Dominion of Pakistan. Following the division of pre-partition Punjab and Bengal provinces, rioting broke out between Sikhs, Hindus and Muslims in several parts of India, including Punjab, Bengal and Delhi, leaving some 500,000 dead. Also, this period saw one of the largest mass migrations ever recorded in modern history, with a total of 12 million Hindus, Sikhs and Muslims moving between the newly created nations of India and Pakistan.

GEOGRAPHY OF INDIA

India, the major portion of the Indian subcontinent, sits atop the Indian tectonic plate, a minor plate within the Indo-Australian Plate.India's defining geological processes commenced seventy-five million years ago, when the Indian subcontinent, then part of the southern supercontinent Gondwana, began a northeastwards drift—lasting fifty million years—across the then unformed Indian Ocean. The subcontinent's subsequent collision with the Eurasian Plate and subduction under it, gave rise to the Himalayas, the planet's highest mountains, which now abut India in the north and the north-east. In the former seabed immediately south of the emerging Himalayas, plate movement created a vast trough, which, having gradually been filled with river-borne sediment, now forms the Indo-Gangetic Plain.

To the west of this plain, and cut off from it by the Aravalli Range, lies the Thar Desert. The original Indian plate now survives as peninsular India, the oldest and geologically most stable part of India, and extending as far north as the Satpura and Vindhya ranges in central India. These parallel ranges run from the Arabian Sea coast in Gujarat in the west to the coal-rich Chota Nagpur Plateau in Jharkhand in the east. To their south, the remaining peninsular landmass, the Deccan Plateau, is flanked on the left and right by the coastal ranges, Western Ghats and Eastern Ghats respectively; the plateau contains the oldest rock formations in India, some over one billion years old. Constituted in such fashion, India lies to the north of the equator between 6°44' and 35°30' north latitude and 68°7' and 97°25' east longitude.

India's coast is 7,517 kilometers (4,671 mi) long; of this distance, 5,423 kilometers (3,370 mi) belong to peninsular India, and 2,094 kilometers (1,301 mi) to the Andaman, Nicobar, and Lakshadweep Islands. According to the Indian naval hydrographic charts, the mainland coast consists of the following: 43% sandy beaches, 11% rocky coast including cliffs, and 46% mudflats or marshy coast.

Major Himalayan-origin rivers that substantially flow through India include the Ganges and the Brahmaputra, both of which drain into the Bay of Bengal. Important tributaries of the Ganges include the Yamuna and the Kosi, whose extremely low gradient causes disastrous floods every year. Major peninsular rivers whose steeper gradients prevent their waters from flooding include the Godavari, the Mahanadi, the Kaveri, and the Krishna, which also drain into the Bay of Bengal; and the Narmada and the Tapti, which drain into the Arabian Sea. Among notable coastal features of India are the marshy Rann of Kutch in western India, and the alluvial Sundarbans delta, which India shares with Bangladesh. India has two archipelagos: the Lakshadweep, coral atolls off India's south-western coast; and the Andaman and Nicobar Islands, a volcanic chain in the Andaman Sea.

India's climate is strongly influenced by the Himalayas and the Thar Desert, both of which drive the monsoons. The Himalayas prevent cold Central Asian katabatic winds from blowing in, keeping the bulk of the Indian subcontinent warmer than most locations at similar latitudes. The Thar Desert plays a crucial role in attracting the moisture-laden southwest summer monsoon winds that, between June and October, provide the majority of India's rainfall. Four major climatic groupings predominate in India: tropical wet, tropical dry, subtropical humid, and montane.

ECONOMY OF INDIA

The **economy of India**, measured in USD exchange-rate terms, is the twelfth largest in the world, with a GDP of around $1 trillion (2008). It recorded a GDP growth rate of

9.1% for the fiscal year 2007–2008 which makes it the second fastest big emerging economy, after China, in the world. At this rate of sustained growth many economists forecast that India would, over the coming decades, have a more pronounced economic effect on the world stage. Despite this phenomenal rate of growth, India's large population has a per capita income of $2,659, measured by PPP, and $978, measured in nominal terms (revised 2007 estimate). The World Bank classifies India as a low-income economy.

India's economy is diverse, encompassing agriculture, handicrafts, textile, manufacturing, and a multitude of services. Although two-thirds of the Indian workforce still earn their livelihood directly or indirectly through agriculture, services are a growing sector and play an increasingly important role in India's economy. The advent of the digital age, and the large number of young and educated populace fluent in English, is gradually transforming India as an important 'back office' destination for global outsourcing of customer services and technical support. India is a major exporter of highly-skilled workers in software and financial services, and software engineering. Other sectors like manufacturing, pharmaceuticals, biotechnology, nanotechnology, telecommunication, shipbuilding, aviation , tourism and retailing are showing strong potentials with higher growth rates.

India followed a socialist-inspired approach for most of its independent history, with strict government control over private sector participation, foreign trade, and foreign direct investment. However, since the early 1990s, India has gradually opened up its markets through economic reforms by reducing government controls on foreign trade and investment. The privatisation of publicly owned industries and the opening up of certain sectors to private and foreign interests has proceeded slowly amid political debate.

India faces a fast-growing population and the challenge of reducing economic and social inequality. Poverty remains a serious problem, although it has declined significantly since independence. India's economic history can be broadly divided into three eras, beginning with the pre-colonial period lasting up to the 17th century. The advent of British colonisation started the colonial period in the 17th century, which ended with independence in 1947. The third period stretches from independence in 1947 until now.

PRE-COLONIAL

The citizens of the Indus Valley civilisation (based around the river Indus in modern day Pakistan and Northern and Western India), a permanent and predominantly urban settlement that flourished between 2800 BC and 1800 BC, practised agriculture, domesticated animals, used uniform weights and measures, made tools and weapons, and traded with other cities. Evidence of well planned streets, a drainage system and water supply reveals their knowledge of urban planning, which included the world's first urban sanitation systems and the existence of a form of municipal government.

The 1872 census revealed that 99.3% of the population of the region constituting present-day India resided in villages, whose economies were largely isolated and self-sustaining, with agriculture the predominant occupation. This satisfied the food requirements of the village and provided raw materials for hand-based industries, such as textiles, food processing and crafts. Although many kingdoms and rulers issued coins, barter was prevalent. Villages paid a portion of their agricultural produce as revenue to the rulers, while its craftsmen received a part of the crops at harvest time for their services.

Religion, especially Hinduism, and the caste and the joint family systems, played an influential role in shaping economic activities. The caste system functioned much like medieval European guilds, ensuring the division of labour, providing for the training of apprentices and, in some cases, allowing manufacturers to achieve narrow specialization. For instance, in certain regions, producing each variety of cloth was the speciality of a particular sub-caste.

Textiles such as muslin, Calicos, shawls, and agricultural products such as pepper, cinnamon, opium and indigo were exported to Europe, the Middle East and South East Asia in return for gold and silver.

Assessment of India's pre-colonial economy is mostly qualitative, owing to the lack of quantitative information. One estimate puts the revenue of Akbar's Mughal Empire in 1600 at £17.5 million, in contrast with the total revenue of Great Britain in 1800, which totalled £16 million. India, by the time of the arrival of the British, was a largely traditional agrarian economy with a dominant subsistence sector dependent on primitive technology. It existed alongside a competitively developed network of commerce, manufacturing and credit. After the fall of the Mughals, India was administered by Maratha Empire. The maratha empire's budget in 1740s, at its peak, was Rs. 100 million. After the loss at Panipat, the maratha empire disintegrated into confederate states of Gwalior, Baroda, Indore, Jhansi, Nagpur, Pune and Kolhapur. Gwalior state had a budget of Rs. 30M. However, at this time, British East India company entered the Indian political theatre. Until, 1857, when India was firmly under the British crown, the country remained in a state of political instability due to internecine wars and conflicts.

COLONIAL

Colonial rule brought a major change in the taxation environment from revenue taxes to property taxes resulting in mass impoverishment and destitution of the great majority of farmers. It also created an institutional environment that, on paper, guaranteed property rights among the colonizers, encouraged free trade, and created a single currency with fixed exchange rates, standardized weights and measures, capital markets, a well developed system of railways and telegraphs, a civil service that aimed to be free from political interference, and a common-law, adversarial legal system. India's colonisation by the British coincided with major changes in the world economy—industrialisation, and significant growth in production and trade. However, at the end of colonial rule, India inherited an economy that was one of the poorest in the developing world, with industrial development stalled, agriculture unable to feed a rapidly growing population, one of the world's lowest life expectancies, and low rates of literacy.

An estimate by Cambridge University historian Angus Maddison reveals that India's share of the world income fell from 22.6% in 1700, comparable to Europe's share of 23.3%, to a low of 3.8% in 1952. While Indian leaders during the Independence struggle, and left-nationalist economic historians have blamed colonial rule for the dismal state of India's economy in its aftermath, a broader macroeconomic view of India during this period reveals that there were sectors of growth and decline, resulting from changes brought about by colonialism and a world that was moving towards industrialisation and economic integration.While the exact sectors of growth and decline is of questionable importance, the overall effect of the changes brought about by colonialism, and India's degree of industrialisation and economic integration of India under the British rule on India's economy can be assessed from the kind of economy India inherited after the end of the colonial rule in India.

INDEPENDENCE TO 1991

Indian economic policy after independence was influenced by the colonial experience (which was seen by Indian leaders as exploitative in nature) and by those leaders' exposure to Fabian socialism. Policy tended towards protectionism, with a strong emphasis on import substitution, industrialization, state intervention in labour and financial markets, a large public sector, business regulation, and central planning. Jawaharlal Nehru, the first prime minister, along with the statistician Prasanta Chandra Mahalanobis, carried on by Indira Gandhi formulated and oversaw economic policy. They expected favourable outcomes from this strategy, because it involved both public and private sectors and was based on direct and indirect state intervention, rather than the more extreme Soviet-style central command system. The policy of concentrating simultaneously on capital- and technology-intensive heavy industry and subsidising manual, low-skill cottage industries was criticized by economist Milton Friedman, who thought it would waste capital and labour, and retard the development of small manufacturers.

India's low average growth rate from 1947–80 was derisively referred to as the Hindu rate of growth, because of the unfavourable comparison with growth rates in other Asian countries, especially the "East Asian Tigers".

AFTER 1991

In the late 80s, the government led by Rajiv Gandhi eased restrictions on capacity expansion for incumbents, removed price controls and reduced corporate taxes. While this increased the rate of growth, it also led to high fiscal deficits and a worsening current account. The collapse of the Soviet Union, which was India's major trading partner, and the first Gulf War, which caused a spike in oil prices, caused a major balance-of-payments crisis for India, which found itself facing the prospect of defaulting on its loans. In response, Prime Minister Narasimha Rao along with his finance minister Manmohan Singh initiated the economic liberalisation of 1991. The reforms did away with the Licence Raj (investment, industrial and import licensing) and ended many public monopolies, allowing automatic approval of foreign direct investment in many sectors. Since then, the overall direction of liberalisation has remained the same, irrespective of the ruling party, although no party has tried to take on powerful lobbies such as the trade unions and farmers, or contentious issues such as reforming labour laws and reducing agricultural subsidies.

Since 1990 India has emerged as one of the wealthiest economies in the developing world; during this period, the economy has grown constantly, but with a few major setbacks. This has been accompanied by increases in life expectancy, literacy rates and food security.

While the credit rating of India was hit by its nuclear tests in 1998, it has been raised to investment level in 2007 by S&P and Moody's. In 2003, Goldman Sachs predicted that India's GDP in current prices will overtake France and Italy by 2020, Germany, UK and Russia by 2025 and Japan by 2035. By 2035, it was projected to be the third largest economy of the world, behind US and China.

CURRENCY SYSTEM

The rupee is the only legal tender accepted in India. The exchange rate as of May 23, 2008 is about 38.695 to a US dollar, 67.335 to a Euro, and 82.004 to a UK pound. The Indian rupee is accepted as legal tender in the neighboring Nepal and Bhutan, both of which peg their currency to that of the Indian rupee. The rupee is divided into 100 paise. The highest-denomination banknote is the 1,000 rupee note; the lowest-denomination coin in circulation is the 25 paise coin.

NATURAL RESOURCES

India's total cultivable area is 1,269,219 km² (56.78% of total land area), which is decreasing due to constant pressure from an ever growing population and increased urbanisation.

India has a total water surface area of 314,400 km² and receives an average annual rainfall of 1,100 mm. Irrigation accounts for 92% of the water utilisation, and comprised 380 km² in 1974, and is expected to rise to 1,050 km² by 2025, with the balance accounted for by industrial and domestic consumers. India's inland water resources comprising rivers, canals, ponds and lakes and marine resources comprising the east and west coasts of the Indian ocean and other gulfs and bays provide employment to nearly 6 million people in the fisheries sector. In 2008, India had the world's third largest fishing industry.

India's major mineral resources include Coal (fourth-largest reserves in the world), Iron ore, Manganese, Mica, Bauxite, Titanium ore, Chromite, Natural gas, Diamonds, Petroleum, Limestone and Thorium (world's largest along Kerala's shores). India's oil reserves, found in Bombay High off the coast of Maharashtra, Gujarat, and in eastern Assam meet 25% of the country's demand.

Rising energy demand concomitant with economic growth has created a perpetual state of energy crunch in India. India is poor in oil resources and is currently heavily dependent on coal and foreign oil imports for its energy needs. Though India is rich in Thorium, but not in Uranium, which it might get access to if a nuclear deal with US comes to fruition. India is rich in certain energy resources which promise significant future potential - clean / renewable energy resources like solar, wind, biofuels (jatropha, sugarcane).

PHYSICAL INFRASTRUCTURE

Development of infrastructure was completely in the hands of the public sector and was plagued by corruption, bureaucratic inefficiencies, urban-bias and an inability to scale investment.

India's low spending on power, construction, transportation, telecommunications and real estate, at $31 billion or 6% of GDP in 2002 had prevented India from sustaining higher growth rates. This had prompted the government to partially open up infrastructure to the private sector allowing foreign investment which has helped in a sustained growth rate of close to 9% for the past six quarters. India holds second position in the world in roadways' construction, more than twice that of China. As of 2005 the electricity production was at 661.6 billion kWh with oil production standing at 785,000 bbl/day. India's prime import partners are: China 8.7%, US 6%, Germany 4.6%, Singapore 4.6%, Australia 4% as of 2006 CIA FactBook As of 15 January 2007, there were 2.10 million broadband lines in India. Low tele-density is the major hurdle for slow pickup in broadband services. Over 76% of the broadband lines were via DSL and the rest via cable modems.

FINANCIAL INSTITUTIONS

India inherited several institutions, such as the civil services, Reserve Bank of India, railways, etc., from its British rulers. Mumbai serves as the nation's commercial capital, with the Reserve Bank of India (RBI), Bombay Stock Exchange (BSE) and the National Stock Exchange (NSE) located here. The headquarters of many financial institutions are also located in the city.

The RBI, the country's central bank was established on 1 April 1935. It serves as the nation's monetary authority, regulator and supervisor of the financial system, manager of exchange control and as an issuer of currency. The RBI is governed by a central board, headed by a governor who is appointed by the Central government of India. The BSE Sensex or the BSE Sensitive Index is a value-weighted index composed of 30 companies with April 1979 as the base year (100). These companies have the largest and most actively traded stocks and are representative of various sectors, on the Exchange. They account for around one-fifth of the market capitalisation of the BSE. The Sensex is generally regarded as the most popular and precise barometer of the Indian stock markets. Incorporated in 1992, the National Stock Exchange is one of the largest and most advanced stock markets in India. The NSE is the world's third largest stock exchange in terms of transactions. There are a total of 23 stock exchanges in India, but the BSE and NSE comprise 83% of the volumes. The Securities and Exchange Board of India (SEBI), established in 1992, regulates the stock markets and other securities markets of the country.

SECTORS

Agriculture

India ranks second worldwide in farm output. Agriculture and allied sectors like forestry, logging and fishing accounted for 16.6% of the GDP in 2007, employed 60% of the total workforce and despite a steady decline of its share in the GDP, is still the largest economic sector and plays a significant role in the overall socio-economic development of India. Yields per unit area of all crops have grown since 1950, due to the special emphasis placed on agriculture in the five-year plans and steady improvements in irrigation, technology, application of modern agricultural practices and provision of agricultural credit and subsidies since Green revolution in India. However, international comparisons reveal that the average yield in India is generally 30% to 50% of the highest average yield in the world.

The low productivity in India is a result of the following factors:

- Illiteracy, general socio-economic backwardness, slow progress in implementing land reforms and inadequate or inefficient finance and marketing services for farm produce.
- The average size of land holdings is very small (less than 20,000 m^2) and is subject to fragmentation, due to land ceiling acts and in some cases, family disputes. Such small holdings are often over-manned, resulting in disguised unemployment and low productivity of labour.
- Adoption of modern agricultural practices and use of technology is inadequate, hampered by ignorance of such practices, high costs and impracticality in the case of small land holdings.
- Irrigation facilities are inadequate, as revealed by the fact that only 52.6% of the land was irrigated in 2003–04, which result in farmers still being dependent on rainfall, specifically the Monsoon season. A good monsoon results in a robust growth for the economy as a whole, while a poor monsoon leads to a sluggish growth. Farm credit is regulated by NABARD, which is the statutory apex agent for rural development in the subcontinent.

Industry

India is fourteenth in the world in factory output. They together account for 27.6% of the GDP and employ 17% of the total workforce. However, about one-third of the industrial labour force is engaged in simple household manufacturing only.

Economic reforms brought foreign competition, led to privatisation of certain public sector industries, opened up sectors hitherto reserved for the public sector and led to an expansion in the production of fast-moving consumer goods.

Post-liberalisation, the Indian private sector, which was usually run by oligopolies of old family firms and required political connections to prosper was faced with foreign competition, including the threat of cheaper Chinese imports. It has since handled the change by squeezing costs, revamping management, focusing on designing new products and relying on low labour costs and technology.

Services

India is fifteenth in services output. It provides employment to 23% of work force, and it is growing fast, growth rate 7.5% in 1991–2000 up from 4.5% in 1951–80. It has the largest share in the GDP, accounting for 55% in 2007 up from 15% in 1950. Business services (information technology, information technology enabled services, business process outsourcing) are among the fastest growing sectors contributing to one third of the total output of services in 2000. The growth in the IT sector is attributed to increased specialisation, availability of a large pool of low cost, but highly skilled, educated and fluent English-speaking workers. On the supply side and on the demand side, increased demand from foreign consumers interested in India's service exports or those looking to outsource their operations. India's IT industry, despite contributing significantly to its balance of payments, accounted for only about 1% of the total GDP or 1/50th of the total services.

SOCIO-ECONOMIC CHARACTERISTICS

Poverty

Large numbers of India's people live in abject poverty. Wealth distribution in India is improving since the liberalization and with the end of the socialist rule termed as the license raj. While poverty in India has reduced significantly, official figures estimate that 27.5% of Indians still lived below the national poverty line in 2004-2005. A 2007 report by the state-run National Commission for Enterprises in the Unorganised Sector (NCEUS) found that 65% of Indians, or 750 million people, lived on less than 20 rupees per day with most working in "informal labour sector with no job or social security, living in abject poverty."

Since the early 1950s, successive governments have implemented various schemes, under planning, to alleviate poverty, that have met with partial success. All these programmes have relied upon the strategies of the *Food for work* programme and *National Rural Employment Programme* of the 1980s, which attempted to use the unemployed to generate productive assets and build rural infrastructure. In August 2005, the Indian parliament passed the *Rural Employment Guarantee Bill*, the largest programme of this type in terms of cost and coverage, which promises 100 days of minimum wage employment to every rural household in 200 of India's 600 districts. The question of whether economic reforms have reduced poverty or not has fuelled debates without generating any clear cut answers and has also put political pressure on further economic reforms, especially those involving the downsizing of labour and cutting agricultural subsidies.

Occupations and unemployment

Agricultural and allied sectors accounted for about 57% of the total workforce in 1999–2000, down from 60% in 1993–94. While agriculture has faced stagnation in growth, services have seen a steady growth. Of the total workforce, 8% is in the organised sector, two-thirds of which are in the public sector. The NSSO survey estimated that in 1999–2000, 106 million, nearly 10% of the population were unemployed and the overall unemployment rate was 7.32%, with rural areas doing marginally better (7.21%) than urban areas (7.65%).

Unemployment in India is characterized by chronic underemployment or disguised unemployment. Government schemes that target eradication of both poverty and unemployment (which in recent decades has sent millions of poor and unskilled people into urban areas in search of livelihoods) attempt to solve the problem, by providing financial assistance for setting up businesses, skill honing, setting up public sector enterprises, reservations in governments, etc. The decreased role of the public sector after liberalization has further underlined the need for focusing on better education and has also put political pressure on further reforms.

Regional imbalance

One of the critical problems facing India's economy is the sharp and growing regional variations among India's different states and territories in terms of per capita income, poverty, availability of infrastructure and socio-economic development.

The five-year plans have attempted to reduce regional disparities by encouraging industrial development in the interior regions, but industries still tend to concentrate around urban areas and port cities After liberalization, the more advanced states are better placed to benefit from them, with infrastructure like well developed ports, urbanisation and an educated and skilled workforce which attract manufacturing and service sectors. The union and state governments of backward regions are trying to reduce the disparities by offering tax holidays, cheap land, etc., and focusing more on sectors like tourism, which although being geographically and historically determined, can become a source of growth and is faster to develop than other sectors.

DEMOGRAPHICS

With an estimated population of 1.13 billion, India is the world's second most populous country. Almost 70% of Indians reside in rural areas, although in recent decades migration to larger cities has led to a dramatic increase in the country's urban population. India's largest cities are Mumbai (formerly Bombay), Delhi, Kolkata (formerly Calcutta), Chennai (formerly Madras), Bengaluru (formerly Bangalore), Hyderabad and Ahmedabad.

India is the second most culturally, linguistically and genetically diverse geographical entity after the African continent. India is home to two major linguistic families: Indo-Aryan (spoken by about 74% of the population) and Dravidian (spoken by about 24%). Other languages spoken in India come from the Austro-Asiatic and Tibeto-Burman linguistic families. Hindi, with the largest number of speakers, is the official language of the union. English, which is extensively used in business and administration, has the status of a 'subsidiary official language.' The constitution also recognises in particular 21 other languages that are either abundantly spoken or have classical status. The number of dialects in India is as high as 1,652.

Over 800 million Indians (80.5%) are Hindu. Other religious groups include Muslims (13.4%), Christians (2.3%), Sikhs (1.9%), Buddhists (0.8%), Jains (0.4%), Jews, Zoroastrians, Bahá'ís and others. Tribals constitute 8.1% of the population.

India's literacy rate is 64.8% (53.7% for females and 75.3% for males). The state of Kerala has the highest literacy rate (91%); Bihar has the lowest (47%). The national human sex ratio is 944 females per 1,000 males. India's median age is 24.9, and the population growth rate of 1.38% per annum; there are 22.01 births per 1,000 people per year.

CULTURE

India's culture is marked by a high degree of syncretism and cultural pluralism. It has managed to preserve established traditions while absorbing new customs, traditions, and ideas from invaders and immigrants and spreading its cultural influence to other parts of Asia.

Indian architecture is one area that represents the diversity of Indian culture. Much of it, including notable monuments such as the Taj Mahal and other examples of Mughal architecture and South Indian architecture, comprises a blend of ancient and varied local traditions from several parts of the country and abroad. Vernacular architecture also displays notable regional variation.

Indian music covers a wide range of traditions and regional styles. Classical music largely encompasses the two genres – North Indian Hindustani, South Indian Carnatic traditions and their various offshoots in the form of regional folk music. Regionalised forms of popular music include filmi and folk music; the syncretic tradition of the *bauls* is a well-known form of the latter.

Indian dance too has diverse *folk* and *classical* forms. Among the well-known folk dances are the *bhangra* of the Punjab, the *bihu* of Assam, the *chhau* of West Bengal, Jharkhand and Orissa and the *ghoomar* of Rajasthan. Eight dance forms, many with narrative forms and mythological elements, have been accorded classical dance status by India's *National Academy of Music, Dance, and Drama*. These are: *bharatanatyam* of the state of Tamil Nadu, *kathak* of Uttar Pradesh, *kathakali* and *mohiniyattam* of Kerala, *kuchipudi* of Andhra Pradesh, *manipuri* of Manipur, *odissi* of Orissa and the *sattriya* of Assam.

Theatre in India often incorporates music, dance, and improvised or written dialogue. Often based on Hindu mythology, but also borrowing from medieval romances, and news of social and political events, Indian theatre includes the *bhavai* of state of Gujarat, the *jatra* of West Bengal, the *nautanki* and *ramlila* of North India, the *tamasha* of Maharashtra, the *terukkuttu* of Tamil Nadu, and the *yakshagana* of Karnataka.

The Indian film industry is the largest in the world. Bollywood, based in Mumbai, makes commercial Hindi films and is the most prolific film industry in the world. Established traditions also exist in Bengali, Kannada, Malayalam, Marathi, Tamil, and Telugu language cinemas.

The earliest works of Indian literature were transmitted orally and only later written down. These included works of Sanskrit literature – such as the early Vedas, the epics Mahâbhârata and Ramayana, the drama *Abhijñânaúâkuntalam* (The Recognition of Sakuntalâ), and poetry such as the *Mahâkâvya* – and the Tamil language *Sangam* literature. Among Indian writers of the modern era active in Indian languages or English, Rabindranath Tagore won the Nobel Prize in 1913.

Indian cuisine is characterized by a wide variety of regional styles and sophisticated use of herbs and spices. The staple foods in the region are rice (especially in the south and the east) and wheat (predominantly in the north). Spices originally native to the Indian subcontinent that are now consumed world wide include black pepper; in contrast, hot chili peppers, popular across India, were introduced by the Portuguese.

Traditional Indian dress varies across the regions in its colours and styles and depends on various factors, including climate. Popular styles of dress include draped garments such as sari for women and dhoti or lungi for men; in addition, stitched clothes such as salwar kameez for women and kurta-pyjama and European-style trousers and shirts for men, are also popular.

Many Indian festivals are religious in origin, although several are celebrated irrespective of caste and creed. Some popular festivals are Diwali, Thai Pongal, Holi, Onam, Vijayadashami, Durga Puja, Eid ul-Fitr, Bakr-Id, Christmas, Buddha Jayanti and Vaisakhi. India has three national holidays. Other sets of holidays, varying between nine and twelve, are officially observed in individual states. Religious practices are an integral part of everyday life and are a very public affair.

Traditional Indian family values are highly respected, although urban families now prefer the nuclear family structure due to the socio-economic constraints imposed by traditional joint family system.

GOVERNMENT OF INDIA

The Constitution of India, the longest and the most exhaustive constitution of any independent nation in the world, came into force on January 26, 1950. The preamble of the constitution defines India as a sovereign, socialist, secular, democratic republic. India has a quasi-federal form of government and a bicameral parliament operating under a Westminster-style parliamentary system. It has three branches of governance: the Legislature, Executive, and Judiciary.

The President of India is the official head of state elected indirectly by an electoral college for a five-year term. The Prime Minister is, however, the *de facto* head of government and exercises most executive powers. The Prime Minister is appointed by the President and, by convention, is the candidate supported by the party or political alliance holding the majority of seats in the lower house of Parliament.

The legislature of India is the bicameral Parliament, which consists of the upper house called the Rajya Sabha (Council of States) and the lower house called the Lok Sabha (House of People). The Rajya Sabha, a permanent body, has 245 members serving staggered six year terms. Most are elected indirectly by the state and territorial legislatures in proportion to the state's population. The 543 of the Lok Sabha's 545 members are directly elected by popular vote to represent individual constituencies for five year terms. The other two members are nominated by the President from the Anglo-Indian community if, in his opinion, the community is not adequately represented.

The executive branch consists of the President, Vice-President, and the Council of Ministers (the Cabinet being its executive committee) headed by the Prime Minister. Any minister holding a portfolio must be a member of either house of parliament. In the Indian parliamentary system, the executive is subordinate to the legislature, with the Prime Minister and his Council being directly responsible to the lower house of the parliament.

India has a unitary three-tier judiciary, consisting of the Supreme Court, headed by the Chief Justice of India, twenty-one High Courts, and a large number of trial courts. The Supreme Court has original jurisdiction over cases involving fundamental rights and over disputes between states and the Centre, and appellate jurisdiction over the High Courts. It is judicially independent, and has the power to declare the law and to strike down union or state laws which contravene the Constitution. The role as the ultimate interpreter of the Constitution is one of the most important functions of the Supreme Court.

Chapter 2

Pakistan

Pakistan, officially the **Islamic Republic of Pakistan**, is a country located in South Asia, Southwest Asia, Middle East and converges with Central Asia and the Middle East. It has a 1,046 kilometer (650 mile) coastline along the Arabian Sea and Gulf of Oman in the south, and is bordered by Afghanistan and Iran in the west, India in the east and China in the far northeast.

The region forming modern Pakistan was home to the ancient Indus Valley Civilization and then, successively, recipient of ancient Vedic, Persian, Indo-Greek and Islamic cultures. The area has witnessed invasions and settlement by the Persians, Greeks, Arabs, Turks, Afghans and the Mongols. It was a part of British Raj from 1858 to 1947, when the Pakistan Movement for a state for Muslims, led by Muhammad Ali Jinnah and the Muslim League resulted in the independence and creation of the state of Pakistan, that comprised the provinces of Sindh, Northwest Frontier Province, West Punjab, Balochistan and East Bengal. With the adoption of its constitution in 1956, Pakistan became an Islamic republic. In 1971, a civil war in East Pakistan resulted in the independence of Bangladesh. Pakistan's history has been characterized by periods of economic growth, military rule and political instability.

Pakistan is the sixth most populous country in the world and has the second largest Muslim population in the world after Indonesia. The country is listed among the "Next Eleven" economies. Pakistan is a founding member of the Organization of the Islamic Conference, South Asian Association for Regional Cooperation, Developing 8 Countries and the Economic Cooperation Organization. It is also a member of the United Nations, Commonwealth of Nations, World Trade Organization, G33 developing countries, Group of 77 developing nations, major non-NATO ally of the United States and is a nuclear state.

HISTORY OF PAKISTAN

The **history of Pakistan** as a modern nation began with independence from British India on 14 August 1947, although the region has been inhabited continuously for at least two million years; its ancient history includes some of the oldest settlements of South Asia and some of its major civilizations. The political history of eventual birth of the country began in the aftermath of the Indian Rebellion of 1857, which culminated in 90 years of direct rule by the British Crown, and, subsequently, spawned a successful freedom struggle led by the Indian National Congress and the All India Muslim League. The latter was founded in 1906 to protect Muslim interests and rose to popularity in the late 1930s amid fears of neglect and under-representation of Muslims in politics. On 29 December 1930, the poet Muhammad Iqbal called for an autonomous "state in northwestern India for Indian Muslims". Muhammad Ali Jinnah espoused the *Two Nation Theory* and led the Muslim League to adopt the *Lahore Resolution* of 1940, demanding the formation of an independent Pakistan.

Pakistan became independent as a Muslim-majority state with two wings to the east and northwest of India respectively. Independence resulted in communal riots across India and Pakistan — as millions of Muslims moved to Pakistan and millions of Hindus and Sikhs moved to India. Disputes arose over several princely states including Kashmir and Jammu whose ruler had acceded to India following an invasion by tribesmen from Pakistan. This lead to the First Kashmir War (1948) which ended with India occupying roughly two-thirds of the state and Pakistan occupying the remainder. A republic was declared in 1956 but was stalled by a coup d'etat by Ayub Khan (1958–69), who ruled during a period of internal instability and a second war with India in 1965. Economic grievances and political dissent in East Pakistan led to violent political tensions and army repression, escalating into civil war followed by the Indo-Pakistani War of 1971 and ultimately the secession of East Pakistan as the independent state of Bangladesh.

Civilian rule resumed from 1972 to 1977 under Zulfikar Ali Bhutto, until he was deposed by General Zia-ul-Haq, who became the country's third military president. Pakistan's secular policies were replaced by the Islamic Shariah legal code, which increased religious influences on the civil service and the military. With the death of General Zia in a plane crash in 1988, Benazir Bhutto, daughter of Zulfikar Ali Bhutto, was elected as the first female Prime Minister of Pakistan. Over the next decade, she alternated power with Nawaz Sharif, as the country's political and economic situation worsened. Military tensions in the Kargil conflict with India were followed by a Pakistani military coup d'état in 1999 in which General Pervez Musharraf assumed executive powers. In 2001, Musharraf named himself President after the forced resignation of Rafiq Tarar. After the 2002 parliamentary elections, Musharraf transferred executive powers to newly elected Prime Minister Zafarullah Khan Jamali, who was succeeded in the 2004 Prime-Ministerial election by Shaukat Aziz, followed by a temporary period in office by Chaudhry Shujaat Hussain. On 15 November 2007 the National Assembly completed its term and a caretaker government was appointed with the former Chairman of the Senate, Muhammad Mian Soomro as Prime Minister. The assassination of Benazir Bhutto resulted in the general elections being postponed until 18 February 2008.

PREHISTORY

Mehrgarh, (7000-5500 BCE), on the Kachi plain of Balochistan, is an important Neolithic site discovered in 1974, with early evidence of farming and herding, and dentistry. Early residents lived in mud brick houses, stored grain in granaries, fashioned tools with copper ore, cultivated barley, wheat, jujubes and dates, and herded sheep, goats and cattle, while later residents (5500-2600 BCE) engaged in crafts, including flint knapping, tanning, bead production, and metalworking. The site was occupied continuously until about 2600 BCE, but climatic changes between 2600 and 2000 BCE caused the area to become more arid. Mehrgarh was abandoned in favour of the Indus valley, where a new civilization was in the early stages of development.

The Indus Valley civilization developed between 3300-1700 BCE on the banks of the Indus River and at its peak had as many as five million inhabitants in hundreds of settlements extending as far as the Arabian Sea, southern and eastern Afghanistan, southeastern Iran and the Himalayas. The major urban centers were at Dholavira, Harappa, Lothal, Mohenjo-daro, and Rakhigarhi, as well as an offshoot called the Kulli culture (2500-2000 BCE) in southern Balochistan, which had similar settlements, pottery and other artifacts. The Indus Valley civilisation has been tentatively identified as proto-Dravidian, but this cannot be confirmed until the Indus script is fully deciphered. The civilization collapsed abruptly around 1700 BCE, possible due to a cataclysmic earthquake or the drying up of the Ghaggar-Hakra river or due to the invasion of Aryans.

In the early part of the second millennium BCE, Indo-European tribes from Central Asia or the southern Russian steppes migrated into the region, and settled in the Sapta Sindhu area between the Kabul River and the Upper Ganges-Yamuna rivers. The resulting Vedic culture lasted until the middle of the first millennium BCE when there were marked linguistic, cultural and political changes. During the Vedic culture, the hymns of the Rigveda were composed and the foundations of Hinduism were laid. The city of Taxila, in northern Pakistan, became important in Hinduism (and later in Buddhism); according to Hindu tradition, the Mahâbhârata epic was first recited at Taxila at the snake sacrifice Yagna of King Janamejaya, one of the heroes of the story.

EARLY HISTORY

The Indus plains formed the most populous and richest satrapy of the Persian Achaemenid Empire for almost two centuries, starting from the reign of Darius the Great (522-485 BCE). Its heritage influenced the region e. g. adoption of Aramaic script, which the Achaemenids used for the Persian language; but after the end of Achaemenid rule, other scripts became more popular, such as Kharocmhî (derived from Aramaic) and Greek. The interaction between Hellenistic Greece and Buddhism began when Alexander the Great overthrew the Achaemenid empire in 334 BCE, and marched eastwards. Eventually, after defeating King Porus in the fierce Battle of the Hydaspes (near modern Jhelum), he conquered much of the Punjab region. But, his battle weary troops refused to advance further into India to engage the formidable army of Nanda Dynasty and its vanguard of trampling elephants, new monstorities to the invaders. Therefore, Alexander proceeded southwest along the Indus valley. Along the way, he engaged in several battles with smaller kingdoms before marching his army westward across the Makran desert towards modern Iran. Alexander founded several new Macedonian/Greek settlements in Gandhara and Punjab.

During the time of his campaigns on the Indus plain, Alexander had found an ally in Chandragupta Maurya, a fugitive general from Magadha empire of the Nandas, who later raised his own military force and ultimately overthrew the Nanda Dynasty - using Macedonian tactics - and founded the Mauryan dynasty in Magadha, that lasted about 180 years. After Alexander's death in 323BCE, his *Diadochi* (generals) divided the empire, with Seleucus setting up the Seleucid Kingdom, which included the Indus plain. Chandragupta Maurya took advantage of this fragmentation of Greek power and captured the Punjab and Gandhara. Later, the eastern part of the Seleucid Kingdom broke away to form the Greco-Bactrian Kingdom (third–second century BCE). Chandragupta's grandson, Ashoka the Great, (273-232 BCE) expanded the Mauryan empire to its greatest extent covering most of South Asia. He converted to Buddhism after feeling remorse for his bloody conquest of Kalinga in eastern India. His Edicts were written on pillars in Aramaic (the lingua franca of the Achaemenid Empire) or in Kharosthî.

Greco-Buddhism (or Græco-Buddhism) was the syncretism between the culture of Classical Greece and Buddhism in the area of modern Afghanistan and Pakistan, between the fourth century BCE and the fifth century CE. It influenced the artistic development of Buddhism, and in particular Mahayana Buddhism, before it spread to central and eastern Asia, from the 1st century CE onward. Demetrius (son of the Greco-Bactrian king Euthydemus) invaded northern India in 180 BCE as far as Pataliputra and established an Indo-Greek kingdom. To the south, the Greeks captured Sindh and nearby coastal areas, completing the invasion by 175 BCE and confining the Sungas to the east. Meanwhile, in Bactria, the usurper Eucratides killed Demetrius in a battle. Although the Indo-Greeks lost part of the Gangetic plain, their kingdom lasted nearly two centuries.

The Indo-Greek Menander I (reigned 155-130 BCE) drove the Greco-Bactrians out of Gandhara and beyond the Hindu Kush, becoming a king shortly after his victory. His territories covered Panjshir and Kapisa in modern Afghanistan and extended to the Punjab region, with many tributaries to the south and east, possibly as far as Mathura. The capital Sagala (modern Sialkot) prospered greatly under Menander's rule and Menander is one of the few Bactrian kings mentioned by Greek authors. The classical Buddhist text Milinda Pañha, praises Menander, saying there was "none equal to Milinda in all India". His empire survived him in a fragmented manner until the last independent Greek king, Strato II, disappeared around 10 CE. Around 125 BCE, the Greco-Bactrian king Heliocles, son of Eucratides, fled from the Yuezhi invasion of Bactria and relocated to Gandhara, pushing the Indo-Greeks east of the Jhelum River. Various petty kings ruled into the early first century CE, until the conquests by the Scythians, Parthians and the Yuezhi, who founded the Kushan dynasty. The last known Indo-Greek ruler was Theodamas, from the Bajaur area of Gandhara, mentioned on a 1st century CE signet ring, bearing the Kharocmhî inscription *"Su Theodamasa"* (*"Su"* was the Greek transliteration of the Kushan royal title *"Shau"* ("Shah" or "King")).

The Indo-Scythians were descended from the Sakas (Scythians) who migrated from southern Siberia to Kashmir and Arachosia from the middle of the 2nd century BCE to the 1st century BCE. They displaced the Indo-Greeks and ruled a kingdom that stretched from Gandhara to Mathura and Scythian tribes spread further into northwest India and the Iranian plateau.

The Parni were a nomadic Central Asian tribe who overthrew the Persian Seleucids and annexed much of the Indus region. Following the decline of the central Parthian authority after clashes with the Roman Empire, a local Parthian leader, Gondophares established the Indo-Parthian Kingdom in the 1st century CE. The kingdom was ruled from Taxila and covered much of modern southeast Afghanistan, Pakistan and northwestern India.

The Kushan kingdom founded by King Heraios, and greatly expanded by his successor, Kujula Kadphises. Kadphises' son, Vima Takto conquered territory now in India, but lost much of the west of the kingdom to the Parthians. The fourth Kushan emperor, Kanishka I, (circa 127 CE) had a winter capital at Purushapura (Peshawar) and a summer capital at Kapisa (Bagram). The kingdom linked the Indian Ocean maritime trade with the commerce of the Silk Road through the Indus valley. At its height, the empire extended from the Aral Sea to northern India, encouraging long-distance trade, particularly between China and Rome. Kanishka convened a great Buddhist council in Kashmir, marking the start of the pantheistic Mahayana Buddhism and its scission with Nikaya Buddhism.

The art and culture of Gandhara are the best known expressions of the interaction of Greek and Buddhist cultures, which continued over several centuries until the fifth century CE White Hun invasions. Over the next few centuries, the White Huns, Indo-Parthians, and Kushans shared control of the Indus plain while the Persian Sassanid Empire dominated the south and southwest. The mingling of Indian and Persian cultures in the region gave rise to the Indo-Sassanid culture, which flourished in Balochistan and western Punjab. The Gupta Empire arose in northern India around the second century CE and included much of the lower Indus area as a province. The Gupta era was marked by a local Hindu revival, whose impact was felt in distant Punjab/Sindh region, although Buddhism continued to flourish. According to Arab chroniclers, the Rai Dynasty of Sindh (c.489-632), established a great kingdom with Ror (modern Sukkur) as its capital and, at its zenith, under Rai Diwaji (Devaditya), ruled over the Sindh region and beyond. Devadittya was a great patron of Buddhism, which flourished. This kingdom was taken over by Brahman dynasties, whose unpopularity among Buddhist subjects contributed towards the consolidation of Arab conquerors' base in Sindh.

THE MUSLIM PERIOD

In 712 CE, a Syrian Muslim chieftain called Muhammad bin Qasim conquered most of the Indus region for the Umayyad empire, but the instability of the empire resulted in effective control only over Sind and southern Punjab. The provincial capital of "As-Sindh" was at Al-Mansurah, 72 km north of modern Hyderabad. There was gradual conversion to Islam in the south, especially amongst the native Buddhist majority, but in areas north of Multan, Buddhists, Hindus and other non-Muslim groups remained numerous.

In 997 CE, Mahmud of Ghazni conquered the bulk of Khorasan, marched on Peshawar in 1005, and followed it by the conquests of Punjab (1007), Balochistan (1011), Kashmir (1015) and Qanoch (1017). By the end of his reign in 1030, Mahmud's empire extended from Kurdistan in the west to the Yamuna river in the east, and the Ghaznavid dynasty lasted until 1187. Contemporary historians such as Abolfazl Beyhaqi and Ferdowsi described extensive building work in Lahore, as well as Mahmud's support and patronage of learning, literature and the arts.

In 1160, Muhammad Ghori conquered Ghazni from the Ghaznavids and became its governor in 1173. He marched eastwards into the remaining Ghaznavid territory and Gujarat in the 1180s, but was rebuffed by Gujarat's Solanki rulers. In 1186-7, he conquered Lahore, bringing the last of Ghaznevid territory under his control and ending the Ghaznavid empire. Muhammad Ghori returned to Lahore after 1200 to deal with a revolt of the Rajput Ghakkar tribe in the Punjab. He suppressed the revolt, but was killed during a Ghakkar raid on his camp on the Jhelum River in 1206. Muhammad Ghori's successors established the first Indo-Islamic dynasty, the Delhi Sultanate.

The Mamluk Dynasty, (*mamluk means "slave" and referred to the Turkic slave soldiers who became rulers throughout the Islamic world*), seized the throne of the Sultanate in 1211. Several Turko-Afghan dynasties ruled their empires from Delhi: the Mamluk (1211-90), the Khalji (1290-1320), the Tughlaq (1320-1413), the Sayyid (1414-51) and the Lodhi (1451-1526). Although some kingdoms remained independent of Delhi - in Gujarat, Malwa (central India), Bengal and Deccan - almost all of the Indus plain came under the rule of these large Indo-Islamic sultanates. Perhaps the greatest contribution of the sultanate was its temporary success in insulating South Asia from the Mongol invasion from Central Asia in the thirteenth century; nonetheless the sultans eventually lost Afghanistan and western Pakistan to the Mongols.

The sultans (emperors) of Delhi enjoyed cordial relations with Muslim rulers in the Near East but owed them no allegiance. While the sultans ruled from urban centers, their military camps and trading posts provided the nuclei for many towns that sprang up in the countryside. Close interaction with local populations led to cultural exchange and the resulting "Indo-Islamic" fusion has left a lasting imprint and legacy in South Asian architecture, music, literature, life style and religious customs. In addition, the language of Urdu (literally meaning "horde" or "camp" in various Turkic dialects) was born during the Delhi Sultanate period, as a result of the mingling of speakers of Sanskritic prakrits, Persian, Turkish and Arabic languages.

From the 16th to the 19th century CE the formidable Mughal empire covered much of South Asia and played a major role in the economic and cultural development of the region. The empire was one of the three major Islamic states of its day and sometimes contested its northwestern holdings such as Qandahar against the Uzbeks and the Safavid Persians. The Mughals were descended from Persianized Central Asian Turks (with significant Mongol admixture). The third emperor, Akbar the Great, was both a capable ruler and an early proponent of religious and ethnic tolerance and favored an early form of multiculturalism. For a short time in the late 16th century, Lahore was the capital of the empire. The architectural legacy of the Mughals in Lahore includes the Shalimar Gardens built by the fifth emperor, Shahjahan, and the Badshahi Mosque built by the sixth emperor, Aurangzeb.

In 1739, the Persian emperor Nader Shah invaded India, defeated the Mughal Emperor Mohammed Shah, and occupied most of Balochistan and the Indus plain. After Nadir Shah's death, the kingdom of Afghanistan was established in 1747, by one of his generals, Ahmad Shah Abdali and included Kashmir, Peshawar, Daman, Multan, Sind and Punjab. In the south, a succession of autonomous dynasties (the Daudpotas, Kalhoras and Talpurs) had asserted the independence of Sind, from the end of Aurangzeb's reign. Most of Balochistan came under the influence of the Khan of Kalat, apart from some coastal areas such as Gwadar which were ruled by the Sultan of Oman.

The Sikh Confederacy (1748-1799) was a group of small states in the Punjab which emerged in a political vacuum created by rivalry between the Mughals, Afghans and Persians. The Confederacy drove out the Mughals, repelled several Afghan invasions and in 1764 captured Lahore. However after the retreat of Ahmed Shah Abdali, the Confederacy suffered instability as disputes and rivalries emerged. The Sikh empire (1799-1849) was formed on the foundations of the Confederacy by Ranjit Singh who proclaimed himself "*Sarkar-i-Wala*", and was referred to as the Maharaja of Lahore. His empire eventually extended as far west as the Khyber Pass and as far south as Multan. Amongst his conquests were Kashmir in 1819 and Peshawar in 1834, although the Afghans made two attempts to recover Peshawar. After the Maharaja's death the empire was weakened by internal divisions and political mismanagement. The British annexed the Sikh empire in 1849 after two Anglo-Sikh wars.

INDEPENDENCE STRUGGLE

The concept of an independent Muslim nation emerged gradually from the aftermath of the Indian Rebellion of 1857. In 1885, the Indian National Congress was founded as a forum, which later became a party, to promote a nationalist cause. Although the Congress attempted to include the Muslim community in the independence struggle and some Muslims were very active in the Congress, the majority of Muslim leaders did not trust the party, viewing it as a "Hindu-dominated" organization. Some Muslims felt that an independent united India would inevitably be "ruled by Hindus", and that there was a need to address the issue of the Muslim identity within India. Thus in 1877, Syed Ameer Ali formed the Central National Muhammadan Association to work towards the political advancement of the Muslims, but the organisation declined towards the end of the nineteenth century. A turning point came in 1900 when the British administration in the United Provinces (now Uttar Pradesh), acceded to Hindu demands and made Hindi, written in the Devanagari script, the official language. The Muslims feared that the Hindu majority would seek to suppress Muslim culture and religion in an independent India. The All-India Muslim League was founded on December 30th, 1906, on the sidelines of the annual All India Muhammadan Educational Conference in Shahbagh, Dhaka. The meeting was attended by three thousand delegates and presided over by Nawab Viqar-ul-Mulk. It addressed the issue of legitimate safeguards for Muslims and finalised a programme. A resolution, moved by Nawab Salimullah and seconded by Hakim Ajmal Khan.

The constitution and principles of the League were contained in the "*Green Book*", written by Maulana Mohammad Ali. Its goals at this stage did not include establishing an independent Muslim state, but rather concentrated on protecting Muslim liberties and rights, promoting understanding between the Muslim community and other Indians, educating the Muslim and Indian community at large on the actions of the government, and discouraging violence. However, several factors over the next thirty years, including sectarian violence, led to a re-evaluation of the League's aims. Among those Muslims in the Congress who did not initially join the League was Muhammed Ali Jinnah, a prominent Bombay lawyer and statesman. This was because the first article of the League's platform was "*To promote among the Mussalmans (Muslims) of India, feelings of loyalty to the British Government*". In 1907, a vocal group of Hindu hard-liners within the Indian National Congress movement separated from it and started to pursue a pro-Hindu movement openly.

This group was spearheaded by the famous trio of Lal-Bal-Pal - Lala Lajpat Rai , Bal Gangadhar Tilak and Bipin Chandra Pal of Punjab, Bombay and Benagal provinces respectively. Their influence spread rapidly among other like minded Hindus - they called it Hindu nationalism - and it became a cause of serious concern for Muslims. However, Jinnah did not join the League until 1913, when it changed its platform to one of Indian independence as a reaction against the British decision - taken under the enormous pressure and vociferous protests of the Hindu majority - to reverse the 1905 Partition of Bengal, which the League regarded as a betrayal of the Bengali Muslims. Even at this stage, Jinnah believed in Muslim-Hindu co-operation to achieve an independent, united India, although he argued that Muslims should be guaranteed one-third of the seats in any Indian Parliament.

The League gradually became the leading representative body of Indian Muslims. Jinnah became its president in 1916, and negotiated the Lucknow Pact with the Congress leader, Bal Gangadhar Tilak, by which Congress conceded the principle of separate electorates and weighted representation for the Muslim community. However, Jinnah broke with the Congress in 1920 when the Congress leader, Mohandas Gandhi, launched a law violating Non-Cooperation Movement against the British, which a temperamentally law abiding barrister Jinnah disapproved of. Jinnah also became convinced that the Congress would renounce its support for separate electorates for Muslims, which indeed it did in 1928. In 1927, the British proposed a constitution for India as recommended by the Simon Commission, but they failed to reconcile all parties.

The British then turned the matter over to the League and the Congress, and in 1928 an All-Parties Congress was convened in Delhi. The attempt failed, but two more conferences were held, and at the Bombay conference in May, it was agreed that a small committee should work on the constitution. The prominent Congress leader Motilal Nehru headed the committee, which included two Muslims, Syed Ali Imam and Shoaib Quereshi; Motilal's son, Pt Jawaharlal Nehru, was its secretary. The League, however, rejected the committee's report, the so called Nehru Report, arguing that its proposals gave too little representation (one quarter) to Muslims – the League had demanded at least one-third representation in the legislature. Jinnah announced a "parting of the ways" after reading the report, and relations between the Congress and the League began to sour.

THE RISE OF THE LEAGUE

The election of Ramsay MacDonald's Labour government in 1929 in Britain, already weakened by the First World War, fuelled new hopes for progress towards self-government in India. Gandhi travelled to London, claiming to represent all Indians and criticising the League as sectarian and divisive. Round-table talks were held, but these achieved little, since Gandhi and the League were unable reach a compromise. The fall of the Labour government in 1931 ended this period of optimism. By 1930 Jinnah had despaired of Indian politics and particularly of getting mainstream parties like the Congress to be sensitive to minority priorities. A fresh call for a separate state was then made by the famous writer, poet and philosopher Allama Muhammad Iqbal, who in his presidential address to the 1930 convention of the Muslim League said that he felt that a separate Muslim state was essential in an otherwise Hindu-dominated South Asia.

The name was coined by Cambridge student and Muslim nationalist Choudhary Rahmat Ali, and was published on January 28, 1933 in the pamphlet *Now or Never*. He saw it as an acronym formed from the names of the *"homelands"* of Muslims in northwest India — **P** for Punjab, **A** for the Afghan areas of the region, **K** for Kashmir, **S** for Sindh and **tan** for Balochistan, thus forming *"Pakstan"*. An **i** was later added to the English rendition of the name to ease pronunciation, producing *"Pakistan"*. In Urdu and Persian the name encapsulates the concept of *"pak"* (*"pure"*) and *"stan"* (*"land"*) and hence a *"Pure Land"*. In the 1935, the British administration proposed to hand over substantial power to elected Indian provincial legislatures, with elections to be held in 1937. After the elections the League took office in Bengal and Punjab, but the Congress won office in most of the other provinces, and refused to share power with the League in provinces with large Muslim minorities.

Mean while, Muslim ideologues for separatism also felt vindicated by the presidential address of V.D. Savarkar at the 19th session of the famous Hindu nationalist party Hindu Mahasabha in 1937. In it, this legendary revolutionary - popularly called Veer Savarkar and known as the iconic father of the Hindutva ideology - propounded the seminal ideas of his Two Nation Theory or Hindu-Muslim exclusivism, which influenced Jinnah profoundly.

In 1940, Jinnah called a general session of the Muslim League in Lahore to discuss the situation that had arisen due to the outbreak of the Second World War and the Government of India joining the war without consulting Indian leaders. The meeting was also aimed at analyzing the reasons that led to the defeat of the Muslim League in the general election of 1937 in the Muslim majority provinces. In his speech, Jinnah criticized the Indian National Congress and the nationalist Muslims, and espoused the Two-Nation Theory and the reasons for the demand for separate Muslim homelands. Sikandar Hayat Khan, the Chief Minister of Punjab, drafted the original resolution, but disavowed the final version, that had emerged after endless redrafting by the Subject Committee of the Muslim League. The final text unambiguously rejected the concept of a United India because of increasing inter-religious violence and recommended the creation of an independent Muslim state. The resolution was moved in the general session by *Shere-Bangla* A. K. Fazlul Huq, the Chief Minister of Bengal, supported by Chaudhry Khaliquzzaman and other Muslim leaders and was adopted on 23 March 1940.In 1941 it became part of the Muslim League's constitution. However, in early 1941, Sikandar explained to the Punjab Assembly that he did not support the final version of the resolution. The sudden death of Sikandar in 1942 paved the way over the next few years for Jinnah to emerge as the recognised leader of the Indian Muslims. In 1943, the Sind Assembly passed a resolution demanding the establishment of a Muslim homeland. Talks between Jinnah and Gandhi in 1944 in Bombay failed to achieve agreement and there were no more attempts to reach a single-state solution.

The Second World War had broken the back of both Britain and France and disintigration of their colonial empires was expected soon. With the election of another sympathetic Labour government in Britain in 1945, Indians were seeing independence within reach. But, Gandhi and Nehru were not receptive to Jinnah's proposals and were also adamantly opposed to dividing India, since they knew that the Hindus, who saw India as one indivisible entity, would never agree to such a thing. In the Constituent Assembly elections of 1946, the League won 425 out of 496 seats reserved for Muslims (and about 89.2% of Muslim votes) on a policy of creating an independent state of Pakistan, and with an implied threat of secession if this was not granted. By 1946 the British had neither the will, nor the financial resources or military power, to hold India any longer.

Political deadlock ensued in the Constituent Assembly, and the British Prime Minister, Clement Attlee, sent a Cabinet Mission to India to mediate the situation. When the talks broke down, Attlee appointed Louis Mountbatten as India's last Viceroy, to negotiate the partition of India and immediate British withdrawal. Mountbatten, of imperial blood and a world war admiral, handled the problem as a campaign. Ignorant of the complex ground realities in British India, he rashly preponed the date of transfer of power and told Gandhi and Nehru that if they did not accept partition there would be civil war in his opinion and he would rather consider handing over power to individual provinces and the rulers of princely states. This forced the hands of Congress leaders and the "Independence of India Act 1947" provided for the two dominions of Pakistan and India to become independent on the 14th and 15th of August 1947 respectively. This result was despite the calls for a third Osmanistan in the early 1940s.

INDEPENDENCE

On the 14th and 15th of August, 1947, British India was partitioned into the new independent Dominions of Pakistan and India respectively, with both dominions joining the British Commonwealth. However, the ill conceived and controversial decision to partition Punjab and Bengal, two of the biggest provinces, between India and Pakistan had disastrous consequences. This partition created inter-religious violence of such magnitude that exchange of population along religious lines became a necessity in these provinces. More than two million people migrated across the new borders and more than one hundred thousand died in the spate of communal violence, that spread even beyond these provinces. The partition also resulted in tensions over Kashmir leading to the Indo-Pakistani War of 1947. The post-independence political history of Pakistan has been characterised by several periods of authoritarian military rule and continuing territorial disputes with India over the status of Kashmir, and with Afghanistan over the Pashtunistan issue.

In 1948, Jinnah declared in Dhaka that Urdu would be the only state language of Pakistan. This sparked protests in East Bengal (later East Pakistan), where Bengali was spoken by most of the population. The Bengali Language Movement reached its peak on 21 February 1952, when police and soldiers opened fired near the Dhaka Medical College on students protesting for Bengali to receive equal status with Urdu. Several protesters were killed, and the movement gained further support throughout East Pakistan. Later, the Government agreed to provide equal status to Bengali as a state language of Pakistan, a right later codified in the 1956 constitution.

In 1953 at the instigation of religious parties, anti-Ahmadiyya riots erupted, killing scores of Ahmadi Muslims and destroying their properties. The riots were investigated by a two-member court of inquiry in 1954, which was criticised by the Jamaat-e-Islami, one of the parties accused of inciting the riots. This event led to the first instance of martial law in the country and began the inroad of military intervention in the politics and civilian affairs of the country, something that remains to this day.

FIRST MILITARY ERA (1958-1971)

The Dominion was dissolved on 23 March, 1956 and replaced by the Islamic Republic of Pakistan with the last Governor-General, Iskandar Mirza, as the first president. Just two years later the military took control of the nation. Field Marshal Ayub Khan became president and began a new system of government called *Basic Democracy* with a new constitution, by which an electoral college of 80,000 would select the President. Ayub Khan almost lost the controversial 1965 presidential elections to Fatima Jinnah. During Ayub's rule, relations with the United States and the West grew stronger. Pakistan joined two formal military alliances — the Baghdad Pact (later known as CENTO) which included Iran, Iraq, and Turkey to defend the Middle East and Persian Gulf against the Soviet Union; and SEATO which covered South-East Asia. However, the United States adopted a policy of denying military aid to both India and Pakistan during the Indo-Pakistani War of 1965 over Kashmir and the Rann of Kutch.

Between 1947 and 1971, Pakistan consisted of two geographically separate regions, West Pakistan and East Pakistan. During the 1960s, there was a rise in Bengali nationalism in East Pakistan, and of allegations that economic development and hiring for government jobs favoured West Pakistan. An independence movement in East Pakistan began to gather ground. After a nationwide uprising in 1969, General Ayub Khan stepped down from office, handing power to General Yahya Khan, who promised to hold general elections at the end of 1970. On the eve of the elections, a cyclone struck East Pakistan killing approximately 500,000 people. Despite the tragedy and the additional difficulty experienced by affected citizens in reaching the voting sites, the elections were held and the results showed a clear division between East and West Pakistan. The Awami League, led by Sheikh Mujibur Rahman, won a majority with 167 of the 169 East Pakistani seats, but with no seats in West Pakistan, where the Pakistan Peoples Party led by Zulfikar Ali Bhutto, won 85 seats. However, Yahya Khan and Bhutto refused to hand over power to Mujib.

Meanwhile, Mujib initiated a civil disobedience movement, which was strongly supported by the general population of East Pakistan, including most government workers. A round-table conference between Yahya, Bhutto, and Mujib was convened in Dhaka, which, however, ended without a solution. Soon thereafter, the West Pakistani Army commenced Operation Searchlight, an organized crackdown on the East Pakistani army, police, politicians, civilians, and students in Dhaka. Mujib and many other Awami League leaders were arrested, while others fled to neighbouring India. On 27th March 27 1971, Major Ziaur Rahman, a Bengali war-veteran of the East Bengal Regiment of the Pakistan Army, declared the independence of East Pakistan as the new nation of Bangladesh on behalf of Mujib. The crackdown widened and escalated into a guerrilla warfare between the Pakistani Army and the Mukti Bahini (Bengali "freedom fighters"). Although the killing of Bengalis was unsupported by the people of West Pakistan, it continued for 9 months. India supplied the Bengali rebels with arms and training, and, in addition, hosted more than 10 million Bengali refugees who had fled the turmoil.

In March, 1971, India's Prime Minister, Indira Gandhi expressed sympathy for the East Pakistani independence movement, opening India's borders to refugees and providing other assistance. Following a period of covert and overt intervention by Indian forces, open hostilities broke out between the two countries on December 3, 1971. In East Pakistan, the Pakistani Army led by General A. A. K. Niazi, had already been weakened and exhausted by the Mukti Bahini's guerrilla warfare. Outflanked and overwhelmed, the Pakistani army in the eastern theatre surrendered on December 16, 1971, with nearly 90,000 soldiers taken as prisoners of war. The figures of the Bengali civilian death toll from the war vary greatly, depending on the sources. Although Pakistan's official report, by its Hamood-ur-Rahman Commission, places the figure at only 26,000, other sources put the number between 1.25 to 1.5 million. Highest figure, reported in the media, is 3 million.

The result was the emergence of the new nation of Bangladesh. Discredited by the defeat, General Yahya Khan resigned. Bhutto was inaugurated as president and chief martial law administrator on 20 December, 1971.

SECOND DEMOCRATIC ERA (1971-1977)

Civilian rule returned after the war, when General Yahya Khan handed over power to Zulfikar Ali Bhutto. In 1972, Pakistani intelligence learned that India was close to developing a nuclear bomb, and in response, Bhutto formed a group of engineers and scientists, headed by nuclear scientist Abdus Salam — who later won the Nobel Prize for physics — to develop nuclear devices. In 1973, Parliament approved a new constitution. Pakistan was alarmed by the Indian nuclear test of 1974, and Bhutto promised that Pakistan would also have a nuclear device "even if we have to eat grass and leaves."

During Bhutto's rule, a serious rebellion also took place in Balochistan province and led to harsh suppression of Baloch rebels with purported assistance from the Shah of Iran lending air support in order to avoid a spilling over the conflict into Iranian Balochistan. The conflict ended later after an amnesty and subsequent stabilization by the provincial military ruler Rahimuddin Khan. In 1974, Bhutto succumbed to increasing pressure from religious parties and helped Parliament to declare the Ahmadiyya adherents as non-Muslims. Elections were held in 1977, with the People's Party won but this was challenged by the opposition, which accused Bhutto of rigging the vote. General Muhammad Zia-ul-Haq took power in a bloodless coup and Bhutto was later executed, after being convicted of authorizing the murder of a political opponent, in a controversial 4-3 split decision by the Supreme Court.

SECOND MILITARY ERA (1977-1988)

Pakistan had been a US ally for much of the Cold War, from the 1950s and as a member of CENTO and SEATO. The Soviet invasion of Afghanistan renewed and deepened the US-Pakistan alliance. The Reagan administration in the United States helped supply and finance an anti-Soviet insurgency in Afghanistan, using Pakistan as a conduit.

In retaliation, the Afghan secret police, KHAD, carried out a large number of terrorist operations against Pakistan, which also suffered from an influx of illegal weapons and drugs from Afghanistan. In the 1980s, as the front-line state in the anti-Soviet struggle, Pakistan received substantial aid from the United States as it took in millions of Afghan (mostly Pashtun) refugees fleeing the Soviet occupation.

The influx of so many refugees - the largest refugee population in the world - had a heavy impact on Pakistan and its effects continue to this day. General Zia's martial-law administration gradually reversed the socialist policies of the previous government, and also introduced strict Islamic law in 1978, often cited as the contributing factor in the present climate of sectarianism and religious fundamentalism in Pakistan. Ordinance XX was introduced to limit the freedom of the Ahmadi's to call themselves Muslims in Pakistan. Further, in his time, secessionist uprisings in Balochistan were put down violently but successfully by the provincial governor, General Rahimuddin Khan.

General Zia lifted martial law in 1985, holding non-partisan elections and handpicking Muhammad Khan Junejo to be the new Prime Minister, who readily extended Zia's term as Chief of Army Staff until 1990. Junejo however gradually fell out with Zia as his administrative independence grew; for example, Junejo signed the Geneva Accord, which Zia greatly frowned upon. After a large-scale blast at a munitions dump in Ojhri, Junejo vowed to bring to justice those responsible for the significant damage caused, implicating several senior generals. Zia dismissed the Junejo government on several charges in May 1988 and called for elections in November 1988. However, General Zia died in a plane crash on August 17 1988.

THIRD DEMOCRATIC ERA (1988-1999)

From 1988 to 1999, Pakistan was ruled by civilian governments, alternately headed by Benazir Bhutto and Nawaz Sharif, who were each elected twice and removed from office on charges of corruption. During the late 1990s, Pakistan was one of three countries which recognized the Taliban government and Mullah Mohammed Omar as the legitimate ruler of Afghanistan. Allegations have been made of Pakistan and other countries providing economic and military aid to the group from 1994 as a part of supporting the anti-Soviet alliance. It is alleged that some post-invasion Taliban fighters were recruits drawn from Pakistan's madrassahs. Economic growth declined towards the end of this period, hurt by the Asian financial crisis, and economic sanctions imposed on Pakistan after its first tests of nuclear devices in 1998. The Pakistani testing came shortly after India tested nuclear devices and increased fears of a nuclear arms race in South Asia. The next year, the Kargil Conflict in Kashmir threatened to escalate to a full-scale war.

In the election that returned Nawaz Sharif as Prime Minister in 1997, his party received a heavy majority of the vote, obtaining enough seats in parliament to change the constitution, which Sharif amended to eliminate the formal checks and balances that restrained the Prime Minister's power. Institutional challenges to his authority led by the civilian President Farooq Leghari, military chief Jehangir Karamat and Chief Justice Sajjad Ali Shah were put down and all three were forced to resign - Shah doing so after the Supreme Court was stormed by Sharif partisans.

THIRD MILITARY ERA (1999 - 2007)

On 12 October, 1999, Sharif attempted to dismiss army chief Pervez Musharraf and install ISI director Ziauddin Butt in his place, but senior generals refused to accept the decision. Musharraf, who was out of the country, boarded a commercial airliner to return to Pakistan. Sharif ordered the Jinnah International Airport to prevent the landing of the airliner, which then circled the skies over Karachi. In a coup, the generals ousted Sharif's administration and took over the airport. The plane landed with only a few minutes of fuel to spare, and General Musharraf assumed control of the government. He arrested Sharif and those members of his cabinet who took part in this conspiracy. American President Bill Clinton had felt that his pressure to force Sharif to withdraw Pakistani forces from Kargil, in Indian-controlled Kashmir, was one of the main reasons for disagreements between Sharif and the Pakistani army. Clinton and King Fahd then pressured Musharraf to spare Sharif and, instead, exile him to Saudi Arabia, guaranteeing that he would not be involved in politics for ten years. Sharif lived in Saudi Arabia for more than six years before moving to London in 2005.

On May 12, 2000 the Supreme Court of Pakistan ordered the Government to hold general elections by October 12, 2002. In an attempt to legitimize his presidency and assure its continuance after the impending elections, Musharraf held a controversial national referendum on April 30, 2002, which extended his presidential term to a period ending five years after the October elections. Musharraf strengthened his position by issuing a Legal Framework Order in August 2001 which established the constitutional basis for his continuance in office. The general elections were held in October 2002 and the centrist, pro-Musharraf PML-Q won a majority of the seats in Parliament. However, parties opposed to the Legal Framework Order effectively paralysed the National Assembly for over a year. The deadlock ended in December 2003, when Musharraf and some of his parliamentary opponents agreed upon a compromise, and pro-Musharraf legislators were able to muster the two-thirds majority required to pass the Seventeenth Amendment, which retroactively legitimized Musharraf's 1999 coup and many of his subsequent decrees. In a vote of confidence on 1st January 2004, Musharraf won 658 out of 1,170 votes in the Electoral College of Pakistan, and according to Article 41(8) of the Constitution of Pakistan, was elected to the office of President.

While economic reforms undertaken during his regime have yielded some results, social reform programmes and his liberal views, e.g. on reforming extremist versions of the practices prevalent in Islam, appear to have met with resistance. Musharraf's power is threatened by extremists who have grown in strength since the September 11, 2001 attacks and who are particularly angered by Musharraf's close political and military alliance with the United States, including his support of the 2001 invasion of Afghanistan.

Musharraf has survived several assassination attempts by terrorist groups believed to be part of Al-Qaeda, including at least two instances where the terrorists had inside information from a member of his military security. Pakistan continues to be involved in a dispute over Kashmir, with allegations of support of terrorist groups being levelled against Pakistan by India, while Pakistan charges that the Indian government abuses human rights in its use of military force in the disputed region. What makes this dispute a source of special concern for the world community is, that both India and Pakistan possess nuclear weapons. It had led to a nuclear standoff in 2002, when Kashmiri-militants (supposedly backed by the ISI) attacked the Indian parliament. In reaction to this, serious diplomatic tensions developed and India and Pakistan deployed 500,000 and 120,000 troops to the border respectively. While the Indo-Pakistani peace process has since made progress, it is sometimes stalled by infrequent insurgent activity in India (including the 11 July 2006 Mumbai train bombings). Pakistan also has been accused of contributing to nuclear proliferation; indeed, its leading nuclear scientist, Abdul Qadeer Khan, admitted to selling nuclear secrets, though he denied government knowledge of his activities.

After the U.S.A. led invasion of Afghanistan, the Pakistani government, as an ally, sent thousands of troops into the mountainous region of Waziristan in 2002, in search of bin-Laden (whom U.S.A. blames for master-minding the so called 9/11-events) and other heavily armed al-Qaeda members, who had allegedly taken refuge there. In March 2004, heavy fighting broke out at Azam Warsak (near the South Waziristan town of Wana), between Pakistani troops and these militants (estimated to be 400 in number), who were entrenched in several fortified settlements. It was speculated that bin Laden's deputy Ayman al-Zawahiri was among those trapped by the Pakistani Army. On September 5, 2006 a truce was signed with the militants and their local rebel supporters, (who called themselves the Islamic Emirate of Waziristan), in which the rebels were to cease supporting the militants in cross-border attacks on Afghanistan in return for a ceasefire and general amnesty and a hand-over of border-patrolling and check-point responsibilities, till then handled by the Pakistan Army.

Former prime minister Nawaz Sharif attempted to return from exile on September 10, 2007 but was arrested on corruption charges after landing at Islamabad International Airport. Sharif was then put on a plane bound for Jeddah, Saudi Arabia, whilst outside the airport there were violent confrontations between Sharif's supporters and the police. This did not deter another former prime minister, Benazir Bhutto, from returning on October 18, 2007 after an eight year exile in Dubai and London, to prepare for the parliamentary elections to be held in 2008. However, on the same day, two suicide bombers attempted to kill Bhutto as she travelled towards a rally in Karachi. Bhutto escaped unharmed but there were 136 casualties and at least 450 people were injured.

On November 3, 2007, General Musharraf proclaimed a state of emergency and sacked the Chief Justice of Pakistan, Justice Iftikhar Muhammad Choudhry along with other 14 judges of the Supreme Court. Lawyers launched a protest against this action but they were arrested. All private media channels were banned including foreign channels. Musharraf declared that the state of emergency would end on December 16, 2007. On November 28, 2007, General Musharraf retired from the Army and the following day was sworn in for a second presidential term.

On November 25, 2007, Nawaz Sharif made a second attempt to return from exile, this time accompanied by his brother, the former Punjab chief minister, Shahbaz Sharif. Hundreds of their supporters, including a few leaders of the party were detained before the pair arrived at Lahore International Airport. The following day, Nawaz Sharif filed his nomination papers for two seats in the forthcoming elections whilst Benazir Bhutto filed for three seats including one of the reserved seats for women.

On December 27, 2007, Benazir Butto was leaving an election rally in Rawalpindi when she was assassinated by a gunman who shot her in the neck and set off a bomb, killing 20 other people and injuring several more. The exact sequence of the events and cause of death became points of political debate and controversy, because, although early reports indicated that Bhutto was hit by shrapnel or the gunshots, the Pakistani Interior Ministry stated that she died from a skull fracture sustained when the explosion threw Bhutto against the sunroof of her vehicle. Bhutto's aides rejected this claim and insisted that she suffered two gunshots prior to the bomb detonation. The Interior Ministry subsequently backtracked from its previous claim. However, a subsequent investigation, aided by the Scotland Yard of U.K., supported the "hitting the sun-roof"" as the cause of her death. The Election Commission, after a meeting in Islamabad, announced that, due to the assassination of Benazir Bhutto, the elections, which had been scheduled for 8 January 2008, would take place on 18 February.

A General Election was held in Pakistan, according to the revised schedule, on February 18, 2008,). Pakistan's two big and main opposition parties, the Pakistan Peoples Party (PPP) and the Pakistan Muslim League (N) (PML (N)), won majority of seats in the election and formed a government. Although, the Pakistan Muslim League (Q) (PML (Q)) actually was second in the popular vote, the PPP and PML (N) have formed the new coalition-government. On August 7 The deadlock between ruling parties ended when the coalition government of Pakistan decided to move for the impeachment of the President and then head for the restoration of the deposed judiciary. Moreover they have decided that the President of Pakistan now faces charges of weakening the federation, creating economic impasse and violating the constitution.

After that President Pervaiz Musharraf has begun consultation with his allies and with his legal team on the implication of the impeachment and says he is ready to reply to the charges levied upon him by the coalition parties. Also He had been required to seek the vote of confidence from the senate and parliament

On August 18, 2008, President Pervez Musharraf announced in a televised address to the nation that he had decided to resign after nine years in power.

GOVERNMENT AND POLITICS OF PAKISTAN

The government of Pakistan was based on the Government of India Act (1935) for the first nine years after independence. The first Constitution of Pakistan was adopted in 1956, but was suspended in 1958 by General Ayub Khan. The Constitution of 1973 - suspended in 1977, by Zia-ul-Haq, but re-instated in 1991 - is the country's most important document, laying the foundations of government. Pakistan is a semi-presidential federal democratic republic with Islam as the state religion. The bicameral legislature comprises a 100-member Senate and a 342-member National Assembly. The President is the Head of State and the Commander in Chief of the Armed Forces and is elected by an electoral college. The prime minister is usually the leader of the largest party in the National Assembly. Each province has a similar system of government with a directly elected Provincial Assembly in which the leader of the largest party or alliance becomes Chief Minister. Provincial Governors are appointed by the President.

The Pakistani military has played an influential role in mainstream politics throughout Pakistan's history, with military presidents ruling from 1958–71, 1977–88 and from 1999 onwards. The leftist Pakistan Peoples Party, led by Zulfikar Ali Bhutto, emerged as a major political player during the 1970s. Under the military rule of Muhammad Zia-ul-Haq, Pakistan began a marked shift from the British-era secular politics and policies, to the adoption of Shariat and other laws based on Islam. During the 1980s, the anti-feudal, pro-Muhajir Muttahida Qaumi Movement (MQM) was started by unorthodox and educated urban dwellers of Sindh and particularly Karachi. The 1990s were characterized by coalition politics dominated by the Pakistan Peoples Party and a rejuvenated Muslim League.

In the October 2002 general elections, the Pakistan Muslim League (Q) (PML-Q) won a plurality of National Assembly seats with the second-largest group being the Pakistan Peoples Party Parliamentarians (PPPP), a sub-party of the PPP. Zafarullah Khan Jamali of PML-Q emerged as Prime Minister but resigned on 26 June 2004 and was replaced by PML-Q leader Chaudhry Shujaat Hussain as interim Prime Minister. On 28 August 2004 the National Assembly voted 191 to 151 to elect the Finance Minister and former Citibank Vice President Shaukat Aziz as Prime Minister. The Muttahida Majlis-e-Amal, a coalition of Islamic religious parties, won elections in North-West Frontier Province, and increased their representation in the National Assembly - until their defeat in the 2008 elections.

Pakistan is an active member of the United Nations (UN) and the Organisation of the Islamic Conference (OIC), the latter of which Pakistan has used as a forum for *Enlightened Moderation*, a plan to promote a renaissance and enlightenment in the Muslim world. Pakistan is also a member of the major regional organisations of the South Asian Association for Regional Cooperation (SAARC) and the Economic Cooperation Organisation (ECO). In the past, Pakistan has had mixed relations with the United States; in the early 1950s, Pakistan was the United States' "most allied ally in Asia" and a member of both the Central Treaty Organisation (CENTO) and the Southeast Asia Treaty Organisation (SEATO). Also, during the Soviet-Afghan War in the 1980s Pakistan was a crucial US ally. But relations soured in the 1990s, when sanctions were applied by the US over suspicions of Pakistan's nuclear activities. However, the September 11, 2001 attacks and the subsequent War on Terrorism have seen an improvement in US–Pakistan ties, especially after Pakistan ended its support of the Taliban regime in Kabul. This was evidenced by a drastic increase in American military aid, which saw Pakistan take in $4 billion more in three years after the 9/11 attacks than in the three years before.

On 18 February 2008, Pakistan held its general elections after being postponed from 8 January 2008. The Pakistan Peoples Party won the majority of the votes and formed an alliance with the Pakistan Muslim League (N). They nominated and elected Yousaf Raza Gilani as Prime Minister of Pakistan

On 18 August 2008, President Musharraf resigned as President of Pakistan, claiming it was a "difficult decision", but the impeachment scandal threatened to remove him anyway.

GEOGRAPHY OF PAKISTAN

Pakistan covers 340,403 square miles (881,640 km), approximately the combined land areas of France and the United Kingdom, with its eastern regions located on the Indian tectonic plate and the western and northern regions on the Iranian plateau and Eurasian landplate. Apart from the 1,046 kilometre (650 mi) Arabian Sea coastline, Pakistan's land borders total 6,774 kilometres—2,430 kilometres (1,509 mi) with Afghanistan to the northwest, 523 kilometres (325 mi) with China to the northeast, 2,912 kilometres (1,809 mi) with India to the east and 909 kilometres (565 mi) with Iran to the southwest.

The different types of natural features range from the sandy beaches, lagoons, and mangrove swamps of the southern coast to preserved beautiful moist temperate forests and the icy peaks of the Himalaya, Karakoram and Hindu Kush mountains in the north. There are an estimated 108 peaks above 7,000 metres (23,000 ft) high that are covered in snow and glaciers. Five of the mountains in Pakistan (including Nanga Parbat) are over 8,000 metres (26,000 ft). Indian-controlled Kashmir to the Northern Areas of Pakistan and running the length of the country is the Indus River with its many tributaries. The northern parts of Pakistan attract a large number of foreign tourists. To the west of the Indus are the dry, hilly deserts of Balochistan; to the east are the rolling sand dunes of the Thar Desert. The Tharparkar desert in the southern province of Sindh, is the only fertile desert in the world. Most areas of Punjab and parts of Sindh are fertile plains where agriculture is of great importance.

The climate varies as much as the scenery, with cold winters and hot summers in the north and a mild climate in the south, moderated by the influence of the ocean. The central parts have extremely hot summers with temperatures rising to 45 °C (113 °F), followed by very cold winters, often falling below freezing. Officially the highest temperature recorded in Pakistan is 50.55 °C (122.99 °F) at Pad Idan. There is very little rainfall ranging from less than 250 millimetres to more than 1,250 millimetres (9.8–49.2 in), mostly brought by the unreliable south-westerly monsoon winds during the late summer. The construction of dams on the rivers and the drilling of water wells in many drier areas have temporarily eased water shortages at the expense of down-gradient populations.

ECONOMY OF PAKISTAN

Pakistan is a nation with a diverse economy that include textiles, chemicals, food processing, agriculture and other industries. It is the 40th largest economy in the world.

The economy has suffered in the past from decades of internal political disputes, a fast growing population, mixed levels of foreign investment, and a costly, ongoing confrontation with neighboring India. However, IMF-approved government policies, bolstered by foreign investment and renewed access to global markets, have generated solid macroeconomic recovery the last decade. Substantial macroeconomic reforms since 2000, most notably at privatizing the banking sector have helped the economy. Pakistan has seen a growing middle class population since then and poverty levels have decreased by 10% since 2001. GDP growth, spurred by gains in the industrial and service sectors, remained in the 6-8% range in 2004-06. In 2005, the World Bank named Pakistan the top reformer in its region and in the top 10 reformers globally.

Islamabad has steadily raised development spending in recent years, including a 52% real increase in the budget allocation for development in FY07, a necessary step toward reversing the broad underdevelopment of its social sector. The fiscal deficit - the result of chronically low tax collection and increased spending, including reconstruction costs from the devastating Kashmir earthquake in 2005 was manageable. Development in urban areas of Pakistan has remained high but is low in rural areas.

Inflation remains the biggest threat to the economy, jumping to more than 9% in 2005 before easing to 7.9% in 2006. In 2008, following the surge in global petrol prices inflation in Pakistan has reached as high as 12.0%. The central bank is pursuing tighter monetary policy while trying to preserve growth. Foreign exchange reserves are bolstered by steady worker remittances, but a growing current account deficit - driven by a widening trade gap as import growth outstrips export expansion - could draw down reserves and dampen GDP growth in the medium term.

ECONOMIC HISTORY

First five decades

This is a chart of trend of gross domestic product of Pakistan at market prices estimated by the International Monetary Fund with figures in millions of Pakistani Rupees.

Pakistan was a very poor and predominantly agricultural country when it gained independence in 1947. Pakistan's average economic growth rate since independence has been higher than the average growth rate of the world economy during the period. Average annual real GDP growth rates were 6.8% in the 1960s, 4.8% in the 1970s, and 6.5% in the 1980s. Average annual growth fell to 4.6% in the 1990s with significantly lower growth in the second half of that decade.

Industrial-sector growth, including manufacturing, was also above average. In the late 1960s Pakistan was seen as a model of economic development around the world, and there was much praise for its economic progression. Later, economic mismanagement in general, and fiscally imprudent economic policies in particular, caused a large increase in the country's public debt and led to slower growth in the 1990s. Two wars with India in 1965 and 1971 adversely affected economic growth. In particular, the latter war brought the economy close to recession, although economic rebounded sharply until the nationalizations of the mid-1970s.

Economic resilience

Historically, Pakistan's overall economic output (GDP) has grown every year since a 1951 recession. Despite this record of sustained growth, Pakistan's economy had, until a few years ago, been characterized as unstable and highly vulnerable to external and internal shocks. However, the economy proved to be unexpectedly resilient in the face of multiple adverse events concentrated into a four-year period —

- the Asian financial crisis;
- economic sanctions — according to Colin Powell, Pakistan was "sanctioned to the eyeballs";
- global recession;
- severe rioting in the port city of Karachi;
- a severe drought — the worst in Pakistan's history, lasting for many years (about four);
- heightened perceptions of risk as a result of military tensions with India — with as many as 1 million troops on the border, and predictions of impending (potentially nuclear) war;
- the post-9/11 military action in neighboring Afghanistan, with a massive influx of refugees from that country;
- the 2005 Pakistan earthquake

Despite these adverse events, Pakistan's economy kept growing, and economic growth accelerated towards the end of this period. This resilience has led to a change in perceptions of the economy, with leading international institutions such as the IMF, World Bank, and the ADB praising Pakistan's performance in the face of adversity.

Recent economic history

Pakistan's economic outlook has brightened in recent years in conjunction with rapid economic growth and a dramatic improvement in its foreign exchange position as a result of its current account surplus and a consequent rapid growth in hard currency reserves.

The state-owned firm in early 2002 signed agreements with five international telecom companies for terminating additional international incoming traffic to capture the grey market by using voice over Internet protocol (VoIP) technology from the US and Europe into Pakistan.

The conditionality of the IMF program, which was suspended in July 1999 and resumed later during the administration of Pervez Musharraf. Having improved its finances, Pakistan's government announced in 2004 that it would no longer require IMF assistance, and the assistance program ended in that year.

Average urban wages in 2007 hover around $4-5 per day.

With accelerating economic growth, economists are now emphasizing a different range of problems. According to Ahmed Rashid, the World Bank Country Director for Pakistan,

> *Now Pakistan faces higher quality problems—the problems of success. Demand has risen faster than supply. This has shown up in high inflation and a zooming trade deficit. The "tight fiscal, easy money" formula to get growth going needs to be "tight fiscal, tight money and credit" to sustain rapid growth. Idle domestic production capacity allowed the rising demand to be accommodated by rising capacity utilization in cement, steel, fertilizer, textiles, automobiles and motorcycles. Now that capacity is more than fully utilized, resulting in backlogs and imports.*

Musharraf's economic agenda continues to include measures to widen the tax net, privatize public sector assets, and improve its balance of trade. Pakistan has made governance reforms, privatization, and deregulation the cornerstones of its economic revival.

Although it received a positive endorsement from international financial institutions such as the World Bank, the International Monetary Fund and the Asian Development Bank, as well as improved credit ratings from Standard & Poor's and Moody's.

Pakistan's current account surplus had put upward pressure on the Pakistani rupee, which rose from 64 rupees per dollar to 57 rupees per dollar. The State Bank of Pakistan (the central bank) stabilized the rise by lowering interest rates and buying dollars. After short-term Pakistani T-bond rates fell below 2%, with government borrowing having declined, banks greatly expanded their lending to businesses and consumers. Construction activity, sales of durable goods such as trucks and automobiles, and housing purchases have all jumped to record levels. Private sector credit expanded by 28.5% in 2003, and continues to expand despite monetary restraints — the SBP imposed interest-rate increases to moderate money supply and prevent "overheating".

Pakistan's nominal gross domestic product (GDP) in 1997 was US$ 75.3 billion. Five years later in 2002, the country's nominal GDP came down to US$ 71.5 billion. During this five-year period, the real GDP grew by a meagre 3.0 per cent on an average. Pakistan government's debt was 82 per cent of its GDP in 2002. Over one-third of the government's revenue was being used up in making interest payments on the national debt. The near stagnant economy suddenly started showing miraculous growth in 2002 after lifting of economic sanctions imposed after Pakistan's 1998 nuclear tests. The economy grew at 5.1 per cent in 2003, 6.4 per cent in 2004 and 7.0 per cent in 2005. The US$ 72 billions economy of 2002 has swelled into a US$ 108 billion economy in 2005. During 1997-2002 Pakistan's average export growth has been 1.2 per cent per year and increased to 13 per cent per year during 2003-05. Pakistan's debt as a percentage of the GDP came down to 59 per cent in 2005 from 82 per cent in 2002. Pakistan government's interest payment as a percentage of revenue collection came down to 23 per cent in 2005 as compared to 35 per cent in 2002. The foreign economic aid since 9/11, especially from the USA, has contributed most to the country's economic progress.

According to the Asian Development Bank, the first half of FY2006 was marked by a slowdown in both industry and agriculture in Pakistan. Output of cotton declined by an estimated 10.9 per cent from an all-time high of 14.6 million bales harvested in FY2005. Production of sugarcane, another major summer crop, is also estimated lower than last year. The growth of large-scale manufacturing slowed to 8.7 per cent in the first quarter of FY2006 from 24.9 per cent in the same period of last year, primarily due to capacity constraints and the high-base effect. Among individual industries in the first quarter, growth of textiles tumbled to 7.2 per cent from 29.6 per cent year on year. Automobile assembly and electronics, which have shown the fastest expansion among sub-sectors in the last 2-3 years, also decelerated. Inflation accelerated in FY2005 after five years of price stability. Annual inflation, based on the consumer price index, more than doubled to 9.3 per cent from 4.6 per cent, mainly because of higher food prices and rising house rents. Due to a sharp increase in domestic oil prices, transport costs also jumped. Core — nonfood, non-oil — inflation also doubled, from 3.7 per cent to 7.4 per cent.

Pakistan is a middle income country. Its economy is among the fastest-growing in the world as its economy has reached the size of $140 billion from a mere $70 billion a few years earlier, Federal Advisor on Finance Dr Salman Shah informed the media. Per capita income now stands at $808.

The Economic Survey of Pakistan for 2006-2007 has concluded the country's economy recorded 7.3 percent growth, . Former Prime Minister Shaukat Aziz said that Pakistan's economy should continue to grow every year at about seven percent and he also assured that many measures will be taken to give the economy a further boost. He promised privitization of companies and he also invested in the economy by allowing free education for under 16's and also came up with a scheme to pay girls two hundred rupees a month as an incentive to attend school. Also in the next five years many foreign universities from different European nations have announced they will be opening campuses in Pakistan.

Macroeconomic reform and prospects

According to many sources, the Pakistani government has made substantial economic reforms since 2000, and medium-term prospects for job creation and poverty reduction are the best in nearly a decade.

Government revenues have greatly improved in recent years, as a result of economic growth, tax reforms - with a broadening of the tax base, and more efficient tax collection as a result of self-assessment schemes and corruption controls in the Central Board of Revenue - and the privatization of public utilities and telecommunications. Pakistan is aggressively cutting tariffs and assisting exports by improving ports, roads, electricity supplies and irrigation projects. Islamabad has doubled development spending from about 2% of GDP in the 1990s to 4% in 2003, a necessary step towards reversing the broad underdevelopment of its social sector.

Liberalization in the international textile trade has already yielded benefits for Pakistan's exports, and the country also expects to profit from freer trade in agriculture. As a large country, Pakistan hopes to take advantage of significant economies of scale, and to replace China as the largest textile manufacturer as the latter China moves up the value-added chain. These industries play to Pakistan's relative strengths in low labor costs.

Growing stability in the nation's monetary policies has contributed to a reduction in money-market interest rates, and a great expansion in the quantity of credit, changing consumption and investment patterns in the nation. Pakistan's domestic natural gas production, and its significant use of CNG in automobiles, has cushioned the effect of the oil-price shock of 2004-2005. Pakistan is also moving away from the doctrine of import substitution which some developing countries (such as Iran) dogmatically pursued in the twentieth century. The Pakistani government is now pursuing an export-driven model of economic growth successfully implemented by South East Asia and now highly successful in China.

In 2005, the World Bank reported that

"Pakistan was the top reformer in the region and the number 10 reformer globally — making it easier to start a business, reducing the cost to register property, increasing penalties for violating corporate governance rules, and replacing a requirement to license every shipment with two-year duration licenses for traders."

In addition, reduced tensions with India and the ongoing peace process raise new hopes for a prosperous and stable South Asia, with more intra-regional trade. However, due to global economic crisis in year 2007-2008 the economic progress has been adveresely affected and unemployment has increased.

Shahid Javed Burki, former vice president of World Bank and who was in charge of the bank's Latin American division when Mexico was hit by the crisis in 1994, said Pakistan is facing symptoms that preceded the Mexican financial crisis more than 10 years ago. He points to the nation's current account deficit, 'excessive' speculative business activity and weak banking system. In a direct comparison with Indian economy, Pakistan's economy is 1/10th in size however, Pakistan by virtue of its area and population is approximately 1/5th to India's area and population. A lot more needs to be done to raise the standard of the rural and tribal people.

THE ECONOMY TODAY

Stock market

In the first four years of the twenty-first century, Pakistan's KSE 100 Index was the best-performing stock market index in the world as declared by the international magazine "Business Week".

The stock market capitalisation of listed companies in Pakistan was valued at $45,937 million in 2005 by the World Bank. As a result, the corporate sector of Pakistan has grown dramatically in significance in recent times.

Manufacturing and finance

Pakistan's manufacturing sector has experienced double-digit growth in recent years, with large-scale manufacturing growing by 18% in 2003. A reduction in the fiscal deficit has resulted in less government borrowing in the domestic money market, lower interest rates, and an expansion in private sector lending to businesses and consumers. Foreign exchange reserves continued to reach new levels in 2003, supported by robust export growth and steady worker remittances.

Growing middle class

Measured by purchasing power, Pakistan has a 30 million strong middle class, according to Dr. Ishrat Husain, Ex-Governor (2 December 1999 - 1 December 2005) of the State Bank of Pakistan. It is a figure that correlates with research by Standard Chartered Bank which estimates that Pakistan possesses a "a middle class of 30 million people that Standard Chartered estimates now earn an average of about $10,000 a year." In addition, Pakistan has a growing upper class with relatively high per capita incomes.

On measures of income inequality, the country ranks slightly better than the median. In late 2006, the Central Board of Revenue estimated that there were almost 2.8 million income-tax payers in the country.

Poverty alleviation expenditures

Pakistan government spent over 1 trillion Rupees (about $16.7 billion) on poverty alleviation programs during the past four years, cutting poverty from 35 percent in 2000-01 to 24 percent in 2006. Rural poverty remains a pressing issue, as development there has been far slower then in the major urban areas.

Demographics

With a per capita GDP of over $3000 (PPP, 2006) compared with $2600 (PPP, 2005) in 2005 the World Bank considers Pakistan a medium-income country, it is also recorded as a "Medium Development Country" on the Human Development Index 2007. Pakistan has a large informal economy, which the government is trying to document and assess. Approximately 49% of adults are literate, and life expectancy is about 64 years. The population, about 168 million in 2007, is growing at about 1.80%.

Relatively few resources in the past had been devoted to socio-economic development or infrastructure projects. Inadequate provision of social services, high birth rates and immigration from nearby countries in the past have contributed to a persistence of poverty. An influential recent study concluded that the fertility rate peaked in the 1980s, and has since fallen sharply. Pakistan has a family-income Gini index of 41, close to the world average of 39.

Employment

The high population growth in the past few decades has ensured that a very large number of young people are now entering the labor market. Even though it is among the seven most populous Asian nations, Pakistan has a lower population density than Bangladesh, Japan, India, and the Philippines. In the past, excessive red tape made firing from jobs, and consequently hiring, difficult. Significant progress in taxation and business reforms has ensured that many firms now are not compelled to operate in the underground economy.

In late 2006, the government launched an ambitious nationwide service employment scheme aimed at disbursing almost $2 billion over five years.

Tourism

Tourism in Pakistan in Pakistan is a growing industry. Major attractions include ruins of Indus valley civilisation and mountain resorts in the Himalayas. Himalayan and Karakoram range (which includes K2, the second highest mountain peak in the world, attracts adventurers and mountaineers from around the world.

Revenue

The Board of Revenue has collected nearly one trillion Rupees($14.1 billion) in taxes in the 2007-2008 financial year.

CURRENCY SYSTEM

Rupee

The basic unit of currency is the Rupee, which is divided into 100 paisas. Since the turn of the century, a strengthening economy and large current-account surplus has caused the rupee's exchange rate to rise in value. In response, Pakistan's central bank has prevented the rupee from rising too much, by lowering interest rates and buying dollars, in order to preserve the country's export competitiveness. As of 2005, one US dollar is approximately equal to 60 rupees. Currently the newly printed 5,000 rupee note is the largest denomination in circulation. Recently the SBP has introduced all new design notes of Rs. 5, 10, 20, 100, 500, 1000, 5000 denomination, while the work of Rs.10,000 note is in progress which will help the banking industry in keeping few notes in saving accounts. The new notes have been designed using the euro technology and are made in good bright colors.

INDUSTRY

Pakistan ranks forty-first in the world and fifty-fifth worldwide in factory output. Pakistan's industrial sector accounts for about 24% of GDP. Cotton textile production and apparel manufacturing are Pakistan's largest industries, accounting for about 66% of the merchandise exports and almost 40% of the employed labour force. Other major industries include cement, fertilizer, edible oil, sugar, steel, tobacco, chemicals, machinery, and food processing.

The government is privatizing large-scale parastatal units, and the public sector accounts for a shrinking proportion of industrial output, while growth in overall industrial output (including the private sector) has accelerated. Government policies aim to diversify the country's industrial base and bolster export industries.

Mining and quarrying

The country has immense reserves of various minerals and natural resources. Important minerals found in Pakistan are gypsum, limestone, chromites, iron ore, rock salt, silver, gold, precious stones, gems, marble, copper, coal, graphite, sulphur, fire clay, silica. The salt range in Punjab Province has the largest deposit of pure salt found anywhere in the world. Balochistan province is a mineral rich area having substantial mineral, oil and gas reserves which have not been exploited to their full capacity or fully explored, recent government policies have begun to develop this region of the country and to tap into the immense resources found there. The province has significant quantities of copper, chromite and iron, and pockets of antimony and zinc in the south and gold in the far west. Natural gas was discovered near Sui in 1952, and the province has been gradually developing its oil and gas projects over the past fifty years.

Major reserves of copper and gold in Balochistan's Rekodiq area have been discovered in early 2006. The Rekodiq mining area has proven estimated reserves of 2 billion tons of copper and 20 million ounces of gold. According to the current market price, the value of the deposits has been estimated at about $65 billion, which would generate thousands of jobs.

The discovery has ranked Rekodiq among the world's top seven copper reserves. The Rekodiq project is estimated to produce 200,000 tons of copper and 400,000 ounces of gold per year, at an estimated value of $1.25 billion at current market prices. The copper and gold are currently traded at about $5,000 per ton and $600 per ounce respectively in the international market.

North West Frontier Province accounts for at least 78% of the marble production in Pakistan. Pakistan is home to some of the most finest and purest grades of marble, granite and slate found in the world. Much of the grade A Marble that is exported out of European countries like Italy actually have their origins in Pakistan which previously lacked fine polishing and processing machinery. The Government has taken steps to invest in this crucial sector with the recent establishment of a *Marble City* within Balochistan.

The Federal Bureau of Statistics provisionally valued this sector at Rs.211,851 million in 2005 thus registering over 99% growth since 2000.

Fuel extraction industry

Pakistan's first oil field was discovered in the late 1952 in Baluchistan near a giant gas field at Sui in Balochistan. The Toot oilfield was discovered in the early 1960s the Islamabad in the Punjab. Production has steadily increased since then.

Pakistan's first gas field was the giant gas field at Sui in Balochistan which was discovered in the late 1952.

Pakistan is also a major producer of Bituminous coal, Sub-bituminous coal and Lignite. Coal mining started in the British colonial era and has continued to be used by Pakistani industries after independence in 1947.

Pakistan produced about 45 tonnes of Uranium in 2006.

Manufacturing

In FY 2002-03, real growth in manufacturing was 7.7%. In the twelve months ending 30 June 2004, large-scale manufacturing grew by more than 18% compared to the previous twelve-month period. The textile and garment industry's share in the economy along with its contribution to exports, employment, foreign-exchange earnings, investment and value added make it Pakistan's single largest manufacturing sector. The industry is comprised of 453 textile mills: 50 integrated units; and 403 spinning units, with 9.33 million spindles and 148,000 rotors, The capacity utilization was 83% for spindles and 47% for rotors during 2003.

The Federal Bureau of Statistics provisionally valued large-scale manufacturing at Rs.981,518 million in 2005 thus registering over 138% growth since 2000 while small-scale manufacturing was valued at Rs.356,835 million in 2005 thus registering over 80% growth since 2000.

Construction

After the devastating 2005 Kashmir earthquake Pakistan has instituted stricter building codes. The cost of construction in Pakistan will increase 30 to 50% due to implementation of a new building code which requires strengthening of structures to withstand earthquake of 8 to 8.5 magnitude. The demand for cement has increased due to reconstruction after the earthquake. The price of cement has increased by 50% and Pakistan government banned export of cement to lower the prices and the reconstruction costs.

Dubai Ports World, announced on June 1, 2006 that it will spend $10 billion to develop transport infrastructure and real estate in Pakistan. Dubai Ports World is also discussing the possibility of the company taking over operational management of Gwadar port in Balochistan.

Emaar Properties, announced on May 31, 2006 three real estate developments in the cities of Islamabad and Karachi in Pakistan. The projects, with a total investment of $2.4 billion, will include a series of master planned communities that will set new benchmarks in commercial, residential and retail property within Pakistan.

In addition the conglomerate signed an unprecedented $43 billion deal to develop two island resorts - Bundal Island and Buddo Island - over the next decade.

The Federal Bureau of Statistics provisionally valued this sector at Rs.178,819 million in 2005 thus registering over 88% growth since 2000.

Electricity, gas and water supply

Pakistan has extensive energy resources, including fairly sizable natural gas reserves, some proven oil reserves, coal (Pakistan has the fourth-largest coal reserves in the world), and a large hydropower potential. However, the exploitation of energy resources has been slow due to a shortage of capital and domestic political constraints. Domestic petroleum production totals only about half the country's oil needs, and the need to import oil has contributed to Pakistan's trade deficits and past shortages of foreign exchange.

The current government has announced that privatization in the oil and gas sector is a priority, as is the substitution of indigenous gas for imported oil, especially in the production of power. Pakistan is a world leader in the use of compressed natural gas (CNG) for personal automobiles.

The short-term national energy demand has expanded significantly since 2001 due to massive rise in sales of durable goods like refrigerators, washing machines, split air conditioners, *et al.*

In 2004, Access Group International announced plans to invest $1 billion over the next 5 years in solar cell manufacture and wind farms. MOUs have been signed with Alternate Energy Development Board. In early 2005, the government approved a 25-year Energy Security Plan to boost electric capacity eightfold.

The Canadian conglomerate Cathy Oil and Gas signed a memorandum of understanding in late 2006 to invest $5 billion in oil and gas exploration, development, production and commercialisation in Pakistan.

The World Bank estimates that it takes about 32 days only to get an electrical connection in Pakistan.

The Federal Bureau of Statistics provisionally valued this sector at Rs.215,662 million in 2005 thus registering over 62% growth since 2000.

SERVICES SECTOR

Pakistan's service sector accounts for about 53.3% of GDP. Transport, storage, communications, finance, and insurance account for 24% of this sector, and wholesale and retail trade about 30%. Pakistan is trying to promote the information industry and other modern service industries through incentives such as long-term tax holidays.

The government is acutely conscious of the immense job growth opportunities in service sector and has launched aggressive privatisation of telecommunications, utilities and banking despite union unrest.

DEMOGRAPHY OF PAKISTAN

Pakistan had an estimated population of 172,800,000 as of July 2008, making it the world's sixth largest population and placing it higher than Russia and lower than Brazil. Pakistan is expected to have a population of around 208 million by the year 2020 because of the high growth rate. Population projections for Pakistan are relatively difficult because of the apparent differences in the accuracy of each census and the inconsistencies between various surveys related to the fertility rate, but it is likely that the rate of growth peaked in the 1980s and has since declined significantly. The population was estimated at 162,400,000 on July 1, 2005, with a fertility rate of 34 per thousand, a death rate of 10 per thousand, and the rate of natural increase at 2.4%. Pakistan also has a high infant mortality rate of 70 per thousand births.

In November of 2006 China and Pakistan signed a Free Trade Agreement hoping to triple bilateral trade from $4.2 billion (USD) to $15 billion (USD) within the next five years. Pakistan's exports in 2007 amounted to $20.58 billion (USD).

For Pakistan to be a Developed Nation it would take 159 years. This is considering Pakistan's annual growth rate was to be calculated at 4.9%.

The major ethnic groups are - Punjabis (44.68% of the population), Pashtuns (15.42%),Sindhis (14.1%), Seraikis (8.38%), Muhajirs (7.57%), Balochis (3.57%) and others

(6.08%). As of early 2007, about 2 million registered Afghan refugees remain in Pakistan as a result of the on going war and instability in Afghanistan.

Although spoken only by a minority of Pakistanis, Urdu is the national language and *lingua franca* of Pakistan, while English is the official language, used in the Constitution and widely used by businesses, educated urban classes and most universities. Punjabi is the largest indigenous language and is spoken by over 60 million people, but has no official recognition in the country. Other significant languages spoken in Pakistan include (in order of number of speakers): Pashto, Sindhi, Saraiki, and Balochi; English is mostly spoken by educated peoples.

The demographics of religion in Pakistan were significantly altered in 1947 by the migration of Muslims from India to Pakistan, and that of Hindus and Sikhs of Pakistan to India. Census data indicates that 96% of the population are Muslims, (nearly 77% are Sunni Muslims and 20% are Shi'a Muslims). Minority religions include Hinduism (1.85%), Christianity (1.6%), as well as much smaller numbers of Sikhs (Around 0.04%), Parsis, Ahmadis, Buddhists, Jews, Bahá'ís, and Animists (mainly the Kalasha of Chitral). Pakistan is the second most populous Muslim-majority country and also has the second largest Shi'a population in the world.

SOCIETY AND CULTURE OF PAKISTAN

Pakistan has a rich and unique culture that has preserved established traditions throughout history. Many cultural practices, foods, monuments, and shrines were inherited from the rule of Muslim Mughal and Afghan emperors. The national dress of shalwar qamiz is originally of Central Asian origin derived from Turko-Iranian nomadic invaders and is today worn in all parts of Pakistan. Women wear brightly coloured shalwar qamiz, while men often wear solid-coloured ones. In cities western dress is also popular among the youth and the business sector.

Pakistani society is largely multilingual and 96% Muslim, with high regard for traditional family values, although urban families have grown into a nuclear family system due to the socio-economic constraints imposed by the traditional joint family system. Recent decades have seen the emergence of a middle class in cities like Karachi, Lahore, Rawalpindi, Hyderabad, Faisalabad, and Peshawar that wish to move in a more liberal direction, as opposed to the northwestern regions bordering Afghanistan that remain highly conservative and dominated by centuries-old regional tribal customs. Increasing globalization has increased the influence of "Western culture" with Pakistan ranking 46th on the A.T. Kearney/FP Globalization Index. There are an approximated four million people of Pakistani descent living abroad, with close to a half-million expatriates living in the United States, around a million living in Saudi Arabia and nearly one million in the United Kingdom, all providing burgeoning cultural connections.

The variety of Pakistani music ranges from diverse provincial folk music and traditional styles such as Qawwali and Ghazal Gayaki to modern forms fusing traditional and western music, such as the synchronisation of Qawwali and western music by the world renowned Nusrat Fateh Ali Khan. In addition Pakistan is home to many famous folk singers such as the late Alam Lohar, who is also well known in Indian Punjab. The arrival of Afghan refugees in the western provinces has rekindled Pashto and Persian music and established Peshawar as a hub for Afghan musicians and a distribution centre for Afghan music abroad. State-owned Pakistan Television Corporation (PTV) and Pakistan Broadcasting Corporation were the dominant media outlets, but there are now numerous private television channels. Various American, European, and Asian television channels and films are available to the majority of the Pakistani population via private Television Networks, cable, and satellite television. There are also small indigenous film industries based in Lahore and Peshawar (often referred to as Lollywood). Although Bollywood films have been banned from being played in public cinemas since 1965, Indian film stars are still generally popular in Pakistan due to the fact that Pakistanis are easily able to buy Bollywood films from local shops for private home viewing. But recently Pakistan allowed selected Bollywood films to be shown in Pakistani cinemas.

There are many festivals celebrated annually in Pakistan - which may or may not be observed as national public holidays - e.g. Pakistan Day (23 March), Independence Day (14 August), Defence of Pakistan Day (6 September), Pakistan Air Force Day (7 September), the anniversaries of the birth (25 December, a national holiday) and death (11 September) of Quaid-e-Azam, birth of Allama Iqbal (9 November) and the birth (30 July) and death (8 July) of Madar-e-Millat. Labour Day, (also known as May Day), is also observed in Pakistan on May 1 and is a public holiday. Several important religious festivals are celebrated by Pakistani Muslims during the year; the celeberation days depend on the lunar Islamic calendar. Ramadan, the ninth month of the calendar, is characterised by daytime fasting for 29 or 30 days and is followed by the festival of Eid ul-Fitr.

In a second festival, Eid ul-Adha, an animal is sacrificed in remembrance of the actions of Prophet Abraham (Arabic: Ibrahim) and the meat is shared with friends, family, and the less fortunate. Both Eid festivals are public holidays, serving as opportunities for people to visit family and friends, and for children to receive new clothes, presents, and sweets. Muslims also celebrate Eid-e-Milad-un-Nabi - the birthday of the prophet Muhammad - in the third month of the calendar (Rabi' al-Awwal) and mark the Day of Ashurah on the 9th and 10th days of the first month (Muharram) to commemorate the martyrdom of Husayn bin Ali. Hindus, Buddhists, Sikhs, and Christians in Pakistan also celebrate their own festivals and holidays. Sikhs come from across the world to visit several holy sites in Punjab, including the shrine of Guru Nanak, the founder of Sikhism, at Hasan Abdal in Attock District, and his birthplace, at Nankana Sahib. There are also several regional and local festivals, such as the Punjabi festival of Basant, which marks the start of spring and is celebrated by kite flying.

The architecture of the areas now constituting Pakistan can be designated to four distinct periods — pre-Islamic, Islamic, colonial and post-colonial. With the beginning of the Indus civilization around the middle of the 3rd millennium B.C., an advanced urban culture developed for the first time in the region, with large structural facilities, some of which survive to this day. Mohenjo-daro, Harappa and Kot Diji belong to the pre-Islamic era settlements. The rise of Buddhism and the Persian and Greek influence led to the development of the Greco-Buddhist style, starting from the 1st century CE. The high point of this era was reached with the culmination of the Gandhara style. An example of Buddhist architecture is the ruins of the Buddhist monastery Takht-i-Bahi in the northwest province.

The arrival of Islam in today's Pakistan meant a sudden end of Buddhist architecture. However, a smooth transition to predominantly pictureless Islamic architecture occurred. The most important of the few completely discovered buildings of Persian style is the tomb of the Shah Rukn-i-Alam in Multan. During the Mughal era design elements of Islamic-Persian architecture were fused with and often produced playful forms of the Hindustani art. Lahore, occasional residence of Mughal rulers, exhibits a multiplicity of important buildings from the empire, among them the Badshahi mosque, the fortress of Lahore with the famous Alamgiri Gate, the colourful, still strongly Persian seeming Wazir Khan Mosque as well as numerous other mosques and mausoleums. Also the Shahjahan Mosque of Thatta in Sindh originates from the epoch of the Mughals. In the British colonial period, predominantly functional buildings of the Indo-European representative style developed from a mixture of European and Indian-Islamic components. Post-colonial national identity is expressed in modern structures like the Faisal Mosque, the Minar-e-Pakistan and the Mazar-e-Quaid.

The literature of Pakistan covers the literatures of languages spread throughout the country, namely Urdu, Sindhi, Punjabi, Pushto, Baluchi as well as English in recent times and in the past often Persian as well. Prior to the 19th century, the literature mainly consisted of lyric poetry and religious, mystical and popular materials. During the colonial age the native literary figures, under the influence of the western literature of realism, took up increasingly different topics and telling forms. Today, short stories enjoy a special popularity. The national poet of Pakistan, Muhammad Iqbal, wrote mainly in the Persian language, and additionally in Urdu. His works are concerned mostly with Islamic philosophy. Iqbal's most well-known work is the Persian poem volume Asrar-i-Khudi ("the secrets of the even"). The most famous works of early Urdu literature originated in the 14th century. The most well-known representative of the contemporary Urdu literature of Pakistan is Faiz Ahmed Faiz. Sufi Shah Abdul Latif is considered one of the most outstanding mystical poets. Mirza Kalich Beg has been termed the father of modern Sindhi prose. In Punjabi, naats and qawaalis are delivered. The Pushto literature tradition is a cultural link between Pakistan and neighbouring Afghanistan. Extensive lyric poetry and epic poems have been published in Pushto. In Baluchi language songs and ballads are popular.

Chapter 3

Sri Lanka

Sri Lanka, officially the **Democratic Socialist Republic of Sri Lanka** is an island nation in South Asia, located about 31 kilometres (19.3 mi) off the southern coast of India. It is home to around twenty million people.

Because of its location in the path of major sea routes, Sri Lanka is a strategic naval link between West Asia and South East Asia, and has been a center of Buddhist religion and culture from ancient times. Today, the country is a multi-religious and multi-ethnic nation, with more than a quarter of the population following faiths other than Buddhism, notably Hinduism, Christianity and Islam. The Sinhalese community forms the majority of the population, with Tamils, who are concentrated in the north and east of the island, forming the largest ethnic minority. Other communities include the Muslim Moors and Malays and the Burghers.

Famous for the production and export of tea, coffee, coconuts and rubber, Sri Lanka boasts a progressive and modern industrial economy and the highest per capita income in South Asia. The natural beauty of Sri Lanka's tropical forests, beaches and landscape, as well as its rich cultural heritage, make it a world famous tourist destination.

After over two thousand years of rule by local kingdoms, parts of Sri Lanka were colonized by Portugal and the Netherlands beginning in the 16th century, before the control of the entire country was ceded to the British Empire in 1815. During World War II, Sri Lanka served as an important base for Allied forces in the fight against the Japanese Empire. A nationalist political movement arose in the country in the early 20th century with the aim of obtaining political independence, which was eventually granted by the British after peaceful negotiations in 1948.

HISTORY OF SRI LANKA

Traditionally, the recorded History of Sri Lanka boasts of 25 chronicled centuries. However, the inhabitation of the country goes back much further, to the Balangoda People, about 32,000 - 3000 BC. Most of Sri Lanka's History is based on the Book called

Mahavamsa. However, there have been instances where historic rock inscriptions have been contrary to the Mahavamsa.

The Iron age in Sri Lanka begins about 1000 BC. Anuradhapura has been continuously settled since about 900 BC.

In the 6th century BC, Sri Lankans developed a unique hydraulic civilization, producing the largest reservoirs and dams up until the 20th century, enormous pyramid-like Stupa (Dagaba) architecture, within a culture nourished by Buddhism. It was forced to deal with South Indian invasions in the tenth century and European expansions in the sixteenth century.

Historical chronicles are found in stone writings ('sel lipi'), ola leaf writings ('Hela Atuva') and also in great Indian chronicles as Mahabharata and the Ramayana. The main historical written evidence is the Mahavamsa, also including Dipavamsa & Chulavamsa, their Burmese versions, as well as the parallel Indian records. The island presently known as "Sri Lanka" was originally known to the Sinhalese as "Sinhale" or "Heladiva".

In the 5th century B.C., Indo-Aryan emigrated from India, mixed with the Hela people and later Buddhism was established and helped develop the Sinhalese culture in Sri Lanka. According to Buddist scriptures the Buddha is said to have visited the island on three occasions to see the Naga Kings, thought to be Tamil speakers and who at one time ruled various kingdoms throughout all of North and South India before being driven out by the Aryan invaders. Prior to this period in time. More than 70% of Sinhalese populace considers itself to be Buddhist. Along with the Sinhalese, there is a Tamil Hindu population on this island.

There is a long-standing relationship between Sinhalese, Tamils, Moors, Malayans, Burghers, Ja (Javanese), Veddahs and other hundreds of inhabitants and cultural groups of Sri Lanka, which has ensured an extremely close relationship between the groups and cultures.

PREHISTORY

The island is estimated to have been colonised by the Balangoda People (named after the area where their remains were discovered) about 34,000 years ago. They have been identified as a group of Mesolithic hunter gatherers who lived in caves. Several of these caves including the well known Batadombalena and the Fa-Hien Rock cave have yielded many artefacts that points to them being the first inhabitants of the island.

The Balangoda People appear to have been responsible for creating Horton Plains, in the central hills, by burning the trees in order to catch game. However, discovery of Oats and Barley on the plains dating to about 15,000 BC suggest they may have engaged in agriculture.

Several minute granite tools of about 4 centimeters in length, earthenware and remnants of charred timber, and clay burial pots that date back to the Stone Age Mesolithic

Man who lived 8000 years ago have been discovered during recent excavations around a cave at Varana Raja Maha vihara & also in Kalatuwawa area.

Cinnamon, which is native to Sri Lanka, was in use in Ancient Egypt in about 1500 BC, suggesting that there were trading links with the island. It is possible that Biblical Tarshish was located on the island (James Emerson Tennent identified it with Galle).

A large settlement appears to have been founded before 900 BC at the site of Anuradhapura and signs of an Iron Age culture have also been found. The size of the settlement was about 15 hectares at that date, but it expanded to 50 ha, to 'town' size within a couple of centuries. A similar site has been discovered at Aligala in Sigiriya.

It is suspected that the hunter gatherer people known as the Wanniyala-Aetto or Veddas, who still live in the Central, Uva and North-Eastern parts of the island, are relatively direct descendants of the first inhabitants (Balangoda man). They may have migrted to the island from the main land around the time humans spread from Africa to other parts of the world. The Ramayana epic, composed possibly between the 2nd and 4th centuries BC, states that Lanka was created by the divine sculptor Vishwakarma for Kubera, the lord of wealth. Ravana, usurped the throne of Kubera after defeating him in a battle. Ramayana recounts how Rama invaded the island through the Mannar causeway with the help of Sugreeva (the king of a Vanara (monkey) Army) and Hanuman the minister of Sugreeva, to save his abducted wife Sita from Ravana, the King of Sri Lanka.

The earliest chronicles the Dipavamsa and Mahavamsa say that, before the migration of Vijaya, tribes of Yakkhas (demon worshippers), Nagas (cobra worshippers) and devas (god worshippers) inhabited the island. Pottery has been found at Anuradhapura, bearing Brahmi script and non-Brahmi writing, dating back to 600 BC. One of the oldest examples of the script.

LEGENDARY AND EARLY HISTORY (500 - 250 BC)

Pali Chronicles and the arrival of Vijaya

The Pali chronicles, i.e., the Dipavamsa, Mahavamsa, Thupavamsa and the Chulavamsa as well as a large collection of stone inscriptions, the Indian Epigraphical records, the Burmese versions of the chronicles etc., provide an exceptional record for the history of Sri Lanka from about the 6th century B.C. The Mahavamsa, written circa 5th century A. D. by the monk Nagasena, using the Dipavamsa, the Attakatha and other written sources available to him, correlates well with the Indian history of the period, with King Asoka's dates of reign actually discovered through the Mahavamsa. The account of the period prior to Asoka's coronation (given in the Mahavamsa as 218 years after the Buddha's death) seems to be part legend. Thus the history begins with the arrival of Vijaya and his 700 followers. Vijaya, is a Kalinga(ancient Orissa) prince, the eldest son of King Sinhabahu (means:-"*Man with Lion arms*") and Queen Sinhasivali, who were siblings born by a mythical union between a lion and a human princess.

The historian contrives the chronology to claim that Vijaya landed on the same day as the death of the Buddha, giving added significance to Vijaya's arrival. The story of Vijaya and Kuveni (the local reigning queen) is reminiscent of Greek legend, and may have a common source in Indo-European folk tales. Vijaya landed near Mahathitha (Manthota or Mannar), and, according to the Mahavamsa, named the Island "Thambaparni" ('copper-colored palms), a name which entered into Ptolemy's map of the ancient world. Tamirabharani is the old name for the second longest river (known as Malwatu Oya in Sinhala and Aruvi Aru in Tamil); it was a main supply route connecting the capital, Anuradhapura to Mahathitha (Mannar), used by Greek ships and Chinese ships travelling on the Silk Route. Mahathitha was an ancient port, linking the Indian coast and the Persian gulf with Sri Lanka, and frequented by sea-faring people in pre-Vijayan times.

The present day Sihalese (and even some Tamils) are a mixture of the indegenous people and other groups that came to the island from various parts of India. The Sinhalese recognize the Vijayan Indo-Aryan influence/civilization and Buddism (that was already in existence prior to the arrival of Vijaya), that set them appart from other groups in neighbouring south India. One must take into consideration that Vijaya's subsequent queens were from Madurai, south India.

Saka-Murunda

Ancient epigraphic inscriptions found at Anuradhapura and some other places in Sri Lanka attest *Muridi* (Muruda = Murunda), *Meraya* (Maurya? or else *the inhabitants from Meru in Hindukush*?) etc.

Tamils

The Tamils are known to be the descendents of people that migrated from south Indian Cholan and Pandayan dynasties. It is not yet established if the Naga tribe were in fact early Tamils who has lived in Srilanka since pre-history. They are predominantly Hindu (or Catholic).

Senan and Guttakan were the first Tamil rulers (2nd century BC). They left no evidence except for the allusion in the Mahavamsa. The intermingling of Tamil and Sinhala people, especially after the 12th century is evidenced by the Sinhalization of many Tamil place names and the tamilization of Sinhala toponyms. Although the Mahavamsa only mentions the name Sinhala after the 12th Century. It could also be said that the Sinhalese language is a diluted form of pali.

There is also a reference to Dravidian community *Dameda* (Damila or Tamil), and another reference to *Jhavaka* (?) and *Mileka* (=Mlechha).

Kambojas

Of these several ethnic groups, the Kaboja (or Kamboja, Kambodjin) find mention in seven or eight ancient inscriptions, whereas term Daemeda is referenced four times,

Mileka occurs twice and the Muridi, Meraya and Jhavaka occur only once. The Sihalavatthu, a Pali text of about the fourth century, also attests a group of people called the Kambojas living in Rohana. The third story of this text, called *Metteyya-vatthu,* reveals that the Elder named Maleyya was residing in *Kamboja-gama,* in the province (Janapada) of Rohana on the Island of Tambapanni (Sri Lanka). Further, there is an ancient evidence from Mahavamsa that the Yonas or Yavanas (Greeks), the next door neighbors of the Kambojas in the north-west, had also their settlement in *Pandukabhaya* in Anuradhapura.

The ancient inscriptions reveal that the Kambojas were actively involved in trade since there is reference to one 'Grand Trade Guild of the Kambojas' (*Kabojhiya-mahapugiyana*) and one 'Sangha of the Kambojas' (*Gota-Kabojhi(ya]na*) in Anuradhapura. Scholars have dated these epigraphic inscriptions to at least third century BCE (or probably earlier). This may imply that the Aryan speakers of Sri Lankan population may have materially descended from the north-western Kambojas and partly from the Saka (Murinda) and the Yavana colonists.. Plenty of evidence exists there that the Kambojas who inhabited a region bordering the upper Indus, had at one time established themselves in a country near Sind from where they, accompanied by the Yavanas, had finally reached Ceylon in pre-Christian times.

FEUDAL SRI LANKA (250 BC-1600 AD)

Anuradhapura dynasty

DEVANAMPIYA TISSA (250-210 BC). A Sinhalese King of Mauriya clan. His links with Emperor Asoka led to the introduction of Buddhism by Mahinda (son of Asoka) in 247? BC. Sangamitta, (sister of Mahinda) brought a Bodhi sapling via Jambukola(Sambiliturei). There is no evidence in the history of King Ashoka about his having had a son by the name of Mahinda (or by any other name) or a daughter by the name of Sangamitta (or by any other name). This king's reign was crucial to Theravada Buddhism, and for Sri Lanka.

ELARA 205-161 BC, a South Indian Tamil invader who ruled "Pihiti Rata", i.e., Sri Lanka north of the mahaweli, after killing King Asela. During Elara's time, KelaniTissa was a sub-king of Maya Rata (south-west) and KavanTissa was a **regional sub-king** of Ruhuna (South-east). Kavantissa built Tissa Maha Vihara, Dighavapi Tank and many shrines in Seruvila. DUTU GEMUNU (GAMINI) 161-137 BC – Eldest son of King Kavan Tissa, who was a young man 25 years of age, defeated the South Indian Tamil Invader Elara (over 64 years of age) in single combat, described in the Mahavamsa. Dutugamunu is depicted as a Sinhala "Asoka". The Ruwanwelisaya, built by this king is a dagaba of pyramid-like proportions. It was an engineering marvel.

Five Tamil Chiefs: PULAHATHA deposed by BAHIYA, deposed by PANAYAMARA, deposed by PILAYAMARA, murdered by DATHIYA 88 BC – deposed by Valagambahu, **ending Tamil rule**. VALAGAMBAHU I 89-77 BC – restored the Dutugamunu dynasty. The Mahavihara Theravada -Abhayagiri(pro-Mahayana) doctrinal disputes arose at this time. The Tripitaka was written in Pali at Aluvihara, Matale. CHORA NAGA (Mahanaga) 63-51 BC; poisoned by his consort Anula. Queen Anula 48-44 BC – Widow of Chora Naga and Kuda Tissa, *first Queen of Lanka*. She had many lovers who were poisoned by her. She was finally killed by: KUTTAKANNA TISSA. VASABHA 67-111 AD – Vallipuram gold plate; he fortified Anuradhapura and built eleven tanks; many edicts. GAJABAHU I 114-136 – invaded the Chola kingdom and brought back captives. He recovered the tooth relic of the Buddha.

MAHASENA 274-301 AD – The Theravada (Maha Vihara) was persecuted and Mahayana surfaced. Later the King returned to the Maha Vihara. **Pandu** 429 AD - **first of seven Pandiyan rulers**, ending with Pithya, 455; DHATUSENA 455-473 AD, his uncle, **Mahanama** wrote the Mahavamsa, he built "Kalaweva". His son KASHYAPA 470-488 AD, built the famous sigiriya rock palace. Some 700 rock graffiti give a glimpse of ancient Sinhala.

Lambakanna

MANAVAMMA 684-718 AD – seized the throne with Pallava help. Manavamsa introduced Pallava patronage for three centuries. By the 9th century, with the Pandyan ascendancy in southern India, Anuradhapura was sacked. However, the Sinhalese invaded Pandya using a rival prince, and Madurai itself was sacked. MAHINDA V 982-1029 AD – was the last Sinhala monarch of Anuradhapura. He fled to Ruhuna, where, in 1007, the Chola took him to prison and he died in India.

Chola empire

The great Raja Raja Cholan I, and his great son Rajendra Cholan I, defeated all of the Sinhalese kings and sub-kings who ruled over Sinhlala kingdoms on the island and brought the entire island under South Indian Tamil control. The Sinhala king Mahinda V and his family were captured and taken to Chola Naadu. Tamils ruled the entire island for the next 140 years.

Polonnaruwa rule

VIJAYABAHU I 1055-1110 AD, recaptured the whole Island, and established Polonnaruwa as the new capital. King Vijaya Bahu married from the Kalinga (Orissa) Royal Family a second queen, and had a son Vikrama Bahu and a daughter Ratnavali. His sister, Mitta, married a Pandya Prince who had three sons, the eldest being Manabharana. He married Ratnavali. Their son was PARAKRAMA BAHU I 1153-1186 AD – Grandson of Vijaya Bahu I, Prince of Sinhala-Pandyan-Kalinga descent, son of Manabharana and Vijaya Bahu's sister, Mitta. He was a very powerful king, noted for his engineering, naval power, art, culture, many Sinhala inscriptions, and even a Tamil edict in Uruthota (Kayts). The Chulavamsa was written by **Dharmakirthi**, updating the Mahavamsa to include Parakramabahu. It was a great age since the epic Anuradhapura period.

DAMBADENIYA KINGDOM

Jaffna kingdom

The Jaffna kingdom (1215-1619 CE), also known as Kingdom of Aryacakravarti came into existence after the invasion of Magha, who is said to have been from Kalinga, in South India. It eventually became a tribute paying feudatory of the Pandyan Empire in modern South India in 1250, but later become independent with the fragmentation of the Pandyan control. For a brief period, in the early to middle fourteenth century, it was an ascendant power in the island of Sri Lanka when all regional kingdoms accepted subordination. However, the kingdom was eventually overpowered by the rival Kotte Kingdom, around 1450.

It was freed of Kotte control in 1467; its subsequent rulers directed their energies towards consolidating its economic potential by maximising revenue from pearls and elephant exports and land revenue. It was less feudal than most of other regional kingdoms in the island of Sri Lanka of the same period. During this period, important local Tamil literature was produced and Hindu temples were built including an academy for language advancement.

The arrival of the Portuguese colonial power to the island of Sri Lanka in 1505, and its strategic location in the Palk Strait connecting all interior Sinhalese kingdoms to South India, created political problems. Many of its kings confronted and ultimately made peace with the Portuguese colonials. In 1617, Cankili II, an usurper to the throne, confronted the Portuguese but was defeated, thus bringing the kingdom's independent existence to an end in 1619.

COLONIAL ERA (1517-1948)

Portuguese era

The first Europeans to visit Sri Lanka in modern times were the Portuguese: Francisco de Almeida arrived in 1505, finding the island divided into seven warring kingdoms and unable to fend off intruders. The Portuguese founded a fort at the port city of Colombo in 1517 and gradually extended their control over the coastal areas. In 1592 the Sinhalese moved their capital to the inland city of Kandy, a location more secure against attack from invaders. Intermittent warfare continued through the 16th century.

Many lowland Sinhalese were forced to convert to Christianity while the coastal Moors were religiously persecuted and forced to retreat to the Central highlands. The Buddhist majority disliked Portuguese occupation and its influences and welcomed any powei who might rescue them. In 1602, therefore, when the Dutch captain Joris Spilberg landed, the king at Kandy appealed to him for help.

Dutch era

It was in 1638 that the Dutch attacked in earnest, and not until 1656 that Colombo fell. By 1660 the Dutch controlled the whole island except the kingdom of Kandy. The

Dutch persecuted the Catholics but left the Buddhists, Hindus and Moslems alone. However, they taxed the people far more heavily than the Portuguese had done. A mixed Dutch-Sinhalese people known as Burgher peoples are the legacy of Dutch rule.

In 1659, the British sea captain Robert Knox landed by chance on Sri Lanka and was captured by the king of Kandy. He escaped 19 years later and wrote an account of his stay. This helped to bring the island to the attention of the British.

British rule

During the Napoleonic Wars the United Kingdom, fearing that French control of the Netherlands might deliver Sri Lanka to the French, occupied the coastal areas of the island (which they called Ceylon) with little difficulty in 1796. In 1802 by the Treaty of Amiens the Dutch part of the island was formally ceded to Britain, and became a crown colony. In 1803 the British invaded the Kingdom of Kandy in the 1st Kandyan War, but were bloodily repulsed. In 1815 Kandy was occupied in the 2nd Kandyan War, finally ending Sri Lankan independence. Following the bloody suppression of the Uva Rebellion or 3rd Kandyan War in 1817–1818, a treaty in 1818 preserved the Kandyan monarchy (Nayaks of Kandy) as a British dependency.

The Kandyan peasantry were stripped of their lands by the Wastelands Ordinance, a modern enclosure movement and reduced to penury. The British found that the uplands of Sri Lanka were very suited to coffee, tea and rubber cultivation, and by the mid 19th century Ceylon tea had become a staple of the British market, bringing great wealth to a small class of white tea planters. To work the estates, the planters imported large numbers of Tamil workers as indentured labourers from south India, who soon made up 10% of the island's population. These workers had to work in slave-like conditions and to live in line rooms, not very different from cattle sheds.

The British colonialists favoured the semi-European Burghers, certain high-caste Sinhalese and the Tamils who were mainly concentrated to the north of the country, exacerbating divisions and enmities which have survived ever since. Nevertheless, the British also introduced democratic elements to Sri Lanka for the first time in its history. The Burghers were given some degree of self-government as early as 1833. It was not until 1909 that constitutional development began with a partly-elected assembly, and not until 1920 that elected members outnumbered official appointees. Universal suffrage was introduced in 1931, over the protests of the Sinhalese, Tamil and Burgher elite who objected to the common people being allowed to vote.

INDEPENDENCE MOVEMENT (1935 TO 1970)

Ceylon National Congress (CNC) was founded to agitate for greater autonomy. The party soon split along ethnic and caste lines. Prof. K. M. de Silva, the famous Peradeniya historian has pointed out that the refusal of the Ceylon Tamils to accept minority status to be one of the main causes which broke up the Ceylon National Congress. The CNC did not seek independence or "Swaraj". What may be called the independence movement broke into two streams, viz., the "constitutionalists", who sought independence by gradual modification of the status of Ceylon, and the more radical groups associated with the Colombo Youth League, Labour movement of Goonasinghe, and the Jaffna Youth Congress. These organizations were the first to raise the cry of Swaraj, or outright independence, following the Indian example, when Nehru, Sarojini Naidu and other Indian leaders visited Ceylon in 1926.

The efforts of the constitutionalists led to the arrival of the Donoughmore Commission reforms (1931) and the Soulbury Commission recommendations, which essentially upheld the 1944 draft constitution of the Board of ministers headed by D. S. Senanayake. The Marxist Lanka Sama Samaja Party (LSSP), which grew out of the Youth Leagues in 1935, made the demand for outright independence a corner stone of their policy. Its deputies in the State Council, N.M. Perera and Philip Gunawardena, were aided in this struggle by other less radical members like Natesa Iyer and Don Alwin Rajapaksa. They also demanded the replacement of English as the official language by Sinhala and Tamil. The Marxist groups were a tiny minority and yet their movement was viewed with grave suspicion by the British administration. The heroic (but ineffctive) attempts to rouse the public against the British Raj in revolt would have led to certain bloodshed and a delay in independence. British state papers released in the 1950s show that the Marxist movement had a very negative impact on the policy makers at the Colonial office.

The Soulbury Commission was the most important result of the agitation for constitutional reform in the 1930s. The Tamil leadership had by then fallen into the hands of G. G. Ponnambalam who had rejected the "Ceylonese identity". Ponnamblam had declared himself a "proud Dravidian", and attempted to establish an independent identity for the Tamils. Ponnamblam was a politician who attacked the Sinhalese, and their historical chronicle known as the Mahavamsa. One such inflamed attack in Navalapitiya led to the first Sinhala-Tamil riot in 1939. Ponnambalam opposed universal franchise, supported the caste system, and claimed that the protection of Tamil rights requires the Tamils (15% of the population in 1931) having an equal number of seats in parliament to that of the Sinhalese (~72% of the population).

This "50-50" or "balanced representation" policy became the hall mark of Tamil politics of the time. Ponnambalam also accused the British of having established colonization in "traditional Tamil areas", and having favoured the Buddhists by the buddhist temporalities act. The Soulbury Commission rejected these submissions by Ponnambalam, and even noted their unacceptable communal character. Sinhalese writers pointed out the large immigration of Tamils to the southern urban centers, especially after the opening of the Jaffna-Colombo railway. Meanwhile, Senanayake, Baron Jayatilleke, Oliver Gunatilleke and others lobbied the Soulbury Commission without confronting them officially. The unofficial submissions contained what was to later become the draft constitution of 1944.

The close collaboration of the D. S. Senanayake government with the war-time British administration led to the support of Lord Mount-Batton. His dispatches and a telegram to the Colonial office supporting Independence for Ceylon have been cited by historians as having helped the Senanayake government to secure the independence of Sri Lanka. The shrewd cooperation with the British as well as diverting the needs of the war market to Ceylonese markets as a supply point, managed by Oliver Goonatilleke, also led to a very favourable fiscal situation for the newly independent government.

SECOND WORLD WAR

During World War II, Sri Lanka was a front-line British base against the Japanese. The opposition to the war in Sri Lanka was orchestrated by the Marxist organisations. The LSSP leaders of the pro-independence agitation were arrested by the Colonial authorities. On 5 April 1942, The Japanese Navy bombed Colombo. This led to the fleeing of the Indian merchants who dominated the commercial sector in Colombo, removing a great political problem that had faced the Senanayake government. The Marxist leaders also escaped to India, where they participated in the struggle there. The movement in Ceylon was minuscule, limited to the English educated intelligentsia and trade unions, mainly in the urban centers.

These groups were led by Robert Gunawardena, Philip's brother. In stark contrast to this "heroic" but ineffective approach to the war, the Senanayake government took advantage of the war to establish excellent rapport with the commanding elite. Ceylon became a main center of the war, with Mountbatten using Colombo as its headquarters. Oliver Goonatilleka successfully exploited the markets for the country's rubber and other agricultural products to replenish the treasury. They also used the war period to continue to agitate for independence, using the opportunities offered by the war to establish their "friendship" with Britain.

Meanwhile, the Marxists, who analysed that this was an imperialist war which should be followed by the proletarian revolution, followed a path of agitation totally unrelated to their negligible combat strength, and diametrically opposite to the "constitutionalist" approach of Senanayake and other leaders. A very small garrison on the Cocos Islands, manned by Ceylonese, mutinied. It has been claimed that the LSSP had some hand in it, although this is far from clear. Three of the mutineers were the only British Commonwealth troops to be shot for mutiny during the Second World War. Two members of the Governing Party, Junius Richard Jayawardene and Dudley Senanayake held discussions with the Japanese with a view to collaboration to oust the British. Sri Lankans in Singapore and Malaysia formed the 'Lanka Regiment' of the Indian National Army.

However, the constitutionalists led by D. S. Senanayake succeeded in winning independence. The Soulbury constitution was essentially what Senanayake's board of ministers had drafted in 1944. The promise of Dominion status, and independence itself, had been given by the Colonial office.

POST WAR

The Sinhalese leader Don Stephen Senanayake left the CNC on the issue of independence, disagreeing with the revised aim of 'the achieving of freedom', although his real reasons were more subtle. He subsequently formed the United National Party (UNP) in 1946, when a new constitution was agreed on, based on the behind-the -curtain lobbying of the Soulbury commission. At the elections of 1947, the UNP won a minority of the seats in Parliament, but cobbled together a coalition with the Sinhala Maha Sabha of Solomon Bandaranaike and the Tamil Congress of G.G. Ponnambalam. The successful inclusions of the Tamil-communalist leader Ponnambalam, and his Sinhala counterpart Bandaranaike were a remarkable political balancing act by Senanayake. However, the vacuum in Tamil Nationalist politics created by Ponnamblam's transition to a moderate opened the field for the Tamil Arasu Kachchi, a Tamil soverignist party (renderd into English as the "Federal" party) led by S. J. V. Chelvanaykam, the lawyer son of a Christian minister.

POLITICAL INDEPENDENCE

Dominion status, raised to independence itself followed on 4 February 1948, with military treaties with Britain (the upper ranks of the armed forces were initially British) and British air and sea bases remaining intact. Senanayake became the first Prime Minister of Sri Lanka. In 1949, with the concurrence of the leaders of the Ceylon Tamils, the UNP government disenfranchised the Indian Tamil plantation workers. This was the price that Senanayake had to pay, to obtain the support of the Kandyan Sinhalese who felt threatened by the demographics of the tea estates, where the inclusion of the "Indian Tamils" would have meant electoral defeat for the Kandyan leaders. Senanayke died in 1952 after falling from a horse.

He was succeeded by his son Dudley Senanayake, the minister of Agriculture. However, in 1953 - following a massive general strike or 'Hartal' by the Left parties against the UNP, Dudley Senanayake resigned. He was followed by John Kotelawala, a very senior politician and an uncle of Dudley. Kotelawala did not have the enormous personal prestige or the adroit political acumen of D. S. Senanayake. He brought to the fore, the issue of national languages that D. S. Senanayake had adroitly kept on the back burner. He antagonized the Tamils and the Sinhalese by stating conflicting policies with regard to the status of Sinhala and Tamil as official languages. He also antagonized the Buddhist lobby by attacking politically active Buddhist Monks who were Bandaranaike's supporters.

In 1956 the UNP was defeated at elections (being reduced to 8 seats in Parliament) by the Mahajana Eksath Peramuna, which included the Sri Lanka Freedom Party (SLFP) led by Solomon Bandaranaike and the Viplavakari Lanka Sama Samaja Party of Philip Gunawardena. Bandaranaike was a politician who had nursed the Sinhala nationalist lobby since the 1930s. He replaced English with Sinahala only as the official language.

He was the chief Sinhalese spokesmen who attempted to counter the communal politics unleashed by G. G. Ponnambalam. In 1957 British bases were removed and Sri Lanka officially became a non-aligned country. The Paddy Lands Act, the brainchild of Philip Gunawardena was passed, giving those working the land greater rights vis-a-vis absentee landlords.

Bandaraike entered into a pact with Chelvanayagam of the Tamil-based Tamil Arasu Kachchi to secure more rights for the Tamils, but this was opposed by G. G. Ponnambalam and by JR Jayawardene of the UNP. The latter organised a "March to Kandy" in protest. This triggered hostility from the Tamil minority which soon led to disturbances, culminating in serious riots in 1958.

Philip Gunawardena, while in government, continued to organize strikes in the Colombo port. He was removed from the government as the right-wing of the governing coalition grew into the ascendent. The right-wing forces also conspired against the government. This was the time when McCarthyism was rampant in the United States, and Mossadeq had also been assassinated in Iran. Bandaranaike was assassinated in September 1959. His successor Wijayananda Dahanayake, an ex-LSSP member from Galle, was unable to hold the government together, and elections in March 1960 brought the UNP under Dudley Senanayake back to office, but without a working parliamentary majority.

Fresh elections in July saw Bandaranaike's widow, Sirimavo Bandaranaike, lead the SLFP to power and become the world's first elected female head of government. Her government avoided further confrontations with the Tamils, but its socialist policies of nationalization led to a cut-off of United States aid and a growing economic crisis. After an attempted coup-d'etat by right-wing Army and Police officers who were mainly non-buddhists, aimed at bringing the UNP back to power, Bandaranaike nationalised the oil companies. This led to a boycott of the country by the oil cartels, which was broken with aid from the Kansas oil producers co-operative. In 1964 she formed a coalition government with the LSSP, a Trotskyist party with Dr N.M. Perera as Minister of Finance.

Dissatisfaction with the economic situation brought the UNP under Senanayake back to office in 1965, but this government fared no better, since the underlying cause of Sri Lanka's problems were the declining market, the exploding population resulting from advanced health services and social welfare. Its traditional commodity exports, tea, coffee and rubber could not match the costs of importing food and maintaining the welfare economy. In 1968 Bandaranaike formed a coalition, the United Front with the LSSP and the Communist Party of Sri Lanka, which swept the 1970 polls on a platform of socialism.

INDEPENDENT REPUBLIC (1970 TO PRESENT)

Under Bandaranaike the country became a republic, the Free Sovereign and Independent Republic of Sri Lanka, the Senate was abolished and the position of Sinhala as the official language (with Tamil as a second language) was confirmed. Full independence was established as the last remaining ties of subjection to the UK were broken (e.g. the Privy Council was no longer a body of appeal above the Supreme Court). The British-owned plantations were nationalised in order to fulfil the election pledges of the Marxist program and to "prevent the ongoing dis-investment by the owning companies".

An attempt was made at economic independence, with a five-year plan to achieve industrial development. However, this was stymied due to a shortage of foreign exchange, a very expensive welfare program, and the oil crisis of 1974. These were combined with an unprecedented drought which severely affected the harvest of rice, the staple food of the people. Strides forward were made in the fields of heavy industry, automotive spares and electronics. The strongly centralized economy, functioning via a set of state corporations grew very sluggishly.

In 1971 a group variously labelled Maoist or Guevarist, the People's Liberation Front (JVP) launched a rebellion. It was led by Rohana Wijeweera, a marxist who had his education at the Lumumba University in the Soviet Union. This movement was not connected with the traditional Sri Lankan Marxist parties which were then in power. Most of the "insurgents" were unemployed literate youth who were the product of the post-independence population explosion. Although the JVP rebellion was brutally suppressed, the JVP found a place in Sri Lankan politics as a voice of leftist Sinhalese nationalism, along with the right-wing movement in the UNP associated with Cyril Matthew. Militant Tamil Chauvinist movements, e.g., the Pulip Padai, had been launched in Trincomalee in 1965. The Jaffna university was "ethnically cleansed" of non-Tamils in 1976, and the city itself began to be subject to similar "ethnic cleansing", eliminating Muslim and Sinhala residents.

The extreme-Tamil groups rejected and physically eliminated the main Colombo-Tamil leadership of the Tamil United Liberation Front (TULF). Tamil public servants or members of parliament working with the government were harassed. The mayor of Jaffna was assassinated in 1975. The militants claimed their independence, their rights, and their "traditional homeland", and formed armed separatist groups such as the Liberation Tigers of Tamil Eelam ('Tamil Tigers'), demanding an independent Tamil state called Eelam. Much of this had the implicit and material support of politicians in India. The country began to slide towards a civil war in which a unique cyanide-carrying suicide brigade appeared.

NEW CONSTITUTION

By 1977 the voters were tired of Bandaranaike's socialist policies and elections returned the UNP to power under Junius Jayewardene on a manifesto pledging a market economy and "a free ration of 8 seers (kilograms) of cereals". The SLFP and the left-wing parties were virtually wiped out in Parliament (although they garnered 40% of the popular vote), leaving the Tamil United Liberation Front, led by Appapillai Amirthalingam, as the official opposition. This created a dangerous ethnic cleavage in Sri Lankan politics.

Bandaranaike had her civic rights removed by an act of Parliament. In 1978 Jayewardene introduced a new constitution making Sri Lanka a presidential 'Democratic Socialist' republic, with himself as executive President. In 1980 he crushed a general strike by the trade-union movement, jailing its leaders. When the UNP member for the parliamentary constituency of Kalawana was removed on an election petition by his Communist opponent, Jayawardene allowed him to continue sitting in the house.

In 1977, Colombo abandoned state controlled economic policies and its import substitution trade policy for market-oriented policies and export-oriented trade. This included the opening of free-trade zones with a heavy emphasis on exports of garments from these zones.

Elections to District Councils in 1981 were marred by the open theft of ballot boxes in Jaffna. The Jaffna Library, the repository of thousands of valuable documents was burned down by thugs alleged to be linked with the government.

President Jayawardene had the constitution amended (one of 13 amendments during his 10 years in office) to allow presidential elections to be held early, in 1982. The main opposition candidate, Hector Kobbekaduwa was garlanded with onions by the farmers of the Jaffna peninsular, impoverished by the policy of unrestricted imports.

The Presidential election, held amidst widespread acts of electoral malpractice (Hector Kobbekaduwa arrived at the polling station only to find his vote had already been cast) resulted in Jayawardene's re-election. He followed this with an infamous plebiscite on postponing parliamentary elections for six years. Associates of Kobbekaduwa, such as TB Ilangaratne and Vijaya Kumaratunga, were jailed as 'Naxalites', a political creed unheard of in Sri Lanka, before or since. The Commissioner of Elections, in his report on the referendum, reported that it was flawed.

In 1983 following a demonstration against the US establishment of a military base in Diego Garcia, former MP Vivienne Goonewardena was physically assaulted at a police station. Her fundamental rights application in this matter was upheld by the Supreme Court in an act of judicial independence. Following this, thugs stoned the houses of the Supreme Court judges who had made the ruling and the police officer who had been convicted had his fine paid by the government and received a promotion.

CIVIL WAR (1983 TO PRESENT)

In July 1983 communal riots took place due to the ambush and killing of 13 Sri Lankan Army soldiers by the Tamil Tiger Terrorists. Using the voters list which contained the exact addresses of Tamils, the Tamil community faced a severe backlash from the Sinhalese rioters including the destruction of shops. It was rumoured that people behind the riots were government thugs supported by Jayewardene and his cabinet. While many Sinhalese were involved in the mob, many other Sinhalese kept Tamil neighbours in their homes to protect them from the rioters. During these riots the government did nothing to control the mob. Conservative government estimates put the death toll at

400 with 150,000 leaving the country resulting in a Tamil Diaspora in Canada, UK, Australia and other western countries.

Jayewardene held office until 1989, ruling as a virtual dictator under emergency powers. In 1987, following an army offensive in the Vadamarachchi peninsular, India started getting deeply involved in the ethnic conflict. A convoy sent by India was stopped in Sri Lankan waters by the Sri Lankan Navy and the Indian Air Force retaliated with an air drop of supplies onto the Jaffna peninsular. While the UNP organised street protests against India, Jayawardene declared that he would defend the country's independence to the last bullet.

However, the air drop also caused Jayawardene to reconsider his position and he then accepted the offer of Indian Prime Minister Rajiv Gandhi of a Peace Accord. Rajiv Gandhi's offer to send troops into Sri Lanka was deeply unpopular with the Sinhalese and, although initially popular with the Tamils, led to an outbreak of hostilities between the Tamil Tigers and the Indian Peace Keeping Force (IPKF) - Eelam War II.

In 1989 Jayewardene was succeeded by his own choice as President, Ranasinghe Premadasa, who asked for the Indian troops to be withdrawn - which was later done by Indian Prime Minister V.P. Singh. Premadasa was assassinated by a Tamil Tiger suicide bomber in 1993. Rajiv Gandhi had already met a similar fate in 1991.

Premadasa was succeeded by Dingiri Banda Wijetunga, with Ranil Wickremasinghe as Prime Minister. In August 1994 the People's Alliance under Bandaranaike's daughter Chandrika Kumaratunga won legislative elections on a platform of concessions to the Tamils and a 'balanced economy'. Kumaratunga became Prime Minister and in November she was elected President, appointing her 78-year-old (but still active) mother Prime Minister. A ceasefire ensued, which broke down after several months - the beginning of Eelam War III. Under the Bandaranaikes the war dragged on, with the military unable to defeat the separatists and the government opposed to negotiations. By 2000 an estimated 65,000 people had been killed in the conflict.

At Presidential elections in 1999, former Prime Minister Wickremesinghe of the UNP contested on a platform of no concessions to the Tamils, but was defeated by Kumaratunga. A 180-degree turn in UNP policy occurred and in December 2001 the UNP returned to office on a policy of a negotiated settlement with the Tigers, with Wickremasinghe as Prime Minister. A cease fire began, the first long cessation of hostilities since the beginning of the conflict. But the 1978 constitution left the Prime Minister with little power against a hostile President, and Kumaratunga did all she could to frustrate Wickremesinghe's government. In March 2004 she dismissed Wickremesinghe and called fresh elections, which returned the SLFP to office under Mahinda Rajapakse.

By 2005 there had been no further progress towards either a military or political solution. The assassination of Foreign Minister Lakshman Kadirgamar in August 2005, by the LTTE (although they denied responsibility), further hardened attitudes. His successor was Anura Bandaranaike, the President's brother and putative political heir. Twenty years of civil conflict had done immense damage to Sri Lankan society and the economy, which has fallen behind other Asian economies, although it remains the second most prosperous nation in South Asia.

In elections held on 17 November 2005, Mahinda Rajapakse, the son of Don Alwin Rajapaksa, was elected President, defeating Wickremasinghe. He appointed Ratnasiri Wickremanayake Prime Minister and Mangala Samaraweera Foreign Minister. Negotiations with the LTTE stalled and low-intensity conflict began. The violence dipped off after talks in February, but escalated in April; it remains to be seen whether or not the conflict will revert to full-scale war.

On August 2006 Red Cross evacuated 150 foreigners from Jaffna region after one month of fighting between the LTTE and the government.

GEOGRAPHY OF SRI LANKA

The island of Sri Lanka lies in the Indian Ocean, to the southwest of the Bay of Bengal and to the southeast of the Arabian Sea. It is separated from the Indian subcontinent by the Gulf of Mannar and the Palk Strait. According to Hindu mythology, a land bridge to the Indian mainland, known as Rama's Bridge, was constructed during the time of Rama by the vanara architect Nala. Often referred to as Adam's Bridge, it now amounts to only a chain of limestone shoals remaining above sea level. According to colonial British reports, this is a natural causeway which was formerly complete, but was breached by a violent storm in 1480. The width of the Palk Strait is small enough for the coast of Sri Lanka to be visible from the furthest point near the Indian town of Rameswaram. The tear drop shaped island consists mostly of flat-to-rolling coastal plains, with mountains rising only in the south-central part. Amongst these are Sri Pada (Adams Peak) and the highest point Pidurutalagala, at 2,524 meters (8,281 ft). The Mahaweli ganga (Mahaweli river) and other major rivers provide fresh water to the population.

Sri Lanka's climate can be described as tropical, and quite hot. Its position between 5 and 10 north latitude endows the country with a warm climate, moderated by ocean winds and considerable moisture. The mean temperature ranges from a low of 16 °C (61 °F) in Nuwara Eliya in the Central Highlands (where frost may occur for several days in the winter) to a high of 32 °C (90 °F) in Trincomalee on the northeast coast (where temperatures may reach 38 °C (100 °F)). The average yearly temperature for the country as a whole ranges from 28° to 30 °C (82–86 °F). Day and night temperatures may vary by 4 to 7 °C (7–13 °F). In January, the coolest month, many people wear coats and sweaters in the highlands and elsewhere. May, the hottest period, precedes the summer monsoon rains.

The rainfall pattern is influenced by the monsoon winds of the Indian Ocean and Bay of Bengal, which encounter the slopes of the Central Highlands, they unload heavy rains on the mountain slopes and the southwestern sector of the island. Some of the windward slopes receive up to 2,500 millimetres (98 in) of rain per month, but the leeward slopes in the east and northeast receive little rain. Periodic squalls occur and sometimes tropical cyclones bring overcast skies and rains to the southwest, northeast, and eastern parts of the island. Between December to March, monsoon winds come from the northeast, bringing moisture from the Bay of Bengal. Humidity is typically higher in the southwest and mountainous areas and depends on the seasonal patterns of rainfall. At Colombo, for example, daytime humidity stays above 70% all year, rising to almost 90 percent during the monsoon season in June. Anuradhapura experiences a daytime low of 60% during the monsoon month of March, but a high of 79% during the November and December rains. In the highlands, Kandy's daytime humidity usually ranges between 70 and 79%.

GOVERNMENT AND POLITICS OF SRI LANKA

Politics of Sri Lanka takes place in a framework of a presidential representative democratic republic, whereby the President of Sri Lanka is both head of state and head of government, and of a multi-party system. Executive power is exercised by the government. Legislative power is vested in both the government and parliament. Since decennia the party system is dominated by the socialist Sri Lanka Freedom Party and the conservative United National Party. The Judiciary is independent of the executive and the legislature. The Politics of Sri Lanka reflect the historical and political differences between the two main ethnic groups, the majority Sinhala and the minority Tamils, who are concentrated in the north and east of the island.

At independence in 1948, Sri Lanka, then called Ceylon, was a Commonwealth realm, with the monarch represented by the Governor General. The Parliament was bicameral, consisting of a Senate and a House of Representatives. In 1971, the Senate was abolished, and the following year, Ceylon was renamed Sri Lanka, and became a republic within the Commonwealth, with the last Governor General becoming the first President of Sri Lanka. Under the first republican Constitution, the unicameral legislature was known as the National State Assembly.

In 1978, a new Constitution was adopted, which provided for an executive President, and the legislature was renamed Parliament.

POLITICAL CONDITIONS

Sri Lanka's two major political parties — the United National Party and the Sri Lanka Freedom Party — embrace democratic values, international nonalignment, and encouragement of Sinhalese culture. Past differences between the two on foreign and economic policy have narrowed. Generally, the SLFP envisions a broader role for the state, and the UNP a broader role for capitalism.

Sri Lanka has a multi-party democracy that enjoys surprising stability given the high levels of political violence, especially that which occurred under the UNP regime of 1977-1993. Recent elections have seen decreasing election violence between the SLFP and the UNP, compared to the period 1977-1994. Elections have been cleaner, without the rampant impersonation and vote-rigging which characterised the 1982 Presidential Election, the notorious Referendum of the same year, the Presidential Election of 1988 and the General Election of 1989.

The president (Mrs C.B.Kumaratunaga SLFP) dissolved the parliament in February 2004 after a two year term (though the parliament was elected for a 6 year term.) The election was held on 2 April 2004. The SLFP in alliance with the JVP secured the most seats by a single party but failed to achieve a majority. One of the ironies of the alliance was that the Presidents husband had in fact been assaninated by a member of the JVP. As a result of the alliance they lost the very first vote in parliament; that of appointment of the speaker. As a result the parliament did not pass a single bill from February to May.

EXECUTIVE BRANCH

The President, directly elected for a six-year term, is head of state, head of government, and commander in chief of the armed forces. The election occurs under the Sri Lankan form of the contingent vote. Responsible to Parliament for the exercise of duties under the constitution and laws, the president may be removed from office by a two-thirds vote of Parliament with the concurrence of the Supreme Court.

The President appoints and heads a cabinet of ministers responsible to Parliament. The President's deputy is the prime minister, who leads the ruling party in Parliament. A parliamentary no-confidence vote requires dissolution of the cabinet and the appointment of a new one by the President.

LEGISLATIVE BRANCH

The **Parliament** has 225 members, elected for a six year term, 196 members elected in multi-seat constituencies and 29 by proportional representation. The president may summon, suspend, or end a legislative session and dissolve Parliament. Parliament reserves the power to make all laws. The primary modification is that the party that receives the largest number of valid votes in each constituency gains a unique "bonus seat". The president may summon, suspend, or end a legislative session and dissolve Parliament any time after it has served for one year. Parliament reserves the power to make all laws. Since its independence in 1948, Sri Lanka has remained a member of the Commonwealth of Nations.

Parliament was dissolved on February 7, 2004 by President Chandrika Bandaranaike Kumaratunga. Elections were held on April 04 and the new Parliament convened on April 23 and elected Mahinda Rajapaksa as the Prime Minister. Mr Mahinda Rajapakse was elected to the post of President on November 17, 2005. The cabinet appointed by him was comical, with over one hundred members of parliament receiving ministerial portfolios. Many of the public were amused by the fact that there were now four Ministers for Nation Building. In particular because the ministers themselves seemed puzzled by what this broad potfolio involved. Mr G.Rajapakse(The Presidents brother) was appointed Minister of Defense. The Labour Minister, Mr Mervin De Silva resigned in 2007 following reports that he assaulted several journalists. He is also reputed to associate with drug dealers.

POLITICAL PARTIES AND ELECTIONS

In August 2005, the Supreme Court ruled that Presidential Elections would be held in November 2005, resolving a long-running dispute on the length of President Kumaratunga's term. Mahinda Rajapaksa was nominated the SLFP candidate and former Prime Minister Ranil Wickremesinghe UNP candidate. The Election was held on November 17, 2005, and Mahinda Rajapaksa was elected the fifth Executive President of Sri Lanka with a 50.29% of valid votes, compared to Ranil Wickremesinghe's 48.43%. Mahinda Rajapaksa took oath as President on November 19, 2005. Ratnasiri Wickremanayake was appointed the 22nd Prime Minister on November 21, 2005, to fill the post vacated by Mahinda Rajapaksa. He was previously Prime Minister in 2000.

ADMINISTRATIVE DIVISIONS

Local government is divided into two parallel structures, the civil service, which dates to colonial times, and the provincial councils, which were established in 1987.

Civil Service Structure

The country is divided into 25 districts, each of which has a district secretary (the GA, or Government Agent) who is appointed. Each district comprises 5-16 divisions, each with a DS, or divisional secretary, again, appointed. At a village level Grama Niladari (Village Officers), Samurdhi Niladari (Development Officers) and agriculture extension officers work for the DSs.

Provincial Council Structure

Under the Indo-Sri Lankan Accord of July 1987—and the resulting 13th amendment to the constitution—the Government of Sri Lanka agreed to devolve some authority to the provinces. Provincial councils are directly elected for 5-year terms. The leader of the council majority serves as the province's Chief Minister with a board of ministers; a provincial governor is appointed by the president.

The Provincial Councils have full statute making power with respect to the Provincial Council List, and shared statute making power respect to the Concurrent List. While all matters set out in the Reserved List are under the central government.

Local Government structure

Below the provincial level are elected Municipal Councils and Urban Councils, responsible for municialities and cities respectively, and below this level Pradeshiya Sabhas (village councils), again elected. There are: 18 Municipal Councils: Sri Jayawardanapura Kotte, Colombo, Kandy, Jaffna, Galle, Matara, Dehiwala-Mount Lavinia, Anuradhapura, Gampaha, Moratuwa, Ratnapura, Kurunegala, Nuwara Eliya, Badulla, Batticaloa, Kalmune, Negombo. 42 Urban Councils: 270 Pradeshiya Sabhas: (The above statistics include the new local government authorities established by the government in January 2006.)

JUDICIAL BRANCH

Sri Lanka's judiciary consists of a Supreme Court, Court of Appeal, High Court, and a number of subordinate courts. Sri Lanka's legal system reflects diverse cultural influences. Criminal law is fundamentally British. Basic civil law is Roman-Dutch, but laws pertaining to marriage, divorce, and inheritance are communal, known as respectively as Kandyan, *Thesavalamai* (Jaffna Tamil) and Muslim (Roman-Dutch law applies to Low-country Sinhalese, Estate Tamils and others).

TAMIL CONFLICT

Rajapaksa offers less autonomy than Wickremasinghe to the northeast, home to most of Sri Lanka's 3.2 million ethnic Tamils. His narrow victory was accused of being engineered by the Liberation Tigers of Tamil Eelam (LTTE) who want Tamil Eelam to be an independent country. The LTTE boycotted the election, thereby preventing thousands of Tamils from voting, and so Wickremasinghe, whose election promises included a Federal state to the North and East, from taking power.

ECONOMY OF SRI LANKA

With an economy of $27.4 billion ($95.5 billion PPP estimate), and a per capita GDP of about $4,700 (PPP), Sri Lanka has mostly enjoyed strong growth rates in recent years.

The main economic sectors of the country are tourism, tea export, apparel, textile, rice production and other agricultural products. In addition to these economic sectors overseas employment contributes highly in foreign exchange, most of them from middle-east.

After getting political independence from British colonialism in February 1948, the economy of the country has been affected by Tsunami and couple of insurrections such as 1971, 1987-89 and ongoing civil war. The parties which ruled the country after 1948 does not implement any national plan or policy on economy, then time to time it was effected with left and right wing economic practices. The government during 1970-77 period applied pro-left economic policies and practices then after 1977 to 1994 UNP rule and 1994-2004 SLFP rule applied pro-right policies. After 2004 the UPFA government is highly concentrating on mass production of domestic consumption such as rice, grain and other agricultural products.

Sri Lanka began to shift away from a socialist orientation in 1977. Since then, the government has been deregulating, privatizing, and opening the economy to international competition. Twenty years of civil war has no doubt slowed economic growth, diversification and liberalization, and the leftist Janatha Vimukthi Peramuna (JVP) uprisings, especially the second in the late 1980s, also caused extensive upheavals.

Following the quelling of the JVP, increased privatization, reform, and a stress on export-oriented growth helped revive the economy's performance, taking GDP growth to 7% in 1993. Economic growth has been uneven in the ensuing years as the economy faced a multitude of global and domestic economic and political challenges. Overall, average annual GDP growth was 5.2% over 1991-2000. In 2001, however, GDP growth was negative 1.4%—the first contraction since independence. The economy was hit by a series of global and domestic economic problems and affected by terrorist attacks in Sri Lanka and the United States. The crises exposed the fundamental policy failures and structural imbalances in the economy and the need for bold reforms. The year ended in parliamentary elections in December, which saw the election of a more pro-capitalism party to Parliament (while the socialist leaning Sri Lanka Freedom Party retained the Presidency).

The government of Prime Minister Ranil Wickremasinghe of the United National Party has indicated a strong commitment to economic and social sector reforms, deregulation, and private sector development. In 2002, Sri Lanka commenced a gradual recovery. Early signs of a peace dividend were visible throughout the economy—Sri Lanka has been able to reduce defense expenditures and begin to focus on getting its large, public sector debt under control. In addition, the economy has benefited from lower interest rates, a recovery in domestic demand, increased tourist arrivals, a revival of the stock exchange, and increased foreign direct investment (FDI). In 2002, economic growth bounced up to 4%, helped by strong service sector growth. Agriculture staged a partial recovery. At present Agriculture in Sri Lanka needs keen attention as it directed towards disastorus situation. Industrial sector growth, however, faltered for the second consecutive year due to weak demand and lower prices for Sri Lanka's exports. The government was able to exert fiscal control, and inflation trended down. Total FDI inflows during 2002 were about $246 million and are expected to exceed $300 million in 2003.

The largest share of FDI has been in the services sector. Good progress was made under the Stand By Arrangement, which was resumed by the International Monetary Fund (IMF). These measures, together with peaceful conditions in the country, have helped restore investor confidence and created conditions for the government to embark on extensive economic and fiscal reforms and seek donor support for a poverty reduction and growth strategy. However, the resumption of the civil-war in 2005 led to a steep increase defence expenditures. The increased violence and lawlessness also prompted some donor countries to cut back on aid to the country. Sri Lanka has also accumulated a 9.2 % deficit and the central bank has not intervened since late 2006 to print more currency. A sharp rise in world petroleum prices combined with fallout from the civil war has led to inflation hitting 20%.

CURRENCY

Sri Lanka had switched to a floating currency after a worsening currency crisis due to sterilized intervention in January 2001. Foreign reserves had been exhausted defending the rupee from free fall during the 1990s. By 2004, sterilized intervention was resumed to prevent further depreciation of the rupee and was eased off in 2005 after a rush of foreign aid due to the tsunami. By 2006, sterilized intervention was restarted as the rupee lost further ground. The IMF categorizes the Sri Lankan rupee as a managed float. By 2006, the rupee depreciated by 5 % and depreciated a further 4.2 % within the first half of 2007. This has been due to flight of capital out of the country because of rising uncertainty and resumption of the longstanding civil war. The rupee has been under pressure due to widening trade and budget deficit, increased cost of living, cost of fuel imports and rising inflation. The rising uncertainty has given rise to a thriving black market for trading between dollars and rupees. Official trading through the central bank has been problematic for many traders, coming under increasing moral persuasion to avoid selling rupees for the sake of national interests.

LABOUR

More than 20% of the 6.1 million-strong labor force, excluding the north and east, is unionized. Trade union membership is on the decline. There are more than 1,650 registered trade unions, many of which have 50 or fewer members, and 19 federations. Many unions have political affiliations. The Ceylon Workers Congress (CWC) and Lanka Jathika estate workers union are the two largest unions representing workers in the heavily unionized plantation sector. The president of the CWC also is Minister of Livestock Development and Estate Infrastructure.

The CWC's agenda includes political issues, such as citizenship status for stateless Indian Tamils. Some of the stronger and more influential trade unions include the Ceylon Mercantile Union, Sri Lanka Nidhahas Sevaka Sangamaya, Jathika Sevaka Sangayama, Ceylon Federation of Trade Unions, Ceylon Bank Employees Union, Union of Post and Telecommunication Officers, Conference of Public Sector Independent Trade Unions, and the JVP-aligned Inter-Company Trade Union. The unemployment rate has declined in recent years and hovers at 10%. The rate of unemployment among high school and college graduates, however, remains proportionally higher than the rate for less-educated workers. The government has embarked on educational reforms it hopes will lead to better preparation of students and fewer mismatches between graduates and jobs. In addition, it also has begun a youth corps program to provide employment skills to the unemployed.

FINANCIAL INSTITUTIONS

The **Central Bank of Sri Lanka** is the monetary authority of Sri Lanka was established in 1950. The Central Bank is responsible for the conduct of monetary policy in the country and also has the supervisory powers over the financial system.

The **Colombo Stock Exchange** (CSE) is the main stock exchange in Sri Lanka. It is one of the most modern exchanges in South Asia, providing a fully automated trading platform. The vision of the CSE is to contribute to the wealth of the nation by creating value through securities. The headquarters of the CSE have been located at the World Trade Center Towers in Colombo since 1995 and it also has branches across the country in Kandy, Matara,Kurunegala and Negombo.

Transportation and roads

Most Sri Lankan cities and towns are connected by the Sri Lanka Railways, the state-run national railway operator. The Ceylon Transport Board is the state-run agency responsible for operating public bus services across the island.

The total length of Sri Lankan roads exceeds 11,000 kilometres (6,840 mi), with a vast majority of them being paved. The government has launched several highway projects to bolster the economy and national transport system, including the Colombo-Katunayake Expressway, the Colombo-Kandy (Kadugannawa) Expressway, the Colombo-Padeniya Expressway and the Outer Circular Highway to ease Colombo's traffic congestion.

Energy

The production of electricity in the country mostly done by the hydro power stations situated in central highlands.

ECONOMIC SECTORS

Tea industry

The **tea industry** is one of the main foreign exchange gaining industry in Sri Lanka also became the world's leading exporter in 1995 shared 23% of the total export higher than Kenya shared 22%. The central highlands of the country, low temperature climate through out the year, annual rainfall and the level of humidity are more favorable geographical factors for production in high quality tea. The industry was introduced to the country in 1867 by James Taylor, the British planter who arrived in 1852.

Recently, Sri Lanka has become one of the countries exporting fair trade tea to the UK and other countries. It is reckoned that such projects could reduce rural poverty.

Tourism

Tourism is one of the main foreign exchange gaining industry in Sri Lanka. There are major tourist attractions are focused around the islands famous beaches located in the southern and eastern parts of the country, also ancient World Heritage Sites located in the interior of the country and thr lush green resorts located in the mountainous regions attracts tourism.

Apparel and textile industry

The apparel industry of the country which producing high quality ready made garments and the main exporters are USA and Europe. There are about 900 factories throughout country serves world's leading fashion designing companies like Victoria's Secret, Liz Claiborne and Tommy Hilfiger.

Agriculture

The agricultural sector of the country which producing domestic consumption such as rice, coconut and grain also a part of the culture since 2500 years. The tea industry which existing since 1867 is not a part of this sector of agriculture, it is mainly focusing on export market rather than domestic use in the country.

GLOBAL ECONOMIC RELATIONS

Exports to the United States, Sri Lanka's most important market, were valued at $1.8 billion in 2002, or 38% of total exports. For many years, the United States has been Sri Lanka's biggest market for garments, taking more than 63% of the country's total garment exports. India is Sri Lanka's largest supplier, with exports of $835 million in 2002. Japan, traditionally Sri Lanka's largest supplier, was its fourth-largest in 2002 with exports of $355 million. Other leading suppliers include Hong Kong, Singapore, Taiwan, and South Korea. The United States is the 10th-largest supplier to Sri Lanka; U.S. exports amounted to $218 million in 2002, according to Central Bank trade data—U.S. Customs data places U.S. exports to Sri Lanka at $166 million in 2002. Wheat accounted for 14% of U.S. exports to Sri Lanka in 2002, down from the previous year.

CREDIT RATING AND COMMERCIAL BORROWING

Sri Lanka had applied for credit ratings from international agencies in its efforts to apply for loans from international markets in 2005 after the election of Mahinda Rajapakse as president. Standard and Poor's has rated Sri Lanka a "B+" speculative ("junk") rating, four grades below investment grade. Fitch has rated Sri Lanka with "BB-" which is three grades below investment grade. Standard and Poor's maintains Sri Lanka is constrained by providing widespread subsidies, a bloated public sector, transfers to loss-making state enterprises, and high interest local and international burdens. Standard and Poor's estimates public sector debt has reached 95 % of GDP, in comparison to CIA estimates of 89 % of GDP. Sri Lanka in mid-2007 sought to borrow $500 million from international markets to shore up the deteriorating exchange rate and reduce pressure on repayment of the domestic debt market. The head of the opposition UNP, Ranil Wickremasinghe has warned that such intense borrowing is unsustainable and will not repay these loans once elected to power.

FOREIGN ASSISTANCE

Sri Lanka is highly dependent on foreign assistance, and several high-profile assistance projects were launched in 2003. The most significant of these resulted from an aid conference in Tokyo in June 2003; pledges at the summit, which included representatives from the IMF, World Bank, Asian Development Bank, Japan, the European Union and the United States totaled $4.5 billion.

DEMOGRAPHY OF SRI LANKA

Sri Lanka is an island in the Indian Ocean about 28 kilometers (18 mi.) off the southeastern coast of India with a population of about 20 million. Density is highest in the southwest where Colombo, the country's main port and industrial center, is located. The net population growth is about 0,7%. Sri Lanka is ethnically, linguistically, and religiously diverse.

PEOPLE

Sinhalese make up 73.8% of the population and are concentrated in the densely populated southwest. Sri Lanka Tamils, citizens whose ancestors have lived on the island for centuries, total about 18% and live predominantly in the north and east. However accurate census figures with regards the Sri Lankan Tamil community have been difficult to quantify, given that large areas of northern Sri Lanka are under rebel control and that large numbers of tamils have fled abroad.

Indian Tamils are a distinct ethnic group and comprise 5.1% of the population. The British brought them to Sri Lanka in the 19th century as tea and rubber plantation workers, and they remain concentrated in the "tea country" of south-central Sri Lanka. In accordance with a 1964 agreement with India, Sri Lanka granted citizenship to 230,000 "stateless" Indian Tamils in 1988. Under the pact, India granted citizenship to the remainder, some 200,000 of whom now live in India. Another 75,000 Indian Tamils, who themselves or whose parents once applied for Indian citizenship, now wish to remain in Sri Lanka. The government has stated these Tamils will not be forced to return to India, although they are not technically citizens of Sri Lanka.

Other minorities include Muslims (both Moors, who are descendants of Arabs; and Malays from South East Asia), at about 8.3% of the population; Burghers, who are descendants of European colonists, principally from Portugal, the Netherlands and the UK; and aboriginal Veddahs.

RELIGION

Most Sinhalese are Buddhist; most Tamils are Hindu. The Malays and Moors are Muslim. Sizable minorities of both Sinhalese and Tamils are Christians, most of whom are Roman Catholic. The Burgher population is mostly Roman Catholic or Presbyterian.

The Veddahs have Animist and Buddhist practices. The 1978 constitution, while assuring freedom of religion, grants primacy to Buddhism.

LANGUAGES

Sinhala, an Indo-European language, is the native tongue of the Sinhalese. Tamils speak Tamil, a Dravidian language. The Moors speak an Arab-Tamil dialect, consisting of a large number of Arabic words while The Malays speak Sri Lankan Creole Malay. Many of the Burghers speak Sri Lankan Indo-Portuguese although its use has declined and all speak Sinhala. The Veddahs speak a language closely related to Sinhala. Use of English has declined since independence, but it continues to be spoken by many in the middle and upper middle classes, particularly in Colombo. The government is seeking to reverse the decline in the use of English, mainly for economic but also for political reasons. Both Sinhala and Tamil are official languages.

SRI LANKAN CULTURE

The culture of Sri Lanka has been influenced by many things in the past. Mostly it has been influenced by religion and colonialization by the Dutch, the Portuguese and the British.

NEW YEAR

The Sinhalese new year (Sinhala and Tamil new year) is a very important cultural practise in the island, the festival which falls in April (the month of Bak) when the sun moves from the Meena Rashiya (House of Pisces) to the Mesha Rashiya (House of Aries) Sri Lankans begin celebrating their National New Year Aluth Avurudhu in Sinhala and Puththandu in Tamil. However, unlike the usual practice where the new year begins at midnight, the National New Year begins at the time determined by the astrologers. Not only the beginning of the new year but the conclusion of the old year is also specified by the astrologers. And unlike the customary ending and beginning of new year, there is a period of a few hours in between the conclusion of the Old Year and the commencement of the New Year, which is called the "nona gathe" (neutral period). During this time one is expected to keep off and take a break from all types of work and engage solely in relaxing religious activities and traditional games. Many children and adults wear traditional outfits not in fashion.

GLOBALIZATION

Throughout the past centuries Sri Lanka has been going through a dramatic make over. A vast majority of the Sri Lankan community were only influenced by their own traditional food and nothing more. But, due to economical growth and intense competition in developed countries, companies have taken themselves overseas to developing nations, in an attempt to achieve a positive global presence (competitive advantage). Consequently, this method has caused a major ripple effect in countries like Sri Lanka like never before. Currently in some of the major cities in Sri Lanka you should prepare yourself to be dazzled (some may say loss of identity) by the assimilation/influence of western culture into Sri Lankan community. You can now find the presence of American taste represented by McDonalds, Pizza Hut and Kentucky Fried Chicken, Dominos Pizza and so on.

Sri Lanka's cuisine mainly consists of boiled or steamed rice served with curry. Another well-known rice dish is Kiribath, meaning "milk rice." Curries in Sri Lanka are not just limited to meat- or fish-based dishes, there are also vegetable and even fruit curries. A typical Sri Lankan meal consists of a "main curry" (fish, chicken, or mutton), as well as several other curries made with vegetable and lentils. Side-dishes include pickles, chutneys and "sambols" which can sometimes be fiery hot. The most famous of these is the coconut sambol, made of ground coconut mixed with chillies, dried Maldive fish and lime juice. This is ground to a paste and eaten with rice, as it gives zest to the meal and is believed to increase appetite.

In addition to sambols, Sri Lankans eat "mallung", chopped leaves mixed with grated coconut and red onions. Coconut milk is found in most Sri Lankan dishes to give the cuisine its unique flavor.

Sri Lanka has long been renowned for its spices. In the 15th and 16th centuries, traders from all over the world who came to Sri Lanka brought their native cuisines to the island, resulting in a rich diversity of cooking styles and techniques. Lamprais—rice boiled in stock with a special curry, accompanied by "frikkadels" (meatballs), all of which is then wrapped in a banana leaf and baked—is a Dutch-influenced Sri Lankan dish. Dutch and Portuguese sweets also continue to be popular. British influences include roast beef and roast chicken.

Sri Lankans use spices liberally in their dishes and typically do not follow an exact recipe: thus, every cook's curry will taste slightly different. Furthermore, people from different regions of the island (for instance, hill-country dwellers versus coastal dwellers) traditionally cook in different ways. Sri Lankan cuisine is known to be among the world's spiciest, due to the high use of different varieties chillies referred to as amu miris, kochchi miris, and maalu miris (capsicum) among others. It is generally accepted for tourists to request that the food is cooked with a lower chillie content to cater for the more sensitive Western pallette. Food cooked for public occasions typically uses less chillie than food cooked in the home, the latter where the food is cooked with the chillie content preferable to the occupants.

RELIGION IN SRI LANKA

Sri Lanka's culture also revolves around religion. The Buddhist community of Sri Lanka observe Poya Days, which are also important days of prayers to the Hindus, once per month according to the Lunar calendar. The Hindus and Muslims also observe their own holidays. Sri Lankans are very religious because the history of the island has been involved with religion numerous times. There are many Buddhist temples in Sri Lanka and many mosques, Hindu temples and churches all across the island. The religious preference of an area could be determined by the number of religious institutions in the area. The North and the East of the island has many mosques and Hindu temples because a large Tamil and Muslim population resides in those areas. Many churches could be found along the southern coast line because many living in those areas are Roman Catholic or Christian. The interior of the island is mostly the Buddhist population and there are many Buddhists residing in all parts of the island because they are the largest religious group in Sri Lanka.

Sri Lanka has a multi ethnic and multi religious population. Buddhism constitutes the religious faith of about 70% of the population of the island, most of whom follow the Theravada school of Buddhism. According to traditional Sri Lankan chronicles, Buddhism was introduced into Sri Lanka in the 2nd century BCE by Venerable Mahinda, the son of the Emperor Ashoka, during the reign of Sri Lanka's King Devanampiyatissa. During this time, a sapling of the Bodhi Tree under which the Buddha attained enlightenment was brought to Sri Lanka and the first monasteries were established under the sponsorship of the Sri Lankan king. The Pali Canon (*Thripitakaya*), having previously been preserved as an oral tradition, was first committed to writing in Sri Lanka around 30 BC.

Sri Lanka has the longest continuous history of Buddhism of any Buddhist nation, with the Sangha having existed in a largely unbroken lineage since its introduction in the 2nd century BCE. During periods of decline, the Sri Lankan monastic lineage was revived through contact with Thailand and Burma. Periods of Mahayana influence, as well as official neglect under colonial rule, created great challenges for Theravada Buddhist institutions in Sri Lanka, but repeated revivals and resurgences — most recently in the 19th century — have kept the Theravada tradition alive for over 2000 years.

The second largest religion is Hinduism. Hinduism was primarily established in Sri Lanka by migrants and often invaders from southern India, and Hindus now constitute seven to fifteen percent of the population, mostly of the Shaivite school. Followers of Islam comprise approximately eight percent of the population, having been brought to the island by Arab traders over the course of many centuries European colonists introduced Christianity to the country in the 16th century, and the religion has been adopted by around six percent of the population. There also was a small population of Zoroastrian immigrants from India (Parsis) who settled in Ceylon during the period of British rule. As a result of emigration, few remain, yet they have played a significant role in the growth of the country. The former finance minister of Sri Lanka, Nariman Choksy, was a Parsi. Other famous Parsi families in Sri Lanka include the Captain family and the Pestongee family.

Religion plays an important part in the life and culture of Sri Lankans. The Buddhist majority observe Poya Days, once per month according to the Lunar calendar. The Hindus and Muslims also observe their own holidays. There are many Buddhist temples in Sri Lanka and many mosques, Hindu temples and churches across the island, especially in areas where respective communities are concentrated. Buddhists are distributed across most parts of the island except in the north. Hindus are concentrated in north, east, and central high lands. Christians, particularly Roman Catholics are mainly concentrated along the western coastal belt. Muslims are concentrated in several pockets along the coast and in interior. All religious communities are represented in western province and in other urban centers in sizable numbers.

SPORTS CULTURE IN SRI LANKA

Sports play a very big part in Sri Lankan culture. Sri Lanka's main sport is Volley Ball. But after the age of Englishmens Cricket being the popular sport event in Sri Lanka. Every child in Sri Lanka knows how to play cricket, and there are many cricket fields scattered across the island for children and adults to play the sport. The biggest pastime of the Sri Lankan population, after cricket, is watching the Sri Lankan National Team playing cricket. It is common for businesses to shut down when very big matches are televised. This was the case in 1996 when the Sri Lankan team beat Australia in the finals to win the Cricket World Cup. The whole country shut down as though there were a curfew imposed upon the whole island.

MUSIC OF SRI LANKA

The two single biggest influences on Sri Lankan music are from Buddhism and Portuguese colonizers. Buddhism arrived in Sri Lanka after the Buddha's visit in 300 BC, while the Portuguese arrived in the 15th century, bringing with them cantiga ballads, ukuleles and guitars, along with African slaves, who further diversified the musical roots of the island. These slaves were called kaffrinha, and their dance music was called baila. Traditional Sri Lankan music includes the hypnotic Kandyan drums - drumming was and is very much a part and parcel of music in both Buddhist and Hindu temples in Sri Lanka.

TEA CULTURE IN SRI LANKA

Being one of the largest producers of tea in the world, Sri Lankans drink a lot of tea. Many Sri Lankans drink at least three cups a day. Sri Lanka is also one of the best tea producing countries in the World and the Royal Family of the United Kingdom has been known to drink Ceylon tea. Tea is served whenever a guest comes to a house, it is served at festivals and gatherings. It is served almost anywhere in Sri Lanka.

SRI LANKAN CUISINE

The cuisine of Sri Lanka draws influence from that of India, as well as colonists and foreign traders. Rice, which is usually consumed daily, can be found at any special occasion, while spicy curries are favourite dishes for dinner and lunch. A very popular alcoholic drink is toddy, made from palm tree sap. Rice and curry refers to a range of Sri Lankan dishes. Sri Lankans also eat Hoppers which can be found anywhere in Sri Lanka.

Many Sri Lankans eat short eats as a snack which is a variety of hamburgers, hot dogs, Chinese rolls, patties and pastries. Also, Sri Lankan Chicken Waffles are popular.

It also should be noted that much of Sri Lanka's urban areas now are filled with many American fast food corporations, such as McDonald's. Although many, especially elders and those who stubbornly stick to their cultural cuisine, reject this, many of the younger generation have started to take a liking to this new American cuisine.

Chapter 4

Bangladesh

Bangladesh, officially the People's Republic of Bangladesh is a country in South Asia. It is bordered by India on all sides except for a small border with Burma to the far southeast and by the Bay of Bengal to the south. Together with the Indian state of West Bengal, it makes up the ethno-linguistic region of Bengal. The name *Bangladesh* means "Country of Bengal" in the official Bengali language.

The borders of present-day Bangladesh were established with the partition of Bengal and India in 1947, when the region became the eastern wing of the newly-formed Pakistan. However, it was separated from the western wing by 1,600 kilometres (1,000 mi) across India. Political and linguistic discrimination as well as economic neglect led to popular agitations against West Pakistan, which led to the war for independence in 1971 and the establishment of Bangladesh. However, the new state had to endure famines, natural disasters and widespread poverty, as well as political turmoil and military coups. The restoration of democracy in 1991 has been followed by relative stability and economic progress.

Bangladesh is among the most densely populated countries in the world and has a high poverty rate. Geographically the country straddles the fertile Ganges-Brahmaputra Delta and is subject to annual monsoon floods and cyclones. The government is a parliamentary democracy; however, political rule has been suspended under emergency law since 11 January 2007. Bangladesh is a member of the Commonwealth of Nations, SAARC, BIMSTEC, the OIC, and the D-8. As the World Bank notes in its July 2005 Country Brief, the country has made significant progress in human development in the areas of literacy, gender parity in schooling and reduction of population growth.

HISTORY OF BANGLADESH

Bangladesh became one of the last major nation states following its secession in 1971 from the nation of Pakistan, which achieved its independence from the British Empire alongwith India in (1947). The region's history combines Indo-Aryan, Austro-Asiatic, Dravidian, Mughal, Arab, Persian, Turkic and British influences. Bangladesh today including its surrounding territories (present day Indian states of West Bengal, Orissa, Bihar, Meghalya, Assam and Tripura)territory historically was known as Bengal, was part of the Mughal Empire for more than five centuries and then the Bengal Presidency and finally the British Empire. A.K. Fazlul Haque, Huseyn Shaheed Suhrawardy, Abdul Hamid Khan Bhasani and finally Sheikh Mujibur Rahman struggled to lead the Bengali nation to independence in 1971. Since independence, successive following governments have led to define Bangladesh's democracy to this day.

ANCIENT PERIOD

The Alpine civilization

Remnants of civilization in the greater Bengal region date back three millennia. The civilization that flourished in this region before the Aryan conquest was the Alpine civilization. The Alpines (Eastern Bracycephalic) from Taklamakan Desert in Central Asia settled in eastern India (Bengal, Orissa and the plains of Assam) and formed the main elements of today's Bengali people. The Alpines were divided into various indigenous tribes: Vanga (south Bengal), Pundra (north Bengal), and Rarh/Suhma (West Bengal) according to their respective Totems.

Not much is known about this civilization. Some deprecatory references indicate that the primitive people in Bengal were different in ethnicity and culture from the Vedic beyond the boundary of Aryandom and who were classed as 'Dasyus'. The Bhagavata Purana classes them as sinful people while Dharmasutra of Bodhayana prescribes expiatory rites after a journey among the Pundras and Vangas. However, the Alpines successfully resisted the Vedic Aryan invaders for about a millennium. It was only in the 4th century BCE when Aryanism started to flow into this region with the Mauryan conquest.

Overseas colonization

According to Mahavamsa, Vijaya Singha, a Vanga prince, conquered Lanka (modern day Sri Lanka) in 544 BC and gave the name "Sinhala" to the country. Bengali people also colonized Laat (Gujarat), Madras and the Indonesian archipelago. The Chera, Tamil, Andhra and Karnataka people are also said to be connected with the Bengalis.

A few Naga worshipping peoples — Marana, Chera, Pangalathirayar — migrated from Bengal to South India and established their own kingdoms there. Lac Long Quan, a Naga warrior migrated from *bôn-lang*(Bengal) to Anam (Vietnam) conquered the land (7th century BCE) and renamed it according to the name of his motherland (bon-lang). The kings of Lac Long's line were known as *bôns* (Bongs) and they ruled Anam up to the 3rd century BCE.

Gangaridai Empire

In 326 BCE, with the invasion of Alexander the Great the region again came to prominence. The Greek and Latin historians suggested that Alexander the Great withdrew from India anticipating the valiant counter attack of the mighty Gangaridai and Prasioi empires that were located in the Bengal region. Alexander, after the meeting with his officer, Coenus, was convinced that it was better to return. Diodorus Siculus mentions Gangaridai to be the largest and the most powerful empire in India whose king possessed an army of 20,000 horses, 200,000 infantry, 2,000 chariots and 4,000 elephants trained and equipped for war. The allied forces of Gangaridai and Prasii (Nanda Empire) were preparing a massive counter attack against the forces of Alexander on the banks of Ganges. Gangaridai according to the Greek accounts kept on flourishing at least up to the 1st century AD.

Early Middle Ages

The pre-Gupta period of Bengal is shrouded with obscurity. Before the conquest of Samudragupta Bengal was divided into two kingdoms: Pushkarana and Samatata. Chandragupta II had to defeat a confederacy of Vanga kings. Bengal became a part of the Gupta Empire. However, the Mrigashikhaban Stupa of Varendra is a strong proof that the Guptas themselves had originated from Bengal. This implies that the Guptas were Bengali and the Gupta Empire was in fact a Bengali empire. Even today the origin of the Guptas is still hotly debated.

Gupta Empire

Maharaja Sri-Gupta the founder of the dynasty probably ruled a portion of Northern or Central Bengal. Later, the Guptas extended their dominion as far as Magadha, Prayaga, and Saket (Ayodhya). Samudragupta and Chandragupta II were two celibrated kings of the empire. The Gupta Age is often considered as the Golden Age of India by modern historians. The Gupta Empire, already weakened by the Hephthalite invasions, was finally brought to an end by Yasodharman of Malwa. Factions of the Gupta dynasty, however, survived in Bengal where they later formed the Gauda Kingdom.

Gauda Kingdom

By the sixth century, the Gupta Empire ruling over the northern Indian subcontinent was largely broken up. Eastern Bengal became the Vanga Kingdom while the Gauda kings rose in the west with their capital at Karnasuvarna (Murshidabad). The first two kings of an independent Gauda kingdom, Kumargupta and Damodargupta, consolidated their power in Gaur and Magadha. Mahasengupta the greatest king of this dynasty expanded his kingdom to the Brahmaputra valley in Assam and to Malava in Central India. Shashanka, the successor of Mahasengupta, unified the smaller principalities of Bengal (Gaur, Vanga, Samatata) and vied for regional power with Harshavardhana in northern India. But this burst of Bengali power did not last beyond his death, as Bengal descended afterwards into a period marked by disunity and foreign invasion.

The Pala Empire

The first independent Buddhist king of Bengal, Gopala I, came to power in 750 in Gaur. Gopala founded the Buddhist Pala dynasty which lasted for four centuries (750-1120 AD), ushering in a period of relative stability and prosperity.

At its peak, under Dharmapala, the empire extended into much of Bihar and once more wrestled for control of the subcontinent. He conquered Bhoja (Berar), Matsya (Jaipur), Madra (Central Punjab), Kuru (Thaneswar), Yadu (Mathura and Dwaraka), Avanti (Malwa), Yavana (Muslims of Sindh/Multan), Gandhara (Kabol valley), Kambojja (Northern Bengal ruled by Barman kings — later after the fall of Kambojja, another Kambojja was born: Cambodia, ruled by Barmans) and Kira (Kangra).

Devapala the Great, successor of Dharmapala, expanded his empire farther up to Assam and Utkala in the east, Kamboja in the north-west and Deccan in the south. He exterminated the Utkalas, conquered the Pragjyotisha (Assam), shattered the pride of the Huna, and humbled the lords of Gurjara, Pratiharas and the Dravidas.

The Pala Empire can be considered as the "Roman Empire of Bengal". Never had the Bengali people reached such height of power and glory and never had they influenced the outside world to that extent. Palas were responsible for the introduction of Mahayana Buddhism in Tibet, Bhutan and Myanmar. The pre-dominant Pala sculptures and the proto-Bangla scripts of the Sailendra Empire (Malaya, Java, Sumatra) of the late 8th century attest that the Sailendra dynasty originated from Bengal.

The death of Devapala ended the period of ascendancy of the Pala Empire and several independent dynasties and kingdoms emerged during this time, including the Khadgas, Devas, the Chandras, and Varmanas.

Mahipala I rejuveneted the reign of the Palas. He recovered north Bengal from the Kambojas and survived the invasions of Rajendra Chola and the Chalukyas. Mahipala I did not join the Hindu confederacy against Mahmud of Ghazni.

After Mahipala I the Pala dynasty again saw its decline until Ramapala, the last great ruler of the dynasty, managed to retrieve the position of the dynasty to some extent. He crushed the Varendra rebellion and extended his empire farther to Kamarupa, Orissa and Northern India.

The Palas were followed by the Sena dynasty who brought the East and West Bengal under one ruler only during the twelfth century. The Sena dynasty brought a revival of Hinduism and cultivated Sanskrit literature.

LATE MIDDLE AGES - ARRIVAL OF ISLAM

Islam made its first appearance in Bengal during the twelfth century AD when Sufi missionaries arrived. Later occasional Muslim invaders reinforced the process of conversion by building mosques, madrassas and Sufi Khanqahs. Beginning in 1202 a military commander from the Delhi Sultanate, Ikhtiar Uddin Muhammad bin Bakhtiar Khilji, overran Bihar and Bengal as far east as Rangpur, Bogra and the Brahmaputra River. The defeated Laksman Sen and his two sons moved to a place then called Vikramapur (south of Dhaka), where their diminished dominion lasted until the late thirteenth century.

Turkic dynasties

The period after Bakhtiar Khilji's death in 1206 devolved into infighting among the Khiljis - representative of a pattern of succession struggles and intra-empire intrigues during later Turkish regimes. Ghiyasuddin Iwaz Khalji prevailed and extended the Sultan's domain south to Jessore and made the eastern Bang province a tributary. The capital was made at Lakhnauti on the Ganges near the older Bengal capital of Gaur. He managed to make Kamarupa, Orissa and Trihut pay tribute to him. But he was later defeated by Shams-ud-Din Iltutmish.

The weak successors of Iltutmish encouraged the local governors to declare independence. Bengal was sufficiently remote from Delhi that its governors would declare independence on occasion, styling themselves as Sultans of Bengal. It was during this time that Bengal earned the name "Bulgakpur" (land of the rebels). Tughral Togun Khan added Oudh and Bihar to Bengal. Mughisuddin Yuzbak also conquered Bihar and Oudh from Delhi but was killed during an unsuccessful expedition in Assam.

Two Turkish attempts to push east of the broad Jamuna and Brahmaputra rivers were repulsed, but a third led by Mughisuddin Tughral conquered the Sonargaon area south of Dhaka to Faridpur, bringing the Sen Kingdom officially to an end by 1277. Mughisuddin Tughral repulsed two massive attacks of the sultanate of Delhi before finally being defeated and killed by Ghiyas ud din Balban.

Ilyas Shahi dynasty

Ilyas Shah founded an independent dynasty that lasted from 1342-1487 which successfully repulsed attempts by Delhi to rein them in. They continued to reel in the territory of modern-day Bengal, reaching to Khulna in the south and Sylhet in the east. The sultans advanced civic institutions and became more responsive and "native" in their outlook, cut loose from Delhi. Considerable architectural projects were completed in Gaur including the massive Adina Mosque and the 1479 Darasbari Mosque which still stands in Bangladesh near the border. The Sultans of Bangalah were patrons of Bengali literature and began a process in which a common Bengali culture and identity would coalesce.

The Ilyas Shahi Dynasty was interrupted by an uprising of the Hindus under Ganesh. However the Ilyas Shahi dynasty was restored by Nasiruddin Mahmud Shah, which was finally overthrown by the Habshi (Abyssinian) slaves of the sultanate.

Hussain Shahi dynasty

The Habshi rule gave way to the Hussain Shahi dynasty that ruled from 1494-1538. Alauddin Hussain Shah, considered as the greatest of all the sultans of Bengal for the cultural renaissance during his reign, conquered Kamarupa, Kamata, Jajnagar, Orissa and extended the sultanate all the way to the port of Chittagong, which witnessed the arrival of the first Portuguese merchants.

Nasiruddin Nusrat Shah gave refuge to the Afghan lords during the invasion of Babur though he remained neutral. However Nusrat Shah made a treaty with Babur and saved Bengal from a Mughal invasion.

The last Sultan of the dynasty, who continued to rule from Gaur, had to contend with rising Afghan activity on his northwestern border. Eventually, the Afghans broke through and sacked the capital in 1538 where they remained for several decades until the arrival of the Mughals.

Afghan rule

Sher Shah Suri established the Sur dynasty in Bengal. After the battle of Chausa he declared himself independent Sultan of Bengal and Bihar. Sher Shah was the only Muslim Sultan of Bengal to establish an empire in northern India. The Afghan rule in Bengal remained for 44 years. Their most impressive achievement was Sher Shah's construction of the Grand Trunk Road connecting Sonargaon, Delhi and Peshawar.

The Sur dynasty was followed by the Karrani dynasty. Sulaiman Karrani annexed Orissa to the Muslim sultanate permanently. Daud Shah Karrani declared independence from Akbar which led to four years of bloody war between the Mughals and the Afghans. The Mughal onslaught against the Afghan Sultan ended with the battle of Rajmahal in 1576, led by Khan Jahan. However, the Afghans and the local landlords (Baro Bhuyans) led by Isa Khan resisted the Moghul invasion.

MUGHAL PERIOD

Bengal came once more under the suzerainty of Delhi as the Mughals conquered it in 1576. Not far from Sonargaon, Dhaka rose from the mists of obscurity as a Mughal provincial capital. But it remained remote and thus a difficult to govern region—especially the section east of the Brahmaputra River—outside the mainstream of Mughal politics. The Bengali ethnic and linguistic identity further crystallized during this period, since the whole of Bengal was united under an able and long-lasting administration. Furthermore its inhabitants were given sufficient autonomy to cultivate their own customs and literature.

In 1612, during Emperor Jahangir's reign, the defeat of Sylhet completed the Mughal conquest of Bengal, except for Chittagong. At this time the capital was established at Dhaka. Chittagong was later annexed in order to stifle Arakanese raids from the east. A well-known Dhaka landmark, Lalbagh Fort, was built during Aurangzeb's sovereignty.

History repeated itself as the frontier Bengal province broke off from a Delhi-based empire around the time Aurangzeb's death in 1707. Murshid Quli Khan ended Dhaka's century of grandeur as he shifted the capital to Murshidabad ushering in a series of independent Bengal Nawabs. Nawab Alivardi Khan showed military skill during his wars with the Marathas. He completely routed the Marathas from Bengal. He crushed an uprising of the Afghans in Bihar and made the British pay 150,000 Tk for blocking Mughal and Armenian trade ships.

EUROPEANS IN BENGAL

Portuguese traders and missionaries were the first Europeans to reach Bengal in the latter part of the fifteenth century. They were followed by representatives of the Dutch, the French, and the British East India Company. The Mughal Subahdar of Bengal Kasim Khan Mashadi completely destroyed the Portuguese forces in the Battle of Hoogly (1632). About 10,000 Portuguese men and women died in the battle and 4,400 were sent captive to Delhi.

During Aurangzeb's reign, the local Nawab sold three villages, including one then known as Calcutta, to the British. Calcutta was Britain's first foothold in Bengal and remained a focal point of their economic activity. The British gradually extended their commercial contacts and administrative control beyond Calcutta to the rest of Bengal. Job Charnock was one of the first dreamers of a British empire in Bengal. He almost waged war against the Mughal authority of Bengal which led to the Anglo-Mughal war of Bengal (1686-1690). Shaista Khan, the Nawab of Bengal, defeated the British in the battles of Hoogly, Baleshwar, and Hijly and expelled the British from Bengal. Captain William Heath with a naval fleet moved towards Chittagong but it was a failure and he had to retreat to Madras.

BRITISH RULE

The British East India Company gained official control of Bengal following the Battle of Palashey in 1757. This was the first conquest, in a series of engagements that ultimately lead to the expulsion of other European competitors, the defeat of the Mughals and the consolidation of the subcontinent under the rule of a corporation — an unique event in imperialistic history. Kolkata (Anglicized as "Calcutta") on the Hooghly became a major trading port for Bamboo, Tea, Sugar cane, Spices, Cotton Muslin and Jute produced in Dhaka, Rajshahi, Khulna and Kushtia and parts of the rest of Bengal.

Scandals and the bloody rebellion known as the Bengal Mutiny prompted the British government to intervene in the affairs of the East India Company. In 1858, authority in India was transferred from the Company to the crown and the rebellion was brutally suppressed. Rule of India was organized under a Viceroy and continued a pattern of economic exploitation. Famine racked the subcontinent many times, including at least two major famines in Bengal. The British Raj was politically organized into seventeen provinces—of which Bengal was one of the most significant—most headed by a governor.

For a brief period in the early twentieth century, an abortive attempt was made to divide Bengal into two zones, West Bengal and East Bengal & Assam.

CREATION OF PAKISTAN

As the independence movement throughout British-controlled India began in the late nineteenth century gained momentum during the twentieth century, Bengali politicians played an active role in Mohandas Gandhi's Congress Party and Mohammad Ali Jinnah's Muslim League, exposing the opposing forces of ethnic and religious nationalism. By exploiting the latter, the British probably intended to distract the independence movement, for example by partitioning Bengal in 1905 along religious lines. The split only lasted for seven years. At first the Muslim League sought only to ensure minority rights in the future nation. In 1940 the Muslim League passed the Lahore Resolution which envisaged one or more Muslim majority states in South Asia.

Non-negotiable was the inclusion of the Muslim parts of Punjab and Bengal in these proposed states. The stakes grew as a new Viceroy Lord Mountbatten was appointed expressly for the purpose of effecting a graceful British exit. Communal violence in Noakhali and Calcutta sparked a surge in support for the Muslim League, which won a majority of Bengal's Muslim seats in the 1946 election. Accusations have been made that Hindu and Muslim nationalist instigators were involved in the latter incident. At the last moment Huseyn Shaheed Suhrawardy and Sarat Chandra Bose came up with the idea of an independent and unified Bengal state, which was endorsed by Jinnah. This idea was vetoed by the Indian National Congress.

British India was partitioned and the independent states of India and Pakistan were created in 1947; the region of Bengal was divided along religious lines. The predominantly Muslim eastern half of Bengal became the East Bengal (later renamed East Pakistan) state of Pakistan and the predominantly Hindu western part became the Indian state of West Bengal.

Pakistan's history from 1947 to 1971 was marked by political instability and economic difficulties. In 1956 a constitution was at last adopted, making the country an "Islamic republic within the Commonwealth". The nascent democratic institutions foundered in the face of military intervention in 1958, and the government imposed martial law between 1958 and 1962, and again between 1969 and 1971.

Almost from the advent of independent Pakistan in 1947, frictions developed between East and West Pakistan, which were separated by more than 1,000 miles of Indian territory. East Pakistanis felt exploited by the West Pakistan-dominated central government. Linguistic, cultural, and ethnic differences also contributed to the estrangement of East from West Pakistan.

When Mohammad Ali Jinnah died in September 1948, Khwaja Nazimuddin became the Governor General of Pakistan while Nurul Amin was appointed the Chief Minister of East Bengal. Nurul Amin continued as the Chief Minister of East Bengal until 2 April 1954. The abolition of the Zamindari system in East Bengal (1950) and the Language Movement were two most important events during his tenure.

THE BENGALI LANGUAGE MOVEMENT

The question as to what would be the state language of Pakistan was raised immediately after its creation. The central leaders and the Urdu-speaking intellectuals of Pakistan declared that Urdu would be the state language of Pakistan, just as Hindi was the state language of India. However, Bengalis strongly resisted attempts to impose Urdu as the sole official language of Pakistan, and the students and intellectuals of East Pakistan, demanded that Bengali (Bangla) be made one of the state languages, arguing that it was in any case the native language of the majority (54% native speakers as opposed to 7% native Urdu speakers) in the whole of Pakistan.

The Bengali Language Movement began in 1948 and reached its climax in a demonstration on 21 February 1952 at which several demonstrators were killed by police. After a lot of controversy over the language issue, the final demand from East Pakistan was that Bangla must be the official language and the medium of instruction in East Pakistan, and that for the central government it would be one of the state languages along with Urdu. The first movement on this issue was mobilised by Tamaddun Majlish headed by Professor Abul Kashem. Gradually many other non-communal and progressive organisations joined the movement, which finally turned into a mass movement, and ended in the adoption of Bengali as one of the state languages of Pakistan.

POLITICS: 1954 - 1970

The first election for East Bengal Provincial Assembly was held between 8 March and 12 March 1954. The Awami Muslim League, Krishak-Sramik Party and Nezam-e-Islam formed the United Front, on the basis of 21-points agenda.

Notable pledges contained in the 21-points were:

- making Bengali one of the main state languages
- autonomy for the province
- reforms in education
- independence of the judiciary
- making the legislative assembly effective

The United Front won 215 out of 237 Muslim seats in the election. The ruling Muslim League got only nine seats. Khilafat-E-Rabbani Party got one, while the independents got twelve seats. Later, seven independent members joined the United Front while one joined the Muslim League.

There were numerous reasons for the debacle of the Muslim League. Above all, the Muslim League regime angered all sections of the people of Bengal by opposing the demand for recognition of Bangla as one of the state languages and by ordering the massacre of 1952.

The United Front got the opportunity to form the provincial government after winning absolute majority in the 1954 election. Of the 222 United Front seats, the Awami Muslim League had won 142, Krishak-Sramik Party 48, Nezam-i-Islam 19, and Ganatantri Dal 13.

The major leaders of the United Front were Huseyn Shaheed Suhrawardy and Maulana Abdul Hamid Khan Bhasani of Awami Muslim League and A. K. Fazlul Huq of Krishak-Sramik Party. Suhrawardy and Bhasani did not take part in the election and Fazlul Huq was invited to form the government. But a rift surfaced at the very outset on the question of formation of the cabinet. The unity and solidarity among the component parties of the United Front soon evaporated. Finally, on 15 May, Fazlul Huq arrived at an understanding with the Awami Muslim League and formed a 14-member cabinet with five members from that party.

But this cabinet lasted for only fourteen days. The Muslim League could not concede defeat in the elections in good grace. So, they resorted to conspiracies to dismiss the United Front government. In the third week of May, there were bloody riots between Bengali and non-Bengali workers in different mills and factories of East Bengal. The United Front government was blamed for failing to control the law and order situation in the province.

Fazlul Huq was then quoted in an interview taken by *The New York Times* correspondent John P Callaghan and published in a distorted form that he wanted the independence of East Bengal. Finally, on 29 May 1954, the United Front government was dismissed by the central government and Governor's rule was imposed in the province, which lasted till 2 June 1955.

Curiously enough within two months of his sacking, Fazlul Huq was appointed the central Home Minister. As Home Minister, Fazlul Huq utilised his influence to bring his party to power in East Bengal. Naturally, the United Front broke up. The Muslim members of the United Front split into two groups. In 1955 the Awami Muslim League adopted the path of secularism and non-communalism, erased the word 'Muslim' from its nomenclature and adopted the name "Awami League".

Great differences began developing between the two wings of Pakistan. While the west had a minority share of Pakistan's total population, it had the largest share of revenue allocation, industrial development, agricultural reforms and civil development projects. Pakistan's military and civil services were dominated by the fair-skinned, Persian-cultured Punjabis and Afghans. Only one regiment in the Pakistani Army was Bengali. And many Bengali Pakistanis could not share the natural enthusiasm for the Kashmir issue, which they felt was leaving East Pakistan more vulnerable and threatened as a result.

INDEPENDENCE

After the Awami League won all the East Pakistan seats of the Pakistan's National Assembly in the 1970-71 elections, West Pakistan opened talks with the East on constitutional questions about the division of power between the central government and the provinces, as well as the formation of a national government headed by the Awami League.

The talks proved unsuccessful, however, and on March 1, 1971, Pakistani President Yahya Khan indefinitely postponed the pending National Assembly session, precipitating massive civil disobedience in East Pakistan.

On March 4, a group of students, lead by Abdur Rob, of Dhaka University raised the new (proposed) flag of Bangla.

On March 7, there was a historical public gathering in Paltan Maidan to hear the guideline for the revolution and independence from Shaikh Mujib, the frontier leader of movement that time. Although he avoided the direct speech of independence as the talks were still underway, he influenced the mob to prepare for the separation war. The speech is still considered a key moment in the war of liberation, and is remembered for the phrase, "Ebarer Shongram Muktir Shongram, Ebarer Shongram Shadhinotar Shongram...." ("This revolution is for victory, this revolution is for freedom....").

After the military crackdown by the Pakistan army began on the night of March 25, 1971 Sheikh Mujib Mujibur Rahman was arrested and the political leaders dispersed, mostly fleeing to neighbouring India where they organized a provisional government afterwards. The people were at a loss. At this crucial moment with a sudden forced political vacuum, the Eighth East Bengal Regiment under the leadership of Major Ziaur Rahman revolted against the Pakistan Army and took up the Bangladesh flag as its mainstay on the night of March 26 - March 27, 1971. Major Zia declared, on behalf of the Great Leader Sheikh Mujibur Rahman, the independence of Bangladesh.

The Bangladesh Government was formed in Meherpur, adjacent to Indian border. There the war plan was sketched.

A war force was established named "Muktibahini". M. A. G. Osmani was assigned as the Chief of the force. The land sketched into 11 sectors under 11 sector commanders. Major Ziaur Rahman was the sector commander of Chittagong-Comilla region.

The training and most of the arms-ammunitions were arranged by the Meherpur government which were supported by India.

As fighting grew between the Pakistan Army and the Bengali Mukti Bahini ("freedom fighters"), an estimated ten million Bengalis, mainly Hindus, sought refuge in the Indian states of Assam, Tripura and West Bengal.

The crisis in East Pakistan produced new strains in Pakistan's troubled relations with India. The two nations had fought a war in 1965, mainly in the west, but the refugee pressure in India in the fall of 1971 produced new tensions in the east. Indian sympathies lay with East Pakistan, and on December 3, 1971, India intervened on the side of the Bangladeshis. On December 16, 1971, Pakistani forces surrendered, and Bangla Desh ("Country of Bangla") was finally established the following day. The new country changed its name to Bangladesh on January 11, 1972 and became a parliamentary democracy under a constitution. Shortly thereafter on March 19 Bangladesh signed a friendship treaty with India.

POST-INDEPENDENCE

Sheikh Mujibur Rahman, 1972-75

Sheikh Mujibur Rahman came to office with immense personal popularity but had difficulty transforming this popular support into the political strength needed to function as head of government. The 1972 constitution adopted as state policy the Awami League's (AL) four basic principles of nationalism, secularism, socialism, and democracy.

The first parliamentary elections were held in March 1973, with the Awami League winning a massive majority. The new Bangladesh government focused on relief, rehabilitation, and reconstruction of the economy and society. In December 1974, in the face of continuing economic deterioration and mounting civil disorder, Mujib proclaimed a state of emergency, limited the powers of the legislative and judicial branches, and instituted a one-party system.

Despite some improvement in the economic situation during the first half of 1975, criticism of Mujib grew. In August 1975, Mujib, and most of his family, were assassinated by mid-level army officers. A new government, headed by former Mujib associate Khandakar Moshtaque, was formed.

Ziaur Rahman, 1975-81

Successive military coups resulted in the emergence of Army Chief of Staff Gen. Ziaur Rahman ("Zia") as strongman. He pledged the army's support to the civilian government headed by President Chief Justice Sayem. Acting at Zia's behest, Sayem dissolved Parliament, and instituted the Martial Law Administration (MLA).

Zia sought to revitalize the demoralized bureaucracy, to begin new economic development programs, and to emphasize family planning. In November 1976, Zia became Chief Martial Law Administrator (CMLA) and assumed the presidency upon Sayem's retirement five months later, promising national elections in 1978.

As President, Zia announced a 19-point program of economic reform and began dismantling the MLA. Zia won a five-year term in June 1978 elections, with 76% of the vote. Democracy and constitutional order were fully restored when the ban on political parties was lifted, new parliamentary elections were held in February 1979. The AL and the Bangladesh Nationalist Party (BNP), founded by Zia, emerged as the two major parties.

In May 1981, Zia was assassinated in Chittagong by dissident elements of the military. The conspirators were either taken into custody or killed. Vice President Justice Abdus Sattar was sworn in as acting president, and elected president as the BNP's candidate six months later. Sattar followed the policies of his predecessor and retained essentially the same cabinet.

Hussain Mohammed Ershad, 1982-90

In March 1982 Army Chief of Staff Lt. Gen. H.M. Ershad suspended the constitution and declared martial law citing pervasive corruption, ineffectual government, and economic mismanagement. The following year, Ershad assumed the presidency, and won overwhelming public support for his regime in a national referendum in March 1985, although turnout was small. Political life was liberalized through 1985 and 1986, and the Jatiya (National) Party was established as Ershad's vehicle for the transition back to democracy.

Parliamentary elections were held in May 1986, but were boycotted by the BNP, now led by President Zia's widow, Begum Khaleda Zia. The Jatiya Party won a modest majority of the 300 elected seats in the National Assembly. The participation of the Awami League — led by the late President Mujib's daughter, Sheikh Hasina Wajed — lent the elections some credibility, despite widespread charges of voting irregularities.

Ershad retired from military service in preparation for the presidential elections in October 1986, and won 84% of the vote. Protesting that martial law was still in effect, both the BNP and the AL refused to put up opposing candidates. In November 1986, martial law was lifted, and the opposition parties took their elected seats in the National Assembly.

In July 1987, after the government hastily pushed through a bill to include military representation on local administrative councils, the opposition walked out of Parliament. As the opposition organized protest marches and nationwide strikes, the government arrested scores of opposition activists. After declaring a state of emergency, Ershad dissolved Parliament and scheduled fresh elections for March 1988.

The elections were held despite an opposition boycott, and the ruling Jatiya Party won 251 of the 300 seats. The Parliament passed a large number of bills, including in June 1988 a controversial constitutional amendment making Islam Bangladesh's state religion.

On December 6, 1990, following general strikes, increased campus protests, public rallies, and a general disintegration of law and order, Ershad resigned. On February 27, 1991, an interim government headed by Acting President Chief Justice Shahabuddin Ahmed oversaw what most observers believed to be the nation's most free and fair elections to that date.

Khaleda Zia, 1991-96

The center-right BNP won a plurality of seats and formed a government with Khaleda Zia, widow of Ziaur Rahman, becoming prime minister. The electorate approved changes to the constitution, formally re-creating a parliamentary system and returning governing power to the office of the prime minister, as in Bangladesh's original 1972 constitution.

In March 1994, controversy over a parliamentary by-election, which the opposition claimed the government had rigged, led to general strikes and an indefinite boycott of Parliament by the opposition. In late December 1994, the opposition resigned en masse from Parliament, and pledged to boycott national elections scheduled for February 15, 1996.

In February, Khaleda Zia was re-elected by a landslide in voting boycotted by the three main opposition parties. In March 1996, following escalating political turmoil, the Parliament amended the constitution to allow a neutral caretaker government to assume power and conduct new parliamentary elections.

Sheikh Hasina, 1996-2001

Elections were held in June 1996 which were found by international and domestic election observers to be free and fair. The Awami League won a plurality of the seats, and formed the government with support from the Jatiya Party of deposed president Ershad. AL leader Sheikh Hasina became Prime Minister.

In June 1999, the BNP and other opposition parties again began to boycott Parliament, and stage nationwide general strikes. A four-party opposition alliance formed at the beginning of 1999 announced that it would boycott parliamentary by-elections and local government elections.

In July 2001, the Awami League government stepped down to allow a caretaker government to preside over parliamentary elections. In August, Khaleda Zia and Sheikh Hasina agreed to respect the results of the election, join Parliament win or lose, foreswear the use of hartals (violently enforced strikes) as political tools, and if successful in forming a government allow for a more meaningful role for the opposition in Parliament. The caretaker government was successful in containing the violence, which allowed a parliamentary general election to be held on October 1, 2001.

Khaleda Zia, 2001-2006

The four-party alliance led by the BNP won over a two-thirds majority in Parliament. Begum Khaleda Zia was sworn in on October 10, 2001, as Prime Minister for the third time.

On August 17, 2005, near-synchronized blasts of improvised explosive devices in 63 out of 64 administrative districts targeted mainly government buildings and killed two persons. An extremist Islamist group named Jama'atul Mujahideen, Bangladesh (JMB) claimed responsibility for the blasts, which aimed to press home JMB's demand for a replacement of the secular legal system with Islamic sharia courts. Hundreds of senior and mid-level JMB leaders were arrested.

In February 2006, after sporadic boycotts, the AL returned to Parliament, demanded early elections and requested significant changes in the electoral and caretaker government systems to stop alleged moves by the ruling coalition to rig the next election. Dialogue between the Secretaries General of the main ruling and opposition parties failed to sort out the electoral reform issues.

Caretaker Government, October 2006-present

On January 3, 2007, the Awami League announced it would boycott the January 22 parliamentary elections. The AL planned a series of country-wide general strikes and transportation blockades.

On January 11, 2007, President Iajuddin Ahmed declared a state of emergency, resigned as Chief Adviser, and indefinitely postponed parliamentary elections. On January 12, 2007, former Bangladesh Bank governor Fakhruddin Ahmed was sworn in as the new Chief Adviser, and ten new advisers (ministers) were appointed. Under emergency provisions, the government suspended certain fundamental rights guaranteed by the constitution and detained a large number of politicians and others on suspicion of involvement in corruption and other crimes. The government announced elections will occur in late 2008.

In the summer of 2007 the government arrested Sheikh Hasina and Khaleda Zia, Bangladesh's two most influential political leaders, on charges of corruption. Hasina and Zia have challenged the cases filed against them under the Emergency Power Rules, which deny the accused the right to bail. While the cases are under judicial review, the two leaders continue to be imprisoned as of March 2008.

GOVERNMENT AND POLITICS OF BANGLADESH

Politics of Bangladesh takes place in a framework of a parliamentary representative democratic republic, whereby the Prime Minister of Bangladesh is the head of government, and of a multi-party system. Executive power is exercised by the government. Legislative power is vested in both the government and parliament. The Constitution of Bangladesh was written in 1972 and has undergone thirteen amendments.

EXECUTIVE BRANCH

The President is the head of state , a largely ceremonial post. The real power is held by the Prime Minister, who is the head of government. The president is elected by the legislature every five years and has normally limited powers that are substantially expanded during the tenure of a caretaker government, mainly in controlling the transition to a new government. Bangladesh has instituted a unique system of transfer of power; at the end of the tenure of the government, power is handed over to members of a civil society for three months, who run the general elections and transfer the power to elected representatives. This system was first practiced in 1991 and adopted to the constitution in 1996.

The prime minister is ceremonially appointed by the president and must be a member of parliament (MP), commanding the confidence of the majority of the MPs. The cabinet is composed of ministers selected by the prime minister and appointed by the president.

LEGISLATIVE BRANCH

The legislature is a unicameral, 300-seat body, the Jatiyo Sangshad. The 300 members are elected by universal suffrage at least every 5 years. There is universal suffrage for all citizens at the age of 18.

"On 16 May 2004, the Jatiyo Sangshad (the national parliament) passed the 14th constitutional amendment to reintroduce quotas for women (article 65). The number of seats in parliament is to be raised to 345, 45 (13%) of which will be reserved for women in the next parliament. The seats will be allocated to parties in proportion to their overall share of the vote. This quota system replaces the previous quota law which expired in 2001. Until 2001 a system of reserved seats for women was used, where 30 seats out of 330 were reserved to women (chosen by indirect election by the 300 directly elected MPs). This provision of guaranteeing women reserved seats expired in April 2001.

This quota system was first introduced by the 1972 Constitution (originally providing for 15 reserved seats for women, out of 315 seats, for a period of 10 years). In 1978 a presidential proclamation enlarged the number of reserved seats to 30 and extended the period of reservation to 15 years from the date of promulgation of the constitution of the Republic in December 1972. The constitutional provision lapsed in 1987 and was re-incorporated in the constitution by an amendment in 1990 to be effective for 10 years from the first meeting of the legislature next elected. This provision also lapsed in 2001. The Parliament elected in October 2001 does not have reserved seats for women. Women's groups are lobbying for these seats to become directly elected positions and for the number of reserved seats to be increased" (International Institute for Democracy and Electoral Assistance). The 8th Parliament had its first sitting on 28 October 2001.

POLITICAL PARTIES AND ELECTIONS

The two major parties in Bangladesh are the Bangladesh Nationalist Party (BNP) and Bangladesh Awami League. BNP finds its allies among Islamist parties like Jamaat-e-Islami Bangladesh while Awami League aligns itself traditionally with leftist and secularist parties. Another important player is the Jatiya Party, headed by former military ruler Ershad. The Awami League-BNP rivalry has been bitter and punctuated by protests, violence and murder. Student politics is particularly strong in Bangladesh, a legacy from the liberation movement era. Almost all parties have highly active student wings, and students have been elected to the Parliament.

Two radical Islamist parties, Jagrata Muslim Janata Bangladesh (JMJB) and Jama'atul Mujahideen Bangladesh (JMB), were banned in February 2005 by Bangladesh Nationalist Party (BNP). Since then, a series of bomb attacks took place in the country and have been blamed on those groups, and hundreds of suspected members have been detained in numerous security operations, including the head the of those two parties in 2006. The first recorded case of a suicide bomb attack in Bangladesh took place in November 2005.

JUDICIAL BRANCH

The highest judiciary body is the Supreme Court, whose Chief Justice and judges are recommended by the Prime Minister and formally appointed by the President. The judiciary has come under criticism for lack of independence. Indeed, magistrates for lower courts are selected via the same process for all members of the civil service, an office which is run by the executive. In the summer of 2007, a new law has been enacted to redress this problem. Laws are loosely based on English common law, but family laws such as marriage and inheritance are based on religious scripts, and hence differ from one religious community to another.

HISTORY

Provisional government

The provisional government of the new nation of Bangladesh was formed in Dhaka with Justice Abu Sayeed Choudhury as President, and Sheikh Mujibur Rahman ("Mujib")—who was released from Pakistani prison in early 1972—as Prime Minister.

1972-1975 Sheikh Mujibur Rahman

Mujib came to office with immense personal popularity, but had difficulty transforming this popular support into the political strength needed to function as head of government. The new constitution, which came into force in December 1972, created a strong executive prime minister, a largely ceremonial presidency, an independent judiciary, and a unicameral legislature on a modified Westminster model. The 1972 constitution adopted as state policy the Awami League's (AL) four basic principles of nationalism, secularism, socialism, and democracy.

The first parliamentary elections held under the 1972 constitution were in March 1973, with the Awami League winning a massive majority. No other political party in Bangladesh's early years was able to duplicate or challenge the League's broad-based appeal, membership, or organizational strength. Relying heavily on experienced civil servants and members of the Awami League, the new Bangladesh Government focused on relief, rehabilitation, and reconstruction of the economy and society. Economic conditions remained precarious, however. In December 1974, Mujib decided that continuing economic deterioration and mounting civil disorder required strong measures. After proclaiming a state of emergency, Mujib used his parliamentary majority to win a constitutional amendment limiting the powers of the legislative and judicial branches, establishing an executive presidency, and instituting a one-party system, the Bangladesh Krishak Sramik Awami League (BAKSAL), which all members of Parliament were obliged to join.

Despite some improvement in the economic situation during the first half of 1975, implementation of promised political reforms was slow, and criticism of government policies became increasingly centered on Mujib. In August 1975, Mujib, and most of his family, were assassinated by mid-level army officers. His daughter, Sheikh Hasina, happened to be out of the country. A new government, headed by former Mujib associate Khandakar Moshtaque, was formed.

1975-1981 Ziaur Rahman

Successive military coups resulted in the emergence of Army Chief of Staff Gen. Ziaur Rahman ("Zia") as strongman. He pledged the army's support to the civilian government headed by President Chief Justice Sayem. Acting at Zia's behest, Sayem dissolved Parliament, promising fresh elections in 1977, and instituted martial law.

Acting behind the scenes of the Martial Law Administration (MLA), Zia sought to invigorate government policy and administration. While continuing the ban on political parties, he sought to revitalize the demoralized bureaucracy, to begin new economic development programs, and to emphasize family planning. In November 1976, Zia became Chief Martial Law Administrator (CMLA) and assumed the presidency upon Sayem's retirement 5 months later, promising national elections in 1978.

As President, Zia announced a 19-point program of economic reform and began dismantling the MLA. Keeping his promise to hold elections, Zia won a 5-year term in June 1978 elections, with 76% of the vote. In November 1978, his government removed the remaining restrictions on political party activities in time for parliamentary elections in February 1979. These elections, which were contested by more than 30 parties, marked the culmination of Zia's transformation of Bangladesh's Government from the MLA to a democratically elected, constitutional one. The AL and the Bangladesh Nationalist Party (BNP), founded by Zia, emerged as the two major parties. The constitution was again amended to provide for an executive prime minister appointed by the president, and responsible to a parliamentary majority.

In May 1981, Zia was assassinated in Chittagong by dissident elements of the military. The attempted coup never spread beyond that city, and the major conspirators were either taken into custody or killed. In accordance with the constitution, Vice President Justice Abdus Sattar was sworn in as acting president. He declared a new national emergency and called for election of a new president within 6 months—an election Sattar won as the BNP's candidate. President Sattar sought to follow the policies of his predecessor and retained essentially the same cabinet, but the army stepped in once again.

1982-1990 Hussain Mohammed Ershad

Army Chief of Staff Lt. Gen. Hussain Mohammed Ershad assumed power in a bloodless coup in March 1982. Like his predecessors, Ershad suspended the constitution and—citing pervasive corruption, ineffectual government, and economic mismanagement—declared martial law. The following year, Ershad assumed the presidency, retaining his positions as army chief and CMLA. During most of 1984, Ershad sought the opposition parties' participation in local elections under martial law. The opposition's refusal to participate, however, forced Ershad to abandon these plans. Ershad sought public support for his regime in a national referendum on his leadership in March 1985. He won overwhelmingly, although turnout was small. Two months later, Ershad held elections for local council chairmen. Pro-government candidates won a majority of the posts, setting in motion the President's ambitious decentralization program. Political life was further liberalized in early 1986, and additional political rights, including the right to hold large public rallies, were restored. At the same time, the Jatiya (People's) Party, designed as Ershad's political vehicle for the transition from martial law, was established.

Despite a boycott by the BNP, led by President Zia's widow, Begum Khaleda Zia, parliamentary elections were held on schedule in May 1986. The Jatiya Party won a modest majority of the 300 elected seats in the national assembly. The participation of the Awami League—led by the late Prime Minister Mujib's daughter, Sheikh Hasina Wazed—lent the elections some credibility, despite widespread charges of voting irregularities.

Ershad resigned as Army Chief of Staff and retired from military service in preparation for the presidential elections, scheduled for October. Protesting that martial law was still in effect, both the BNP and the AL refused to put up opposing candidates. Ershad easily outdistanced the remaining candidates, taking 84% of the vote. Although Ershad's government claimed a turnout of more than 50%, opposition leaders, and much of the foreign press, estimated a far lower percentage and alleged voting irregularities.

Ershad continued his stated commitment to lift martial law. In November 1986, his government mustered the necessary two-thirds majority in the national assembly to amend the constitution and confirm the previous actions of the martial law regime. The President then lifted martial law, and the opposition parties took their elected seats in the national assembly.

In July 1987, however, after the government hastily pushed through a controversial legislative bill to include military representation on local administrative councils, the opposition walked out of Parliament. Passage of the bill helped spark an opposition movement that quickly gathered momentum, uniting Bangladesh's opposition parties for the first time. The government began to arrest scores of opposition activists under the country's Special Powers Act of 1974. Despite these arrests, opposition parties continued to organize protest marches and nationwide strikes. After declaring a state of emergency, Ershad dissolved Parliament and scheduled fresh elections for March 1988.

All major opposition parties refused government overtures to participate in these polls, maintaining that the government was incapable of holding free and fair elections. Despite the opposition boycott, the government proceeded. The ruling Jatiya Party won 251 of the 300 seats. The Parliament, while still regarded by the opposition as an illegitimate body, held its sessions as scheduled, and passed a large number of bills, including, in June 1988, a controversial constitutional amendment making Islam Bangladesh's state religion.

By 1989, the domestic political situation in the country seemed to have quieted. The local council elections were generally considered by international observers to have been less violent and more free and fair than previous elections. However, opposition to Ershad's rule began to regain momentum, escalating by the end of 1990 in frequent general strikes, increased campus protests, public rallies, and a general disintegration of law and order.

On December 6, 1990, Ershad offered his resignation. On February 27, 1991, after 2 months of widespread civil unrest, an interim government oversaw what most observers believed to be the nation's most free and fair elections to date.

1991-1996 Khaleda Zia

The center-right BNP won a plurality of seats and formed a coalition government with the Islamic party Jamaat-e-Islami Bangladesh, with Khaleda Zia, widow of Ziaur Rahman, obtaining the post of Prime Minister. Only four parties had more than 10 members elected to the 1991 Parliament: The BNP, led by Prime Minister Begum Khaleda Zia; the AL, led by Sheikh Hasina; the Jamaat-e-Islami (JI), led by Golam Azam; and the Jatiya Party (JP), led by acting chairman Mizanur Rahman Choudhury while its founder, former President Ershad, served out a prison sentence on corruption charges. The electorate approved still more changes to the constitution, formally re-creating a parliamentary system and returning governing power to the office of the prime minister, as in Bangladesh's original 1972 constitution. In October 1991, members of Parliament elected a new head of state, President Abdur Rahman Biswas.

In March 1994, controversy over a parliamentary by-election, which the opposition claimed the government had rigged, led to an indefinite boycott of Parliament by the entire opposition. The opposition also began a program of repeated general strikes to press its demand that Khaleda Zia's government resign and a caretaker government supervise a general election. Efforts to mediate the dispute, under the auspices of the Commonwealth Secretariat, failed. After another attempt at a negotiated settlement failed narrowly in late December 1994, the opposition resigned en masse from Parliament. The opposition then continued a campaign of Marches, demonstrations, and strikes in an effort to force the government to resign. The opposition, including the Awami League's Sheikh Hasina, pledged to boycott national elections scheduled for February 15, 1996.

In February, Khaleda Zia was re-elected for the second term by a landslide in voting boycotted and denounced as unfair by the three main opposition parties. In March 1996, following escalating political turmoil, the sitting Parliament enacted a constitutional amendment to allow a neutral caretaker government to assume power conduct new parliamentary elections; former Chief Justice Mohammed Habibur Rahman was named Chief Advisor (a position equivalent to prime minister) in the interim government. New parliamentary elections were held in June 1996 and were won by the Awami League; party leader Sheikh Hasina became Prime Minister.

1996-2001 Sheikh Hasina

Sheikh Hasina formed what she called a "Government of National Consensus" in June 1996, which included one minister from the Jatiya Party and another from the Jatiyo Samajtantric Dal, a very small leftist party. The Jatiya Party never entered into a formal coalition arrangement, and party president H.M. Ershad withdrew his support from the government in September 1997. Only three parties had more than 10 members elected to the 1996 Parliament: The Awami League, BNP, and Jatiya Party. Jatiya Party president, Ershad, was released from prison on bail in January 1997.

Although international and domestic election observers found the June 1996 election free and fair, the BNP protested alleged vote rigging by the Awami League. Ultimately, however, the BNP party decided to join the new Parliament. The BNP soon charged that police and Awami League activists were engaged in large-scale harassment and jailing of opposition activists. At the end of 1996, the BNP staged a parliamentary walkout over this and other grievances but returned in January 1997 under a four-point agreement with the ruling party. The BNP asserted that this agreement was never implemented and later staged another walkout in August 1997. The BNP returned to Parliament under another agreement in March 1998.

In June 1999, the BNP and other opposition parties again began to abstain from attending Parliament. Opposition parties have staged an increasing number of nationwide general strikes, rising from 6 days of general strikes in 1997 to 27 days in 1999. A four-party opposition alliance formed at the beginning of 1999 announced that it would boycott parliamentary by-elections and local government elections unless the government took steps demanded by the opposition to ensure electoral fairness. The government did not take these steps, and the opposition has subsequently boycotted all elections, including municipal council elections in February 1999, several parliamentary by-elections, and the Chittagong city corporation elections in January 2000. The opposition demands that the Awami League government step down immediately to make way for a caretaker government to preside over paliamentary and local government.

2001-2006 Khaleda Zia

Khaleda Zia won a second term in 2001. Her coalition included several Islamist parties, a fact which was criticized by those who feared post-9/11 Islamic radicalism and de-secularization in Bangladesh. Islamist violence targeting courts and imposing social strictures became a serious problem as Zia's term wore on. It came to a head in 2005 with the first suicide bombing and a coordinated bombing. This problem abated as two parties were outlawed and the leaders of the movement were rounded up.

2006-present caretaker government

An election was scheduled for the end of 2006, however it did not take place. The caretaker government was accused of BNP bias by Hasina and her coalition, who fomented nationwide protests and shutdowns. In January 2007, the head of the caretaker government stepped down, many believe under pressure from the military.

Fakhruddin Ahmed, former World Bank economist, was selected to replace him and has committed himself to rooting out corruption and preparing a better voter list. Emergency law was declared and a massive campaign to crack down on corruption is underway. By July 2007 some 200,000 people had been arrested. The government says it will hold elections before the end of 2008.

In April, Ahmed's administration attempted to reform the political parties by exiling Hasina and Zia, but they backed down amid domestic and international protestations. Hasina, who had been visiting her children in the US, was allowed to return but she faced serious charges, including involvement in the assassination of four political rivals. In July, she was taken into custody after two businessmen testified that she had extorted 80 million taka (US$1.16 million) from them. This provoked angry protests from her supporters; even her bitter rival Khalida Zia, as well as six British MPs and MEPs, called for her release. Khaleda herself faces charges of tax evasion.

ADMINISTRATIVE DIVISIONS

At the local government level, the country is divided into divisions, districts, subdistricts, unions, and villages. Local officials are elected at the union level. All larger administrative units are run by members of the civil service.

GEOGRAPHY OF BANGLADESH

Bangladesh is a low-lying, riverine country located in South Asia with a largely marshy jungle coastline of 710 kilometers (440 mi) on the northern littoral of the Bay of Bengal. Formed by a delta plain at the confluence of the Ganges (Padma), Brahmaputra (Jamuna), and Meghna Rivers and their tributaries, Bangladesh's alluvial soil is highly fertile, but vulnerable to flood and drought. Hills rise above the plain only in the Chittagong Hill Tracts in the far southeast and the Sylhet division in the northeast. Straddling the Tropic of Cancer, Bangladesh has a tropical monsoon climate characterized by heavy seasonal rainfall, high temperatures, and high humidity. Natural disasters, such as floods, toradoes, and tidal bores affect the country yearly. Bangladesh also is affected by major cyclones – on average 16 times a decade. One cyclone struck the southeastern coast in May 1991, killing 136,000 people. The cyclone Sidr struck the southwestern coast on November

15, 2007 affecting not only the coastal districts of the administrative division Khulna but also about half of the tropical forest Sundarbans.

The physiography of Bangladesh is varied and has an area characterized by two distinctive features: a broad deltaic plain subject to frequent flooding, and a small hilly region crossed by swiftly flowing rivers. The country has an area of 144,000 square kilometers and extends 820 kilometers north to south and 600 kilometers east to west. Bangladesh is bordered on the west, north, and east by a 2,400-kilometer land frontier with India and, in the southeast, by a short land and water frontier (193 km) with Burma (Myanmar). On the south is a highly irregular deltaic coastline of about 580 kilometers, fissured by many rivers and streams flowing into the Bay of Bengal. The territorial waters of Bangladesh extend 12 nautical miles, and the exclusive economic zone of the country is 200 nautical miles (370 km).

Roughly 80 % of the landmass is made up of fertile alluvial lowland called the Bangladesh Plain. The plain is part of the larger Plain of Bengal, which is sometimes called the Lower Gangetic Plain. Although altitudes up to 105 meters above sea level occur in the northern part of the plain, most elevations are less than 10 meters above sea level; elevations decrease in the coastal south, where the terrain is generally at sea level. With such low elevations and numerous rivers, water—and concomitant flooding—is a predominant physical feature. About 10,000 square kilometers of the total area of Bangladesh is covered with water, and larger areas are routinely flooded during the monsoon season.

The only exceptions to Bangladesh's low elevations are the Chittagong Hills in the southeast, the Low Hills of Sylhet in the northeast, and highlands in the north and northwest. The Chittagong Hills constitute the only significant hill system in the country and, in effect, are the western fringe of the north-south mountain ranges of Burma and eastern India. The Chittagong Hills rise steeply to narrow ridge lines, generally no wider than 36 meters, with altitudes from 600 to 900 meters above sea level. At 1,052 meters altitude, the highest elevation in Bangladesh is found at Mowdok, in the southeastern part of the hills. Fertile valleys lie between the hill lines, which generally run north-south. West of the Chittagong Hills is a broad plain, cut by rivers draining into the Bay of Bengal, that rises to a final chain of low coastal hills, mostly below 200 meters, that attain a maximum elevation of 350 meters. West of these hills is a narrow, wet coastal plain located between the cities of Chittagong in the north and Cox's Bazar in the south.

About 67% of Bangladesh's nonurban land is arable. Permanent crops cover only 2%, meadows and pastures cover 4%, and forests and woodland cover about 16%. The country produces large quantities of quality timber, bamboo, and sugarcane. Bamboo grows in almost all areas, but high-quality timber grows mostly in the highland valleys. Rubber planting in the hilly regions of the country was undertaken in the 1980s, and rubber extraction had started by the end of the decade. A variety of wild animals are found in the forest areas, such as in the Sundarbans on the southwest coast, which is the home of the world-famous Royal Bengal Tiger. The alluvial soils in the Bangladesh Plain are generally fertile and are enriched with heavy silt deposits carried downstream during the rainy season.

HUMAN GEOGRAPHY

Urbanization is proceeding rapidly, and it is estimated that only 30% of the population entering the labor force in the future will be absorbed into agriculture, although many will likely find other kinds of work in rural areas. The areas around Dhaka and Comilla are the most densely settled. The Sundarbans, an area of coastal tropical jungle in the southwest and last wild home of the Bengal Tiger, and the Chittagong Hill Tracts on the southeastern border with Burma and India, are the least densely populated.

CLIMATE

Bangladesh has a tropical monsoon climate characterized by wide seasonal variations in rainfall, high temperatures, and high humidity. Regional climatic differences in this flat country are minor. Three seasons are generally recognized: a hot, muggy summer from March to June; a hot, humid and rainy monsoon season from June to November; and a warm-hot, dry winter from December to February. In general, maximum summer temperatures range between 38 and 41 °C. April is the hottest month in most parts of the country. January is the coolest (but still hot) month, when the average temperature for most of the country is 16-20 °C during the day and around 10°C at night.

Winds are mostly from the north and northwest in the winter, blowing gently at one to three kilometers per hour in northern and central areas and three to six kilometers per hour near the coast. From March to May, violent thunderstorms, called northwesters by local English speakers, produce winds of up to 60 kilometers per hour. During the intense storms of the early summer and late monsoon season, southerly winds of more than 160 kilometers per hour cause waves to crest as high as 6 meters in the Bay of Bengal, which brings disastrous flooding to coastal areas.

Heavy rainfall is characteristic of Bangladesh. With the exception of the relatively dry western region of Rajshahi, where the annual rainfall is about 1600 mm, most parts of the country receive at least 2300 mm of rainfall per year. Because of its location just south of the foothills of the Himalayas, where monsoon winds turn west and northwest, the region of Sylhet in northeastern Bangladesh receives the greatest average precipitation. From 1977 to 1986, annual rainfall in that region ranged between 3280 and 4780 mm per year. Average daily humidity ranged from March lows of between 55 and 81 % to July highs of between 94 and 100 %, based on readings taken at selected stations nationwide in 1986.

About 80 % of Bangladesh's rain falls during the monsoon season. The monsoons result from the contrasts between low and high air pressure areas that result from differential heating of land and water. During the hot months of April and May hot air rises over the Indian subcontinent, creating low-pressure areas into which rush cooler, moisture-bearing winds from the Indian Ocean. This is the southwest monsoon, commencing in June and usually lasting through September. Dividing against the Indian landmass, the monsoon flows in two branches, one of which strikes western India. The other travels up the Bay of Bengal and over eastern India and Bangladesh, crossing the plain to the north and northeast before being turned to the west and northwest by the foothills of the Himalayas.

Natural calamities, such as floods, tropical cyclones, tornadoes, and tidal bores—destructive waves or floods caused by flood tides rushing up estuaries—ravage the country, particularly the coastal belt, almost every year. Between 1947 and 1988, 13 severe cyclones hit Bangladesh, causing enormous loss of life and property. In May 1985, for example, a severe cyclonic storm packing 154 kilometer-per-hour winds and waves 4 meters high swept into southeastern and southern Bangladesh, killing more than 11,000 persons, damaging more than 94,000 houses, killing some 135,000 head of livestock, and damaging nearly 400 kilometers of critically needed embankments.

Annual monsoon flooding results in the loss of human life, damage to property and communication systems, and a shortage of drinking water, which leads to the spread of disease. For example, in 1988 two-thirds of Bangladesh's 64 districts experienced extensive flood damage in the wake of unusually heavy rains that flooded the river systems. Millions were left homeless and without potable water. Half of Dhaka, including the runways at the Zia International Airport—an important transit point for disaster relief supplies—was flooded. About 2 million tons of crops were reported destroyed, and relief work was rendered even more challenging than usual because the flood made transportation of any kind exceedingly difficult. A tornado in April 1989 killed more than 600 people (possibly many more; it may have been the deadliest tornado in world history).

There are no precautions against cyclones and tidal bores except giving advance warning and providing safe public buildings where people may take shelter. Adequate infrastructure and air transport facilities that would ease the sufferings of the affected people had not been established by the late 1980s. Efforts by the government under the Third Five-Year Plan (1985-90) were directed toward accurate and timely forecast capability through agrometeorology, marine meteorology, oceanography, hydrometeorology, and seismology. Necessary expert services, equipment, and training facilities were expected to be developed under the United Nations Development Programme.

RIVER SYSTEMS

The rivers of Bangladesh mark both the physiography of the nation and the life of the people. About 700 in number, these rivers generally flow south. The larger rivers serve as the main source of water for cultivation and as the principal arteries of commercial transportation. Rivers also provide fish, an important source of protein. Flooding of the rivers during the monsoon season causes enormous hardship and hinders development, but fresh deposits of rich silt replenish the fertile but overworked soil. The rivers also drain excess monsoon rainfall into the Bay of Bengal. Thus, the great river system is at the same time the country's principal resource and its greatest hazard.

The profusion of rivers can be divided into five major networks. The Jamuna-Brahmaputra is 292 kilometers long and extends from northern Bangladesh to its confluence with the Padma. Originating as the Yarlung Zangbo Jiang in China's Xizang Autonomous Region (Tibet) and flowing through India's state of Arunachal Pradesh, where it becomes known as the Brahmaputra ("Son of Brahma"), it receives waters from five major tributaries that total some 740 kilometers in length. At the point where the Brahmaputra meets the Tista River in Bangladesh, it becomes known as the Jamuna. The Jamuna is notorious for its shifting subchannels and for the formation of fertile silt islands (chars). No permanent settlements can exist along its banks.

The second system is the Padma-Ganges, which is divided into two sections: a 258-kilometer segment, the Ganges, which extends from the western border with India to its confluence with the Jamuna some 72 kilometers west of Dhaka, and a 126-kilometer segment, the Padma, which runs from the Ganges-Jamuna confluence to where it joins the Meghna River at Chandpur. The Padma-Ganges is the central part of a deltaic river system with hundreds of rivers and streams—some 2,100 kilometers in length—flowing generally east or west into the Padma.

The third network is the Surma-Meghna River System, which courses from the northeastern border with India to Chandpur, where it joins the Padma. The Surma-Meghna, at 669 kilometers by itself the longest river in Bangladesh, is formed by the union of six lesser rivers. Below the city of Kalipur it is known as the Meghna. When the Padma and Meghna join together, they form the fourth river system—the Padma-Meghna—which flows 145 kilometers to the Bay of Bengal.

This mighty network of four river systems flowing through the Bangladesh Plain drains an area of some 1.5 million square kilometers. The numerous channels of the Padma-Meghna, its distributaries, and smaller parallel rivers that flow into the Bay of Bengal are referred to as the Mouths of the Ganges. Like the Jamuna, the Padma-Meghna and other estuaries on the Bay of Bengal are also known for their many chars.

A fifth river system, unconnected to the other four, is the Karnaphuli. Flowing through the region of Chittagong and the Chittagong Hills, it cuts across the hills and runs rapidly downhill to the west and southwest and then to the sea. The Feni, Karnaphuli, Sangu, and Matamuhari—an aggregate of some 420 kilometers—are the main rivers in the region. The port of Chittagong is situated on the banks of the Karnaphuli. The Karnaphuli Reservoir and Karnaphuli Dam are located in this area. The dam impounds the Karnaphuli River's waters in the reservoir for the generation of hydroelectric power.

During the annual monsoon period, the rivers of Bangladesh flow at about 140,000 cubic meters per second, but during the dry period they diminish to 7,000 cubic meters per second. Because water is so vital to agriculture, more than 60 % of the net arable land, some 91,000 km^2, is cultivated in the rainy season despite the possibility of severe flooding, and nearly 40 % of the land is cultivated during the dry winter months. Water resources development has responded to this "dual water regime" by providing flood protection, drainage to prevent overflooding and waterlogging, and irrigation facilities for the expansion of winter cultivation. Major water control projects have been developed by the national government to provide irrigation, flood control, drainage facilities, aids to river navigation and road construction, and hydroelectric power. In addition, thousands of tube wells and electric pumps are used for local irrigation. Despite severe resource constraints, the government of Bangladesh has made it a policy to try to bring additional areas under irrigation without salinity intrusion.

Water resources management, including gravity flow irrigation, flood control, and drainage, were largely the responsibility of the Bangladesh Water Development Board. Other public sector institutions, such as the Bangladesh Krishi Bank, the Bangladesh Rural Development Board, the Bangladesh Bank, and the Bangladesh Agricultural Development Corporation were also responsible for promotion and development of minor irrigation works in the private sector through government credit mechanisms.

ECONOMY OF BANGLADESH

According to the IMF list of 2007, Bangladesh ranked as the 48th largest economy in the world. Although one of the world's poorest and most densely populated countries, Bangladesh has made major strides to meet the food needs of its increasing population, through increased domestic production augmented by imports. The land is devoted mainly to rice and jute cultivation, although wheat production has increased in recent years; the country is largely self-sufficient in rice production. Nonetheless, an estimated 10% to 15% of the population faces serious nutritional risk. Bangladesh's predominantly agricultural economy depends heavily on an erratic monsoonal cycle, with periodic flooding and drought. Although improving, infrastructure to support transportation, communications, and power supply is poorly developed. Bangladesh is limited in its reserves of coal and oil, and its industrial base is weak. The country's main endowments include its vast human resource base, rich agricultural land, relatively abundant water, and substantial reserves of natural gas.

Since independence in 1971, Bangladesh has received more than $30 billion in grant aid and loan commitments from foreign donors, about $15 billion of which has been disbursed. Major donors include the World Bank, the Asian Development Bank, the UN Development Program, the United States, Japan, Saudi Arabia, and west European countries. Bangladesh historically has run a large trade deficit, financed largely through aid receipts and remittances from workers overseas. Foreign reserves dropped markedly in 2001 but stabilized in the $3 to $4 billion range (or about 3 months' import cover). In January 2007, reserves stood at $3.74 billion, and they increased to $5.39 billion by January 2008, according to the Bank of Bangladesh, the central bank.

East Bengal—the region that was to become East Pakistan and later Bangladesh—was a prosperous region of South Asia until modern times. It had the advantages of a mild, almost tropical climate, fertile soil, ample water, and an abundance of fish, wildlife, and fruit. The standard of living compared favorably with other parts of South Asia. As early as the thirteenth century, the region was developing as an agrarian economy. It was not entirely without commercial centers, and Dhaka in particular grew into an important entrepôt during the Mughal Empire. The British, however, on their arrival in the early seventeenth century, chose to develop Calcutta as their commercial and administrative center in South Asia. The development of East Bengal was thereafter limited to agriculture. The colonial infrastructure of the eighteenth and nineteenth centuries reinforced East Bengal's function as the primary producer—chiefly of rice and jute—for processors and traders in Calcutta and beyond.

Some of the same factors that had made East Bengal a prosperous region became disadvantages during the nineteenth and twentieth centuries. As life expectancy increased, the limitations of land and the annual floods increasingly became constraints on economic growth. Traditional agricultural methods became obstacles to the modernization of agriculture. Geography severely limited the development and maintenance of a modern transportation and communications system.

The partition of British India and the emergence of India and Pakistan in 1947 severely disrupted the former colonial economic system that had preserved East Bengal (now East Pakistan) as a producer of jute and rice for the urban industrial economy around Calcutta. East Pakistan had to build a new industrial base and modernize agriculture in the midst of a population explosion. The united government of Pakistan expanded the cultivated area and some irrigation facilities, but the rural population generally became poorer between 1947 and 1971 because improvements did not keep pace with rural population increase. Pakistan's five-year plans opted for a development strategy based on industrialization, but the major share of the development budget went to West Pakistan, that is, contemporary Pakistan. The lack of natural resources meant that East Pakistan was heavily dependent on imports, creating a balance of payments problem. Without a substantial industrialization program or adequate agrarian expansion, the economy of East Pakistan steadily declined. Blame was placed by various observers, but especially those in East Pakistan, on the West Pakistani leaders who not only dominated the government but also most of the fledgling industries in East Pakistan.

Following the violent events of 1971 during the fight for independence, the highest rural population density in the entire world, an annual population growth rate between 2.5 and 3 percent, chronic malnutrition for perhaps the majority of the people, and the dislocation of between 8 and 10 million people who had fled to India and returned to independent Bangladesh by 1972. The new nation had few experienced entrepreneurs, managers, administrators, engineers, or technicians. There were critical shortages of essential food grains and other staples because of wartime disruptions. External markets for jute had been lost because of the instability of supply and the increasing popularity of synthetic substitutes. Foreign exchange resources were minuscule, and the banking and monetary system was unreliable.

Although Bangladesh had a large work force, the vast reserves of undertrained and underpaid workers were largely illiterate, unskilled, and underemployed. Commercially exploitable industrial resources, except for natural gas, were lacking. Inflation, especially for essential consumer goods, ran between 300 and 400 percent. The war of independence had crippled the transportation system. Hundreds of road and railroad bridges had been destroyed or damaged, and rolling stock was inadequate and in poor repair. The new country was still recovering from a severe cyclone that hit the area in 1970 and cause 250,000 deaths. India, by no means a wealthy country and without a tradition of giving aid to other nations, came forward immediately with massive economic assistance in the first months after the fighting ended. Between December 1971 and January 1972, India committed US$232 million in aid to Bangladesh, almost all of it for immediate disbursement.

Bangladeshi leaders slowly began to turn their attention to developing new industrial capacity and rehabilitating its economy. The static economic model adopted by these early leaders, however—including the nationalization of much of the industrial sector—resulted in inefficiency and economic stagnation. Beginning in late 1975, the government gradually gave greater scope to private sector participation in the economy, a pattern that has continued. A few state-owned enterprises have been privatized, but many, including major portions of the banking and jute sectors, remain under government control. Population growth, inefficiency in the public sector, resistance to developing the country's richest natural resources, and limited capital have all continued to restrict economic growth.

In the mid-1980s, there were encouraging, if halting, signs of progress. Economic policies aimed at encouraging private enterprise and investment, denationalizing public industries, reinstating budgetary discipline, and liberalizing the import regime were accelerated. From 1991 to 1993, the government successfully followed an enhanced structural adjustment facility (ESAF) with the International Monetary Fund (IMF) but failed to follow through on reforms in large part because of preoccupation with the government's domestic political troubles. In the late 1990s the government's economic policies became more entrenched, and some of the early gains were lost, which was highlighted by a precipitous drop in foreign direct investment in 2000 and 2001. In June 2003 the IMF approved 3-year, $490-million plan as part of the Poverty Reduction and Growth Facility (PRGF) for Bangladesh that aimed to support the government's economic reform program up to 2006. Seventy million dollars was made available immediately. In the same vein the World Bank approved $536 million in interest-free loans.

ECONOMIC SECTORS

Agriculture

Most Bangladeshis earn their living from agriculture. Although rice and jute are the primary crops, maize and vegetables are assuming greater importance. Due to the expansion of irrigation networks, some wheat producers have switched to cultivation of maize which is used mostly as poultry feed. Tea is grown in the northeast. Because of Bangladesh's fertile soil and normally ample water supply, rice can be grown and harvested three times a year in many areas. Due to a number of factors, Bangladesh's labor-intensive agriculture has achieved steady increases in food grain production despite the often unfavorable weather conditions.

These include better flood control and irrigation, a generally more efficient use of fertilizers, and the establishment of better distribution and rural credit networks. With 28.8 million metric tons produced in 2005-2006 (July-June), rice is Bangladesh's principal crop. By comparison, wheat output in 2005-2006 was 9 million metric tons. Population pressure continues to place a severe burden on productive capacity, creating a food deficit, especially of wheat. Foreign assistance and commercial imports fill the gap. Underemployment remains a serious problem, and a growing concern for Bangladesh's agricultural sector will be its ability to absorb additional manpower. Finding alternative sources of employment will continue to be a daunting problem for future governments, particularly with the increasing numbers of landless peasants who already account for about half the rural labor force.

Manufacturing

Many new jobs - mostly for women - have been created by the country's dynamic private ready-made garment industry, which grew at double-digit rates through most of the 1990s. By the late 1990s, about 1.5 million people, mostly women, were employed in the garments sector. During 2001-2002, export earnings from ready-made garments reached $3,125 million, representing 52% of Bangladesh's total exports.

Eastern Bengal was known for its fine muslin and silk fabric before the British period. The dyes, yarn, and cloth were the envy of much of the premodern world. Bengali muslin, silk, and brocade were worn by the aristocracy of Asia and Europe. The introduction of machine-made textiles from England in the late eighteenth century spelled doom for the costly and time-consuming handloom process. Cotton growing died out in East Bengal, and the textile industry became dependent on imported yarn. Those who had earned their living in the textile industry were forced to rely more completely on farming. Only the smallest vestiges of a once-thriving cottage industry survived.

Investment

The stock market capitalisation of the Dhaka Stock Exchange in Bangladesh crossed $ 10 billion in November 2007. The earliest strategy of the Bangladeshi government was to promote industrialization by making funds available for businessmen through subsidies and national banks. But this plan went awry, as the government lacked the political will to stop financing poorly-performing companies. As a result, the national banks had built large heaps of 'non-performing' loans which are unlikely to be ever repaid. The failure of the national banks discouraged investments by the emerging private financial sector. Currently, Bangladeshi entrepreneurs generally suffer from lack of funding as many banks are reluctant to invest in industry and have instead turned their attention to consumer credit.

Textile sector

Bangladesh's textile industry, which includes knitwear and ready-made garments along with specialised textile products, is the nation's number one export earner. The sector, which employs 2.2 million workers, accounted for 75 per cent of Bangladesh's total exports of US$10.53 billion in FY2005-06, in the process logging a record growth rate of 24.44 per cent. However, since May 2006 the industry has been plagued by on-going industrial unrest, as textile workers, who are among some of the most lowly paid in the world, have staged regular violent demonstrations in a bid to achieve a higher minimum wage, regular rest days and safer working conditions.

Following the worst of the unrest in late May, which saw at least one worker killed as police shot live rounds at protesters, the government formed a Wage Commission, ordering it to report on a suitable new minimum wage in three months.

The Commission, which included business and worker representatives finally released its conclusions on October 9, recommending the wage be set at Tk1,662.50, up from the current level of Tk950, but far below initial worker demands for Tk3,000.

Whether this new wage will placate workers, who allege years of unsafe and abusive conditions remains to be seen. Fresh outbreaks of violence occurred on Oct 2, 3 and 10, but at least some of these protests appear to have stemmed from factory-specific factors, rather than industry wide discontent.

After initially condemning the unrest as the work of outsiders attempting to capture the nation's share of global markets, Bangladesh Garment Manufacturers and Exporters Association (BGMEA) leaders appear to have finally accepted the need to raise wages.

The government also seems to believe some change is necessary. On September 21, 2006 then Ex-Prime Minister Khaleda Zia called on textile firms to ensure the safety of workers by complying with international labor law at a speech inaugurating the Bangladesh Apparel & Textile Exposition (BATEXPO).

External trade

The Bangladesh Garments Manufacturers and Exporters Association (BGMEA) has predicted textile exports will rise from US$7.90 billion earned in 2005-06 to US$15 billion by 2011. In part this optimism stems from how well the sector has fared since the end of textile and clothing quotas, under the Multifibre Agreement, in early 2005.

According to a United Nations Development Programme report "Sewing Thoughts: How to Realise Human Development Gains in the Post-Quota World" Bangladesh has been able to offset a decline in European sales by cultivating new markets in the United States.

"Last year we had tremendous growth. The quota-free textile regime has proved to be a big boost for our factories," said BGMEA president S.M. Fazlul Hoque told reporters, after the sector's 24 per cent growth rate was revealed.

Bangladesh Knitwear Manufacturers and Exporters Association (BKMEA) president Md Fazlul Hoque has also struck an optimistic tone. In an interview with United News Bangladesh he lauded the blistering growth rate, saying "The quality of our products and its competitiveness in terms of prices helped the sector achieve such... tremendous success."

Knitwear posted the strongest growth of all textile products in 2005-06, surging 35.38 per cent to US$2.82 billion. On the downside however, the sector's strong growth came amid sharp falls in prices for textile products on the world market, with growth subsequently dependent upon large increases in volume.

Bangladesh's quest to boost the quantity of textile trade was also helped by US and EU caps on Chinese textiles. The US cap restricts growth in imports of Chinese textiles to 12.5 per cent next year and between 15 and 16 per cent in 2008. The EU deal similarly manages import growth until 2008.

Bangladesh may continue to benefit from these restrictions over the next two years, however a climate of falling global textile prices forces wage rates the centre of the nation's efforts to increase market share.

Prior to the Wage Board's announcement of its recommended minimum wage, the rate had remained unchanged at Tk950 for more than 12 years. Although the government may allow up to three years for the new wage to be implemented, and inevitably there will be compliance issues as manufacturers drag their feet, it seems politically untenable for wages to remain at their current levels given the unprecedented industrial unrest.

In response to the Wage Board's initial draft recommendation of a minimum wage of Tk1,604 to be increased to Tk1,800 after eight months, the BGMEA declared over 50 per cent of factories would be ruined within three months. While this claim is no doubt an exaggeration, the capacity of Bangladesh's textile industry to absorb a significant wage hike as margins become tighter is a key question which hangs over the future of the industry. Bangladesh's textile sector is concentrated in export processing zones in Dhaka and Chittagong. These zones, which are administered by the Bangladesh Export Processing Zone Authority, aim to offer "a congenial investment climate, free from cumbersome procedures" according to Bangladesh Export Promotion Bureau's website.

They offer a range of incentives to potential investors including 10 year tax holidays, duty free import of capital goods, raw materials and building materials, exemptions on income tax on salaries paid to foreign nationals for three years and dividend tax exemptions for the period of the tax holiday.

All goods produced in the zones are able to be exported duty free, in addition to which Bangladesh benefits from the Generalised System of Preferences in US, European and Japanese markets and is also endowed with Most Favoured Nation status from the United States.

Furthermore, Bangladesh imposes no ceiling on investment in the EPZs and allows full repatriation of profits.

The formation of labour unions within the EPZs is prohibited as are strikes.

Bangladesh's exports to the U.S. surpassed $1.9 billion in 1999. Bangladesh also exports significant amounts of garments and knitwear to the EU market.

Bangladesh also has significant jute, leather, shrimp, pharmaceutical, and ceramics industries.

Bangladesh has been a world leader in its efforts to end the use of child labor in garment factories. On July 4, 1995, the Bangladesh Garment Manufacturers Export Association, International Labour Organization, and UNICEF signed a memorandum of understanding on the elimination of child labor in the garment sector. Implementation of this pioneering agreement began in fall 1995, and by the end of 1999, child labor in the garment trade virtually had been eliminated. The labor-intensive process of shipbreaking for scrap has developed to the point where it now meets most of Bangladesh's domestic steel needs. Other industries include sugar, tea, leather goods, newsprint, pharmaceutical, and fertilizer production.

The Bangladesh government continues to court foreign investment, something it has done fairly successfully in private power generation and gas exploration and production, as well as in other sectors such as cellular telephony, textiles, and pharmaceuticals. In 1989, the same year it signed a bilateral investment treaty with the United States, it established a Board of Investment to simplify approval and start-up procedures for foreign investors, although in practice the board has done little to increase investment. The government created the Bangladesh Export Processing Zone Authority to manage the various export processing zones. The agency currently manages EPZs in Adamjee, Chittagong, Comilla, Dhaka, Ishwardi, Karnaphuli, Mongla, and Uttara. An EPZ has also been proposed for Sylhet. The government has given the private sector permission to build and operate competing EPZs-initial construction on a Korean EPZ started in 1999. In June 1999, the AFL-CIO petitioned the U.S. Government to deny Bangladesh access to U.S. markets under the Generalized System of Preferences (GSP), citing the country's failure to meet promises made in 1992 to allow freedom of association in EPZs.

Sylhet is fast becoming the retail capital of Bangladesh, with many shopping centres being built by expatriates to serve fellow expatriates visiting Sylhet and the emerging middleclass. Many of these developments hark back to Britain.

DEMOGRAPHICS OF BANGLADESH

Recent (2005-2007) estimates of Bangladesh's population range from 142 to 159 million, making it the 7th most populous nation in the world. With a land area of 144,000 square kilometers, ranked 94th, the population density is remarkable. A striking comparison is offered by the fact that Russia's population is slightly smaller even though Russia has a land area of 17.5 million square kilometers, at least 120 times bigger than Bangladesh. Indeed Bangladesh has the highest population density in the world, excluding a handful of city-states. Bangladesh's population growth was among the highest in the world in the 1960s and 1970s, when the count grew from 50 to 90 million, but with the promotion of birth control in the 1980s, the growth rate slowed. The total fertility rate is now 3.1 children per woman, compared with 6.2 thirty years ago. The population is relatively young, with the 0–25 age group comprising 60%, while 3% are 65 or older. Life expectancy is 63 years for both males and females.

The majority ethnic group of Bangladesh are the Bengali people, comprising 98% of the population. The remainder are mostly Bihari migrants and indigenous tribal groups. There are thirteen tribal groups located in the Chittagong Hill Tracts, the most populous of the tribes are the Chakmas. The region has been a source for ethnic tension since the inception of Bangladesh. The largest tribal groups outside the Hill Tracts are the Santhals and the Garos (Achiks). There are also Kaibartta, Mundas, Oraons, and Zomi ethnic groups. Human trafficking has been a lingering problem in Bangladesh and illegal immigration has remained a cause of friction with Burma and India.

The official and most widely used language in Bangladesh, as in West Bengal, is Bangla or Bengali, an Indo-Aryan language of Sanskrit origin with its own script. English is used as second language among the middle and upper classes and in higher education. Since a President Order in 1987, Bangla is used for all official correspondence except those that are to foreign recipients.

Health and education levels have recently improved as poverty levels have decreased. Most Bangladeshis are rural, living on subsistence farming. Health problems abound, ranging from surface water contamination, to arsenic contamination of groundwater, and diseases including malaria, leptospirosis and dengue. The literacy rate in Bangladesh is approximately 41%. There is gender disparity, though, as literacy rates are 50% among men and 31% among women, according to a 2004 UNICEF estimate. Literacy has gone up due to many programmes introduced in the country. Among the most successful ones are the *Food for education* (FFE) programme introduced in 1993, and a stipend programme for women at the primary and secondary levels.

CULTURE OF BANGLADESH

The culture of Bangladesh has a unique history, dating back more than 2500 years ago. The land, the rivers and the lives of the common people formed a rich heritage with marked differences from neighboring regions. It has evolved over the centuries, and encompasses the cultural diversity of several social groups of Bangladesh.

The culture of Bangladesh is composite, and over centuries has assimilated influences of Hinduism, Jainism, Buddhism, and Islam. It is manifested in various forms, including music, dance and drama; art and craft; folklores and folktales; languages and literature, philosophy and religion, festivals and celebrations, as also in a distinct cuisine and culinary tradition.

MUSIC, DANCE AND DRAMA

Music and dance style of Bangladesh may be divided into three categories, namely, the classical, folk and the modern. The classical style has been influenced by other prevalent classical forms of music and dances of the Indian subcontinent, and accordingly show some influences dance forms like Bharata Natyam and Kuchipudi. The folk and tribal music and dance forms of Bangladesh are of indigenous origin and rooted to the soil of Bangladesh. Several dancing styles in vogue in the north-eastern part of the Indian subcontinent, like Manipuri and Santhal dances, are also practiced in Bangladesh, but Bangladesh has developed its own distinct dancing styles.

Bangladesh has a rich tradition of folk songs, with lyrics rooted into vibrant tradition and spirituality, mysticism and devotion. Such folk songs also revolve round several other themes, including love themes.

Most prevalent of folk songs and music traditions include Bhatiali, Baul, Marfati, Murshidi and Bhawaiya. Lyricists like Lalon Shah, Hason Raja, Kangal Harinath, Romesh Shill, Abbas Uddin and many unknown anonymous lyrists have enriched the tradition of folk songs of Bangladesh.

In relatively modern context, Rabindra Sangeet and Nazrul geeti form precious cultural heritage of Bangladesh. In recent time, western influences have given rise to several quality rock bands, particularly in urban centers like Dhaka.

Several musical instruments, some of them of indigenous origin, are used in Bangladesh, and major musical instruments used are bamboo flute (banshi), drums (dole), a single stringed instrument named ektara, a four stringed instrument called dotara, a pair of metal bawls used for rhythm effect called mandira. Currently, several musical instruments of western origin like guitar, drums, and saxophone are also used, sometimes alongside the traditional instruments.

Drama remains popular in Bangladesh, including performances of plays by local playwrights, as well as adaptations from writers of Western origin. Jatra, that is, folk drama, is also a part of culture of Bangladesh. In Jatras, legendary plays of heroism, mythological stories, folktales of love and tragedy, and similar countless themes are enacted in open air theatre, and continue to be a popular form of entertainment, in spite of modern influences.

ARTS AND CRAFTS OF BANGLADESH

Fine Arts of Bangladesh

Several artists originated from Bangladesh have gained world-wide familiarity for their artistic contributions. The works of painters like Zainul Abedin, SM Sultan, Quamrul Hassan, Shahabuddin Ahmed, Ronobi and Hashem Khan symbolizes the culture of the country.

Handicrafts of Bangladesh

Handicrafts and cottage industries play a vital role in sustaining the cultural heritage of Bangladesh. The prominent handicrafts in the early and middle ages were textiles, metal works, jewelry, wood works, cane and bamboo works, and clay and pottery. Later, jute and leather became the major raw materials for handicrafts. The most predominant features of Bangladeshi handicrafts are the extensive use of individual skill and the interesting design motifs.

Nakshi Kantha (embroidered quilt), a very popular form of handicraft, is said to be indigenous to Bangladesh. The rural women of the country put together pieces of old cloth with crafty stiches to prepare these quilts to be used in the winter. Although kanthas (quilts) are utilitarian objects, the vivid patterns, borders and motifs often turn them into attractive works of art. In recent years the interest in ethnic arts and crafts has encouraged a kantha revival in the country. Many people now use these quilts for decorative purposes only.

Several, Bangladeshi organizations like Aarong and Probortona export handicrafts from Bangladesh to all over the world. These organizations have played an important role in preserving the handicrafts of Bangladesh and increasing their popularity at home and abroad.

FESTIVALS AND CELEBRATIONS

Festivals and celebrations are integral part of the culture of Bangladesh. Prominent and widely celebrated festivals are Pohela Baishakh, Independence day, National Mourning Day, Eid-ul-Fitr, Eid-ul-Azha, Muharram, Durga puja, and Language Movement Day.

Eid ul-Fitr

As the most important religious festival for the majority Muslims, the celebration of Eid ul-Fitr has become a part of the culture of Bangladesh. The Government of Bangladesh declares holiday for three days on Eid-ul Fitar. People living in towns having their families or parents in villages go to their country homes to meet relatives and celebrate the festival together. All outgoing public transport from the major cities become highly crowded and in many cases the fares tend to rise in spite of government restrictions.

On Eid day, Eid prayers are held all over the country, in open areas like fields or else inside mosques. In Dhaka, the largest Eid prayer is held at the national Eidgah. All major mosques including the Baitul Mukarram also holds prayers. The biggest congregation of Bangladesh is held at Sholakia in Kishoreganj, where about half a million people join the Eid prayer. After the Eid prayers people return home, visit each other's home and eat sweet dishes called *shirni*. Throughout the day gentlemen embrace each other. It is also customary for junior members of the society to touch the feet of the seniors, and seniors returning blessings (sometimes with a small sum of money as a gift).

In the rural areas Eid festival is observed with great fanfare. In some areas Eid fares are arranged. Different types of games including boat race, kabbadi, other traditional Bangladeshi games as well as modern games like football and cricket are played on this occasion.

In urban areas people play music, visit each other's houses and eat special food. Watching movies and television programs has also become an integral part of Eid celebration in urban areas. All local TV channels air special program for several days for this occasion.

Eid ul-Azha

The celebration of Eid ul-Azha is similar to Eid ul-Fitar in many ways. The only big difference is the *Qurbani* or sacrifice of domestic animals on Eid ul-Adha. Numerous temporary marketplaces of different sizes called *Haat* operate in the big cities for sale of Qurbani animals (usually cows and goats).

In the morning on the Eid day, immediately after the prayer, capable people arrange to slaughter their animal of choice. Less affluent people also take part in the festivity by visiting houses of the affluent who are taking part in qurbani. After the qurbani a large portion of the meat is given to the poor people.

Although the religious doctrine allows the sacrifice anytime over a period of three days starting from the Eid day, most people prefer to perform the ritual on the first day of Eid . However, the public holiday spans over three to four days. Many people from the big cities go to their ancestral houses/homes in the villages to share the joy of the festival with friends and relatives.

Pohela Boishakh

Pôhela Boishakh is the first day of the Bangla Calendar. It is usually celebrated on the 14th of April. Pohela Boishakh marked the start day of the crop season. Usually on Pôhela Boishakh, the home is thoroughly scrubbed and cleaned; people bathe early in the morning and dress in fine clothes. They spend much of the day visiting relatives, friends, and neighbours and going to fair. Fairs are arranged in many parts of the country. Various agricultural products, traditional handicrafts, toys, cosmetics, as well as various kinds of food and sweets are sold at these fairs. The fairs also provide entertainment, with singers, dancers and traditional plays and songs. Horseraces, bullraces, bullfights, cockfights, flying pigeons, boat racing were once popular. All gatherings and fairs consist a wide spread of Bengali food and sweets.

The most colourful new year's day festival takes place in Dhaka. Large numbers of people gather early in the morning under the banyan tree at Ramna Park where Chhayanat artists open the day with Rabindranath Tagore's famous song, Esho, he Boishakh, Esho Esho (Come, Year, Come, Come). A similar ceremony welcoming the new year is also held at the Institute of Fine Arts, University of Dhaka. Students and teachers of the institute take out a colourful procession and parade round the campus. Social and cultural organisations celebrate the day with cultural programmes. Newspapers bring out special supplements. There are also special programmes on radio and television.Proir to this day, special discounts on clothes, furniture, electronics and various deals and shopping discounts are available. Special line of sarees, usually cottons, white sarees with red print/embroidery is sold before this day as everyone dresses up for this day. jasmine flowers are also a huge sale for this event which adorns the women's hair.

Language Movement Day

Language Movement Day is a unique part of the culture of Bangladesh. Every year on February 21 this day is observed to pay tribute to the martyrs who sacrificed their lives to establish Bengali as the official language of then East Pakistan in 1952. The mood of the day is sad and humble.

The celebration of Language movement day goes on the entire month of February. Ekushey Book Fair is a book fair arranged to mark this occasion every year. The fair has also become an integral part of the culture of Bangladesh. Authors and readers in Bangladesh eagerly await the fair each year.

To commemorate this movement, Shaheed Minar, a solemn and symbolic sculpture, was erected in the place of the massacre. Today the Shaheed Minar is the centre of cultural activities in Dhaka. On the morning of February 21 each year, people from all walks of life including the national leaders pay tribute to the martyrs by leaving flowers at Shaheed Minar. A very melodious and melancholy song, Amar Bhaier Rokte Rangano, written by Abdul Gaffar Choudhury and composed by Altaf Mahmud, is played repeatedly in electronic media and cultural gatherings throughout the month, and especially on February 21. This song, too, has become a symbolic mark of culture of Bangladesh.

Weddings

A traditional wedding is arranged by Ghotoks (matchmakers), who are typically friends or relatives of the couple. The matchmakers facilitate the introduction, and also help agree the amount of any settlement.

Bengali weddings are traditionally in five parts: first it is the bride and groom's *Mehendi Shondha*,the bride's *Gaye Holud*, the groom's *Gaye Holud*, the *Beeya* and the *Bou Bhaat*. These often take place on separate days. The first event in a wedding is an informal one: the groom presents the bride with a ring marking the "engagement" which is gaining popularity.

For the *mehendi shondha* the bride's side apply henna to each other as well as the bride for the bride's Gaye Holud, the groom's family - except the groom himself - go in procession to the bride's home. The procession traditionally centers on the (younger) female relative and friends of bride, and they are traditionally all in matching clothes, mostly orange in colour. The bride is seated on a dais, and the henna is used to decorate the bride's hands and feet with elaborate abstract designs. The sweets are then fed to the bride by all involved, piece by piece.

The actual wedding ceremony "Beeye" follows the Gaye Holud ceremonies. The wedding ceremony is arranged by the bride's family. On the day, the younger members of the bride's family barricade the entrance to the venue, and demand a sort of admission charge from the groom in return for allowing him to enter. The bride and groom are seated separately, and a Kazi (authorized person by the govt. to perform the wedding), accompanied by the parents and a *Wakil* (witness) from each side formally asks the bride for her consent to the union, and then the groom for his. The bride's side of the family tries to play some kind of practical joke on the groom such as stealing the groom's shoe.

The reception, also known as *Bou-Bhaat* (reception), is a party given by the groom's family in return for the wedding party. It is typically a much more relaxed affair, with only the second-best wedding outfit being worn.

RELIGION IN BANGLADESH

Bangladesh is ethnically homogeneous, with Bengalis comprising 98% of the population. The majority of Bangladeshis (about 88%) are Muslims, and a small number of Hindus, Buddhists and Christians are also in the country.

People of different religions perform there religious rituals with festivity in Bangladesh. The Government has declared National Holidays on all important religious festivals of the four major religion. Durga Puja, Buddha Purnima and Christmas are celebrated with enthusiasm in Bangladesh. All of these form an integral part of the cultural heritage of Bangladesh.

Chapter 5

Nepal

Nepal, officially the **Federal Democratic Republic of Nepal**, also **Republic of Nepal**, is a landlocked country in South Asia. It is bordered by China to the north and by India to the south, east and west. The Himalaya mountain range runs across Nepal's northern and western parts, and eight of the world's ten highest mountains, including the highest, Mount Everest, are within its territory.

The modern state was formed with the Unification of Nepal by Prithvi Narayan Shah on December 21, 1768. Prior to 2006, Nepal was a kingdom. Nepal is now a federal democratic republic. Its recent history has involved struggles for democratic government with periods of direct monarchic rule. From 1996 until 2006, Nepal suffered from a Civil War between government forces and guerrillas of the Communist Party of Nepal (Maoist).

On December 28, 2007, the Interim Parliament passed a bill and declared Nepal to be a *Federal Democratic Republic*. The first meeting of the Constituent Assembly officially implemented that declaration on May 28, 2008.

Nepal is a multi-cultural, multi-linguistic and multi religious country. For a relatively small country, Nepal has a diverse landscape, ranging from the humid Terai plains in the south to the mountainous Himalayas in the north, which makes it a major tourist destination. Hinduism is practiced by a huge majority of the people, but the country also has a strong Buddhist tradition; Lumbini, the birthplace of Buddha Siddhartha Gautama is located in the Terai, one of the three regions of Nepal.

The capital Kathmandu is the largest city in the country. The official language is Nepali and the state currency is the Nepalese Rupee (NPR) Nepal's Flag is the only national flag in the world that is non-quadrilateral in shape. The blue border on the flag of Nepal signifies peace, red stands for the rhododendron, the national flower of Nepal. While the curved moon is symbol of peace and calm nature of Nepalese, the sun represents aggressiveness of Nepalese warriors.

HISTORY OF NEPAL

The **History of Nepal** is characterized by its isolated position in the Himalayas and its two dominant neighbors, India and China. Even though Nepal's heart land was independent through most of its long history, its territorial boundaries have varied greatly over time and internal mosaic of kingdoms restructured often: right from the period of Mahajanapadas, through Greater Nepal to the British Raj.

Due to the arrival of disparate settler groups from outside through the ages, it is now a multi-ethnic, multi-cultural, multi-lingual country. Its population is predominantly Hindu with significant presence of Buddhists, who were in majority at one time in the past. Nepal was split in three kingdoms from the 15th to 18th century, when it was unified under a monarchy. The national language of Nepal is called 'Nepali', a name given - long after unification of Nepal - to the language called Khas Kura.

Modern Nepal experienced a failed struggle for democracy in the 20th century. Since the 1990s, the country has been in civil strife.

Many of the ills of Nepal have been blamed on the royal family of Nepal. In a historical vote for the election of the constituent assembly, Nepalis voted to oust monarchy in Nepal. In June 2008, Nepalis ousted the royal household. Nepal was formally known as the Federal Democratic Republic of Nepal, when it became a federal republic.

EARLY AGES

Prehistory

Neolithic tools found in the Kathmandu Valley indicate that people have been living in the Himalayan region for at least 9,000 years. It appears that a people who were probably of Tibeto-Burman ethnicity lived in Nepal 2,500 years ago.

Legends and Ancient times

Though very little is known about the early history of Nepal, legends and documented references, like the following, reach back to the first millennium BCE:

- The epic Ramayana, which dates from an era before the Mahabharata, states that Mithila, currently known as Janakpur in Nepal, is the birth place of goddess Sita.
- Also, the presence of historical sites, e.g. Valmiki ashram, indicates the presence of Sanatana (eternal) Hindu culture in Nepal at that period.
- The epic Mahabharata mentions the *Kiratas* among the inhabitants of Nepal. Kirati king Yalambar had the dubious honor of being slain in the battle of the Mahabharata, in which gods and mortals fought alongside each other. Legend credits him with meeting Indra, the lord of heaven, who ventured into the Valley in human guise.

- According to some of the chronicles the successors of Nepal were "Cowherd family", whose names often end in *-gupta* and are said to have ruled for some 491 years. They are said to have been followed by the "Buffalo-herder Dynasty", established by an Indian Rajput named Bhul Singh.
- **inscriptions** found on archeological stoneworks, which list mostly the dates and commissioners of these constructions, also communicate royal edicts, religious mantras or historical notes sometimes and, through the corroboration of local myths with such evidence, a people prior to the Licchavi have been identified, known as the Kirata.

Kirat Period

Nepal's recorded history began with the Kiratis, who arrived in the 7th or 8th century BCE from the east. Little is known about them, other than their deftness as sheep farmers and fondness for carrying long knives. The Kirats ruled for about 1225 years (800 BCE-300 CE), their reign had a total of 28 kings during that time. Their first and best remembered king was Yalambar, who finds a reference in the epic Mahabharata.

MEDIAEVAL HISTORY

Birth of Buddhism

One of the earliest confederations of South Asia was that of the Shakya clan, whose capital was Kapilavastu, near the present-day border with the Republic of India. One of its princes was Gautama Buddha, Siddharta Gautama (563–483 BCE), who renounced his royalty to lead an ascetic life and came to be known as the *Buddha* ("the enlightened one"). By 260 BCE, most of North India and southern Nepal were ruled by the Maurya Empire. It was during this period that Buddhism first came to Nepal; it is claimed that Buddha and his disciple Ananda visited the Kathmandu Valley and stayed for a time in Patan. Although not all of Nepal was under Maurya occupation, there is evidence of at least the influence of Maurya Emperor Ashoka the Great, the legendary Buddhist proselytiser and ruler from 273 BCE to 232 BCE. Ashoka was a visitor to Kathmandu in this period and, as a follower of Buddhism, he visited Lumbini, the birthplace of Buddha, and erected stupas in Kathmandu. His daughter married a local prince and further spread the religion. The remains of a Buddhist convent have been found in the Kathmandu Valley.

As the Kirat dynasty came to an end in the valley, parts still remained in the eastern mountains, where they are considered to be the forefathers of today's Limbu and Rai castes.

By 200 CE, Buddhism had waned, and was replaced by Hinduism, brought by the Licchavis, who invaded from northern India and overthrew the last Kirati king. The Hindus also introduced the caste system (which still continues today) and ushered in a classical age of Nepalese art and architecture.

Licchavi rule

It is unclear when exactly the Licchavi kingdom began. From the findings at the ancient capital of Handigaun, it appears that Licchavi rulers were in power on two occasions: from about 200 CE to the 5th century, and from about 750 to 1200 CE. Archaeological evidence for the Licchavi period mainly consists of stonework inscriptions, reckoned on two separate, consecutive eras; the former era evidence, in the Åšaka or Saka era, has an epoch corresponding to 78 CE, whereas the latter, of ACshuvarmâ or Manadeva-II's era, reckons from 576 CE.

In between, in the fourth century CE, the country fell under the influence of Indian Gupta Empire - considered to be a golden period of Hinduism in India - whose cultural diffusion is evident, despite their lack of direct control of Nepal.

First Licchavi rule evidence: A well-preserved life-sized sandstone sculpture of a king named Jaya Varman, discovered in Maligaon in the eastern part of Kathmandu, contains an inscription dating it to the 'samvat' year 107, which most probably is in the Shaka era and is, therefore, from 185 CE; this dating is also supported by the style of the sculpture which is clearly Kushan in origin. It is unclear whether Jaya Varman was a Licchavi or a pre-Licchavi monarch. However, most scholars are agreed that, Licchavi rule of the Kathmandu valley must have begun in the first or second century CE.

Second Licchavi rule evidence: Two known dated inscriptions, both Licchavi, are a broken pillar inscription from Pashupati dated 381 (459 CE), and the Cangu Narayana pillar inscription of King Manadeva in 386 (464 CE).

There is a good and quite detailed description of the kingdom of Nepal in the account of the renowned Chinese Buddhist pilgrim monk, Xuanzang, dating from *c.* 645 CE.

The Licchavi rulers arranged for the documentation of information on politics, society, and the economy in the region. Most of the Licchavi records—written in Sanskrit—are deeds reporting donations to religious foundations, predominantly Hindu temples; and the last such record was added in 733.

The Licchavi dynasty went into decline in the late eighth century and was followed by a Newari era, from 879, although the extent of their control over the entire country is uncertain.

Thakuri rule

By 879, the Licchavi era had petered out and was succeeded by the Thakuri dynasty. A grim period of instability and invasions often referred to as the 'Dark Ages' followed, but Kathmandu Valley's strategic location ensured the kingdom's survival and growth.

MAGAR EMPIRE

Magar is a warrior and martial people that first established it's kingdom in present day western Nepal. They were animistic and shamanic in their religious practices. The Kham Magar of upper Karnali basin and their brethren of mid hills of Nepal had a flourishing and empirical kingdoms. Much archaeological proof of their existence can be found in the western mid hills of Nepal.

Magar have a strong military and warrior traditions. However, their hospitality and concern for the fellow human being is also legendary. The two waves of immigrants became the undoing for Magar empire.

Firstly, the Khasas were welcomed and assimilated within Magar empire. Secondly, following the rout of fundamentalist Brahmin Hindus of the Gangetic plains of India by the advancing Mugal forces, the traditionalist Brahmin Hindus entered Magar empire as refugees. They brought with them Hindu religion.

It is the misfortune of Magar empire and the whole Magar people that these two groups were given sanctuary in Magar empire. The latter group of refugees started to impose their fundamentalist view of Hindu religion upon Magars in Magar kingdoms whereas the former group were given the status of Chettri by the latter group in accordance to their fundamentalist view of Hindu religion.

This left the Magar people to be boxed into the third tier of their own kingdoms. (The first being the fundamentalist refugee Brahmin, the second being newly elevated Chettri, previously the Khasas).

This meant that the once rulers of the Nepali mid hills became the ruled upon. Thus starts the degradation of Magar empire. The introduction of Hinduism in itself became the cataclysmic event in the undoing of the Magar empire.

Malla dynasty

Several centuries later, the Thakuri king, Arideva, founded the Malla dynasty, kick-starting another renaissance of Nepali culture. Despite earthquakes, the occasional invasion, and frequent feuding between the independent city-states of Kathmandu, Patan and Bhaktapur, the dynasty flourished, reaching its zenith in the 15th century under Yaksha Malla.

Chalukaya dynasty

By the late 11th century, southern Nepal came under the occupation of the Chalukaya Empire of southern India. Under the Chalukayas, Nepal's religious establishment changed as the kings patronised Hinduism instead of the prevailing Buddhism.

NEWAR EMPIRE: THREE MEDIEVAL KINGDOMS

Thirteenth century Nepal was occasionally attacked by the rulers of Delhi Sultanate of northern India, and was consequently marked by increased Nepali militarisation. By the late 14th century, much of the country came under the rule of the king Jayasthitimalla, a Newar King, who managed to unite most of the fragmented power bases. This unity was short-lived; in 1482 the territory was carved into three kingdoms : Kathmandu, Patan, and Bhadgaon.

Most of the Nepalese architectural heritage such as temples, palaces including many UNESCO world heritage sites were built by Newars during the rule by Newar Kings. These include Kathmandu Old Palace (Kathmandu Durbar Square), Patan Palace(Patan Durbar Square), Bhaktapur Palace (Bhaktapur Durbar Square) etc.

Between 1717 and 1733, the Nepalese in the west, and also the Bhutanese from the east, attacked Sikkim many times, culminating with the destruction of the capital Rabdentse by the Nepalese. The Sikkim king fled to Tibet.

MODERN PERIOD: GORKHA RULE

After decades of rivalry between the medieval kingdoms, modern Nepal was created in the latter half of the 18th century, when Prithvi Narayan Shah, the ruler of the small principality of Gorkha, formed a unified country from a number of independent hill states. Prithvi Narayan Shah dedicated himself at an early age to the conquest of the Kathmandu valley and the creation of a single state, which he achieved in 1768.

The country was frequently called the Gorkha Kingdom. It is a misconception that the Gurkhas took their name from the Gorkha region of Nepal. The region was given its name after the Gurkhas had established their control of these areas. Gurkha, also spelt as Gorkha, are people from Nepal who take their name from the legendary eighth century Hindu warrior-saint Guru Gorakhnath. Gurkhas claim descent from the Hindu Rajputs and Brahmins of Northern India, who entered modern Nepal from the west.

After Shah's death, the Shah dynasty began to expand their kingdom into what is present day North India. Between 1788 and 1791, Nepal invaded Tibet and robbed Tashilhunpo Monastery of Shigatse. Alarmed, the Chinese emperor Qianlong dispatched a sizeable army that forced the Nepalese to retreat and pay heavy reparations.

After 1800, the heirs of Prithvi Narayan Shah proved unable to maintain firm political control over Nepal. A period of internal turmoil followed.

Rivalry between Nepal and the British East India Company, over the annexation of minor states bordering Nepal, eventually led to the Anglo-Nepalese War (1814–16), in which Nepal suffered a complete rout. The Treaty of Sugauli was signed in 1816, ceding parts of the Nepali territories of Terrai and Sikkim to the British, in exchange for Nepalese autonomy. They have become integral parts of India. As borders between India and Nepal were never clearly defined in the past, the borders at the time of leaving of the British are recognised as the permanent borders.

RANA ADMINISTRATION

Factionalism among the royal family led to a period of instability after the war. In 1846, Queen Rajendralakshmi plotted to overthrow Jang Bahadur, a fast-rising military leader of Indian Rajput ancestry, who was presenting a threat to her power. The plot was uncovered and the queen had several hundred princes and chieftains executed after an armed clash between military personnel and administrators loyal to the queen. This came to be known as the Kot Massacre. However, Bahadur emerged victorious eventually and founded the Rana dynasty; the monarch was made a titular figure, and the post of Prime Minister was made powerful and hereditary, held by a Rana.

The Rana regime, a tightly centralized autocracy, pursued a policy of isolating Nepal from external influences. This policy helped Nepal maintain its national independence during the British colonial era, but it also impeded the country's economic development and modernisation. The Ranas were staunchly pro-British and assisted the British during the Indian Rebellion of 1857, and later in both World Wars.

20TH CENTURY

In 1923 Britain and Nepal formally signed an agreement of friendship, in which Nepal's independence was recognized by the British.

Slavery was abolished in Nepal in 1924.

DEMOCRATIC REFORM

Popular dissatisfaction against the family rule of the Ranas had started emerging from among the few educated people, who had studied in various Indian schools and colleges, and also from within the Ranas, many of whom were marginalised within the Ruling Rana hierarchy. Many of these Nepalese in exile had actively taken part in the Indian Independence struggle and wanted to liberate Nepal as well from the internal autocratic Rana occupation. The political parties like *The Prajaparishad* and *Nepali Congress* were already formed in exile by the leaders like B.P. Koirala, Ganesh Man Singh, Subarna Sumsher Rana, Krishna Prasad Bhattarai,Girija Prasad Koirala and many other patriotic minded Nepalis, who wanted to stage both the military and popular political movement in Nepal, to overthrow the autocratic Rana Regime.

Among the prominent martyrs to die for the cause, executed at the hands of the Ranas, were *Dharma Bhakta Mathema, Shukraraj Shastri, Gangalal Shrestha and Dasharath Chand*. This turmoil culminated in King Tribhuvan, a direct descendant of Prithvi Narayan Shah, fleeing from his "palace prison" in 1950, to newly independent India, touching off an armed revolt against the Rana administration. This eventually ended in the return of the Shah family to power and the appointment of a non-Rana as prime minister. A period of quasi-constitutional rule followed, during which the monarch, assisted by the leaders of fledgling political parties, governed the country. During the 1950s, efforts were made to frame a constitution for Nepal that would establish a representative form of government, based on a British model.

In early 1959, Tribhuvan's son King Mahendra issued a **new constitution**, and the first **democratic elections** for a national assembly were held. The Nepali Congress Party, a moderate socialist group, gained a substantial victory in the election. Its leader,

Bishweshwar Prasad Koirala, formed a government and served as prime minister. After years of power wrangling between the Kings (Tribhuvan and Mahendra) and the government, Mahendra dissolved the democratic experiment in 1960.

ROYAL COUP BY KING MAHENDRA

Declaring parliamentary democracy a failure, King Mahendra carried out a royal coup 18 months later, in 1962. He dismissed the elected Koirala government, declared that a **"partyless" panchayat system** would govern Nepal and promulgated **another new constitution** on December 16, 1962.

Subsequently, the elected Prime Minister, Members of Parliament and hundreds of democratic activists were arrested. (In fact, this trend of arrest of political activists and democratic supporters continued for the entire 30 year period of partyless Panchayati System under King Mahendra and then his son, King Birendra).

The new constitution had established a "partyless" system of panchayats (councils) which King Mahendra considered to be a democratic form of government, closer to Nepalese traditions. As a pyramidal structure, progressing from village assemblies to a Rastriya Panchayat (National Parliament), the panchayat system constitutionalised the absolute power of the monarchy and kept the King as head of state with sole authority over all governmental institutions, including the Cabinet (Council of Ministers) and the Parliament. One-state-one-language became the national policy and all other languages suffered at the cost of the official language, "Nepali", which was the king's language.

King Mahendra was succeeded by his 27 year-old son, King Birendra, in 1972. Amid student demonstrations and anti-regime activities in 1979, King Birendra called for a national referendum to decide on the nature of Nepal's government—either the continuation of the panchayat system with **democratic reforms** or the establishment of a multiparty system. The referendum was held in May 1980, and the panchayat system won a narrow victory. The king carried out the promised reforms, including selection of the prime minister by the Rastriya Panchayat.

People in rural areas had expected that their interests would be better represented after the adoption of parliamentary democracy in 1990. Nepali Congress with support of "Alliance of leftist parties" decided to launch a decisive movement agitational movement, Jana Andolan, which forced the monarchy to accept constitutional reforms and to establish a **multiparty parliament**. In May 1991, Nepal held its first parliamentary elections in nearly 50 years. The Nepali Congress won 110 of the 205 seats and formed the first elected government in 32 years.

Civil Strife

In 1992, in a situation of economic crisis and chaos, with spiralling prices as a result of implementation of changes in policy of the new Congress government, the radical left stepped up their political agitation. A **Joint People's Agitation Committee** was set up by the various groups. A general strike was called for April 6.

Violent incidents began to occur on the evening ahead of the strike. The Joint People's Agitation Committee had called for a 30-minute 'lights out' in the capital, and violence erupted outside Bir Hospital when activists tried to enforce the 'lights out'. At dawn on April 6, clashes between strike activists and police, outside a police station in Pulchok (Patan), left two activists dead.

Later in the day, a mass rally of the Agitation Committee at Tundikhel in the capital Kathmandu was attacked by police forces. As a result, riots broke out and the Nepal Telecommunications building was set on fire; police opened fire at the crowd, killing several persons. The Human Rights Organisation of Nepal estimated that 14 persons, including several on-lookers, had been killed in police firing.

When promised land reforms failed to appear, people in some districts started to organize to enact their own land reform, and to gain some power over their lives in the face of usurious landlords. However, this movement was repressed by the Nepali government, in **"Operation Romeo"** and **"Operation Kilo Sera II"** which took the lives of many of the leading activists of the struggle. As a result, many witnesses to this repression became radicalized.

NEPALESE CIVIL WAR

In February 1996, one of the Maoist parties started a bid to replace the parliamentary monarchy with a so-called people's new democratic republic, through a Maoist revolutionary strategy known as the people's war, which led to the Nepalese Civil War. Led by Dr. Baburam Bhattarai and Pushpa Kamal Dahal (also known as "Prachanda"), the insurgency began in five districts in Nepal: Rolpa, Rukum, Jajarkot, Gorkha, and Sindhuli. The Maoists declared the existence of a provisional "people's government" at the district level in several locations.

Meanwhile, on June 1, 2001, Crown Prince Dipendra went on a shooting-spree, assassinating 11 members of the royal family, including King Birendra and Queen Aishwarya, before shooting himself. Due to his survival he temporarily became king before dying of his wounds, after which Prince Gyanendra (Birendra's brother) inherited the throne as per tradition. Meanwhile, the Maoist rebellion escalated, and in October 2001 the king temporarily deposed the government and took complete control of it. A week later he reappointed another government, but the country was still very unstable: because of the civil war with the Maoists; the various clamouring political factions; the king's attempts to take more control of the government; and worries about the competence of Gyanendra's son and heir, Prince Paras.

In the face of unstable governments and a Maoist siege on the Kathmandu Valley in August 2004, popular support for the monarchy began to wane. On February 1, 2005,

Gyanendra dismissed the entire government and assumed full executive powers, declaring a "state of emergency" to quash the Maoist movement. Politicians were placed under house arrest, phone and internet lines were cut, and freedom of the press was severely curtailed.

The king's new regime made little progress in his stated aim to suppress the insurgents. Municipal elections in February 2006 were described by the European Union as "a backward step for democracy", as the major parties boycotted the election and some candidates were forced to run for office by the army. In April 2006 strikes and street protests in Kathmandu forced the king to reinstate the parliament. A **seven-party coalition** resumed control of the government and stripped the king of most of his powers. As of 15 January 2007 Nepal was governed by an unicameral legislature under an **interim constitution**. On December 24, 2007, seven parties, including the former Maoist rebels and the ruling party, agreed to abolish monarchy and declare Nepal a **Federal Republic**. In the elections held on April 10, 2008, the Maoists secured a simple majority, with the prospect of forming a government to rule the proposed 'Republic of Nepal'.

21ST CENTURY

Declaration of Republic

On May 28, 2008 the newly elected Constituent Assembly declared Nepal a Federal Democratic Republic, abolishing the 240 years old monarchy. The motion for abolition of monarchy was carried by a huge majority; out of 564 members present in the assembly, 560 voted for the motion while 4 members voted against it. Finally, on June 11, 2008 ex-king Gyanendra left the palace. Pushpa Kamal Dahal, popularly known as Parchanda, of the Communist Party of Nepal (Maoist) was elected as the first Prime Minister of the Republic on August 15, 2008 defeating Sher Bahadur Deuba of Nepali Congress.

GEOGRAPHY OF NEPAL

Sandwiched between two Asian giants—China and India—**Nepal** traditionally has been characterized as "a yam caught between two rocks." Noted for its majestic Himalayas, which in Sanskrit means the abode of snow, Nepal is very mountainous and hilly. Its shape is roughly rectangular, about 800 kilometers long and about 100 to 200 kilometers wide, and comprises a total of 147,181 square kilometers of land. It is slightly larger than Bangladesh or the state of Arkansas. Nepal is a landlocked country, surrounded by India on three sides and by China's Xizang Autonomous Region (Tibet) to the north. It is separated from Bangladesh by an approximately 15 kilometer wide strip of India's state of West Bengal, and from Bhutan by the 88 kilometer wide Sikkim, also an Indian state. Such a confined geographical position is hardly enviable. Nepal is almost totally dependent on India for transit facilities and access to the sea—that is, the Bay of Bengal—even for most of the goods coming from China.

For a small country, Nepal has great physical diversity, ranging from the Tarai Plain — the northern rim of the Gangetic Plain situated at about 60 meters above sea level in the south — to the 8850-meter-high Mount Everest, locally known as Sagarmatha (its Nepali name), in the north. From the lowland Tarai belt, landforms rise in successive hill and mountain ranges, including the stupendous rampart of the towering Himalayas, ultimately reaching the Tibetan Plateau beyond the Inner Himalayas. This rise in elevation is punctuated by valleys situated between mountain ranges. Within this maze of mountains, hills, ridges, and low valleys, elevational (altitudinal) changes resulted in ecological variations.

Nepal commonly is divided into three broad physiographic areas: the Mountain Region, the Hill Region, and the Tarai Region. All three parallel each other, from east to west, as continuous ecological belts, occasionally bisected by the country's river systems. These ecological regions were divided by the government into development sectors within the framework of regional development planning.

The rhythm of life in Nepal, as in most other parts of monsoonal Asia, is intricately yet intrinsically intertwined with its physical environment. As scholar Barry Bishop learned from his field research in the Karnali region in the northwest, the livelihood patterns of Nepal are inseparable from the environment.

THE MOUNTAIN REGION

The Mountain Region (called Parbat in Nepali) is situated at 4,000 meters or more above sea level to the north of the Hill Region. The Mountain Region constitutes the central portion of the Himalayan range originating in the Pamirs, a high altitude region of Central Asia. Its natural landscape includes Mount Everest and the other seven of the world's ten highest peaks. In general, the snow line occurs between 5,000 and 5,500 meters. The region is characterized by inclement climatic and rugged topographic conditions, and human habitation and economic activities are extremely limited and arduous. Indeed, the region is sparsely populated, and whatever farming activity exists is mostly confined to the low-lying valleys and the river basins, such as the upper Kali Gandaki Valley.

In the early 1990s, pastoralism and trading were common economic activities among mountain dwellers. Because of their heavy dependence on herding and trading, transhumance was widely practiced. While the herders moved their goths (temporary animal shelters) in accordance with the seasonal climatic rhythms, traders also migrated seasonally between highlands and lowlands, buying and selling goods and commodities in order to generate much needed income and to secure food supplies.

THE HILL REGION

Situated south of the Mountain Region, the Hill Region (called Pahar in Nepali) is mostly between 1,000 and 4,000 meters in altitude. It includes the Kathmandu Valley, the country's most fertile and urbanized area. Two major ranges of hills, commonly known as the Mahabharat Lekh and Siwalik Range (or Churia Range), occupy the region. In addition, there are several intermontane valleys. Despite its geographical isolation and limited economic potential, the region always has been the political and cultural center of Nepal, with decision-making power centralized in Kathmandu, the nation's capital. Because of immigration from Tibet and India, the hill ranges historically have been the most heavily populated area. Despite heavy out-migration, the Hill Region comprised the largest share of the total population in 1991.

Although the higher elevations (above 2,500 meters) in the region are sparsely populated because of physiographic and climatic difficulties, the lower hills and valleys are densely settled. The hill landscape is both a natural and cultural mosaic, shaped by geological forces and human activity. The hills, sculpted by human hands into a massive complex of terraces, are extensively cultivated.

Like the Mountain Region, the Hill Region was a food-deficit area in the early 1990s, although agriculture was the predominant economic activity supplemented by livestock raising, foraging, and seasonal migrating of laborers. The vast majority of the households living in the hills were land-hungry and owned largely pakho (hilly) land. The poor economic situation caused by lack of sufficient land was aggravated by the relatively short growing season, a phenomenon directly attributable to the climatic impact of the region's higher altitude.

As a result, a hill farmer's ability to grow multiple crops was limited. The families were forced to adapt to the marginality, as well as the seasonality, of their environment, cultivating their land whenever they could and growing whatever would survive. Bishop has noted that "as crop productivity decreases with elevation, the importance of livestock in livelihood pursuits . . . increases. For many Bhotia [or Bhote] living in the highlands . . . animal husbandry supplants agriculture in importance." During the slack season, when the weather did not permit cropping, hill dwellers generally became seasonal migrants, who engaged in wage labor wherever they could find it to supplement their meager farm output. Dependence on nonagricultural activities was even more necessary in the mountain ecological belt.

THE TERAI REGION

In complete topographic contrast to the Mountain and Hill regions, the Terai Region, also called Madhesh, is a lowland tropical and subtropical belt of flat, alluvial land stretching along the Nepal-India border, and parallel to the Hill Region. It is the northern extension of the Gangetic Plain in India, commencing at about 300 meters above sea level and rising to about 1,000 meters at the foot of the Siwalik Range. The Terai includes several valleys (dun), such as the Surkhet and Dang valleys in western Nepal, and the Rapti Valley (Chitwan) in central Nepal.

The word terai, a term presumed to be derived from Persian, means "damp," and it appropriately describes the region's humid and hot climate. The region was formed and is fed by three major rivers: the Koshi, the Narayani (India's Gandak River), and the Karnali. A region that in the past contained malaria-infested, thick forests, commonly known as char kose jhadi (dense forests approximately 12 kilometers wide), the Terai was used as a defensive frontier by Nepalese rulers during the period of the British Raj (1858-1947) in India. Today, the majority of Nepal's population and most of the cities and towns are found in this region.

In terms of both farm and forest lands, the Terai is becoming Nepal's richest economic region. Overall, Terai residents enjoy a greater availability of agricultural land than other Nepalese because of the area's generally flat terrain, which is drained and nourished by several rivers. Additionally, it has the largest commercially exploitable forests. In the early 1990s, however, the forests were being increasingly destroyed because of growing demands for timber and agricultural land.

CLIMATE

Nepal has a great deal of variation in climate. Its latitude is about the same as that of Florida, so the low elevation Terai has a tropical and subtropical climate. Above the Terai, the climate is completely different due to higher elevations. The east-west-trending Himalayan ranges to the north and the monsoonal alteration of wet and dry seasons also contribute to local variations in climate. Scholar Sharad Singh Negi identifies five climatic zones in Nepal based on altitude: a tropical and subtropical zone below 1,200 meters (the frost limit in winter), a cool temperate zone between 1,200 and 2,400 meters (where there is at least occasional snowfall in winter), a cold zone betwen 2,400 and 3,600 meters (tree line), a subarctic zone from 3,600 to 4,400 meters, and an arctic zone above 4,400 meters.

In terms of natural vegetational regimes or distribution patterns, altitude again plays a significant role. Below 1,200 meters, the dominant form of vegetation consists of tropical and subtropical forests that have evolved in response to the monsoonal climate. Altitude also affects annual rainfall or precipitation patterns. Up to about 3,000 meters, annual rainfall totals increase with elevation, but above this they decrease with elevation and latitude. Two other patterns can be discerned. First, given the northwestward movement of the moisture-laden summer monsoon (June to September), the amount of annual rainfall generally decreases from east to west, although there are exceptional areas such as the Pokhara Valley in Central Nepal with higher rainfall due to generally lower "hills" to the south and the main Himalayan Range immediately to the north that stops the northward passage of moist air. Second, adabiatic effects increase rainfall on south- and east-facing mountain slopes, with a rain shadow on northern sides. This reaches its climax in the inner Himalayan region and on the Tibetan Plateau. Eastern Nepal receives approximately 2,500 millimeters of rain annually, the Kathmandu area gets about 1,400 millimeters, and western Nepal about 1,000 millimeters.

The towering Himalayas play a critical role, blocking the northwesterly advances of moist, tropical air from the Bay of Bengal, and ultimately leading to its conversion to rain in the summer. In the winter, this range prevents the outbursts of cold air from Inner

Asia from reaching southern Nepal and northern India, thus ensuring warmer winters in these regions than otherwise would be the case.

In addition, there are seasonal variations in the amount of rainfall, depending on the monsoon cycle. Bishop divides the monsoon cycle into four seasons: premonsoon, summer monsoon, postmonsoon, and winter monsoon. The premonsoon season generally occurs during April and May; it is characterized by the highest temperatures, reaching 40 °C during the day in the Terai Region and other lowlands. The hills and mountains, however, remain cool.

The summer monsoon, a strong flow of moist air from the southwest, follows the premonsoon season. For the vast majority of southern Asians, including Nepalese, the term monsoon is synonymous with the summer rainy season, which makes or breaks the lives of hundreds of millions of farmers on the subcontinent. Even though the arrival of the summer monsoon can vary by as much as a month, in Nepal it generally arrives in early June, is preceded by violent lightning and thunderstorms, and lasts through September, when it begins to recede. The plains and lower Himalayas receive more than 70% of their annual precipitation during the summer monsoon. The amount of summer monsoon rain generally declines from southeast to northwest as the maritime wedge of air gradually becomes thinner and dryer. Although the success of farming is almost totally dependent on the timely arrival of the summer monsoon, it periodically causes such problems as landslides; subsequent losses of human lives, farmlands, and other properties (not to mention great difficulty in the movement of goods and people); and heavy flooding in the plains. Conversely, when prolonged breaks in the summer monsoon occur, severe drought and famine often result.

The postmonsoon season begins with a slow withdrawal of the monsoon. This retreat leads to an almost complete disappearance of moist air by mid-October, thus ushering in generally cool, clear, and dry weather, as well as the most relaxed and jovial period in Nepal. By this time, the harvest is completed and people are in a festive mood. The two biggest and most important Hindu festivals— Dashain and Tihar (Dipawali)—arrive during this period, about one month apart. The postmonsoon season lasts until about December.

After the postmonsoon, comes the winter monsoon, a strong northeasterly flow, which is marked by occasional, short rainfalls in the lowlands and plains and snowfalls in the high-altitude areas. The amount of precipitation resulting from the northeast land trade winds varies considerably but increases markedly with elevation. The secondary winter precipitation in the form of snowfalls in the Himalayas is important for generating a sufficient volume of spring and summer meltwaters, which are critical for irrigation in the lower hills and valleys where agriculture predominates. Winter precipitation is also are indispensable for the success of winter crops, such as wheat, barley, and numerous vegetables.

RIVER SYSTEM

Nepal can be divided into three major river systems from east to west: the Koshi River basin, the Narayani River basin (India's Gandak River), and the Karnali River basin. All ultimately become major tributaries of the Ganges River in northern India. After plunging through deep gorges, these rivers deposit their heavy sediments and debris on the plains, thereby nurturing them and renewing their alluvial soil fertility. Once they reach the Tarai Region, they often overflow their banks onto wide floodplains during the summer monsoon season, periodically shifting their courses. Besides providing fertile alluvial soil, the backbone of the agrarian economy, these rivers present great possibilities for hydroelectric and irrigation development. To date Nepal has not made extensive use of its hydorlelectric resourses. All of them make use of the natural elevation differences, diverting water from the river and running it through turbines further downstream.

The latest one is the Kali Gandaki hydroelectricity project a few km north of Tansen. Building dams in Nepal has remained a disputed issue, mainly because of the high risk of earthquakes in the region. None of the river systems support any significant commercial navigation facility. Rather, the deep gorges formed by the rivers represent immense obstacles to establishing the broad transport and communication networks needed to develop an integrated national economy. As a result, the economy in Nepal has remained fragmented. Because Nepal's rivers have not been harnessed for transportation, most settlements in the Hill and Mountain regions remain isolated from each other. As of 1991, trails remained the primary transportation routes in the hills.

The eastern part of the country is drained by the Koshi River, which has seven tributaries. It is locally known as the Sapt Kosi, which means seven Kosi rivers (Tamur, Likhu Khola, Dudh, Sun, Indrawati, Tama, and Arun). The principal tributary is the Arun, which rises about 150 kilometers inside the Tibetan Plateau. The Narayani River drains the central part of Nepal and also has seven major tributaries (Daraudi, Seti, Madi, Kali, Marsyandi, Budhi, and Trisuli). The Kali Gandaki, which flows between the Dhaulagiri Himal and the Annapurna Himal (Himal is the Nepali variation of the Sanskrit word Himalaya), is the main river of this drainage system. The river system draining the western part of Nepal is the Karnali. Its three immediate tributaries are the Bheri, Seti, and Karnali rivers, the latter being the major one. The Maha Kali, which also is known as the Kali and which flows along the Nepal-India border on the west side, and the Rapti River also are considered tributaries of the Karnali.

GOVERNMENT AND POLITICS OF NEPAL

The **politics of Nepal** function within a framework of a republic with a multi-party system. Currently, the positions of President (head of state) and Prime Minister (head of government) are occupied by Ram Baran Yadav and Prachanda, respectively. Executive power is exercised by the President, Prime Minister, and his cabinet, while legislative power is vested in the Constituent Assembly.

Until May 28, 2008, Nepal was a constitutional monarchy. On that date the constitution was altered by the Constituent Assembly to make the country a republic.

POLITICAL CONDITIONS

1990–1996: Parliamentary monarchy

Until 1990, Nepal was an absolute monarchy running under the executive control of the king. Faced with a people's movement against the absolute monarchy, King Birendra, in 1990, agreed to large-scale political reforms by creating a parliamentary monarchy with the king as the head of state and a prime minister as the head of the government.

Nepal's legislature was bicameral consisting of a House of Representatives and a National Council. The House of Representatives consisted of 205 members directly elected by the people. The National Council had 60 members, 10 nominated by the king, 35 elected by the House of Representatives and the remaining 15 elected by an electoral college made up of chairs of villages and towns. The legislature had a five-year term, but was dissolved by the king before its term could end. All Nepalese citizens 18 years and older became eligible to vote.

The executive comprised the King and the Council of Ministers (the Cabinet). The leader of the coalition or party securing the maximum seats in an election was appointed as the Prime Minister. The Cabinet was appointed by the king on the recommendation of the Prime Minister.

Governments in Nepal have tended to be highly unstable; no government has survived for more than two years since 1991, either through internal collapse or parliamentary dissolution by the monarch.

In the first free and fair elections in Nepal in 1991, the Nepali Congress was victorious. The 1994 election defeat of the Nepali Congress Party by the Communist Party of Nepal (Unified Marxist-Leninist) (CPN(UML)) made Nepal the first communist-led monarchy in Asia, with Man Mohan Adhikary prime minister. In mid-1994, parliament was dissolved due to dissension within the Nepali Congress Party. The subsequent general election, held 15 November 1994, gave no party a majority and led to several years of unstable coalition governments. As of the May 1999 general elections, the Nepali Congress Party once again headed a majority government.

There have been three Nepali Congress Party Prime Ministers since the 1999 elections: K.P. Bhattarai (31 May 1999–17 March 2000); Girija Prasad Koirala (20 March 2000–19 July 2001); and Sher Bahadur Deuba (23 July 2001–2003). The final distribution of seats in Parliament gave the Nepali Congress 113; the CPN(UML) 69; the RPP 11; the RJM 5;

the NSP 5; the Workers and Peasants Party 1; and the United People's Front 1. Nepali Congress Party has divided to Nepali Congress Party led by G. P. Koirala and Nepali Congress (Democratic) led by Sher Bahadur Deuba. Amongst the elected MPs, 39 MPs belong to Nepali Congress (Democratic). Former Prime Minister and Influential Leader Krishna Prasad Bhattarai has expressed his support for Nepali Congress (Democratic). Both Congress parties regard Krishna Prasad Bhattarai as their main leader.

King Gyanendra discharged Sher Bahadur Deuba and on 4 June 2003 appointed Surya Bahadur Thapa as Prime Minister.

1996: Maoist insurgency

In February 1996, the Communist Party of Nepal (Maoist) began a violent insurgency in more than 50 of the country's 75 districts. About 11,000 police, civilians, and insurgents have been killed in the conflict since 1996. In July 2001 Prime Minister Deuba announced a cease-fire, which the Maoists pledged to observe, as part of a government effort to seek a negotiated solution to the conflict. Although Maoist-instigated intimidation and extortion continue, the killings have largely subsided since the cease-fire was announced. The government and Maoists held talks in August and September 2001.

Political parties agreed in 1991 that the monarchy would remain to enhance political stability and provide an important symbol of national identity for the culturally diverse Nepali people. The King exercises limited powers, including the right to declare a state of emergency in the event of war or armed revolt, with the advice and consent of the Council of Ministers and the Prime Minister. According to the constitution, the King's declaration of a state of emergency must be approved by a two-thirds majority of the lower house of the Parliament.

2001: Royal massacre

On June 1, 2001, Crown Prince Dipendra was officially reported to have shot and killed his father, King Birendra; his mother, Queen Aishwarya; his brother; his sister, his father's younger brother, Prince Dhirendra; and several aunts, before turning the gun on himself. Although he never regained consciousness before dying, Crown Prince Diprendra was nonetheless the king under the law of Nepalese royal succession. After his death two days later, the late King's surviving brother Gyanendra was proclaimed king.

2005–2007: Suspension of parliament and Loktantra Andolan

On 1 February 2005 King Gyanendra suspended the Parliament, appointed a government led by himself, and enforced martial law. The King argued that civil politicians were unfit to handle the Maoist insurgency. Telephone lines were cut and several high-profile political leaders were detained. Other opposition leaders fled to India and regrouped there. A broad coalition called the Seven Party Alliance (SPA) was formed in opposition to the royal takeover, encompassing the seven parliamentary parties who held about 90% of the seats in the old, dissolved parliament.

The UN-OHCHR, in response to events in Nepal, set up a monitoring program in 2005 to assess and observe the human rights situation there.

On 22 November 2005, the Seven Party Alliance (SPA) of parliamentary parties and the Communist Party of Nepal (Maoist) agreed on a historic and unprecedented 12-point memorandum of understanding (MOU) for peace and democracy. Nepalese from various walks of life and the international community regarded the MOU as an appropriate political response to the crisis that was developing in Nepal. Against the backdrop of the historical sufferings of the Nepalese people and the enormous human cost of the last ten years of violent conflict, the MOU, which proposes a peaceful transition through an elected constituent assembly, created an acceptable formula for a united movement for democracy. As per the 12-point MOU, the SPA called for a protest movement, and the Communist Party of Nepal (Maoist) supported it. This led to a countrywide uprising that started in April 2006. All political forces including civil society and professional organizations actively galvanized the people. This resulted in massive and spontaneous demonstrations and rallies held across Nepal against King Gyanendra's autocratic rule.

The people's participation was so broad, momentous and pervasive that the king feared being overthrown. On 21 April 2006, King Gyanendra declared that "power would be returned to the people". This had little effect on the people, who continued to occupy the streets of Kathmandu and other towns, openly defying the daytime curfew. Finally King Gyanendra announced the reinstatement the House of Representatives, thereby conceding one of the major demands of the SPA, at midnight on 24 April 2006. Following this action the coalition of political forces decided to call off the protests.

Twenty-one people died and thousands were injured during the 19 days of protests. On 19 May 2006, the parliament assumed total legislative power and gave executive power to the Government of Nepal (previously known as His Majesty's Government). Names of many institutions (including the army) were stripped of the "royal" adjective and the Raj Parishad (a council of the King's advisors) was abolished, with his duties assigned to the Parliament itself. The activities of the King became subject to parliamentary scrutiny and the King's properties were subjected to taxation. Moreover, Nepal was declared a secular state abrogating the previous status of a Hindu Kingdom. However, most of the changes have, as yet, not been implemented. On 19 July 2006, the prime minister, G. P. Koirala, sent a letter to the United Nations announcing the intention of the Nepalese government to hold elections to a constituent assembly by April 2007.

DECEMBER 2007 TO MAY 2008: ABOLITION OF THE MONARCHY

On 23 December 2007, an agreement was made for the monarchy to be abolished and the country to become a federal republic with the Prime Minister becoming head of state. Defying political pundits, who had predicted it to be trounced in the April 2008 elections, the Communist Party of Nepal (Maoist) became the largest party amidst a general atmosphere of fear and intimidation from all sides A federal republic was established in May 2008, with only four members of the 601-seat Constituent Assembly voting against the change, which ended 240 years of royal rule in Nepal. The government announced a public holiday for three days, (May 28—May 30), to celebrate the country becoming a federal republic.

LEGISLATIVE BRANCH

Pre-2006

From 1991 to 2002 the **Parliament** (*Sansad*) had two chambers. The **House of Representatives** (*Pratinidhi Sabha*) had 205 members elected for five year term in single-seat constituencies. The **National Council** (*Rashtriya Sabha*) had 60 members, 35 members elected by the Pratinidhi Sabha, 15 representatives of Regional Development Areas and 10 members appointed by the king. Parliament was subsequently dissolved by the king in 2002 on the pretext that it was incapable of handling the Maoists rebels.

From Loktantra Andolan to the Constituent Assembly

After the victory of Loktantra Andolan in the spring of 2006, a unicameral interim legislature replaced the previous parliament. The new body consists both of members of the old parliament as well as nominated members.

JUDICIAL BRANCH

The judiciary is composed of the Supreme Court (Sarbochha Adalat), appellate courts, and various district courts. The Chief Justice of the Supreme Court was appointed by the monarch on recommendation of the Constitutional Council; the other judges were appointed by the monarch on the recommendation of the Judicial Council.

Nepal's judiciary is legally separate from the executive and legislative branches and has increasingly shown the will to be independent of political influence. The judiciary has the right of judicial review under the constitution. The king appointed the chief justice and all other judges to the supreme, appellate, and district courts upon the recommendation of the Judicial Council. All lower court decisions, including acquittals, are subject to appeal. The Supreme Court is the court of last appeal. The king could grant pardons and suspend, commute, or remit any sentence by any court.

ECONOMY OF NEPAL

An isolated, agrarian society until the mid-20th century, Nepal entered the modern era in 1951 without schools, hospitals, roads, telecommunications, electric power, industry, or civil service. The country has, however, made progress toward sustainable economic growth since the 1950s and is committed to a program of economic liberalization.

Nepal has used a series of five-year plans in an attempt to make progress in economic development. It completed its ninth economic development plan in 2002; its currency has been made convertible, and 17 state enterprises have been privatized. Foreign aid accounts for more than half of the development budget. Government priorities over the years have been the development of transportation and communication facilities, agriculture, and industry. Since 1975, improved government administration and rural development efforts have been emphasized.

Agriculture remains Nepal's principal economic activity, employing 80% of the population and providing 37% of GDP. Only about 20% of the total area is cultivable; another 33% is forested; most of the rest is mountainous. Rice and wheat are the main food crops. The lowland Terai region produces an agricultural surplus, part of which supplies the food-deficient hill areas.

Economic development in social services and infrastructure has made progress. A countrywide primary education system is under development, and Tribhuvan University has several campuses. Although eradication efforts continue, malaria had been controlled in the fertile but previously uninhabitable Terai region in the south. Kathmandu is linked to India and nearby hill regions by road and an expanding highway network. The capital was almost out of fuel and transport of supplies caused by a crippling general strike in southern Nepal on February 17, 2008.

Major towns are connected to the capital by telephone and domestic air services. The export-oriented carpet and garment industries have grown rapidly in recent years and together now account for approximately 70% of merchandise exports.

IMPORTS/EXPORTS

Nepal's merchandise trade balance has improved somewhat since 2000 with the growth of the carpet and garment industries. In FY 2000-01 exports posted a greater increase (14%) than imports (4.5%), helping bring the trade deficit down by 4% from the previous year to $749 million. Trade with India rose rapidly after conclusion of the 1996 bilateral trade treaty between the two countries, and now accounts for 43% of all exports. Indian efforts to revise the treaty, which comes up for a 5-year review in December 2001, could dampen Nepal's export growth. The annual monsoon rain, or lack of it, strongly influences economic growth. From 1996 to 1999, real GDP growth averaged less than 4%. The growth rate recovered in 1999, rising to 6% before slipping slightly in 2001 to 5.5%.

Strong export performance, including earnings from tourism, and external aid have helped improve the overall balance-of-payments situation and increase international reserves. Nepal receives substantial amounts of external assistance from India, the People's

Republic of China, the United Kingdom, the United States, Japan, Germany, and the Scandinavian countries. Several multilateral organizations, such as the World Bank, the Asian Development Bank, and the UN Development Programme also provide assistance. In June 1998, Nepal submitted its memorandum on a foreign trade regime to the World Trade Organization and in May 2000 began direct negotiations on its accession.

RESOURCES

Progress has been made in exploiting Nepal's resources, tourism and hydroelectricity with eight of the world's 10 highest mountain peaks, including Mount Everest at 8,850m. In the early 1990s, one large public sector project and a number of private projects were planned; some have been completed. The most significant private sector financed hydroelectric projects currently in operation are the Khimti Khola (60 MW) and the Bhote Koshi Project (36 MW).

The environmental impact of Nepal's hydroelectric projects has been limited by the fact that most are "run-of-river" with only one storage project undertaken to date. The largest under active consideration is the private sector West Seti (750 MW) storage project which is dedicated to exports. Negotiations with India for a power purchase agreement have been underway for several years, but agreement on pricing and capital financing remains a problem. Currently demand for electricity is increasing at 8%-10% a year.

Population pressure on natural resources is increasing. Over-population is already straining the "carrying capacity" of the middle hill areas, particularly the Kathmandu Valley, resulting in the depletion of forest cover for crops, fuel, and fodder and contributing to erosion and flooding. Although steep mountain terrain makes exploitation difficult, mineral surveys have found small deposits of limestone, magnesite, zinc, copper, iron, mica, lead, and cobalt. Nepal is the largest mustard market in Asia.

DEMOGRAPHY OF NEPAL

Perched on the southern slopes of the Himalayan Mountains, State of Nepal is as ethnically diverse as its terrain of fertile plains, broad valleys, terraced hillsides and the highest mountain peaks in the world. The Nepalese are descendants of three major migrations from India, Tibet, and North Burma and Yunnan via Assam.

Among the earliest inhabitants were the Kirat of east mid-region, Newar of the Kathmandu Valley and aboriginal Tharu in the southern Terai region. The ancestors of the Brahman and Chetri caste groups migrated eastward from India Kumaon, Garwal and Kashmir, while other ethnic groups trace their origins to North Burma and Yunnan and Tibet, e.g. the Gurung and Magar in the west, Rai and Limbu in the east, and Sherpa and Bhotia in the north.

In the Terai, a part of the Ganges Basin with 20% of the land, much of the population is physically and culturally similar to the Indo-Aryans of northern India. Indo-Aryan and East Asian looking mixed people live in the hill region. The mountainous region is sparsely populated above 3,000 meters, but in central and western Nepal ethnic Tibetans inhabit even higher semi-arid valleys north of the high Himalaya. Kathmandu Valley, in the middle hill region, constitutes a small fraction of the nation's area but is the most densely populated, with almost 5% of the population.

LANGUAGES

Nepal's diverse linguistic heritage evolved from four major language groups: Indo-Aryan, Tibeto-Burman, Mongolian and various indigenous language isolates. According to the 2001 national census, 92 different living languages are spoken in Nepal (a 93rd category was "unidentified"). The major languages of Nepal (percent spoken as mother tongue) are Nepali (49%), Maithili (12%), Bhojpuri (8%), Tharu (6%), Tamang (5%), Newari/Nepal Bhasa (4%), Magar (3%), Awadhi (2%), Rai (2.79%), Limbu (1%), and Bajjika (1%). The remaining 81 languages are each spoken as mother tongue by less than one percent of the population.

Derived from Sanskrit, Nepali is related to the Indian language Hindi and written in Devanagari script. Nepali is the official, national language and serves as *lingua franca* among Nepalis of different ethnolinguistic groups. Hindi — along with regional dialects Awadhi, Bhojpuri and Maithili — are spoken in the southern Terai Region. Hindi is also widely understood by Nepalese who have worked, studied or traveled in India. Many Nepalese in government and business speak English as well.

RELIGION

Religion is important in Nepal; the Kathmandu Valley alone has more than 2,700 religious shrines. The constitution of Nepal describes the country as a "Hindu Kingdom," although it does not establish Hinduism as the state religion. Nepal's constitution continues long-standing legal provisions prohibiting discrimination against other religions (but also proselytization). Nevertheless until 2006 Nepal remained the only officially Hindu country in the world. The king was deified as the earthly manifestation of the Hindu god, Vishnu. Then on May 19, 2006, the government facing a constitutional crisis, the House of Representatives which had been just reformed, having been previously dissolved, declared Nepal a "secular state".

The 2001 census identified 80.6% of the population as Hindu and 10,7% as Buddhist (although many people labeled Hindu or Buddhist often practice a syncretic blend of Hinduism, Buddhism or animist traditions). 4.2% of the population is Muslim and 3.6% of the population follows the indigenous Kirant Mundhum religion. Christianity is practiced by less than 0.5% of the population.

Buddhist and Hindu shrines and festivals are respected and celebrated by most Nepalis. Certain animist practices of old indigenous religions survive.

ETHNICITY

Nepal's 2001 census enumerated 103 distinct castes and ethnic groups including an "unidentified group". The major caste/ethnic groups identified by the 2001 census are Chetri (15.8%), Hill Brahmin (12.7%), Magar (7.1%), Tharu (6.8%), Tamang (5.6%), Newar (5.5%), Muslim (4.3%), Kami (3.9%), Rai (2.7%), Gurung (2.5%), and Damai/ Dholi (2.4%). The remaining 92 caste/ethnic groups (including the world-famous Sherpa) each constitute less than 2 % of the population.

NEPALESE CULTURE

Nepalese culture is diverse, reflecting different ethnic origins of the people. The Newar community is particularly rich in cultural diversity; they celebrate many festivals, well known for their music and dance.

A typical Nepalese meal is *dal-bhat-tarkari*. *Dal* is a spicy lentil soup, served over *bhat* (boiled rice), served with *tarkari* (curried vegetables) together with *achar* (pickles) or *chutni* (spicy condiment made from fresh ingredients). The Newar community, however, has its own unique cuisine. It consists of non-vegetarian as well as vegetarian items served with alcoholic and non-alcoholic beverages. Mustard oil is the cooking medium and a host of spices, such as cumin, coriander, black peppers, sesame seeds, turmeric, garlic, ginger, methi (fenugreek), bay leaves, cloves, cinnamon, pepper, chillies, mustard seeds etc., are used in the cooking. The cuisine served on festivals is generally the best.

The Newari Music orchestra consists mainly of percussion instruments, though wind instruments, such as flutes and other similar instruments, are also used. String instruments are very rare. There are songs pertaining to particular seasons and festivals. Paahan chare music is probably the fastest played music whereas the Dapa the slowest. There are certain musical instruments such as Dhimay and Bhusya which are played as instrumental only and are not accompanied with songs. The dhimay music is the loudest one. In the hills, people enjoy their own kind of music, playing saarangi (a string instrument), madal and flute. They also have many popular folk songs known as *lok geet* and *lok dohari*.

The Newar dances can be broadly classified into masked dances and non-masked dances. The most representative of Newari dances is Lakhey dance. Almost all the settlements of Newaris organise Lakhey dance at least once a year, mostly in the Goonlaa month. So, they are called Goonlaa Lakhey. However, the most famous Lakhey dance is the Majipa Lakhey dance; it is performed by the Ranjitkars of Kathmandu and the celeberation continues for one whole week that contains the full moon of Yenlaa month. The Lakhey are considered as the saviors of children.

Folklore is an integral part of Nepalese society. Traditional stories are rooted in the reality of day-to-day life, tales of love, affection and battles as well as demons and ghosts and thus reflect local lifestyles, cultures and beliefs. Many Nepalese folktales are enacted through the medium of dance and music.

The Nepali year begins in mid-April and is divided into 12 months. Saturday is the official weekly holiday. Main annual holidays include the National Day, celebrated on the birthday of the king (December 28), Prithvi Jayanti, (January 11), Martyr's Day (February 18) and a mix of Hindu and Buddhist festivals such as dashain in autumn, and *tihar* in late autumn. During tihar, the Newar community also celebrates its New Year as per their local calendar Nepal Sambat.

Most houses in rural lowland of Nepal are made up of a tight bamboo framework and walls of a mud and cow-dung mix. These dwellings remain cool in summer and retain warmth in winter. Houses in the hills are usually made of unbaked bricks with thatch or tile roofing. At high elevations construction changes to stone masonry and slate may be used on roofs.

Chapter 6

Bhutan

The **Kingdom of Bhutan** is a landlocked nation in South Asia. It is located amid the eastern end of the Himalaya Mountains and is bordered to the south, east and west by India and to the north by China. Bhutan is separated from Nepal by the Indian state of Sikkim. The Bhutanese call their country "land of the thunder dragon".

Bhutan is one of the most isolated and least developed nations in the world. Foreign influences and tourism are regulated by the government to preserve the nation's traditional culture, identity and the environment. Accordingly, in 2006 *Business Week* rated Bhutan the happiest country in Asia and the eighth happiest country in the world. The landscape ranges from subtropical plains in the south to the Himalayan heights in the north, with some peaks exceeding 7,000 metres (23,000 ft). The state religion is Vajrayana Buddhism, and the population is predominantly Buddhist, with Hinduism being the second-largest religion. The capital and largest city is Thimphu. After centuries of direct monarchic rule, Bhutan held its first democratic elections in March 2008. Bhutan is a member of the South Asian Association for Regional Cooperation (SAARC).

HISTORY OF BHUTAN

Stone tools, weapons, elephants, and remnants of large stone structures provide evidence that Bhutan was inhabited as early as 2000 BCE, although there are no existing records from that time. Historians have theorized that the state of *Lhomon* (literally, "southern darkness", a reference to the indigenous Mon religion), or *Monyul* ("Dark Land", a reference to the Monpa, the aboriginal peoples of Bhutan) may have existed between 500 BCE and 600 CE.The names *Lhomon Tsendenjong* (Sandalwood Country), and *Lhomon Khashi*, or Southern Mon (country of four approaches) have been found in ancient Bhutanese and Tibetan chronicles.

The earliest transcribed event in Bhutan was the passage of the Buddhist saint Padma Sambhava (also known as Guru Rinpoche) in 747. Bhutan's early history is unclear, because most of the records were destroyed after fire ravaged the ancient capital, Punakha, in 1827. By the 10th century, Bhutan's political development was heavily influenced by its religious history. However, there is no sufficient information stating that all historical records were available before the fire. Various sub-sects of Buddhism emerged which were patronised by the various Mongol warlords. After the decline of the Mongols in the 14th century, these sub-sects vied with each other for supremacy in the political and religious landscape, eventually leading to the ascendancy of the Drukpa sub-sect by the 16th century.

Until the early 17th century, Bhutan existed as a patchwork of minor warring fiefdoms, when the area was unified by the Tibetan lama and military leader Shabdrung Ngawang Namgyal who fled religious prosecution in Tibet. To defend the country against intermittent Tibetan forays, Namgyal built a network of impregnable *dzong* (fortresses), and promulgated a code of law that helped to bring local lords under centralised control. Many such *dzong* still exist and active centers of religion and district administration. After Namgyal's death in 1651, Bhutan fell into civil war. Taking advantage of the chaos, the Tibetans attacked Bhutan in 1710, and again in 1730 with the help of the Mongols. Both assaults were successfully thwarted, and an armistice was signed in 1759.

In the 18th century, the Bhutanese invaded and occupied the kingdom of Cooch Behar to the south. In 1772, Cooch Behar appealed to the British East India Company who assisted them in ousting the Bhutanese, and later in attacking Bhutan itself in 1774. A peace treaty was signed in which Bhutan agreed to retreat to its pre-1730 borders. However, the peace was tenuous, and border skirmishes with the British were to continue for the next 100 years. The skirmishes eventually led to the Duar War (1864–1865), a confrontation over who would control the Bengal Duars. After Bhutan lost the war, the Treaty of Sinchula was signed between British India and Bhutan. As part of the war reparations, the Duars were ceded to the United Kingdom in exchange for a rent of Rs. 50,000. The treaty ended all hostilities between British India and Bhutan.

During the 1870s, power struggles between the rival valleys of Paro and Tongsa led to civil war in Bhutan, eventually leading to the ascendancy of Ugyen Wangchuck, the *ponlop* (governor) of Tongsa. From his power base in central Bhutan, Ugyen Wangchuck defeated his political enemies and united the country following several civil wars and rebellions in the period 1882–1885.

In 1907, an epochal year for the country, Ugyen Wangchuck was unanimously chosen as the hereditary king of the country by an assembly of leading Buddhist monks, government officials, and heads of important families. The British government promptly recognised the new monarchy, and in 1910 Bhutan signed a treaty which "let" Great Britain "guide" Bhutan's foreign affairs. In reality, this did not mean much given Bhutan's historical reticence. It also did not seem to apply to Bhutan's traditional relations with Tibet. The greatest impact of this treaty seems to be the perception that it meant Bhutan was not totally sovereign.

After India gained independence from the United Kingdom on August 15, 1947, Bhutan became one of the first countries to recognise India's independence. A treaty similar to the one of 1910 was signed on August 8, 1949 with the newly independent India.

In 1953, King Jigme Dorji Wangchuck established the country's legislature – a 130-member National Assembly – to promote a more democratic form of governance. In 1965, he set up a Royal Advisory Council, and in 1968 he formed a Cabinet. In 1971, Bhutan was admitted to the United Nations, having held observer status for three years. In July 1972, Jigme Singye Wangchuck ascended to the throne at the age of 16 after the death of his father, Dorji Wangchuck.

In the 1980s, in order to strengthen Bhutan's identity as a nation, the "one nation, one people" campaign was started to foster greater integration of the peripheral ethnic and cultural groups into mainstream Bhutanese society. The age-old code of conduct, known as *Driglam namzha*, and usage of the official national language, Dzongkha, was promoted. At around the same time, a nationwide census revealed a large population of Nepali origin in southern Bhutan. When the government attempted to remove the illegal settlers, there was a violent backlash; numerous acts of terrorism were carried out against government schools, hospitals, offices and neutral southern Bhutanese .

In order to re-establish order in the south, the government drafted many young men and able-bodied civil servants into a militia force. Many southern Bhutanese, including a number of political dissidents, fled to Nepal along with the illegal settlers, where they were admitted into United Nations-run camps and given refugee status. The refugee status notwithstanding, the tone of the dissidents was not necessarily defensive but quite aggressive and chauvinistic . Despite the best efforts of the Bhutanese government Nepal and India, as well as outside parties such as the United Nations, the European Union and the United States, a viable solution to this problem proves to be still elusive. At present, the United States is working towards resettling around 70,000 of these so-called refugees in the US.

In 1998, King Jigme Singye Wangchuck introduced significant political reforms, transferring most of his administrative powers to the Council of Cabinet Ministers and allowing for impeachment of the King by a two-thirds majority of the National Assembly. In late 2003, the Bhutanese army successfully launched a large-scale operation to flush out anti-India insurgents who were operating training camps in southern Bhutan.

In 1999, the government lifted a ban on television and the Internet, making Bhutan one of the last countries to introduce television. In his speech, the King said that television was a critical step to the modernisation of Bhutan as well as a major contributor to the country's Gross National Happiness (Bhutan is the only country to measure happiness), but warned that the "misuse" of television could erode traditional Bhutanese values.

A new constitution was presented in early 2005. In December 2005, Jigme Singye Wangchuck announced that he would abdicate the throne in his son's favour in 2008. On December 14, 2005, he announced that he would be abdicating immediately. Bhutan has now entered a new era of democracy, starting with its first national parliamentary elections in December 2007 and March 2008.

GOVERNMENT AND POLITICS OF BHUTAN

The **Government of Bhutan** was a traditional absolute monarchy, but now developed into a constitutional monarchy. The King of Bhutan is head of state. Executive power is exercised by the Lhengye Shungtsog, the council of ministers. Legislative power is vested in both the government and the National Assembly. A royal edict issued on April 22, 2007 lifted the previous ban on political parties, ordering that they be created, in anticipation of parliamentary elections to be held the following year.The Bhutanese people have historically never had doubts about their nation's sovereignty. Bhutan in fact has never been colonized. However, to the outside world, namely India and before that the British Raj, Bhutan was viewed as less than sovereign for their own geopolitical interests. Bhutan was treated as a suzerainty by the British Raj, during which time the present monarchy was established. Foreign and defence policy was to be decided by the British according to the 1910 Treaty. This did not mean so much to the Bhutanese however due to their policy of self-imposed isolation. In 1949, after Indian independence, Bhutan and India agreed to a ten-article, perpetual treaty which effectively continued the relationship, but with India taking the place of the United Kingdom. That is, India agreed not to interfere in Bhutan's internal relations, while Bhutan agreed "to be guided by the advice of the Government of India in regard to its external relations" (Article 2). The treaty also established free trade and full extradition between the two countries.

While Bhutan sees its destiny as being closely linked with that of India, for which reason it strives to promote excellent relations with it, it has also quietly striven to assert its sovereignty at the same time.

Article 2 of the 1949 treaty has mostly been ignored by both countries as Bhutan confidently handles all of its foreign affairs, including the sensitive border demarcation talks with China.

In February 2007, the Indo-Bhutan Friendship Treaty was substantially revised with all references to phrases such as "will be guided" deleted, thus eliminating the last lingering doubts about the sovereign and independent status of Bhutan.

EXECUTIVE BRANCH

Bhutan's head of state is the Druk Gyalpo ("Dragon King"). Although his title is hereditary, he can be removed by a two-thirds majority vote by the parliament, the unicameral National Assembly, or *Tshogdu*. The candidates to the Council of Ministers

(Lhengye Shungtsog) are nominated by the monarch, elected by the National Assembly. The members serve fixed, five-year terms. There is also a Royal Advisory Council (Lodoi Tsokde), members nominated by the monarch

The Je Khenpo is the highest religious official of Bhutan. He is typically viewed as the closest and most powerful advisor to the King of Bhutan. The 71st and present Je Khenpo is Trulku Jigme Chhoeda. In 1998, the monarch's executive powers were transferred to the council of ministers, or cabinet (*Lhengye Shungtsog*). Candidates for the council of ministers are elected by the National Assembly for a fixed, five-year term, and must be a part of the legislative assembly. The cabinet is headed by the Prime Minister, who is the head of government. The post of Prime Minister rotates each year between the five candidates who secured the highest number of votes. Recently, a new constitution that includes provision for a two-party democratic system was unveiled after four years of preparation. This constitution is likely to be put to the people in a referendum; at the behest of the monarch, the referendum proposes a significant reduction in his powers.

LEGISLATIVE BRANCH

The former Tshogdu had 150 members, 106 members elected at various dates for a three year term in single-seat constituencies, 34 appointed members and 10 representatives of monk body. Suffrage in Bhutan was unique in that each family-unit, rather than individual, had one vote. This has been changed to full universal suffrage as the new Constitution took effect on July 18, 2008 with a new bicameral parliament to take the Tshogdu's place with a National Council (upper house) and a National Assembly (lower house).

JUDICIAL BRANCH

In Bhutan's judicial system, the monarch is the final court of appeal (the "Supreme Court of Appeal"). The Royal High Court of Bhutan is the highest court in the country. The Royal High Court has original jurisdiction over the 20 districts of the nation. Bhutan's legal system is superficially based on Indian law and English common law, but is in fact largely informal. Judicial appointments are made by the monarch, and may be recalled by him at any time.

LEGAL SYSTEM

The criminal justice system is based on trial before a panel of judges, and therefore resembles more the Napoleonic than the British or American systems. The prosecutor, a government employee, seeks to obtain an acknowledgement of culpability from the accused. If this happens quickly, the sentencing may be lenient. If culpability is obvious but the accused refuses to admit to it, the sentence may be correspondingly severe. Judges may dismiss the case for lack of proof at any time. Recent legislation defines required proof of guilt more closely, providing increased protection against trivial or mistaken charges.

Minor criminal offences may be tried by the dzongkhag Drangpon (District Judge). Bhutan has not accepted compulsory International Court of Justice jurisdiction.

ADMINISTRATIVE DIVISIONS

Butan is divided in 20 districts (dzongkhag, singular and plural); Bumthang, Chukha, Dagana, Gasa, Haa, Lhuntse, Mongar, Paro, Pemagatshel, Punakha, Samdrup Jongkhar, Samtse, Sarpang, Thimphu, Trashigang, Trashiyangste, Trongsa, Tsirang, Wangduephodrang, Zhemgang.

GEOGRAPHY OF BHUTAN

The Kingdom of Bhutan is a Himalayan nation, located towards the eastern extreme of the aforementioned mountain range. It is fairly evenly sandwiched between the sovereign territory of two nations: first, the People's Republic of China on the north and northwest. There are approximately 470 kilometers of border with that nation's Tibet Autonomous Region. The second nation is the Republic of India on the south, southwest, and east; there are approximately 605 kilometers with the states of Arunachal Pradesh, Assam, West Bengal, and Sikkim, in clockwise order from the kingdom. Bhutan's total borders amount to 1,075 kilometers. The Kingdom of Nepal to the west, the People's Republic of Bangladesh to the south, and the Union of Myanmar to the southeast are other close neighbours; the former two are separated by only very small stretches of Indian territory.

Bhutan is a very compact nation, but with just a small bit more length than width. The nation's territory totals an approximate 47 000 km^2. Because of its inland, landlocked status, it controls no territorial waters. Its shape, area, and mountainous location are comparable to that of Switzerland.It is now popularly known as Switzerland of Asia. Bhutan's territory used to extend south into present-day Assam, including the protectorate of Cooch Behar, but, starting in 1772, the British East India Company began to push back the borders through a number of wars and treaties, severely reducing Bhutan's size until the Treaty of Sinchulu of 1865, when some border land was ceded back.

The Himalayas dominate the north of the country, where mountain peaks can easily reach seven thousand meters; the highest point is claimed to be the Kula Kangri, at 7 553 m, but detailed topographic studies claim Kula Kangri is wholly in Tibet and modern Chinese measurements claim that Gangkhar Puensum, which has the distinction of being the highest unclimbed mountain in the world, is higher at 7 570 m (vs 7 538 m for Kula Kangri). Weather is extreme in the mountains: the high peaks have perpetual snow, and the lesser mountains and hewn gorges have high winds all year round, making them barren brown wind tunnels in summer, and frozen wastelands in winter. The blizzards generated in the north each winter often drift southward into the central highlands.

The highlands are the most populous part of the nation; the capital of Thimphu lies in the western region. The region is characterized by its many rivers (flowing into India's

Brahmaputra), its isolated valleys that house most of the population, and the expansive forests that cover seventy percent of the nation. Winters are cold, summers are hot; the rainy season is accompanied with frequented landslides.

The valleys of Bhutan are linked by a series of passes ("La" in Dzongkha). Between the Haa valley and Paro Valley is the Chele La (3780m). The Chele La is the highest pass crossed by a Bhutanese highway. The Lateral Road from Thimphu to Punakha crosses the Dochu La (3116m), which features 108 chortens built to commemorate the expulsion of Assamese guerrillas. East of Wangdue Phodrang is the Pele La (3390m). Continuing to the east along the main highway, other major passes include the Yotang La, Shertang La, Wangthang La, Thrumsing La and Kori La (2298m).

The extreme southern strip of the nation consists mostly of tropical plains, more typical of India. It is largely agricultural land, producing mostly rice. Only two percent of Bhutan is arable land, with most of it focused here.

Centuries of isolationism, a small population, and topographical extremes have led to Bhutan maintaining one of the most intact ecosystems in the world. The country ranks amongst the top ten countries in the world in terms of species density (species richness per unit area). Over fifty-five hundred varieties of plantlife exist, including around three-hundred medicinal ones. More than 770 species of avifauna and more than 165 species of mammals are known to exist, including many rare and endangered species like the red panda, snow leopard, and golden langur.

CLIMATE

Bhutan's climate is as varied as its altitudes and, like most of Asia, is affected by monsoons. Western Bhutan is particularly affected by monsoons that bring between 60 and 90 percent of the region's rainfall. The climate is humid and subtropical in the southern plains and foothills, temperate in the inner Himalayan valleys of the southern and central regions, and cold in the north, with year-round snow on the main Himalayan summits.

Temperatures vary according to elevation. Temperatures in Thimphu, located at 2,200 meters above sea level in west-central Bhutan, range from approximately 15°C to 26°C during the monsoon season of June through September but drop to between about -4°C and 16°C in January. Most of the central portion of the country experiences a cool, temperate climate year-round. In the south, a hot, humid climate helps maintain a fairly even temperature range of between 15°C and 30°C year-round, although temperatures sometimes reach 40°C in the valleys during the summer.

Annual precipitation ranges widely in various parts of the country. In the severe climate of the north, there is only about forty millimeters of annual precipitation—primarily snow. In the temperate central regions, a yearly average of around 1,000 millimeters is more common, and 7,800 millimeters per year has been registered at some locations in the humid, subtropical south, ensuring the thick tropical forest, or savanna. Thimphu experiences dry winter months (December through February) and almost no precipitation until March, when rainfall averages 20 millimeters a month and increases steadily thereafter to a high of 220 millimeters in August for a total annual rainfall of nearly 650 millimeters.

Bhutan's generally dry spring starts in early March and lasts until mid-April. Summer weather commences in mid-April with occasional showers and continues through the premonsoon rains of late June. The summer monsoon lasts from late June through late September with heavy rains from the southwest. The monsoon weather, blocked from its northward progress by the Himalayas, brings heavy rains, high humidity, flash floods and landslides, and numerous misty, overcast days. Autumn, from late September or early October to late November, follows the rainy season. It is characterized by bright, sunny days and some early snowfalls at higher elevations. From late November until March, winter sets in, with frost throughout much of the country and snowfall common above elevations of 3,000 meters. The winter northeast monsoon brings gale-force winds down through high mountain passes, giving Bhutan its name— Drukyul, which in the Dzongkha language mean Land of the Thunder Dragon.

RIVER SYSTEMS

Glacial lakes have been rapidly forming on the surface of the debris-covered glaciers in this region during the last few decades. Bhutan has four major river systems: the Drangme Chhu; the Puna Tsang Chhu, also called the Sankosh; the Wang Chhu; and the Amo Chhu. Each flows swiftly out of the Himalayas, southerly through the Dooars to join the Brahmaputra River in India, and thence through Bangladesh where the Brahmaputra (or Jamuna in Bangladesh) joins the mighty Ganges (or Padma in Bangladesh) to flow into the Bay of Bengal. The largest river system, the Drangme Chhu, flows southwesterly from India's state of Arunachal Pradesh and has three major branches: the Drangme Chhu, Mangde Chhu, and Bumthang Chhu.

These branches form the Drangme Chhu basin, which spreads over most of eastern Bhutan and drains the Tongsa and Bumthang valleys. In the Duars, where eight tributaries join it, the Drangme Chhu is called the Manas Chhu. The 320-kilometer-long Puna Tsang Chhu rises in northwestern Bhutan as the Mo Chhu and Pho Chhu, which are fed by the snows from the Great Himalayan Range. They flow southerly to Punakha, where they join to form the Puna Tsang Chhu, which flows southerly into India's state of West Bengal. The tributaries of the 370-kilometer-long Wang Chhu rise in Tibet. The Wang Chhu itself flows southeasterly through west-central Bhutan, drains the Ha, Paro, and Thimphu valleys, and continues into the Duars, where it enters West Bengal as the Raigye Chhu. The smallest river system, the Torsa Chhu, known as the Amo Chhu in its northern reaches, also flows out of Tibet into the Chumbi Valley and swiftly through western Bhutan before broadening near Phuntsholing and then flowing into India.

GLACIERS

Glaciers in northern Bhutan, which cover about 10 percent of the total surface area, are an important renewable source of water for Bhutan's rivers. Fed by fresh snow each winter and slow melting in the summer, the glaciers bring millions of liters of fresh water to Bhutan and downriver areas each year. Glacial melt added to monsoon-swollen rivers, however, also contributes to flooding. Where glacial movement temporary blocks riverflows, downstream areas may be threatened by jokulhlaups.

ECONOMY OF BHUTAN

The Ngultrum is the currency of Bhutan and its value is pegged to the Indian rupee. The rupee is also accepted as legal tender in the country. Though Bhutan's economy is one of the world's smallest, it has grown rapidly in recent years, by eight percent in 2005 and 14 percent in 2006. This was mainly due to the commissioning of the gigantic Tala Hydroelectricity project. As of March 2006, Bhutan's per capita income was US$1,321.

Bhutan's economy is based on agriculture, forestry, tourism and the sale of hydroelectric power to India. Agriculture provides the main livelihood for more than 80 percent of the population. Agrarian practices consist largely of subsistence farming and animal husbandry. Handicrafts, particularly weaving and the manufacture of religious art for home altars, are a small cottage industry. A landscape that varies from hilly to ruggedly mountainous has made the building of roads and other infrastructure difficult and expensive. This, and a lack of access to the sea, has meant that Bhutan has not been able to benefit from significant trading of its produce. Bhutan does not have any railways, though Indian Railways plans to link southern Bhutan to its vast network under an agreement signed in January 2005. Bhutan and India signed a 'free trade' accord in 2008, which additionally allowed Bhutanese imports and exports from third markets to transit India without tariffs. The historic trade routes over the high Himalayas, which connected India to Tibet, have been closed since the 1959 military takeover of Tibet (although smuggling activity still brings Chinese goods into Bhutan).

The industrial sector is in a nascent stage, and though most production is cottage industry type larger industries are being encouraged and some industries such as cement, steel, ferro alloy, etc., have been set up. Most development projects, such as road construction, rely on Indian contract labour. Agricultural produce includes rice, chilies, dairy (some yak, mostly cow) products, buckwheat, barley, root crops, apples, and citrus and maize at lower elevations. Industries include cement, wood products, processed fruits, alcoholic beverages and calcium carbide.

Incomes of over Nu 100,000 per annum are taxed, but very few wage and salary earners qualify. Bhutan's inflation rate was estimated at about three percent in 2003.

Bhutan has a Gross Domestic Product of around USD 2.913 billion (adjusted to Purchasing Power Parity), making it the 162nd largest economy in the world.

Per capita income is around $1,400 , ranked 124th. Government revenues total $272 million, though expenditures amount to $350 million. 60 percent of the budget expenditure, however, is financed by India's Ministry of External Affairs. Bhutan's exports, principally electricity, cardamom, gypsum, timber, handicrafts, cement, fruit, precious stones and spices, total €128 million (2000 est.). Imports, however, amount to €164 million, leading to a trade deficit. Main items imported include fuel and lubricants, grain, machinery, vehicles, fabrics and rice. Bhutan's main export partner is India, accounting for 87.9 percent of its export goods. Bangladesh (4.6 percent) and the Philippines (two percent) are the other two top export partners. As its border with Tibet is closed, trade between Bhutan and China is now almost non-existent. Bhutan's import partners include India (71.3 percent), Japan (7.8 percent) and Austria (three percent).

In a response to accusations in 1987 by a journalist from UK's *Financial Times* that the pace of development in Bhutan was slow, the King said that "Gross National Happiness is more important than Gross National Product." This statement appears to have presaged recent findings by western economic psychologists, including 2002 Nobel Laureate Daniel Kahneman, that question the link between levels of income and happiness. The statement signaled his commitment to building an economy that is appropriate for Bhutan's culture, based on Buddhist spiritual values, and has served as a unifying vision for the economy. In a survey in 2005, 45 percent of Bhutanese reported being very happy, 52 percent reported being happy and only three percent reported not being happy. Based on this data, the Happy Planet Index estimates that the average level of life satisfaction in Bhutan is within the top 10 percent of nations worldwide, and certainly higher than other nations with similar levels of GDP per capita.

DEMOGRAPHY OF BHUTAN

Among the Bhutanese people, several principal ethnic groups may be distinguished. The second dominant group is the Ngalops, a Buddhist group based in the western part of the country. Their culture is closely related to that of Tibet. Much the same could be said of the Sharchops ("Easterners"), the dominant group, who are associated with the eastern part of Bhutan (but who traditionally follow the Nyingmapa rather than the official Drukpa Kagyu form of Himalayan Buddhism). They are called the Western Bhutanese and Eastern Bhutanese respectively. In modern times, with improved transportation infrastructure, there has been much intermarriage between these groups. In the early 1970s, intermarriage between the Lhotshampas and main stream Bhutanese society was encouraged by the government.

The national language is Dzongkha, one of 53 languages in the Tibetan language family. The script, here called *Chhokey* ("Dharma Language"), is identical to classical

Tibetan. In the schools English is the medium of instruction and Dzongkha is taught as the national language. Ethnologue lists 24 languages currently spoken in Bhutan, all of them in the Tibeto-Burman family, except Nepali, an Indo-Aryan language. Until the 1980s, the government sponsored the teaching of Nepali in schools in Southern Bhutan. However, after the armed uprising in the south, Nepali was dropped from the curriculum. The languages of Bhutan are still not well-characterized, and several have yet to be recorded in an in-depth academic grammar.

The literacy rate is 59.5 percent. The country has a median age of 22.3 years. Bhutan has a life expectancy of 62.2 years (61 for males and 64.5 for females) according to the latest data from the World Bank. There are 1,070 males to every 1,000 females in the country.

It is estimated that between two third and three quarter of the Bhutanese population follow Mahayana Buddhism, which is also the state religion. About one quarter to one third are followers of Hinduism. Muslim and non-religious communities account for less than 1 % of the population. The current legal framework in principal guarantees freedom of religion; Proselytism, however, is forbidden by a Royal Government decision.

CULTURE OF BHUTAN

Bhutan has a rich and unique cultural heritage that has largely remained intact due to its isolation from the rest of the world until the early 1960s. One of the main attractions for tourists is the country's culture and traditions. Bhutanese tradition is deeply steeped in its Buddhist heritage. Hinduism is the second dominant religion in Bhutan, being most prevalent in the southern regions. Both religions co-exist peacefully and receive support from the government, and enjoy royal patronage. The government is increasingly making efforts to preserve and sustain the current culture and traditions of the country. Due to its largely unspoilt natural environment and cultural heritage, Bhutan has been referred to as *The Last Shangri-la*.

While the Bhutanese are free to travel abroad, Bhutan is seen to be inaccessible to many foreigners. There is a widespread misconception that Bhutan has set limits on tourist visas. However, it is the high tourist tariff and requirement to go on packaged tours that makes Bhutan an exclusive tourist destination.

The National Dress for Bhutanese men is the *gho*, a knee-length robe tied at the waist by a cloth belt known as the *kera*. Women wear an ankle-length dress, the *kira*, which is clipped at one shoulder and tied at the waist. An accompaniment to the kira is a long-sleeved blouse, the *toego*, which is worn underneath the outer layer. Social status and class determine the texture, colours, and decorations that embellish the garments. Differently coloured scarves and shawls are important indicators of social standing, as Bhutan has traditionally been a feudal society. Jewellery is mostly worn by women, especially during religious festivals and public gatherings. To strengthen Bhutan's identity as an independent country, Bhutanese law requires all Bhutanese citizens to wear the national dress in public areas and as formal wear.

Rice, buckwheat, and increasingly maize, are the staple foods of the country. The diet also includes pork, beef, yak meat, chicken, and mutton. Soups and stews of meat and dried vegetables spiced with chillies and cheese are prepared. *Ema datshi*, made very spicy with cheese and chilies, might be called the national dish for its ubiquity and the pride that Bhutanese have for it. Dairy foods, particularly butter and cheese from yaks and cows, are also popular, and indeed almost all milk is turned to butter and cheese. Popular beverages include butter tea, tea, locally brewed rice wine and beer. Bhutan is the only country in the world to have banned the sale of tobacco.

Bhutan's national sport is archery, and competitions are held regularly in most villages. It differs from Olympic standards not only in technical details such as the placement of the targets and atmosphere. There are two targets placed over 100 meters apart and teams shoot from one end of the field to the other. Each member of the team shoots two arrows per round. Traditional Bhutanese archery is a social event and competitions are organized between villages, towns, and amateur teams. There are usually plenty of food and drink complete with singing and dancing. Attempts to distract an opponent include standing around the target and making fun of the shooter's ability. Darts (*khuru*) is an equally popular outdoor team sport, in which heavy wooden darts pointed with a 10 cm nail are thrown at a paperback-sized target ten to 20 meters away.

Another traditional sport is the *digor*, which can be best described as shot put combined with horseshoe throwing. Cricket has gained remarkable popularity in Bhutan, especially since the heavy influx of Indian Television. Their national cricket team is one of the more successful associate nations in the region. Football is an increasingly popular sport. In 2002, Bhutan's national football team played Montserrat - billed as The Other Final, the match took place on the same day Brazil played Germany in the World Cup Final, but at the time Bhutan and Montserrat were the world's two lowest ranked teams. The match was held in Thimphu's Changlimithang National Stadium, and Bhutan won 4-0. A documentary of the match was made by the Dutch filmmaker Johan Kramer.

Rigsar is the new emergent style of popular music, played on a mix of traditional instruments and electronic keyboards, and dates back to the early 1990s; it shows the influence of Indian popular music, a hybrid form of traditional and Western popular influences. Traditional genres include the *zhungdra* and *boedra*.

Characteristic of the region is a type of castle fortress known as the dzong. Since ancient times, the dzongs have served as the religious and secular administration centres for their respective districts.

Bhutan has numerous public holidays, most of which centre around traditional seasonal, secular and religious festivals. They include the winter solstice (around January

1, depending on the lunar calendar), the lunar New Year (February or March), the King's birthday and the anniversary of his coronation, the official start of monsoon season (September 22), National Day (December 17), and various Buddhist and Hindu celebrations.

Masked dances and dance dramas are common traditional features at festivals, usually accompanied by traditional music. Energetic dancers, wearing colourful wooden or composition face masks and stylized costumes, depict heroes, demons, dæmons, death heads, animals, gods, and caricatures of common people. The dancers enjoy royal patronage, and preserve ancient folk and religious customs and perpetuate the ancient lore and art of mask-making.

Inheritance in Bhutan generally goes in the female rather than the male line. Daughters will inherit their parents' house. A man is expected to make his own way in the world and often moves to his wife's home. Love marriages are common in urban areas, but the tradition of arranged marriages is still common in the villages. Although uncommon, polygamy and polyandry are accepted; often being a device to keep property in a contained family unit rather than dispersing it.

Chapter 7

Maldives

The Maldives, officially the Republic of Maldives, is an island nation consisting of a group of atolls belonging to the Maldive and Suvadive archiplagoes in the Indian Ocean. The Maldives is located south of India's Lakshadweep islands, and about seven hundred kilometres (435 mi) south-west of Sri Lanka. The twenty-six atolls of Maldives' encompass a territory featuring 1,192 islets, two hundred and fifty islands of which are inhabited.

The name "Maldives" may derive from *Maale Dhivehi Raajje* ("The Island Kingdom [under the authority of] Malé")." Some scholars believe that the name "Maldives" derives from the Sanskrit *maladvipa,* meaning "garland of islands", or from *mahila dvipa,* meaning "island of women", but these names are not found in ancient Sanskrit literature. Instead, classical Sanskrit texts mention the "Hundred Thousand Islands" (Lakshadweepa); a generic name which would include not only the Maldives, but also the Laccadives and the Chagos island groups. Another theory suggests that the name "Maldives" derives from the Tamil "mala tivu" meaning "a garland of islands." Some medieval Arab travellers such as Ibn Batuta called the islands "Mahal Dibiyat" from the Arabic word *Mahal* ("palace")." This is the name currently inscribed in the scroll of the Maldive state emblem.

The inhabitants were Buddhist, probably since Ashoka's period, in the 3rd century BC. Islam was introduced in 1153. The Maldives came then under the influence of the Portuguese (1558) and the Dutch (1654) seaborne empires. In 1887 it became a British protectorate. In 1965, the Maldives obtained independence from Britain (originally under the name "Maldive Islands"), and in 1968 the Sultanate was replaced by a Republic. The Maldives is the smallest Asian country in terms of population. It is also the smallest predominantly Muslim nation in the world.

HISTORY OF MALDIVES

Comparative studies of Maldivian oral, linguistic and cultural traditions and customs confirm that the first settlers were Dravidian people from the nearest coasts, most probably fishermen from the southwest coasts of the modern Indian Subcontinent and the western shores of modern Sri Lanka during the early Chera period. One such community is the Giraavaru people who claim ancestry from ancient Tamils. One theory suggests that the Giraavaru islanders may not have been the only early settlers in the Maldives. They are mentioned in ancient legends and local folklore about the establishment of the capital and kingly rule in Malé. The Giraavaru people are considered to be one of the earliest communities of settlers on the islands, predating the Christian era and the arrival of Buddhism on the islands.There are some signs of Arab and east Asian inhabitants mostly in southernmost atolls.

Buddhism came to the Maldives at the time of Emperor Ashoka's expansion and became the dominant religion of the people of the Maldives until the 12th century AD.

Western interest in the archaeological remains of early cultures on the Maldives began with the work of H.C.P. Bell, a British commissioner of the Ceylon Civil Service. Bell was shipwrecked on the islands in 1879, and returned several times to investigate ancient Buddhist ruins. He studied the ancient mounds, called *havitta* or *ustubu* (these names are derived from chaitiya or stupa) by the Maldivians, which are found on many of the atolls.

Although Bell asserted that the ancient Maldivians followed Theravada Buddhism, many local Buddhist archaeological remains now in the Malé Museum display in fact Mahayana and Vajrayana iconography.

According to a legend from the Maldivian Folklore, a prince named Koimala from present day India or Sri Lanka entered the Maldives from the North (Ihavandhu) and, after being welcomed by the Giraavaru people, became the first king from the House of Theemuge. The ancient Maldivian Kings promoted Buddhism and the first Maldive writings and artistic achievements in the form of highly developed sculpture and architecture are from that period. The entire archipelego was conquered by the medieval Chola Tamil emperor Raja Raja Chola I in the early 11th century, becoming a part of the Chola empire. The conversion to Islam is mentioned in the ancient edicts written in copper plates from the end of the 12th century AD. There is also a locally well-known legend about a foreign saint (a Persian from the city of Tabriz or a Moroccan Berber according to the versions) who subdued a demon known as Rannamaari.

Over the centuries, the islands have been visited and their development influenced by sailors and traders from countries on the Arabian Sea and the Bay of Bengal.

Although governed as an independent Islamic sultanate from 1153 to 1968, the Maldives was a British protectorate from 1887 until July 25, 1965. In 1953, there was a brief, abortive attempt to form a republic, but the sultanate was re-imposed. In 1959, objecting to Nasir's centralism, the inhabitants of the three southernmost atolls protested against the government. They formed the United Suvadive Republic and elected, Abdullah Afeef as president and Hithadhoo as capital of this republic.

After independence from Britain in 1965, the sultanate continued to operate for another three years under King Muhammad Fareed. On November 11, 1968, the monarchy was abolished and replaced by a republic, although this was a cosmetic change without any significant alteration in the structures of government. The official name of the country was changed from **Maldive Islands** to the **Maldives** in a progressive manner. Tourism began to be developed on the archipelago about five years later, by the beginning of the 1970s.

In November 1988, a group of Maldivians headed by Mr. Lutfee a small time businessman used Tamil mercenaries from Sri Lanka to stage a coup against President Gayoom. After an appeal by the Maldivian government for help, the Indian military intervened against the mercenaries in order to reinstate Gayyoom in power. On the night of November 3, 1988, the Indian Air Force airlifted a parachute battalion group from Agra and flew them non-stop over 2,000 kilometres (1,240 mi) to the Maldives. The Indian paratroopers landed at Hulule and secured the airfield and restored the Government rule at Malé within hours. The brief, bloodless operation, labelled *Operation Cactus*, also involved the Indian Navy.

On 26 December 2004, the Maldives were devastated by a tsunami following the 2004 Indian Ocean earthquake. Only nine islands were reported to have escaped any flooding, while fifty-seven islands faced serious damage to critical infrastructure, fourteen islands had to be totally evacuated, and six islands were decimated. A further twenty-one resort islands were forced to shut down due to serious damage. The total damage was estimated at over 400 million dollars or some 62% of the GDP. A total of 108 people, including six foreigners, reportedly died in the tsunami. The destructive impact of the waves on the low-lying islands was mitigated by the fact there was no continental shelf or land mass upon which the waves could gain height. The tallest waves were reported 14 feet (4.3 m) high.

ECONOMY OF MALDIVES

In ancient times the Maldives were renowned for the cowries, coir rope, dried tuna fish (Maldive Fish), ambergris (Maavaharu) and coco de mer (Tavakkaashi). Local and foreign trading ships used to load these products in Sri Lanka and transport them to other harbours in the Indian Ocean.

Today Tourism, Maldives' largest industry, accounts for 28% of GDP and more than 60% of the Maldives' foreign exchange receipts. Over 90% of government tax revenue comes from import duties and tourism-related taxes. Fishing is the second leading sector. Agriculture and manufacturing continue to play a lesser role in the economy, constrained by the limited availability of cultivable land and the shortage of domestic labor. Most staple foods must be imported. Industry, which consists mainly of garment production, boat building, and handicrafts, accounts for about 7% of GDP. The Maldivian

Government began an economic reform program in 1989 initially by lifting import quotas and opening some exports to the private sector. Subsequently, it has liberalized regulations to allow more foreign investment. Real GDP growth averaged over 7.5% per year for more than a decade. In late December 2004, a major tsunami left more than 100 dead, 12,000 displaced, and property damage exceeding $300 million. As a result of the tsunami, the GDP contracted by about 3.6% in 2005. A rebound in tourism, post-tsunami reconstruction, and development of new resorts helped the economy recover quickly and showed a 18% increase on 2006. Maldives also enjoys the highest GDP per capita $4,600 (2007 est) among south Asian countries.

FISHERIES

The Maldivian economy was entirely dependent on fishing and other marine products for many centuries. Fishing remains the main occupation of the people and the government gives special priority to the development of the fisheries sector.

The mechanization of the traditional fishing boat called *dhoni* in 1974 was a major milestone in the development of the fisheries industry and the country's economy in general. A fish canning plant was installed in the island of Felivaru in 1977, as a joint venture with a Japanese firm. In 1979, a Fisheries Advisory Board was set up with the mandate of advising the government on policy guidelines for the overall development of the fisheries sector. Manpower development programs were begun in the early 1980s, and fisheries education was incorporated into the school curriculum. Fish aggregating devices and navigational aids were located at various strategic points. Moreover, the opening up of the Exclusive Economic Zone (EEZ) of the Maldives for fisheries has further enhanced the growth of the fisheries sector. Today, fisheries contribute over fifteen percent of the GDP and engage about thirty percent of the country's work force. It is also the second-largest foreign exchange earner after tourism.

COTTAGE INDUSTRIES

The development of the tourism sector gave a major boost to the country's fledging traditional cottage industries such as mat weaving, lacquer work, handicraft, and coir rope making. New industries that have since emerged include printing, production of PVC pipes, brick making, marine engine repairs, bottling of aerated water, and garment production.

POLITICS OF MALDIVES

Politics in the Maldives takes place in the framework of a presidential republic, whereby the President is the head of government. The President heads the executive branch and appoints the cabinet. The President is nominated to a five-year term by a secret ballot of the Majlis (parliament), a nomination which is confirmed by national referendum.

The unicameral Majlis of the Maldives is composed of fifty members serving five-year terms. Two members from each atoll are elected directly by universal suffrage. Eight are appointed by the president, which is the main route through which women enter parliament. The country introduced political parties for the first time in its history in July 2005, six months after the last elections for the parliament. Nearly thirty-six members of the existing parliament joined the Dhivehi Raiyyathunge Party (the Maldivian People's Party) and elected President Gayoom as its leader. Twelve members of parliament became the Opposition and joined the Maldivian Democratic Party. Two members remained independent. In March 2006, President Gayoom published a detailed Roadmap for the Reform Agenda, providing time-bound measures to write a new Constitution, and modernise the legal framework. Under the Roadmap, the government has submitted to the Parliament a raft of reform measures. The most significant piece of legislation passed so far is the Amendment to the Human Rights Commission Act, making the new body fully compliant with the Paris Principles.

The fifty members of parliament sit with an equal number of similarly constituted persons and the Cabinet to form the Constitutional Assembly, which has been convened at the initiative of the President to write a modern liberal democratic constitution for the Maldives. The Assembly has been sitting since July 2004, and has been widely criticised for making very slow progress. The Government and the Opposition have been blaming each other for the delays, but independent observers attribute the slow progress to weak parliamentary traditions, poor whipping (none of the MPs were elected on a party ticket) and endless points of order interventions. Progress has also been slow due to the commitment of the main opposition party, MDP, to depose President Gayoom by direct action ahead of the implementation of the reform agenda, leading to civil unrest in July-August 2004, August 2005 and an abortive putsch in November 2006. Significantly, the leader of the MDP, Ibrahim Ismail (MP for the biggest constituency - Malé) resigned from his party post in April 2005 after having narrowly beat Dr. Mohammed Waheed Hassan only a couple months earlier. He eventually left MDP in November 2006 citing the intransigence of his own National Executive Committee. The government had engaged the services of a Commonwealth Special Envoy Tun Musa Hitam to facilitate all party dialogue, and when the MDP boycotted him, enlisted the services of the British High Commissioner to facilitate a dialogue. The ensuing Westminster House process made some progress but was abandoned as MDP called for the November revolution.

The Roadmap provides the deadline of 31 May 2007 for the Assembly to conclude its work and to pave the way for the first multi-party elections in the country by October 2008. This deadline has not been achieved.

On 19 June 2006, the Assembly voted to hold a public referendum to decide the form of government under the new constitutional settlement. The resulting referendum has led to the public choosing a Presidential Republic.

Attorney General Dr Hassan Saeed, along with Justice Minister Mohamed Jameel Ahmed resigned from cabinet on 5 August 2007 accusing President Maumoon Abdul Qayyoom of deliberately obstructing reform process in the country which Dr Saeed engineered and spearheaded. Dr Saaed is now running against Qayyoom for the Presidency and is seen as his main opponent.

The political structure of the Maldives has remained practically unchanged for centuries. Despite the passage from Monarchy to republic, the contemporary political structure shows a continuity with the feudal past in which power was shared among a few families at the top of the social structure. In some islands, the offices have remained within the same family for generations. The village is ruled by an administrative officer called Katîbu, who serves as the executive headman of the island. Above the Katîbus of every atoll is the AtoÊuveriya (Atoll Chief). The power of these local chiefs is very limited and they take few responsibilities. They are trained to report to the government about the situation in their islands and to merely wait for instructions from the central power and to follow them thoroughly.

JUDICIARY

Al Ustaz Mohamed Rasheed Ibrahim from Fuvahmulah is the present chief justice of Maldives. All judges in the Maldives are appointed by the president. Islamic law is the basis of all judicial decisions.

The Maldives have, in cooperation with the United Nations Development Project (UNDP), undertaken to write the world's first Muslim criminal code. This project would formalize the proceedings of criminal justice in this tiny nation to one of the most comprehensive modern criminal codes in the world. The code has been written and awaits action by the parliament.

Meanwhile, Islam remains the only official religion of The Maldives with popular support of the people of the Republic. The open practice of all other religions are forbidden and such actions are liable to prosecution under the law of the country.

GEOGRAPHY OF MALDIVES

The Maldives holds the record for being the lowest country in the world, with a maximum natural ground level of only 2.3 m (7½ ft), though in areas where construction exists this has been increased to several metres. Over the last century, sea levels have risen about 20 centimetres (8 in); further rises of the ocean could threaten the existence of Maldives.

The first accurate maritime charts of this complex Indian Ocean atoll group were the British Admiralty Charts. In 1834-36 Capt. Robert Moresby, assisted by Lieutenants Christopher and Young, undertook the difficult cartography of the Maldive Islands. The resulting charts were printed as three separate large maps by the Hydrographic Service of the Royal Navy.

A tsunami in the Indian Ocean caused by the 2004 Indian Ocean earthquake caused parts of the Maldives to be covered by sea water and left many people homeless. After the disaster, cartographers are planning to redraw the maps of the islands due to alterations caused by the tsunami.

On April 22, 2008, Maldives President Maumoon Abdul Gayoom pleaded for a cut in global greenhouse gas emissions, warning that rising sea levels could submerge the island nation of Maldives.

The reef is composed of coral debris and living coral. This acts as a natural barrier against the sea, forming lagoons. Other islands, set at a distance and parallel to the reef, have their own protective fringe of reef. An opening in the surrounding coral barrier allows access to the calmer lagoon waters.

The barrier reefs of the islands protect them from the storms and high waves of the Indian Ocean. The Indian Ocean has a great affect on the climate of the country by acting as a heat buffer, absorbing, storing, and slowly releasing the tropical heat. The heat is further mitigated by cool sea breezes.

A layer of humus six inches (152 mm) thick forms the top layer of soil on the islands. Below the humus layer are two feet of sandstone, followed by sand and then fresh water. Due to excessive salt in the soil near the beach, vegetation is limited there to a few plants such as shrubs, flowering plants, and small hedges. In the interior of the island, more vegetation such as mangrove and banyan grow. Coconut palms, the national tree, are able to grow almost everywhere on the islands and are integral to the lifestyle of the natives.

The limited vegetation is supplemented by the abundance of coral reefs and marine life.

DEMOGRAPHY OF MALDIVES

The Maldivian ethnic identity is a blend of the cultures reflecting the peoples who settled on the islands, reinforced by religion and language. The earliest settlers were probably from southern India and Sri Lanka.

Some social stratification exists on the islands. It is not rigid, since rank is based on varied factors, including occupation, wealth, Islamic virtue, and family ties. Traditionally, instead of a complex caste system, like the Vedic one, there was merely a distinction between noble (bçfulhu) and common people in the Maldives. Members of the social elite are concentrated in Malé. Outside of the service industry, this is the only location where the foreign and domestic populations are likely to interact. The tourist resorts are not on islands where the natives live, and casual contacts between the two groups are discouraged.

A census has been recorded since 1905, which shows that the population of the country remained around 100,000 for the first seventy years of the last century. Following independence in 1965, the health status of the population improved so much that the population doubled by 1978, and the population growth rate peaked at 3.4% in 1985. By 2007, the population had reached 300,000, although the census in 2000 showed that the population growth rate had declined to 1.9%. Life expectancy at birth stood at 46 years in 1978, while it has now risen to 72 years. Infant mortality has declined from 127 per thousand in 1977 to 12 today, and adult literacy stands at 99%. Combined school enrollment stands in the high 90s.

As of April 2008, more than 70,000 foreign employees live in the country and another 33,000 illegal immigrants sums up more than one third of Maldivian population. They consist mainly of people from the neighbouring South Asian countries of India, Sri Lanka, Bangladesh and Nepal.

CULTURE OF MALDIVES

Maldivian culture is derived from a number of sources, the most important of which are its proximity to the shores of Sri Lanka and South India. Thus the population is mainly Dravidian from the anthropological point of view.

The language is from Indo-Iranian Sanskritic origin, which points at a later influence from the North of the Subcontinent. According to the legends, the kingly dynasty that ruled the country in the past has its origin there.

Possibly these ancient kings brought Buddhism from the Subcontinent, but it is not clear. In Sri Lanka there are similar legends, but it is improbable that the ancient Maldive royals and Buddhism came both from that island because none of the Sri Lankan chronicles mentions the Maldives. It is unlikely that the ancient chronicles of Sri Lanka would have failed to mention the Maldives if a branch of its kingdom would have extended itself to the Maldive Islands.

Since the 12th cemtury AD there are also influences from Arabia in the language and culture of the Maldives because of the general conversion to Islam in the 12th century, and its location as a crossroads in the central Indian Ocean.

In the island culture there are a few elements of African origin as well from slaves brought to the court by the Royal family and nobles from their Hajj journeys to Arabia in the past. There are islands like Feridhu and Maalhos in Northern Ari Atoll, and Goidhu in Southern Maalhosmadulhu Atoll where many of the inhabitants trace their ancestry to released African slaves.

MUSIC AND DANCE

Culturally Maldivians feel some affinity to Northern India through their language, which is related to the languages of North India. Most older generation Maldivians like to watch Hindi movies and like to listen to Hindi songs. Many popular Maldivian songs are based on Hindi tunes. The reason is that out of a similar language, similar rhythms and cadences develop. In fact it is very easy for Maldivians to fit local lyrics into a Hindi song. Hindi songs are among the most popular songs in Maldives, especially the old ones from Mohammed Rafi, Mukesh, Lata Mangeshkar, Asha Bhonsle. Therefore most local Maldivian dances and songs are based in (or influenced by) North Indian dances Kathak and Hindi songs.

The favourite musical instrument of Maldivians is the bulbul, a kind of horizontal accordion. This instrument is also used to accompany devotional songs, like Maulûd and Maadhaha. The Bodu-Beru (literally "Big Drum") drumming performances, are said to have African roots.

Among the popular celebrations, some include carnival-like costumes like Maali Neshun, Bodu Maali, Bey and Bodu Mas. The costumes are made with palm frond and sack cloth, and some of them look quite spectacular.

MARRIAGE

Maldivian culture shares many aspects of a strong matriarchal tradition with ancient Dravidian culture. A unique feature of Maldivian society is a very high divorce rate by either South Asian or Islamic standards. This is not so in the case of Minicoy Island though, where marriages are more stable.

LOCAL SPIRITUALITY

The Maldives is an exclusively Islamic society. It is common to hear Maldivians refer to their country as a "100 percent Muslim country" . But there is a widespread belief in evil spirits. For protection against such evils, people often resort to various charms and spells. The extent of these beliefs has led some observers to identify a magico-religious system parallel to Islam known as fanditha, which provides a more personal way for the islanders to deal with either actual or perceived problems in their lives. However this is a dying tradition that can be seen in only rural areas.

Chapter 8

Afghanistan

Afghanistan, officially the Islamic Republic of Afghanistan is a landlocked country that is located approximately in the center of Asia. It is variously designated as geographically located within Central Asia, South Asia, and the Middle East. It has religious, ethno-linguistic, and geographic links with most of its neighboring states. It is bordered by Pakistan in the south and east, Iran in the west, Turkmenistan, Uzbekistan and Tajikistan in the north, and China in the far northeast. The name Afghanistan means the *"Land of Afghans."*

Afghanistan is a culturally mixed nation, a crossroads between the East and the West, and has been an ancient focal point of trade and migration. It has an important geostrategical location, connecting South, Central and Southwest Asia. During its long history, the land has seen various invaders and conquerors, while on the other hand, local entities invaded the surrounding vast regions to form their own empires. Ahmad Shah Durrani created the Durrani Empire in 1747, with its capital at Kandahar. Subsequently, the capital was shifted to Kabul and most of its territories ceded to former neighboring countries. In the late 19th century, Afghanistan became a buffer state in "The Great Game" played between the British Indian Empire and Russian Empire. On August 19, 1919, following the third Anglo-Afghan war, the country regained full independence from the United Kingdom over its foreign affairs.

Since the late 1970s Afghanistan has suffered continuous and brutal civil war, which included foreign interventions in the form of the 1979 Soviet invasion and the recent 2001 US-led invasion that toppled the Taliban government. In late 2001 the United Nations Security Council authorized the creation of an International Security Assistance Force (ISAF). This force is composed of NATO troops that are involved in assisting the government of President Hamid Karzai in establishing the writ of law as well as rebuilding key infrastructures in the nation. In 2005, the United States and Afghanistan signed a strategic partnership agreement committing both nations to a long-term relationship. In the meantime, multi-billion US dollars have also been provided by the international community for the reconstruction of the country.

HISTORY OF AFGHANISTAN

Though the modern state of Afghanistan was founded or created in 1747 by Ahmad Shah Durrani, the land has an ancient history and various timelines of different civilizations. Excavation of prehistoric sites by Louis Dupree, the University of Pennsylvania, the Smithsonian Institution and others suggests that humans were living in what is now Afghanistan at least 50,000 years ago, and that farming communities of the area were among the earliest in the world.

Afghanistan is a country at a unique nexus point where numerous Indo-European civilizations have interacted and often fought, and was an important site of early historical activity. Through the ages, the region has been home to various people, among them the Aryan (Indo-Iranian) tribes, such as the Kambojas, Bactrians, Persians, Pashtuns, etc. It also has been conquered by a host of people, including the Median and Persian Empires, Alexander the Great, Kushans, Hepthalites[White Huns], Arabs, Turks, and Mongols. In recent times, invasions from the British, Soviets, and most recently by the United States and their allies have taken place. On the other hand, native entities have invaded surrounding regions in Iranian plateau and Indian subcontinent to form empires of their own.

Between 2000 and 1200 BC, Indo-European-speaking Aryans are thought to have been in the region of northern Afghanistan. It is unlikely that the Aryans themselves originated in Afghanistan although they did migrate from there south towards India and west towards Persia, but they also migrated into Europe via north of the Caspian. These Aryans set up a nation that during the rule of Medes and Achaemenid Persians which became known as Aryânâm Xðaèra or Airyânem Vâejah. Original homelands of the Aryans have been proposed as Anatolia, Kurdistan, Central Asia, Iran, or Northern India, with the directions of the historical migration varying accordingly. Later, during the rule of Ashkanian, Sasanian and after, it was called Erânshahr meaning "Dominion of the Aryans."

It has been speculated that Zoroastrianism might have originated in what is now Afghanistan between 1800 to 800 BC, as Zoroaster lived and died in Balkh. Ancient Eastern Iranian languages, such as Avestan, may have been spoken in this region around the time of the rise of Zoroastrianism. By the middle of the sixth century BC, the Persian Empire of the Achaemenid Persians overthrew the Median Empire and incorporated Afghanistan (known as Arachosia to the Greeks) within its boundaries. Alexander the Great conquered Afghanistan after 330 BCE. Following Alexander's brief occupation, the successor state of the Seleucid Empire controlled the area until 305 BCE, when they gave most of the area to the Mauryan Empire as part of an alliance treaty. During Mauryan rule, Buddhism became the dominant religion in the region. The Mauryans were overthrown by the Sunga Dynasty in 185 BCE, leading to the Hellenistic reconquest of Afghanistan by the Greco-Bactrians by 180 BCE. Much of Afghanistan soon broke away from the Greco-Bactrians and became part of the Indo-Greek Kingdom. The Indo-Greeks were defeated by the Indo-Scythians and expelled from most of Afghanistan by the end of the 2nd century BCE.

During the first century, the Parthian Empire subjugated Afghanistan, but lost it to their Indo-Parthian vassals. In the mid to late 1st century AD the vast Kushan Empire, centered in modern Afghanistan, became great patrons of Buddhist culture. The Kushans were defeated by the Sassanids in the third century. Although various rulers calling themselves Kushans has (generally known as Indo-Sassanids) continued to rule at least parts of the region, they were probably more or less subject to the Sassanids. The late Kushans were followed by the Kidarite Huns who, in turn, were replaced by the short-lived but powerful Hephthalites, as rulers of the region in the first half of the fifth century. The Hephthalites were defeated by the Sasanian king Khosrau I in AD 557, who re-established Sassanid power in Persia. However, the successors of Kushans and Hepthalites established a small dynasty in Kabulistan called Kushano-Hephthalites or Kabul-Shahan/ Shahi, who were later defeated by the Muslim Arab armies and finally conquered by Muslim Turkish armies led by the Ghaznavids.

ISLAMIC CONQUEST OF THE REGION

In the Middle Ages, up to the nineteenth century, Afghanistan was part of a larger region known as Greater Khorasan. Several important centers of Khorâsân are thus located in modern Afghanistan, such as Balkh, Herat, Ghazni and Kabul. It was during this period of time when Islam was introduced and spread in the area.

The region of Afghanistan became the center of various important empires, including that of the Samanids (875–999), Ghaznavids (977–1187), Seljukids (1037–1194), Ghurids (1149–1212), and Timurids (1370–1506). Among them, the periods of Ghaznavids of Ghazni, and Timurids of Heart are considered as some of the most brilliant eras of Afghanistan's history.

In 1219 the region was overrun by the Mongols under Genghis Khan, who devastated the land. Their rule continued with the Ilkhanates [one of 4 Subordinate Mongolian Khanates], and was extended further following the invasion of Timur Lang ("Tamerlane"), a ruler from Central Asia. In 1504, Babur, a descendant of both Timur Lang and Genghis Khan, established the Mughal Empire with its capital at Kabul. By the early 1700s, Afghanistan was controlled by several ruling groups: Uzbeks to the north, Safavids to the west and the remaining larger area by the Mughals or self-ruled by local Afghan tribes.

HOTAKI DYNASTY: FIRST AFGHAN RULE

In 1709, Mir Wais Hotak, a local Afghan (*Pashtun*) from the Ghilzai clan, overthrew and killed Gurgin Khan, the Safavid governor of Kandahar. Mir Wais successfully defeated the Persians, who were attempting to convert the local population of Kandahar from Sunni to the Shia sect of Islam. Mir Wais held the region of Kandahar until his death in 1715 and was succeeded by his son Mir Mahmud Hotaki. In 1722, Mir Mahmud led an

Afghan army to Isfahan (Iran), sacked the city and proclaimed himself King of Persia. However, the great majority still rejected the Afghan regime as usurping, and after the massacre of thousands of civilians in Isfahan by the Afghans – including more than three thousand religious scholars, nobles, and members of the Safavid family – the Hotaki dynasty was eventually removed from power by a new ruler, Nadir Shah of Persia.

DURRANI EMPIRE: BEGINNINGS OF THE "AFGHAN STATE"

In 1738 Nadir Shah and his army, which included four thousand Pashtuns of the Abdali clan, conquered the region of Kandahar; in the same year he occupied Ghazni, Kabul and Lahore. On June 19, 1747, Nadir Shah was assassinated, possibly planned by his nephew Ali Qoli. In the same year, one of Nadir's military commanders and personal bodyguard, Ahmad Shah Abdali, a Pashtun from the Abdali clan, called for a loya jirga following Nadir's death. The Afghans gathered at Kandahar and chose Ahmad Shah as their King. Since then, he is often regarded as the founder of modern Afghanistan. After the inauguration, he changed his title or clans' name to *"Durrani"*, which derives from the Persian word *Durr*, meaning *"Pearl"*.

By 1751 Ahmad Shah Durrani and his Afghan army conquered the entire present-day Afghanistan, Pakistan, Khorasan and Kohistan provinces of Iran, along with Delhi in India. In October 1772, Ahmad Shah retired to his home in Maruf, Kandahar, where he died peacefully. He was succeeded by his son, Timur Shah Durrani, who transferred the capital from Kandahar to Kabul. Timur died in 1793 and was finally succeeded by his son Zaman Shah Durrani.

EUROPEAN INFLUENCE AND THE CREATION OF THE STATE OF AFGHANISTAN

During the nineteenth century, following the Anglo-Afghan wars (fought 1839–42, 1878–80, and lastly in 1919) and the ascension of the Barakzai dynasty, Afghanistan saw much of its territory and autonomy ceded to the United Kingdom. The UK exercised a great deal of influence, and it was not until King Amanullah Khan acceded to the throne in 1919 that Afghanistan re-gained complete independence over its foreign affairs. During the period of British intervention in Afghanistan, ethnic Pashtun territories were divided by the Durand Line. This would lead to strained relations between Afghanistan and British India – and later the new state of Pakistan – over what came to be known as the Pashtunistan debate. The longest period of stability in Afghanistan was between 1933 and 1973, when the country was under the rule of King Zahir Shah.

REPUBLIC

However, in 1973 Zahir Shah's brother-in-law, Mohammed Daoud Khan, launched a bloodless coup and became the first President of Afghanistan.

In 1978 a prominent member of the People's Democratic Party of Afghanistan (PDPA), Mir Akbar Khyber (or "Kaibar"), was killed by the government. The leaders of PDPA apparently feared that Daoud was planning to exterminate them all, especially since most of them were arrested by the government shortly after. Hafizullah Amin and a number of military wing officers of the PDPA managed to remain at large and organised an uprising.

The PDPA, led by Nur Mohammad Taraki, Babrak Karmal and Amin overthrew the regime of Mohammad Daoud, who was killed along with his family. The uprising was known as the Great Saur Revolution ('Saur' means 'April' in Pushto). On 1 May, Taraki became President , Prime Minister and General Secretary of the PDPA. The country was then renamed the Democratic Republic of Afghanistan (DRA), and the PDPA regime lasted, in some form or another, until April 1992.

Some are of the opinion that the 1978 Khalq uprising against the government of Daoud Khan was essentially a resurgence by the Ghilzai tribe of the Pashtun against the Durrani (the tribe of Daoud Khan and the previous monarchy).

Once in power, the PDPA moved to permit freedom of religion and carried out an ambitious land reform, waiving farmers' debts countrywide. They also made a number of statements on women's rights and introduced women to political life. A prominent example was Anahita Ratebzad, who was a major Marxist leader and a member of the Revolutionary Council. Ratebzad wrote the famous *New Kabul Times* editorial (May 28, 1978) which declared: "Privileges which women, by right, must have are equal education, job security, health services, and free time to rear a healthy generation for building the future of the country .... Educating and enlightening women is now the subject of close government attention."

The majority of people in the cities including Kabul either welcomed or were ambivalent to these policies. However, the secular nature of the government made it unpopular with religiously conservative Afghans in the villages and the countryside, who favoured traditionalist 'Islamic' restrictions on women's rights and in daily life.

The U.S. saw the situation as a prime opportunity to weaken the Soviet Union. As part of a Cold War strategy, in 1979 the United States government (under President Jimmy Carter and National Security Advisor Zbigniew Brzezinski) began to covertly fund and train anti-government Mujahideen forces through the Pakistani secret service known as Inter Services Intelligence (ISI), with the intention of provoking Soviet intervention, (according to Brzezinski). The Mujahideen belonged to various different factions, but all shared, to varying degrees, a similarly conservative 'Islamic' ideology.

In March 1979 Hafizullah Amin took over as prime minister, retaining the position of field marshal and becoming vice-president of the Supreme Defence Council. Taraki remained President and in control of the Army on 14 September, Amin overthrew Taraki, who died or was killed.

SOVIET INVASION AND CIVIL WAR

In order to bolster the Parcham faction , the Soviet Union—citing the 1978 Treaty of Friendship, Cooperation and Good Neighborliness that had been signed between the two countries—intervened on December 24, 1979. Over 100,000 Soviet troops took part in the invasion backed by another 100,000 plus and by members of the Parcham faction. Amin was killed and replaced by Babrak Karmal.

The Soviet occupation resulted in the killings of at least 600,000 to 2 million Afghan civilians. Over five million Afghans fled their country to Pakistan, Iran and other parts of the world. Faced with mounting international pressure and great number of casualties on both sides, the Soviets withdrew in 1989.

The Soviet withdrawal from the DRA was seen as an ideological victory in the US, which had backed the Mujahideen through three US presidential administrations in order to counter Soviet influence in the vicinity of the oil-rich Persian Gulf.

Following the removal of the Soviet forces, the US and its allies lost interest in Afghanistan and did little to help rebuild the war-ravaged country or influence events there. The USSR continued to support President Najibullah (former head of the Afghan secret service, *KHAD*) until 1992 when the new Russian government refused to sell oil products to the Najibullah regime.

Because of the fighting, a number of elites and intellectuals fled to take refuge abrcad. This led to a leadership imbalance in Afghanistan. Fighting continued among the victorious Mujahideen factions, which gave rise to a state of warlordism. The most serious fighting during this period occurred in 1994, when over 10,000 people were killed in Kabul alone. It was at this time that the Taliban developed as a politico-religious force, eventually seizing Kabul in 1996 and establishing the Islamic Emirate of Afghanistan. By the end of 2000 the Taliban had captured 95% of the country.

During the Taliban's seven-year rule, much of the population experienced restrictions on their freedom and violations of their human rights. Women were banned from jobs, girls forbidden to attend schools or universities. Communists were systematically eradicated and thieves were punished by amputating one of their hands or feet. Meanwhile, the Taliban managed to nearly eradicate the majority of the opium production by 2001.

2001-PRESENT WAR IN AFGHANISTAN

Following the September 11, 2001 attacks the United States launched Operation Enduring Freedom, a military campaign to destroy the al-Qaeda terrorist training camps inside Afghanistan. The US military also threatened to overthrow the Taliban government for refusing to hand over Osama bin Laden and several al-Qaida members. The US made a common cause with the former Afghan Mujahideen to achieve its ends, including the Northern Alliance, a militia still recognized by the UN as the Afghan government.

In late 2001, US Special Forces invaded Afghanistan to aid anti-Taliban militias, backed by US air strikes against Taliban and Al Qaeda targets, culminating in the seizure of Kabul by the Northern Alliance and the overthrow of the Taliban, with many local warlords switching allegiance from the Taliban to the Northern Alliance.

In December of the same year, leaders of the former Afghan mujahideen and diaspora met in Germany, and agreed on a plan for the formulation of a new democratic government that resulted in the inauguration of Hamid Karzai, an ethnic Pashtun of the Durrani clan (from which the royal family was drawn) from the southern city of Kandahar, as Chairman of the Afghan Interim Authority. Karzai was a top adviser to the UNOCAL corporation, which negotiatied with the Taliban to construct a Central Asia Gas (CentGas) pipeline from Turkmenistan through western Afghanistan to Pakistan.

After a nationwide *Loya Jirga* in 2002, Karzai was chosen by the representatives to assume the title as Interim President of Afghanistan. The country convened a Constitutional Loya Jirga (Council of Elders) in 2003 and a new constitution was ratified in January 2004. Following an election in October 2004, Hamid Karzai won and became the President of the Islamic Republic of Afghanistan. Legislative elections were held in September 2005. The National Assembly – the first freely elected legislature in Afghanistan since 1973 – sat in December 2005, and was noteworthy for the inclusion of women as voters, candidates, and elected members.

As the country continues to rebuild and recover, it is still struggling against poverty, poor infrastructure, large concentration of land mines and other unexploded ordnance, as well as a huge illegal poppy cultivation and opium trade. Afghanistan also remains subject to occasionally violent political jockeying. The country continues to grapple with the Taliban insurgency and the threat of attacks from a few remaining al Qaeda.

At the start of 2007 reports of the Taliban's increasing presence in Afghanistan led the US to consider longer tours of duty and even an increase in troop numbers. According to a report filed by Robert Burns of Associated Press on January 16, 2007, "U.S. military officials cited new evidence that the Pakistani military, which has long-standing ties to the Taliban movement, has turned a blind eye to the incursions." Also, "The number of insurgent attacks is up 300 percent since September, 2006, when the Pakistani government put into effect a peace arrangement with tribal leaders in the north Waziristan area, along Afghanistan's eastern border, a U.S. military intelligence officer told reporters."

GEOGRAPHY OF AFGHANISTAN

Afghanistan is a landlocked and mountainous country in South-Central Asia, with plains in the north and southwest. The highest point is Nowshak, at 7,485 m (24,557 ft) above sea level. Large parts of the country are dry, and fresh water supplies are limited. The endorheic Sistan Basin is one of the driest regions in the world. Afghanistan has a continental climate with hot summers and cold winters. The country is frequently subject to minor earthquakes, mainly in the northeast of Hindu Kush mountain areas. Some 125 villages were damaged and 4000 people killed by the May 30, 1998 earthquake.

At 249,984 sq mi (647,500 km^2), Afghanistan is the world's 41st-largest country (after Myanmar). The country's natural resources include gold, silver, copper, zinc and iron ore in southeastern areas; precious and semi-precious stones such as lapis, emerald and azure in the north-east; and potentially significant petroleum and natural gas reserves in the north. The country also has uranium, coal, chromite, talc, barites, sulfur, lead, and salt. However, these significant mineral and energy resources remain largely untapped due to the effects of the Soviet invasion and the subsequent civil war. Plans are underway to begin extracting them in the near future.

GOVERNMENT AND POLITICS OF AFGHANISTAN

Politics in Afghanistan has historically consisted of power struggles, bloody coups and unstable transfers of power. With the exception of a military junta, the country has been governed by nearly every system of government over the past century, including a monarchy, republic, theocracy and communist state. The constitution ratified by the 2003 Loya jirga restructured the government as an Islamic republic consisting of three branches, (executive, legislature and judiciary).

Afghanistan is currently led by President Hamid Karzai, who was elected in October 2004. The current parliament was elected in 2005. Among the elected officials were former mujahadeen, Taliban members, communists, reformists, and Islamic fundamentalists. 28% of the delegates elected were women, 3 points more than the 25% minimum guaranteed under the constitution. This made Afghanistan, long known under the Taliban for its oppression of women, one of the leading countries in terms of female representation. Construction for a new parliament building began on August 29, 2005.

The Supreme Court of Afghanistan is currently led by Chief Justice Abdul Salam Azimi, a former university professor who had been legal advisor to the president. The previous court, appointed during the time of the interim government, had been dominated by fundamentalist religious figures, including Chief Justice Faisal Ahmad Shinwari. The court had issued numerous questionable rulings, such as banning cable television, seeking to ban a candidate in the 2004 presidential election and limiting the rights of women, as well as overstepping its constitutional authority by issuing rulings on subjects not yet brought before the court. The current court is seen as more moderate and led by more technocrats than the previous court, although it has yet to issue any rulings.

DEMOGRAPHY OF AFGHANISTAN

The **Demographics of Afghanistan** are ethnically and linguistically mixed. This reflects its location astride historic trade and invasion routes leading from Central Asia into South Asia and Southwest Asia. Afghanistan can be considered a country of minorities as there is no group serving as a majority. Rather, Pashtuns are the largest ethnic group followed by Tajiks as the second largest group, then Hazaras, Uzbeks tied for third, followed by the Aimak, Turkmen, Baluch, Nuristani and other small groups. Pashto and Persian (*Dari*) the two official languages of the country. Persian is spoken by at least half of the population and serves as a lingua franca for most. Pashto is spoken widely in the south, east and south west. Uzbek and Turkmen are spoken in the north. Smaller groups throughout the country also speak more than 70 other languages and numerous dialects.

PASHTUNS

The Pashtuns (also known as Pakhtun or Pathan), are people that today reside mainly in southern and eastern Afghanistan and are also located in western Pakistan. Considerable pockets also exist throughout other parts of Afghanistan as Pashtuns have in recent times migrated, or have been forcefully displaced, to northern and western regions. Smaller groups of Pashtuns are also found in Iran. There are many conflicting theories, some contemporary, some ancient, about the origins of the Pashtun people, both among historians and the Pashtun themselves. According to the writer W.K. Frazier Tyler writing in his book Afghanistan, "The word Afghan... first appears in history in the Hudud-al-Alam, a work by an unknown Arab geographer who wrote in 982 AD."

Al-Biruni referred to Afghans as various tribes living on the western frontier mountains of India, which would be the Sulaiman Mountains. According to other sources, these tribes are the lost Jewish tribes that never returned and were converted to islam during the Arab Empire. Thus it is believed that the Pashtuns emerged from the area around the Sulaiman Mountains, and expanded from there. The Afghan identity began to develop as Pashtun identity under the rule of Ahmad Shah Durrani who united the Pashtun (Afghan) chiefdoms in the middle of 18th century. Another boost took place under the rule of Abdur Rahman Khan who with British support further centralized the government. Until the advent of the modern "Afghan" state in the 20th century, the word *Afghan* had been synonymous with *Pashtun*.

TAJIKS

The Persian-speaking Tajiks are closely related to the Persians of Iran and are amongst the oldest inhabitants of the region. They can trace their roots back to the original Eastern Iranian peoples that settled Central Asia in ancient times, such as the Bactrians, Sogdians, Scythians and Parthians, as well as ancient Persians who fled to Central Asia during the Arab Islamic expansion. The Tajiks also comprise the majority population of Tajikistan and are found in large numbers in Uzbekistan and Iran as well as parts of western Pakistan and the Xinjiang province of western China.

Sub-groups of the Tajiks include the Farsiwan and the Qizilbash. The major difference between them is that they are generally of the Shia sect while other Tajiks are of the Sunni sect.

Despite being the indigenous peoples responsible for carrying on civilized society through the centuries, since the Mongol invasion of Central Asia, Tajiks have never ruled from first hand the region that is today Afghanistan — with the exception of the Kartids, the Ganjshakariyyas of Kabulistan and the short 10-month rule of Habibullah Kalakani in 1929.

In modern Afghanistan, Tajiks have been mainly known for being bureaucrats, educators, doctors, teachers, professors, artisans and especially successful merchants and entrepreneurs. Some were also ministers.

HAZARAS

The Hazaras are a Persianized Eurasian people who reside mainly in the Hazarajat region. The Hazara seem to have Mongolian origins with some admixture from surrounding indigenous groups. Linguistically the Hazara speak a dialect of Persian and sometimes their variant is interspersed with more Mongolian words. It is commonly believed by many Afghans that the Hazara are descendants of Genghis Khan's army, which marched into the area during the 12th century. Proponents of this view hold that many of the Mongol soldiers and their family members settled in the area and remained there after the Mongol empire dissolved in the 13th century, converting to Islam and adopting local customs. Unlike most Afghans the Hazara are Shia, which has often set them apart from their neighbors. There are sizeable Hazara communities in Pakistan particularly in Quetta as well as in Iran.

UZBEKS

The Uzbeks are the main Turkic people of Afghanistan and are found mainly in the northern regions of the country. Most likely the Uzbeks migrated with a wave of Turkic invaders and intermingled with local Iranian tribes over time to become the ethnic group they are today. By the 1500s the Uzbeks had settled throughout Central Asia and reached Afghanistan following the conquests of Muhammad Shaybani. Most Uzbeks are Sunni Muslim and are closely related to the Turkmen who also can be found in Afghanistan. The Uzbeks of Afghanistan are usually bilingual, fluent in both Persian and Uzbek. Physically, the Uzbek are generally Mongoloid.

TURKMEN

The Turkmen are the smaller Turkic group who can also be found in neighboring Turkmenistan, Iran particularly around Mashad and Pakistan. Largely Sunni Muslim, their origins are very similar to that of the Uzbeks. Unlike, the Uzbeks, however, the Turkmen are traditionally a nomadic people (though they were forced to abandon this way of life in Turkmenistan itself under Soviet rule). Physically, they are aquiline Mongoloid.

BALUCH

The Baluch are another Iranian ethnic group that numbers around 200,000 in Afghanistan. The main Baloch areas located in Balochistan province in Pakistan and Sistan and Baluchistan province of Iran. Many also live in southern Afghanistan. They are most likely an offshoot of the Kurds and reached Afghanistan sometime between 1000 and 1300 BCE. Mainly pastoral and desert dwellers, the Baluch are also Sunni Muslim.

CULTURE OF AFGHANISTAN

Afghans display pride in their religion, country, ancestry, and above all, their independence. Like other highlanders, Afghans are regarded with mingled apprehension and condescension, for their high regard for personal honor, for their clan loyalty and for their readiness to carry and use arms to settle disputes. As clan warfare and internecine feuding has been one of their chief occupations since time immemorial, this individualistic trait has made it difficult for foreign invaders to hold the region.

Afghanistan has a complex history that has survived either in its current cultures or in the form of various languages and monuments. However, many of the country's historic monuments have been damaged in recent wars. The two famous statues of Buddha in the Bamyan Province were destroyed by the Taliban, who regarded them as idolatrous. Other famous sites include the cities of Kandahar, Heart, Ghazni and Balkh. The Minaret of Jam, in the Hari River valley, is a UNESCO World Heritage site. The cloak worn by Muhammad is stored inside the famous Khalka Sharifa in Kandahar City.

Buzkashi is a national sport in Afghanistan. It is similar to polo and played by horsemen in two teams, each trying to grab and hold a goat carcass. Afghan hounds (a type of running dog) also originated in Afghanistan.

Although literacy levels are very low, classic Persian poetry plays a very important role in the Afghan culture. Poetry has always been one of the major educational pillars in Iran and Afghanistan, to the level that it has integrated itself into culture. Persian culture has, and continues to, exert a great influence over Afghan culture. Private poetry competition events known as "musha'era" are quite common even among ordinary people. Almost every homeowner owns one or more poetry collections of some sort, even if they are not read often.

The eastern dialects of the Persian language are popularly known as "Dari". The name itself derives from "Pârsî-e Darbârî", meaning *Persian of the royal courts*. The ancient term *Darî* – one of the original names of the Persian language – was revived in the Afghan constitution of 1964, and was intended *to signify that Afghans consider their country the cradle of the language.* Hence, the name *Fârsî*, the language of Fârs, is strictly avoided. With this point in mind, we can consider the development of Dari or Persian literature in the political entity known as Afghanistan."

Many of the famous Persian poets of the tenth to fifteenth centuries stem from Khorasan where is now known as Afghanistan. They were mostly also scholars in many disciplines like languages, natural sciences, medicine, religion and astronomy.

- Mawlânâ Rumi, who was born and educated in Balkh in the thirteenth century and moved to Konya in modern-day Turkey

- Rabi'a Balkhi (the first poetess in the History of Persian Poetry, tenth century, native of Balkh)
- Daqiqi Balkhi (tenth century, native of Balkh)
- Farrukhi Sistani (tenth century, the Ghaznavids royal poet)
- Unsuri Balkhi (a tenth/eleventh century poet, native of Balkh)
- Khwaja Abdullah Ansari (eleventh century, from Herat)
- Nasir Khusraw (eleventh century, from Qubadyan near Balkh)
- Anvari (twelfth century, lived and died in Balkh)
- Sanâ'î Ghaznawi (twelfth century, native of Ghazni)
- Jâmî of Herât (fifteenth century, native of Herat in western Afghanistan), and his nephew Abdullah Hatifi Herawi, a well-known poet
- Alî Sher Navâ'î (fifteenth century, Herat).
- Hanzala Badghisi, Zaheer Faryabi, Shahid Balkhi, Maroofi Balkhi, Abul-Mu'ayyed Balkhi, Abu-Shukoor Balkhi

Most of these individuals were of Persian (Tâjîk) ethnicity who still form the second-largest ethnic group in Afghanistan. Also, some of the contemporary Persian language poets and writers, who are relatively well-known in Persian-speaking world, include Ustad Betab, Qari Abdullah, Khalilullah Khalili, Sufi Ghulam Nabi Ashqari, Sarwar Joya, Qahar Asey, Parwin Pazwak and others. In 2003, Khaled Hosseini published The Kiterunner which though fiction, captured much of the history, politics and culture experienced in Afghanistan from the 1930s to present day.

In addition to poets and authors, numerous Persian scientists were born or worked in the region of present-day Afghanistan. Most notable was Avicenna (Abu Alî Hussein ibn Sînâ) whose father hailed from Balkh. Ibn Sînâ, who travelled to Isfahan later in life to establish a medical school there, is known by some scholars as "the father of modern medicine". George Sarton called ibn Sînâ "the most famous scientist of Islam and one of the most famous of all races, places, and times." His most famous works are *The Book of Healing* and *The Canon of Medicine*, also known as the Qanun. Ibn Sînâ's story even found way to the contemporary English literature through Noah Gordon's *The Physician*, now published in many languages. Moreover, according to Ibn al-Nadim, Al-Farabi, a well-known philosopher and scientist, was from the Faryab Province of Afghanistan.

Before the Taliban gained power, the city of Kabul was home to many musicians who were masters of both traditional and modern Afghan music, especially during the Nauroz-celebration. Kabul in the middle part of the twentieth century has been likened to Vienna during the eighteenth and nineteenth centuries.

The tribal system, which orders the life of most people outside metropolitan areas, is potent in political terms. Men feel a fierce loyalty to their own tribe, such that, if called upon, they would assemble in arms under the tribal chiefs and local clan leaders (Khans). In theory, under Islamic law, every believer has an obligation to bear arms at the ruler's call (Ulul-Amr).

Heathcote considers the tribal system to be the best way of organizing large groups of people in a country that is geographically difficult, and in a society that, from a materialistic point of view, has an uncomplicated lifestyle.

ECONOMY OF AFGHANISTAN

Afghanistan is a member of the South Asian Association for Regional Cooperation (SAARC), Economic Cooperation Organization (ECO) and the Organization of the Islamic Conference (OIC). It is an impoverished country, one of the world's poorest and least developed. Two-thirds of the population lives on fewer than 2 US dollars a day. Its economy has suffered greatly from the 1979 Soviet invasion and subsequent conflicts, while severe drought added to the nation's difficulties in 1998–2001.

The economically active population in 2002 was about 11 million (out of a total of an estimated 29 million). As of 2005, the official unemployment rate is at 40%. The number of non-skilled young people is estimated at 3 million, which is likely to increase by some 300,000 per annum.

The nation's economy began to improve since 2002 due to the infusion of multi-billion US dollars in international assistance and investments, as well as remittances from expats. It is also due to dramatic improvements in agricultural production and the end of a four-year drought in most of the country.

The real value of *non-drug* GDP increased by 29% in 2002, 16% in 2003, 8% in 2004 and 14% in 2005. As much as one-third of Afghanistan's GDP comes from growing poppy and illicit drugs including opium and its two derivatives, morphine and heroin, as well as hashish production. Opium production in Afghanistan has soared to a new record in 2007, with an increase on last year of more than a third, the United Nations has said. Some 3.3 million Afghans are now involved in producing opium. In a recent article in the Washington Quarterly, Peter van Ham and Jorrit Kamminga argue that the international community should establish a pilot project and investigate a licensing scheme to start the production of medicines such as morphine and codeine from poppy crops to help it escape the economic dependence on opium.

According to a 2004 report by the Asian Development Bank, the present reconstruction effort is two-pronged: first it focuses on rebuilding critical physical infrastructure, and second, on building modern public sector institutions from the remnants of Soviet style planning to ones that promote market-led development. In 2006, two US companies, Black & Veatch and the Louis Berger Group, have won a US 1.4 billion dollar contract to rebuild roads, power lines and water supply systems of Afghanistan.

One of the main drivers for the current economic recovery is the return of over 4 million refugees from neighbouring countries and the West, who brought with them fresh energy, entrepreneurship and wealth-creating skills as well as much needed funds to start up businesses. What is also helping is the estimated US 2–3 billion dollars in international assistance every year, the partial recovery of the agricultural sector, and the reestablishment of market institutions. Private developments are also beginning to get underway. In 2006, a Dubai-based Afghan family opened a $25 million Coca Cola bottling plant in Afghanistan.

While the country's current account deficit is largely financed with the donor money, only a small portion – about 15% – is provided directly to the government budget. The rest is provided to non-budgetary expenditure and donor-designated projects through the United Nations system and non-governmental organizations. The government had a central budget of only $350 million in 2003 and an estimated $550 million in 2004. The country's foreign exchange reserves totals about $500 million. Revenue is mostly generated through customs, as income and corporate tax bases are negligible.

Inflation had been a major problem until 2002. However, the depreciation of the Afghani in 2002 after the introduction of the new notes (which replaced 1,000 old Afghani by 1 new Afghani) coupled with the relative stability compared to previous periods has helped prices to stabilize and even decrease between December 2002 and February 2003, reflecting the turnaround appreciation of the new Afghani currency. Since then, the index has indicated stability, with a moderate increase toward late 2003.

The Afghan government and international donors seem to remain committed to improving access to basic necessities, infrastructure development, education, housing and economic reform. The central government is also focusing on improved revenue collection and public sector expenditure discipline. The rebuilding of the financial sector seems to have been so far successful. Money can now be transferred in and out of the country via official banking channels. Since 2003, over sixteen new banks have opened in the country, including Afghanistan International Bank, Kabul Bank, Azizi Bank, Standard Chartered Bank, First Micro Finance Bank, and others. A new law on private investment provides three to seven-year tax holidays to eligible companies and a four-year exemption from exports tariffs and duties.

Some private investment projects, backed with national support, are also beginning to pick up steam in Afghanistan. An initial concept design called the City of Light Development, envisioned by Dr. Hisham N. Ashkouri, Principal of ARCADD, Inc. for the development and the implementation of a privately based investment enterprise has been proposed for multi-function commercial, historic and cultural development within the limits of the Old City of Kabul along the Southern side of the Kabul River and along Jade Meywand Avenue, revitalizing some of the most commercial and historic districts in the City of Kabul, which contains numerous historic mosques and shrines as well as viable commercial activities among war damaged buildings. Also incorporated in the design is a new complex for the Afghan National Museum.

According to the US Geological Survey and the Afghan Ministry of Mines and Industry, Afghanistan may be possessing up to 36 trillion cubic feet (1,000 km) of natural gas, 3.6 billion barrels (570,000,000 m) of petroleum and up to 1,325 million barrels (2.107E+8 m) of natural gas liquids. This could mark the turning point in Afghanistan's reconstruction efforts. Energy exports could generate the revenue that Afghan officials need to modernize the country's infrastructure and expand economic opportunities for the beleaguered and fractious population. Other reports show that the country has huge amounts of gold, copper, coal, iron ore and other minerals. The government of Afghanistan is in the process of extracting and exporting its copper reserves, which will be earning $1.2 billion US dollars in royalties and taxes every year for the next 30 years. It will also provide permanent labor to 3,000 of its citizens.

Chapter 9

India-South Asia Historical and Political Relations

INDIA-PAKISTAN RELATIONS

Relations between India and Pakistan are going through one of the worst phases ever since the signing of the Simla Agreement in 1972. Indo-Pakistan relations have seen more low points than high points in the last three decades. However, each time the two countries were at loggerheads on any problem area, the various irritants were absorbed and a decision made to take things forward in a positive manner. If we focus on the last few years, it becomes apparent that bilateral discussions between the two countries stopped after January 1994. This was not only due to tensions between the two countries but also because of compulsions of domestic politics. Even though political leaders on both sides, reiterated their willingness to resume talks over the next couple of years, the atmosphere between the two countries only became conducive for such an exercise in March 1997, when Pakistan-India foreign secretary level talks were held in New Delhi after a gap of three years. While the contrasting approaches of the two sides were evident even at this meeting, there was a ray of hope at the resumption of the negotiating process. The real breakthrough came in May 1997, when Indian Prime Minister I.K.Gujral met Pakistani Prime Minister Nawaz Sharif at Maldives. They took a number of decisions like agreeing to release prisoners from each other's countries, agreeing to establish a hotline between both of them, and most importantly, agreeing to establish working groups to address various outstanding issues upon which the two countries disagreed.

These decisions seemed to augur well for relations between the two countries. It was widely believed that Indo-Pakistan relations were definitely on the mend, especially when foreign secretary level talks were held in Islamabad in June 1997, where it was decided that working groups would be set up to address outstanding issues of concern to both sides. However, this high in relations was not an indication of future trends and it soon became apparent that the two countries could not agree on the mechanics of forming the working groups at appropriate levels in order to take the negotiation process forward. Over the next few months, Islamabad and New Delhi did display their commitment to the dialogue process through various acts of goodwill, like releasing fishermen in each other's custody, easing of travel restrictions etc. However, actions such as these slowly became overshadowed by tensions due to exchange of firing along the LOC in August-September 1997. Foreign secretary level talks were held in New Delhi in September 1997, Nawaz Sharif and I.K. Gujral met in New York in October 1997, Shamshad Ahmad and K.Raghunath met in October 1997 on the sidelines of the Commonwealth Conference in Edinburgh, and I.K. Gujral and Nawaz Sharif met on the sidelines of the trilateral summit at Bangladesh in January 1998. However, no breakthrough was made at any of these meetings due to divergent perspectives on how to approach the working groups issue. Also the political uncertainty in New Delhi due to the toppling of the United Front government placed further discussions on hold. Efforts to return to the negotiating table between the new Indian Prime Minister Vajpayee and Nawaz Sharif did not bear fruit as Pakistan refused to resume talks unless there was substantive negotiation on the Kashmir issue.

Indo-Pak interaction acquired a new context with the nuclear tests of May 1998 when relations hit a new low. Pakistan tried to project the South Asian region as a nuclear flashpoint in the aftermath of the tests and sensitised the Kashmir question by linking it with the nuclear tests. The extreme bitterness and tension between India and Pakistan in the period after the nuclear tests, did bring with it the realisation on both sides that things could not continue in the same manner indefinitely and that a meeting ground had to be found. Things started looking up again as Indian Prime Minister Vajpayee met Pakistani Prime Minister Nawaz Sharif at New York in September 1998. It was decided that foreign secretary level talks would be held between India and Pakistan, and a direct bus service between Lahore and Delhi was proposed. The talks at foreign secretary level held in October and November 1998 did not make concrete advances on major issues. Yet the fact that talks took place held promise for future interaction.

Indo-Pakistan relations hit an all time high with Indian Prime Minister Vajpayee's bus diplomacy, immediately after which there was tremendous goodwill between the two countries. Several issues were concretised in the shape of the various agreements signed at that time. It seemed that the only way to go was "forward." Pakistan's façade of friendliness was completely shattered when the Kargil war ensured the complete breakdown of the high level of trust and goodwill created at Lahore. India's faith was completely lost in any future overtures that may be made by Pakistan. India found its resilience being tested yet again as the Indian Airlines flight was hijacked and taken to Kandahar by Pakistani backed Harkatul Mujahideen. This contemptuous act was the final straw in pushing Indo-Pak relations to their lowest ebb since 1972.

At this moment, it becomes important to not only have an overview of the relationship between the two countries, but also where they may be headed in the forseeable future.

In this paper an attempt has been made to focus on critical events which have had a bearing on Indo-Pakistan relations in the last two years, and in that context, examine the future trends.

THE CONTEXT

No understanding of trends in Indo-Pakistan relations can be complete without understanding the Simla Agreement which is the benchmark of relations between India and Pakistan. It is the Simla Agreement which defines the basic parameters according to which Indo-Pakistan relations have been conducted in the past, and it will hopefully be defining the parameters in the future as well. It is therefore necessary to take a brief look at the provisions of the Simla Agreement to the extent that they have a bearing on critical events in the last two years.

As per the Simla Agreement, the Line of Control, indicating the position of the two armies on the day of cease-fire i.e.December 17, 1971 was delineated by designated military commanders of India and Pakistan. The Simla Agreement desired that, the sanctity of the Line of Control was to be maintained by both sides and both sides agreed that "neither side shall seek to alter it unilaterally, irrespective of mutual differences and legal interpretations." Also, there was a commitment by both countries to respect each other's "territorial integrity and sovereignty" as well as to solve problems between the two countries by peaceful means. The two countries also agreed, "That in accordance with the Charter of the United Nations they will refrain from the threat or use of force against the territorial integrity or political independence of each other." While talks on Kashmir have been held on and off and India had agreed to the concept of a "composite dialogue" the Pakistani army still preferred to violate the LOC and commit aggression against India, violating the very foundations of the Simla Agreement.

Another important aspect of the Simla Agreement to be borne in mind is that the unwritten part of the Simla understanding between then Indian Prime Minister Indira Gandhi and then Pakistani President Zulfiqar Ali Bhutto, was that the LOC would be converted into an international border in due course. This, in a sense meant that even though such an agreement i.e., converting the LOC into an international border, had not yet been arrived at, the LOC was to have the sanctity of an international border.

In another important clause of the Simla Agreement, both India and Pakistan, agreed to "settle their differences by peaceful means through bilateral negotiations or by any other peaceful means mutually agreed upon between them." Pakistan has been resorting to internationalisation of the Kashmir problem at NAM, OIC, ECO and UN meetings. It has been accusing Indian security forces of violating human rights in Jammu and Kashmir. Pakistan, in contravention of the Simla Agreement has urged various countries to mediate between India and Pakistan.

While the Simla Agreement can be regarded as having maintained peace between the two countries and in Jammu and Kashmir for a period of nearly two decades, that peace was broken by Pakistan's proxy war which was launched by "Operation Topac" in 1989.

Ever since 1947, Pakistan made several attempts to seize Kashmir from India, as Kashmir's accession to India remained unacceptable to Pakistan. Pakistan tried to achieve its objective in 1947 by engineering a tribal invasion of Kashmir, which resulted in the Kashmir war of 1947-48. Pakistan tried to achieve the same objective through 'Operation Gibraltar' in 1965 but failed to wrest Kashmir from India. In 1971, when decisive Indian military intervention in the civil war between the two wings of Pakistan helped in the creation of Bangladesh, Pakistan again hoped that Kashmir would be detached from India through the use of force. Pakistan failed to achieve its objective. The military option, one hoped was finally dumped. From July 1972 onwards after the Simla Agreement, the Kashmir situation upto 1989 was peaceful except for the dismissal of the government on the Indian side.

As Pakistan did not succeed in wresting Kashmir from India by the use of military force during the three wars, in the latter half of 1988, Pakistan launched a low intensity operation to create alienation of the Valley from the rest of India. Pakistan abetted full-scale subversion, terrorism, insurrection and insurgency in Jammu and Kashmir. India's belief is borne out by available reports which are based on the findings of various international agencies. The proxy war by Pakistan was stepped up in 1990. Between 1990 and 1998, 5,845 civilians were killed in Jammu and Kashmir while the figure for security forces killed is 1,401. Moreover, large quantities of weapons were found in Jammu and Kashmir from 1988 to 1997. These include 18,378 AK-47s and 2,015 LMGs. The Pakistanis were convinced that such a form of unconventional war would help reinforce and channelise the discontent in the Valley and over a period of time, lead it in the direction of secession from India.

The obvious involvement of Pakistan in the Kashmir Valley, in the form of a methodically planned proxy war, has been a part of Pakistan's scheme to bleed India of its resources without having to get involved in an open conventional military confrontation. In the early years, the most active militant group was the Jammu and Kashmir Liberation Front. However, by 1989-1990, JKLF began to be sidelined by Pakistan as JKLF's favoured "third option", implying independence for the Kashmiris was inconsistent with Pakistan's definition of "self-determination" for the Kashmiris which implied a willingness to join Pakistan. At this time, the Hizb-ul-Mujahideen, which was the military wing of the Jamaat-e-Islami came up as a rival to the JKLF.

Over the years it became obvious that Pakistan was suffering a setback, due to the fast declining Kashmiri support in the Valley to militancy, and things were fast approaching normalcy in Indian Kashmir by 1995-1996. In fact, militant activity gradually shifted to new areas such as Doda, Punch and Rajouri, as the Indian security forces came to have almost complete control of the security situation in the Kashmir Valley. After 1995-1996 the role and participation of foreign militants of Pakistani, Afghanistani and POK origin increased in the Kashmir Valley. In recent years, the Harkatul Mujahideen militants have been involved in fighting in Kashmir. The Harkatul Mujahideen is just a new front for the Harkatul Ansar which was declared a terrorist organisation by the US in 1994.The Harkatul militants operate in Afghanistan and Kashmir, and have strong links with the Jamiat-ul-Ulema-Islam (JUI), as well as the Sipahe Sahaba Pakistan (SSP) in Pakistan.The Lashkar-e-Taiba another dominant militant group which sends its recruits to battle in Kashmir, is the militant wing of the Markaz Dawa wal Irshad, an Ahle Hadith-Wahabi organisation based in Muridke, near Lahore. The Hizbul Mujahideen operates in Kashmir and has strong links with the Jamaat-e-Islami.

It was in this background of about ten years that the two countries exploded their nuclear devices which started a new phase in relations between India and Pakistan.

THE NEW PHASE: POST-POKHRAN, POST-CHAGAI

India-Pakistan relations acquired an entirely new dimension with India conducting its nuclear tests on May 11 and 13, 1998 and Pakistan responding with its own nuclear tests on May 28 and 30. In the midst of vigorous international criticism of both India and Pakistan and demands on both that further tests be abandoned and both countries sign the CTBT, Pakistan did not hesitate to indulge in mudslinging against India for having raised the level of the arms race in the region and for not doing enough to resolve the Kashmir question. India on the other hand, displayed considerable understanding of the motives of Pakistani tests and offered a No-First-Use Agreement. Pakistan while rejecting the No-First-Use proposal by India offered instead a Non-Aggression Pact which India described as irrelevant because of the existence of the Simla Agreement. Pakistan's continuous refusal to consider India's proposal pertaining to no-first-use of nuclear weapons confirms suspicions that Pakistan considers nuclear weapons as not merely means of deterrence but weapons of war which it would not hesitate to use if the need arose. Pakistan's Foreign Secretary, Shamshad Ahmad, during the Kargil crisis stated that, "We will not hesitate to use any weapon in our arsenal to defend our territorial integrity." This factor is amply brought out in General Musharraf's posturing since his takeover.

Pakistan in the post Chagai period actively tried to link the nuclear tests with the Kashmir question, by suggesting that Kashmir being an unresolved issue which has been the cause of frequent wars in the past is now pregnant with the possibilities of a nuclear conflict in the subcontinent. This has been projected by Pakistan as a good enough reason for third party mediation in the Kashmir dispute and Pakistan has been openly making a bid for intervention by the United States, United Kingdom, China, Japan and other countries. India continues to take the position that Pakistan and India between themselves are capable of resolving this dispute bilaterally, also because this is the approach agreed upon by the two countries in the Simla Agreement.

India has been emphasising the fact that both the countries have succeeded in avoiding a war since 1972 despite the fact that Pakistan has had a nuclear weapons capability since 1987 and India since about the same time or later in 1990. There has been a view among senior military leaders in Pakistan that once Pakistan acquired nuclear weapons, this would neutralise Indian conventional military superiority. It would then be possible for Pakistan to snatch Kashmir from India through irregular warfare under the nuclear umbrella without India being able to impose any punishment on Pakistan for the acts. "A Pakistani nuclear capability would paralyse not only the Indian nuclear decision, but also Indian conventional forces, and a bold Pakistani strike to liberate Kashmir might go unchallenged if Indian leadership was indecisive." Former Chief of Army Staff (COAS) Aslam Beg, stated in a seminar that in spite of the battle over Kashmir raging for the past many years, "we have no fear of war, which has been possible because of the nuclear deterrence which exists today in the subcontinent." The launching of the proxy war in Kashmir in 1988 following the acquisition of the bomb and subsequent escalation of the militancy in December 1989 proved this assessment. When both the countries went overtly nuclear in May 1998, Pakistan hoped that its nuclear weapons would deter India from responding to any act of aggression by it in Kashmir. However, despite Pakistan's nuclear weapons, India took on the Pakistani challenge in Kargil and gave a befitting reply. In a sense, the Pakistani bluff was called and India gave clear proof of its determination that it will not brook any violation of its borders, whether there are any nuclear weapons or not in the hands of the enemy.

There has been considerable ambivalence in Pakistan's attitude, on the question of signing the CTBT. In response to external pressures (from the United States, China etc.) that both Pakistan and India should sign the CTBT, India has taken the position that it would not be averse to signing the CTBT subject to negotiations on some of its provisions. Pakistan on the other hand stays with the position that it would sign the CTBT if India does so, even though in July 1998 there were reports that it would delink its attitude towards the CTBT from that of India. Besides, Pakistan's main focus has been on advocating to India a regional test ban treaty. India rejected this idea on the ground that a regional test treaty is not adequate to meet its concerns which are primarily centered around global non-proliferation and which also want to ensure a nuclear abstinence on the part of China.

DIALOGUE PROCESS IN THE POST NUCLEAR PHASE

It becomes important to take a look at the impact of the nuclear tests on the process of dialogue between the two countries. In a climate of newly created tension and suspicions in the wake of nuclear tests by India and Pakistan, both countries felt the need to talk to each other at sufficiently high levels to find a meeting ground and to instill mutual confidence. The dialogue process between India and Pakistan could not be resumed in June 1998 as the two could not agree on the modalities for talks. There was a difference in the interpretation of the June 23,1997 agreement which was signed between the foreign secretaries of India and Pakistan, in Islamabad. This difference occurred over whether the working groups were to address all issues between India and Pakistan, or whether peace and security and Kashmir would be discussed by the foreign secretaries themselves.

The earliest opportunity available after that was at the SAARC Summit in Colombo which was held in end July 1998. Both Prime Minister Vajpayee and Prime Minister Nawaz Sharif stated that they would like to utilise the opportunity to hold a meeting on the margins of the summit to have a candid exchange of views on the post nuclear security situation and if possible agree on a framework of official level talks in the near future. However, the talks held between July 29 and July 30 ended in a stalemate. Meanwhile, the intermittent firing exchanged between Indian and Pakistani troops across the line of control during July 1998 and beginning of August further vitiated the atmosphere between the two countries. Hopes for meaningful interaction between Vajpayee and Nawaz Sharif at Durban on the sidelines of the NAM summit came to naught as Nawaz Sharif stayed away due to domestic compulsions. However, Pakistani Foreign Minister Sartaj Aziz held fruitful talks with Indian Minister of State for External Affairs, Vasundhara Raje, on the sidelines of the summit, and on September 3, it was announced that India and Pakistan had agreed on the modalities for resumption of foreign secretary level talks.

The deadlock in Indo-Pakistan relations was finally broken when Vajpayee met Nawaz Sharif at New York on September 23, 1998 during the UN General Assembly session. It was agreed that the two foreign secretaries would meet in Islamabad from October 15, 1998 to focus on Kashmir and peace and security, including confidence building measures, which were the first two items on the eight point agenda finalised in June 1997, during the foreign secretary level talks in Islamabad. Following this there would be a series of meetings in November 1998 to discuss the six other items on the agenda. The New York meeting also resulted in a host of CBMs. For instance, telephone hotlines between the two prime ministers were to be restored, trade and people to people contact were to be enhanced, the railway link between Kokrapar (Pakistan) and Munnabao (Rajasthan) was to be restarted, a direct bus service between Delhi and Lahore was proposed, visa rules were to be relaxed, and efforts were to be made to stop cross border firing.

The October round of talks in Islamabad did not achieve any major breakthrough, except that the process of dialogue received an impetus. India and Pakistan reiterated their known positions on Kashmir, but agreed to meet again and carry forward the dialogue at the next round of talks between the two foreign secretaries. The Indian side proposed a no-first-use of nuclear weapons agreement, ensuring reliable communication links and greater transparency between the two sides through extending the hotline between the two Directors General of Military Operations to divisional and sector commanders, reviving the hotline between the two foreign secretaries, giving advance notice of missiles tests of over 200 km range and extending the existing agreement on non-attack on each other's nuclear installations to cover economic and population centres, renewal of the invitation to the Pakistani Army Chief to visit India and exchange of officers between the two National Defence Colleges. The Pakistani side spoke of a non-aggression pact, mutual nuclear and ballistic restraint while it remained cool to the no-first-use proposal. The November talks in New Delhi became bogged down due to the usual accusations and counter accusations hurled by India and Pakistan towards each other.

The New Delhi round of talks held in November 1998, included six issues which were Tulbul navigation project, Siachen, Sir Creek, trade, terrorism and drug trafficking and cultural exchanges. With regard to the Tulbul navigation project, the Pakistani Foreign Office spokesman, Tariq Altaf, on his return to Pakistan, accused India of trying to "justify" its "violation" of the 1960 Indus Waters Treaty and rejecting Pakistan's move to settle the dispute through arbitration. During the talks, Pakistan rejected India's proposal for a ceasefire in Siachen, wanting instead to address the question of troop disengagement in the area. Pakistan, during the eighth round of talks on Siachen in November, called for the "redeployment of troops." According to Pakistan, troop pullback should be considered on the basis of the 1989 "agreement". India proposed a package of confidence building measures which would lead to a "comprehensive ceasefire" in the Saltoro range region." India also wanted a "freeze" on the ground positions of troops from both sides to "immediately defuse tension and atmosphere of confrontation in the area." Once the ceasefire had been agreed to in principle specific "modalities" which would make it durable could be discussed in an "agreed framework." It was suggested by India that both sides could establish a "bilateral monitoring mechanism." New Delhi did not agree with the Pakistani proposal of placing an "international monitoring mechanism" to supervise the ceasefire in the Siachen area.

India rejected Pakistan's bid to internationalise the Sir Creek issue, reiterating that all differences between New Delhi and Islamabad after the Simla Accord have to be resolved bilaterally. Wanting to arrive at an early resolution of maritime boundaries, India proposed a new formulation which delinks the charting of maritime frontiers from fixing the land boundary in Sir Creek. India proposed that the two sides should delimit the maritime boundary from the "seaward" side. The two sides could proceed towards land from the extremity of the EEZ limit to a "mutually acceptable limit." Pakistan rejected this approach and insisted that the determination of the land boundary in the Sir Creek area and fixing its maritime borders were inseparable. India and Pakistan discussed a wide range of economic and commercial issues. However, Pakistan insisted that progress in these areas would be restricted till an environment of "peace and security" was created between the two countries. The talks on bilateral economic cooperation were held for the first time since 1989.

The Indian side stressed upon the need to be accorded MFN status by Pakistan, which is obligatory under the rules of the World Trade Organisation. It was suggested that till this came about, Pakistan could consider increasing the list of commodities importable from India. India rejected Pakistan's suggestion of involving the United Nations Military Observer Group (UNMOGIP) or any other international observer along the border in Jammu and Kashmir to verify India's allegations regarding its involvement in cross-border terrorism. India asserted that Pakistan was involved in "destabilising" it by sponsoring terrorism within India. Pakistan countered India's allegations by saying that New Delhi was behind the sectarian strife in its cities. It denied providing material support to Kashmiris and said it was unaware of any terrorist training camps on its soil. On the issue of promotion of friendly exchanges in various fields, India put forth 22 detailed suggestions in the field of art, culture, youth affairs, sports, information and media. The Pakistani delegation promised to consider the proposals during the next round of the dialogue process.

The November round of talks became bogged down due to the usual accusations and counter accusations hurled by India and Pakistan towards each other. In some situations they were not able to move beyond their often stated positions. Pakistan showed its tenacity in trying to bring in third party intervention into what should be bilaterally resolvable issues. However, the effort on both sides to discuss a wide range of issues was itself commendable. There was some amount of progress in the November talks which can be measured by a number of positive developments.

Both countries set up technical committees on the supply of surplus power to India. Certain proposals by India to avoid double taxation were under consideration. The Pakistani proposal for setting up a mechanism for quick information flows on trade and investment was agreed to by India. Pakistan agreed to ensure that visas were issued to Indians within six weeks and that there would be no delay. Both countries agreed to set up a mechanism for regular meetings and exchange of operational information between the Central Bureau of Investigation and Federal Investigating Agency of Pakistan, "for expeditious assistance to each other for combating various kinds of crimes including counterfeiting of currency and cyber crimes." Also there was progress on the proposal for introduction of a bus service between Delhi and Lahore. Both countries agreed to release fishermen in each others custody.

LAHORE BUS DIPLOMACY

The next landmark in Indo-Pak relations was the Indian Prime Minister Vajpayee's visit to Lahore on February 20-21, 1999 on the inaugural run of the Delhi-Lahore bus service. There was an increasing realisation on the part of both Nawaz Sharif and Vajpayee that improvement of relations between the two countries had to be a priority. There was a major effort on the part of both to kick-start such a process and give it direction. Nawaz Sharif being a businessman realised the untapped potential of economic cooperation between the two countries.

The momentum for Vajpayee's visit was generated when the two governments went ahead with the Cricket Test Series despite right wing opposition in both countries. Also, not only was the "hockey diplomacy" between the two countries successful, the delegation of Indian MPs to Islamabad for a parliamentarians' meet organised by the Jung group of newspapers did a fair share to promote confidence between the people of India and Pakistan. Before that, faced with a shortage of sugar, the Indian government cleared imports worth Rs.387 crore from Pakistan. Negotiations between the power ministry officials from both sides led to an agreement for export of 300 MW of power annually to India from Pakistan.

The Lahore Summit led to the signing of the Lahore Declaration by the Prime Ministers of Pakistan and India on February 21,1999, the issuing of the Joint Statement by India and Pakistan, and the Memorandum of Understanding signed by the Foreign Secretaries of India and Pakistan. Both the Lahore Declaration and the MOU referred to mutual adherence to the principles of the UN Charter, as also contained references to the implementation of the Simla Agreement. Both the Lahore Declaration and the MOU agreed to the resolution of all outstanding issues, including that of Jammu and Kashmir. While New Delhi conceded simultaneity in terms of bringing talks on Kashmir onto the agreed agenda, along with other areas of mutual benefit, Islamabad conceded bilateralism. The reference to the "composite and integrated" dialogue process implied that it would not be hostage to any single issue.

Prime Ministers Atal Bihari Vajpayee and Nawaz Sharif, at the end of their summit announced a number of steps including nuclear confidence building measures, for "prevention of conflict" between the two countries. They also agreed that their respective governments reaffirmed their condemnation of terrorism and their determination to combat this problem. The two governments agreed to give advance warning to the other when conducting ballistic missile flight tests. Seeking to minimise the potential of freak nuclear accidents, the two countries agreed to alert the other immediately in case of any "accidental, unauthorised or unexplained incident" on the other side. They also agreed to abide by their unilateral moratorium on nuclear testing. The level of bilateral talks was raised to the Foreign Minister level and the composite dialogue between the two countries' foreign secretaries was to continue. Travel restrictions were to be modified, making people to people contact easier. At a joint press conference the two Prime Ministers said all nuclear issues, including the Comprehensive Test Ban Treaty and a joint strategy for a nuclear weapons free world were discussed. Sharif told newsmen, that Pakistan would hold consultations with India on the issue of granting most favoured nation treatment to New Delhi under the WTO framework.

While hopes were high after the summit both sides had to come down to earth soon. Nawaz Sharif could not be seen to be softening his stance on Kashmir in undue haste. Nawaz Sharif, barely a week after the summit in Lahore, stated, "There would come a time when the talks would have to be superseded in case there is no concrete development in solving the Kashmir issue." Pakistani Foreign Secretary, Shamshad Ahmed, stated, soon after the meetings, that Pakistan is not to blame for the bloodshed in Kashmir. This was in reaction to comments by Vajpayee, who on returning to New Delhi, on February 21, from Pakistan, said that relations between the two neighbours could only improve when killings by Muslim separatists in Kashmir ended. The happenings in Indo-Pakistan relations after Vajpayee's visit give an idea of the existing contradictions present in relations between the two states. Nawaz Sharif brought up the

Kashmir issue when he made a statement that Mr Vajpayee had agreed with Islamabad's view's that the people of Kashmir should have the right of self-determination. This statement was refuted by the Indian PM's office. Again at Dhaka, where Nawaz Sharif had gone for the D-8 summit, he stated that "a solution to Kashmir is a must for achieving peace in a nuclearised South Asia."

The next important event was the meeting between Indian Foreign Minister Jaswant Singh and Pakistani Foreign Minister Sartaj Aziz at Sri Lanka in March 1999, on the sidelines of the SAARC summit. The two foreign ministers agreed on the urgency of taking concrete measures for implementation of the Lahore Declaration, the MOU and the Joint Statement issued during the Lahore summit. The ministers agreed to a six point programme which included setting up of a committee on humanitarian issues to deal with the release of civilian prisoners, relaxation of the visa regime, identifying areas of cooperation in information technology, Y2K and WTO related issues. A sign of progress between the two countries was exhibited when on March 22, 1999, India and Pakistan exchanged prisoners who had been held in their countries for years. India soon announced major steps to ease visa and travel restrictions for several categories of Pakistanis, in an effort to promote people to people contact, as part of the understanding reached at Lahore and Sri Lanka. Further, in the new environment, the Indian navy made a proposal for exchange of goodwill visits with Pakistan's navy, to the Defence Ministry.

The contradiction in Indo-Pak relations became apparent again when, Nawaz Sharif while visiting Rawalpindi stated that, " the Pakistan Army is fully geared and equipped to face any eventuality." His remarks came in the wake of Indian External Affairs Minister, Jaswant Singh's interview to the Pakistani newspaper, The News, in which he ruled out any third party mediation on the Kashmir issue and dismissed Pakistani demands to pull out the army from the Valley as a confidence building measure. On the positive side, a seventy five member business delegation visited FICCI in early April. Also, there was a two day biannual conference of the Pakistan Rangers and the BSF officers.

They along with representatives of the narcotics and border survey departments of both sides, discussed cross border firing, the question of deportation of Indian and Pakistani nationals from each other's country, and agreed to exchange information on the activities of cross border narcotics smugglers. On the business front a fifty eight member Indian business delegation arrived in Karachi on March 7, 1999. The Federation of Indian Export Organisation, (FIEO) President, Navratan Samdria headed the delegation, which met with the Karachi Chamber of Commerce and Industry. Also, the India Pakistan Chamber of Commerce and Industry (IPCCI) was inaugurated on April 10, 1999. The test firing of Agni II on April 11, 1999, by India was communicated to Pakistan a day before, as per the Lahore Declaration. Even while negative statements were emanating from both sides, the basic thrust of these negotiations and agreements was to continue the dialogue and discussions at various levels.

While the Lahore process was the culmination of Nawaz Sharif's efforts towards taking Indo-Pak relations to a new high, it is known that the army in Pakistan was even then uncomfortable with this event, and had in the meanwhile been planning the Kargil adventure. It was reported in July 1999, that "Highly placed sources confirm that the decision to take over the Kargil posts was taken in October last year and preparations started immediately after that." In an article, General Mirza Aslam Beg, the former Chief of Army Staff disclosed that the mujahideen's operation was approved after briefings given to the Prime Minister at GHQ and ISI Headquarters as early as January 1999.

Another Pakistani commentator, in an article published in July 1999, stated that, "It is generally accepted that Kargil was planned last year and its execution began in February just about the time of the Lahore Declaration." Afzal Mahmood, in his article asks the question, "Why did (Pakistan) fail to give the (Lahore) process a good try–which means reasonable time and opportunity to prove its worth as a conflict resolution mechanism? First we accept the concept of bilateralism, glorify the Lahore process and take pride in opening a new chapter in Indo-Pak relations and shortly thereafter embark upon a course of action–ill thought out and rash–that brings us to an eyeball-to-eyeball confrontation with India."

The feeling of euphoria created by the Lahore Summit was completely shattered due to Pakistan's aggression in Kargil which marked an unanticipated downturn in Indo-Pakistan relations.

KARGIL

It becomes meaningful to examine the implications of the Kargil war on Indo-Pak relations. Kargil has to be seen in the context of the proxy war conducted by Pakistan in the last decade. Kargil was in a sense the culmination of the proxy war. The purpose of the Pakistani operation in Kargil is clear. Pakistan wanted to enlarge the conflict in Kashmir, and to bring to the focus of the international community, the danger of another Indo-Pak war, one in which nuclear weapons could be used. By fabricating this kind of danger, Pakistan hoped for international intervention which would succeed in defreezing the Kashmir issue. Pakistan's manifold goals in its offensive in Kargil can be described in the following manner: Firstly, it hoped to cut off the Srinagar-Leh road so that movement of supplies to Leh garrison and Siachen would become impossible. Secondly, it wanted to block Zojila Pass and threaten Kashmir Valley from the north, which would be a new direction to make inroads. Thirdly, it wished to have control over the Himalayan range so that it would have unopposed access for insurgent-terrorists going into the Kashmir Valley and Doda district of Jammu. Fourthly, it wanted to outflank the Indian Army deployed on the LOC in north-western Kashmir and the Siachen glacier through Shyok Valley. Pakistan assumed that India would not retaliate because of the threat of nuclear weapons but India fought and recovered its territory.

The roots of the Kargil episode can be traced back to Pakistan's yearning to mastermind a people's revolt in Kashmir. The people of Kashmir, despite being under duress due to terrorist activities, went in for an elected government in 1996. Pakistan, realising the hopelessness of the situation, opted for military action in Kargil. Pakistan disregarded the peace initiative offered by India in Lahore. It deceived India by simultaneously planning the Kargil operations in great secrecy. The Kargil conflict was a great setback for the peace process and the confidence building measures initiated in the year preceding the Kargil intrusion. The Pakistani forces were found to be composed of Pakistani army units, mercenaries and Afghan war veterans. The Pakistani troops operating across the LOC were identified to be from the 2nd, 3rd, 4th, 5th and 6th Battalions of the Northern Light Infantry. These battalions were augmented by Afghan war veterans and Islamic militants trained by the Lashkar-e-Taiba and Harkatul-ul-Mujahideen, etc. A Pakistani commentator admits that, "

Carried out with the help of religious militants backed by the para-military Northern Light Infantry, the plan, it appears, was to take control of the vacant Indian positions on the Kargil heights, from where military supply routes to Ladakh and Siachen could be blocked." A survey of various articles written by a number of analysts in Pakistan leaves no room for doubt that Pakistan was directly involved in the Kargil war. M.P. Bhandara wrote, "We are told incessantly that the Kargil freedom fighters are genuine Kashmiri freedom fighters. However, is it reasonable to believe that freedom fighters can fight at 15,000 feet above sea level without Pakistani rations, clothing, logistics, ammunition and intelligence support?" Ikram Sehgal stated that, "...though belated we have begun to recognise the sacrifice and valour of the Northern Light Infantry (NLI)...No single unit of our army has inflicted such damage on men, morale and equipment of the Indians in their history as the NLI has done..." Pakistan's Foreign Minister Sartaj Aziz visited New Delhi for talks on June 12, 1999 but the Indian External Affairs Minister made it clear that no negotiations could take place until Pakistan withdrew all infiltrators beyond the LOC. Jaswant Singh also confronted Sartaj Aziz with a taped conversation between two Pakistani generals which confirmed the Pakistan army's involvement in the Kargil fighting.

India's stand was of course vindicated, by the immense international support it received. During the Clinton-Sharif meeting of July 4, 1999, Nawaz Sharif agreed, "that concrete steps will be taken for the restoration of the Line of Control in accordance with the Simla Agreement". Nawaz Sharif by agreeing with President Clinton on this point, admitted not only that Kargil constituted a violation of the Line of Control, but that it was in Pakistan's power to undo this violation. The implicit suggestion was that he would withdraw his forces from Indian Kashmir, to the position as it existed before Pakistan's aggression in Kargil sector across the LOC. In a sense, the Pakistani government accepted the sanctity of the LOC, thereby putting a stamp of approval on it as forming a de facto boundary between India and Pakistan.

According to reports, General Zinni, the chief of US central command, during his visit to Islamabad in the last week of June, 1999, received a firm commitment from the

Pakistani leadership that they were ready to take concrete measures to de-escalate the situation. Faced with a serious economic situation, Pakistan could not afford to antagonise the US which could have withheld the 100 million dollar tranche of the IMF loan due in July. The G8 countries condemned the infiltration and demanded withdrawal of the intruders from the Indian side of the LOC. China stated that both India and Pakistan must exercise restraint and should solve the Kargil problem peacefully through negotiations. Pakistan, of course, continued to deny that its troops were operating across the LOC, even though a meeting was held between the Indian Director General of Military Operations and Pakistan's Director of Military Operations in the second week of July 1999, to chalk out the time frame for Pakistani forces to withdraw from Indian territory. The restraint shown by India in not crossing the LOC, even in the face of severe provocation was widely appreciated by the international community.

All the Pakistani government had to show for itself at the end was an ignominious retreat, without any quid pro quo on Kashmir and a total loss of credibility, not only amongst foreign countries, but within the country itself. The editor's note in the well-known Pakistani newsmagazine, Newsline, stated that, "The Washington agreement confirmed Indian and western allegations that the mujahideen action was backed by Pakistan. Far from internationalising the Kashmir issue, the government's mishandling of the Kargil crisis has diplomatically isolated the country." Another article stated, "That the Kargil adventure was ill-conceived, if not downright foolish, was becoming clear, albeit slowly, even to the congenitally blind. That consequently Pakistan, swallowing its pride and not a few of its brave and gallant words, would sooner or later have to mount a retreat was also becoming clear, especially after Niaz Naik's secret visit to New Delhi which was a desperate bid to get India to agree to some kind of a deal which would provide a face saving way out for us." Air Marshal (retd.) Asghar Khan, admitted that, "In 52 years of its existence, Pakistan has fought four wars with India without a clear objective."

India felt terribly cheated by Pakistan because India had invested a lot of hope and faith in the Lahore process. That something as disastrous as an act of blatant aggression across the LOC in the Kargil sector could have been done by Pakistan so soon after the Lahore Declaration came as a fatal blow to India's hope about improving relations with Pakistan. Disappointment turned into disgust when widespread stories emanated from Pakistan suggesting that the army had specifically sought and obtained Prime Minister Nawaz Sharif's clearance with regard to intrusions in Kargil soon after Nawaz had signed the Lahore Declaration.

HIJACKING INCIDENT

The hijacking of the Indian Airlines plane became a way of subjecting the Indian population to terror tactics in continuation of the Kargil conflict. The Harkatul Mujahideen, the organisation which was responsible for the hijacking, and which was demanding the release of Masood Azhar, its leader, in exchange for Indian hostages, is one of the major militant organisations which is funded by Pakistan for anti-India activities. Taking into account the fact that the Pakistan government and the army have had major links with the Taliban in Afghanistan, and the fact that the Harkatul Mujahideen was involved, shows the backing of the Pakistani government without doubt, even though India did not make public accusations in this regard right in the beginning. The complicity of the Pakistan army and the Taliban was further proved when there was no help in the release of the hostages and India had to concede the demands of the hijackers. While the hijacking incident soured relations between India and Pakistan still further, Pakistan seemed to derive quiet satisfaction from the fact that India was forced to release the hardcore militants who had been under detention in India because of their acts of terrorism.

Pakistan in the initial phase of the hijacking, took the stance that it had extended all possible help in the safe landing of the hijacked airliner at Lahore airport and the Indian High Commissioner G.Parthasarthy was provided a special helicopter at his request for monitoring the ground situation. However, the Indian Airline IC 814 plane took off from Lahore by the time he reached there. Pakistan said that it had allowed the hijacked plane to land at Lahore airport purely on humanitarian grounds, as the captain had warned that the aircraft had almost run short of fuel. In a preliminary reaction to the hijacking incident, Foreign Office spokesman Tariq Altaf stated that under the international laws, Pakistan had no other option but to allow the plane to land. General Pervez Musharraf on December 28, emphasised that Pakistan had "absolutely no involvement" in the hijacking of the Indian airliner. In an interview with CNN, he said, "We do not really know the facts and the people as to who have hijacked (the plane)." He further stated that, Pakistan had cooperated with India totally "and we would like to co-operate with them totally." Foreign Minister Abdul Sattar, in a vain attempt to put Indian fears at rest, went a step further and stated that the hijackers of the Indian Airlines plane would face court proceedings under the international law if they came to Pakistan. He said that, "I can tell you with full responsibility that the hijackers have not entered Pakistan."

All promises made by various officials of Pakistan became undone within the next few days itself. It was reported that the ISPR spokesman Director-General Brigadier Rashid Qureshi, in a statement on January 3, 2000 made it clear that the jailed Islamic terrorist, Maulana Masood Azhar freed by India, in a deal with the hijackers of the Indian Airlines plane could return home if his Pakistani identity was established. However, the same news report went on to admit that Azhar had studied at Karachi's Jamia Uloom Islamia Binori Town, Pakistan's second largest Islamic seminary. It went on to say that Azhar had links with the Harkatul Mujahideen, formerly known as Harkatul Ansar, one of the guerrilla groups fighting in Kashmir and that he was arrested in Kashmir in 1994. According to another report, Mushtaq Ahmad Zargar, founder chief of Al-Umar Mujahideen, one of the several groups fighting in Kashmir, arrived in the POK capital late on January 4, four days after he was released by the Indian government along with two other Kashmiri freedom fighters in exchange for 155 passengers of hijacked Indian Airlines plane on December 31. The report further stated that other mujahideen released were Maulana Masood Azhar and Ahmad Umar Saeed Sheikh, stated to be affiliated with the Harkatul Mujahideen.

Pakistan's support for militant groups engaged in anti-India activities could no longer be hidden, as Maulana Masood Azhar, was allowed to address a Jumatul Wida congregation at Jama Masjid Al-Sadiq in Bahawalpur, where he declared jehad against India, and urged the men in the congregation to sign up to fight against Indian rule in Kashmir. "There is no way open for us other than to fight jehad against India for Kashmir's liberation," he said. Pakistan's real intentions became clear as the adviser to Pakistan's Chief Executive, Javed Jabbar said that Pakistan would not arrest Maulana Masood Azhar. In an interview with New York Times he said, " India had violated all norms of law and justice" by imprisoning Maulana Azhar for six years without finding him guilty of a crime in a court of law. "They have not been able to convict and sentence him. What are we supposed to do? He has not committed any crime on Pakistani territory." Realising the futility of relying on Pakistan to take remedial measures, India officially asked Pakistan on January 15,2000 to extradite the five hijackers of the Indian Airlines Airbus to stand trial for terrorism in India. Pakistan's High Commissioner in Delhi, Ashraf Jehangir Qazi was called to the Foreign Office and the demand was handed over to him by Indian Foreign Secretary Lalit Mansingh.

The hijacking further vitiated the atmosphere between India and Pakistan. This event which showcases Pakistan's aggressive tendencies towards India, coincides with the belligerent posture adopted by Pakistan towards India under the rule of General Musharraf. It becomes important to focus on Pakistan's attitude in the last few months which is a critical factor in the future of Indo-Pakistan relations.

COUP AND AFTERMATH

Nuclear Threats

The vitriolic statements emanating from across the border over the past few months do not bode well for Indo-Pakistan relations. It becomes obvious from such statements that Pakistan considers nuclear weapons as not merely means of deterrence but weapons of war which it would not hesitate to use. General Musharraf talked of the possibility of use of nuclear power if Pakistan's security is threatened. In an interview with CNN, the General, when asked under what conditions would Pakistan use nuclear weapons, said that, "If the security of Pakistan is threatened...that is my short answer." Asked about the guiding principle of Pakistan's policy on the use of nuclear weapons he said, "We have not worked that principle out, but we have worked surely that Pakistan's security will never be compromised."

CTBT

The policy of the Government under General Musharraf is to initiate a national debate on the CTBT issue in order to develop a national consensus before taking any decision.

In an interview with CNN, General Musharraf said that the CTBT would not be signed by Pakistan unless "we develop consensus." He further stated that, "we will see what Pakistan needs and what is in the interest of Pakistan, and only then we will decide our response on the question of the CTBT." Those who favour the CTBT argue that it will not only re-endorse Islamabad's repeated stance of non-proliferation but also lead to the easing of some sanctions imposed on Pakistan after the nuclear tests.

A joint meeting of the Federal Cabinet and the National Security Council , held on December 22, 1999, which was presided over by General Pervez Musharraf, deliberated on the CTBT issue in great detail. Foreign Minister Abdul Sattar noted that if India does not sign, Pakistan would retain the right to conduct tests. "If India conducts another nuclear explosion before the CTBT enters into force, nothing in or outside the treaty can foreclose Pakistan's right to do the same, whether it has signed the treaty or not." Mr Sattar briefed the meeting on the CTBT issue and on the outcome of the Foreign Policy Advisory Board meeting held in the Foreign Office on December 20, in which the same was deliberated upon by analysts and scholars. Mr Sattar also met a number of religious leaders who are vocal in their opposition to the CTBT. Besides taking note of the non-discriminatory nature of the treaty, it was highlighted in the meeting that the treaty only prohibits nuclear tests and it does not "affect possession or enhancement of nuclear capability or production of fissile material."

KASHMIR

Pakistan has been stressing the centrality of the Kashmir issue in its dealings with India. General Pervez Musharraf, while presiding over the 30th session of the Azad Kashmir Council in Islamabad, on December 18, stated that "The recent developments in South Asia have shown that Kashmir is a nuclear flashpoint in the region and the international community has also recognised it." The Chief Executive warned that lasting peace and stability in South Asia is not possible without the solution of the core issue of Kashmir. "Pakistan is willing to solve the Kashmir issue through peaceful means if India shows sincerity for the resolution of the issue," he said. General Musharraf, during his visit to Muzaffarabad on December 27, 1999 stated that "Pakistan is Kashmir and Kashmir is Pakistan." "I want to reiterate that there is a change in the policy towards India. Earlier we used to say that we will negotiate all issues, including Kashmir. But now we will discuss the Kashmir issue first," said the Chief Executive. General Musharraf said he had told the Foreign Office that Kashmir is the core issue and "there is no negotiations, no talks" with India unless the Kashmir issue is discussed." Chief Executive General Pervez Musharraf also sounded a warning that Pakistan will teach India a lesson if it tries to cross the Line of Control (LOC). "Indians are not refraining from crossing the LOC out of any love for Pakistan. They would have done it long before if they could. We will teach them a lesson on the LOC or anywhere else," he said in a wide ranging interview to Nation and Nawai Waqt on January 23, 2000.

NO TRADE

The hardline stance taken by Pakistan is even reflected in the statement of Federal Commerce Minister Abdul Razzak in which he ruled out the possibility of trade with India in the existing regional and political situation, saying that a solution to the Kashmir issue tops the agenda of the present government. "Although both sides could have competitive advantage of trade between two major economies of the subcontinent yet I feel that any such move will be futile before solving the core issue of Kashmir," he said while speaking to newsmen at the Export Promotion Bureau (EPB) office in Lahore.

PROSPECTS FOR INDO-PAKISTAN RELATIONS

Prospects for peace between India and Pakistan are bleak in the forseeable future. In the short term there does not seem to be any hope for improvement in Indo-Pak relations. Any forward movement with Pakistan becomes difficult because of the ideological conflict between India and Pakistan. Pakistan's ideology is contradictory to that of India, and Pakistan's domestic opinion is steeped in that ideology. Also, the Kashmir issue never fails to be a rallying point for governments in power in Pakistan when they want to divert attention from their internal problems. The Indian government has taken a clear stand that there can be no talks till Pakistan stops instigating terrorism across the border into India. This does not seem likely to happen. On the contrary, Pakistan has intensified its jehad against India, and more specifically Kashmir. General Musharraf's statement that hostility would continue even after resolution of the Kashmir issue, seems to imply that the aim of the Pakistani establishment, is not just to get Kashmir, but the destabilisation of the Indian state.

The militant organisations funded by Pakistan like the Lashkar-e-Taiba, Harkat ul Mujahideen and Hizbul Mujahideen are highly motivated. In fact, the chief of the Lashkar-e-Taiba, Mohammad Saeed while addressing a congregation near Muridke in November 1999, declared that the "mujahideen" would continue their jehad in Kashmir till they attained victory and they would never accept any formula for the division of the state. There is a belief in Pakistan that they have been successful in tying up the Indian army in Kashmir. Abdul Sattar who was a hardliner against India, is back in the power structure and the term "Indian hegemonism" is back in vogue. Chief of the Naval Staff Admiral Aziz Mirza stated that, "We have the compulsion to safeguard our maritime interest against an enemy having hegemonic designs," while addressing officers of the Navy at Karachi on October 19, 1999. After Kargil, Pakistan slipped into internal convulsions and is yet to settle down from the consequences of the coup. As regards the question of plebiscite, self-determination on the basis of ethnicity is a dangerous doctrine to apply to Jammu and Kashmir. Pakistan itself will be dismembered if this doctrine is applied across the board, considering the ethnic problems in Baluchistan, Sindh and the North West Frontier Province of Pakistan. Therefore, for Pakistan to be able to agree to a resolution of the Kashmir question will not be easy.

Prime Minister Vajpayee in the beginning said that there was no possibility of talks with the present regime in Pakistan though he was hopeful that the spirit of the Lahore summit between him and then Prime Minister Nawaz Sharif would be revived someday. He stated that the main obstacle to the resumption of talks is the breach of trust between the two countries following the Kargil conflict. Prime Minister Vajpayee has also made it clear that India is not interested in talking with Pakistan till it stops cross border terrorism into India. More recently, the Indian Prime Minister has taken a harder stand and said that unless POK is returned to India we will not talk to Pakistan. Such statements make it obvious that prospects for an early resumption of talks with Pakistan are not very bright.

Even contact on the economic front is going to be difficult in the near future, looking at the positions adopted by both countries. While Pakistan has ruled out the possibility of trade with India, SAARC meetings scheduled to be held in November 1999, at the political level were cancelled because India objected to dealing with the military government in Pakistan. India also rejected a proposal for Pakistani and Indian commerce ministers to meet before the WTO ministerial conference in Seattle in November 1999 end, because it did not want to provide legitimacy to the military government in Pakistan.

While it is going to be a challenge to keep channels of communication open with Pakistan, we cannot dismiss the fact that Musharraf is in power in Pakistan. Though the Commonwealth has suspended Pakistan, it continues to have a seat in the UN and other international fora, most of which seem to treat the new management in Pakistan as just one more change in government. He will continue to have a working relationship with powers which are important to Pakistan- i.e., the US, China, Islamic countries, Western Europe and Japan. Also, the people of Pakistan themselves have welcomed the Musharraf government. There is general support for Musharraf's military regime, excluding a certain section of Nawaz Sharif's Pakistan Muslim League.

It is likely that General Musharraf will remain in power for the forseeable future, as no definite time frame has been given for restoration of democracy in Pakistan. General Musharraf is likely to continue to have a confrontational attitude towards India, and will probably encourage subversion against India. In his speech after assuming office as Chief Executive, General Pervez Musharraf, on October 17, 1999 stated emphatically that, "We shall continue our unflinching moral, political and diplomatic support to our Kashmiri brethren in their struggle to achieve their right of self-determination." He feels that Indo-Pakistan dialogue would be useful only if India discusses the Kashmir issue with Pakistan in a meaningful manner. He has also clarified that his pulling back troops from the Indo-Pakistan frontier will not extend to the LOC in Jammu and Kashmir.

We need to keep in mind that Musharraf has an antagonistic mindset when he deals with India. When dealing with him we need to keep in mind certain features about his background and tread carefully, based on how these factors would influence his thinking and course of action. Mercenaries recruited from different Muslim countries for fighting

Soviet troops in Afghanistan were trained under the charge of General Musharraf in the concerned Directorate of the ISI. In 1987, he became the brigade commander of the Special Services Group which was given the job of pushing back Indian forces from Siachen. He was also in charge of all military and subversive operations against Jammu and Kashmir due to his role as force commander Northern Areas. General Musharraf also played a major role in the fourth major military conflict between India and Pakistan over Kargil.

In the long term, India and Pakistan will have to restart the process of communication with a series of confidence building measures. A broad definition of the concept of CBMs suggests that India and Pakistan have engaged in confidence building exercises since their independence in 1947 although the term came into use in more recent times. One of the most enduring pillars of Indo-Pak CBMs has been the Indus Waters Treaty of September 19, 1960. Adherence to the provisions of this treaty has survived inspite of the ups and downs in the relations between the two countries. There has been support for Track II diplomacy between the two countries in an effort to explore the broad range of dialogue and networking processes available. Track II dialogues "provide a second line of communication between conflicting states and seek to bridge the gap between official government positions by serving as testing grounds for new policy initiatives." Select academics, journalists, businessmen, and retired military officials and civilian officials from India and Pakistan have been holding meetings under what is referred to as the Neemrana process. The Centre for Policy Research in New Delhi has initiated a regional dialogue between the intellectuals of the two states. People-to-people dialogues are promoted by organisations like the India-Pakistan People's Forum. Such dialogues assume even more importance in the present situation where both the governments may have difficulty acting directly and where the foundations need to be prepared for state-to-state diplomacy at a later point.

Both India and Pakistan view each other as adversaries and such images are transmitted not only through the medium of education but also through the print and electronic media. Media needs to focus less on political and social tensions and conflicts in each country and more on positive developments and changes across the border. India and Pakistan share common problems in the energy sector. Both countries suffer from severe shortages of oil and electric power for use in industrial, agricultural and household sectors. Substantial opportunities are there for India and Pakistan to collaborate in jointly exploring, developing, and sharing their energy resources.

In the area of trade and economic relations, India and Pakistan in the post independence period had dismal relations. The two countries have not been able to exploit the existing potential for trade in a wide range of products which could be purchased at a lower cost and with a shorter delivery time. This point has been reiterated in a recent report on India-Pakistan trade, wherein it was stated that though Pakistan fears dumping of various items by India into Pakistan if the Most Favoured Nation

(MFN) status is granted to India, the consumers in Pakistan would be the beneficiaries due to the availability of low priced products. The report also stated that "consumers will benefit from Pakistan-India liberalisation on goods imported from India which are categorised as; goods that are being manufactured in India and whose ex-factory cost is similar to that of any other third country's exports; here the Pakistani consumer will benefit due to low transportation cost."

While these are all examples of meaningful relations in the Indo-Pak context and what would be the ideal level of interaction between the two countries, only time will tell how much of this is achievable. Any forward movement will depend on maintaining a continuity in dialogue which is important for long term success in normalising relations between India and Pakistan.

INDIA AND SRI LANKA RELATIONS

Bilateral relations between the Democratic Socialist Republic of Sri Lanka and the Republic of India have been generally friendly, but were controversially affected by the on-going Sri Lankan civil war and by the failure of Indian intervention during the Sri Lankan civil war. India is the only neighbour of Sri Lanka, separated by the Palk Strait; both nations occupy a strategic position in South Asia and have sought to build a common security umbrella in the Indian Ocean.

India and Sri Lanka established diplomatic relations when the latter gained its independence in 1948. Both nations proceeded to establish extensive cultural, commercial, strategic and defence ties to establish a common sphere of influence in the region, adopting non-alignment to control Western and Soviet influence. The close relationship between the then-Indian Prime Minister Indira Gandhi and then-Sri Lankan Prime Minister Sirimavo Bandaranaike led to the development of strong bilateral relations. In 1971, Indian armed forces helped squash a Communist rebellion against the Sri Lankan government.

INDIAN INTERVENTION IN THE SRI LANKAN CIVIL WAR

In the 1980s, private entities and elements in the state government of Tamil Nadu were believed to be encouraging the funding and training for the Liberation Tigers of Tamil Eelam, a separatist insurgent force. In 1987, faced with growing anger amongst its own Tamils, and a flood of refugees, India intervened directly in the conflict for the first time after the Sri Lankan government attempted to regain control of the northern Jaffna region by means of an economic blockade and military assaults, India supplied food and medicine by air and sea. After subsequent negotiations, India and Sri Lanka entered into an agreement. The peace accord assigned a certain degree of regional autonomy in the Tamil areas with Eelam People's Revolutionary Liberation Front (EPRLF) controlling the regional council and called for the Tamil militant groups to lay down their arms. Further India was to send a peacekeeping force, named the IPKF to Sri Lanka to enforce the disarmament and to watch over the regional council.

Even though the accord was signed between the governments of Sri Lanka and India, with the Tamil Tigers and other Tamil militant groups not having a role in the signing of the accord, most Tamil militant groups accepted this agreement, the LTTE rejected the accord because they opposed the candidate, who belonged to another militant group named Eelam Peoples Revolutionary Liberation Front (EPRLF), for chief administrative officer of the merged Northern and Eastern provinces. Instead the LTTE named three other candidates for the position. The candidates proposed by the LTTE were rejected by India. The LTTE subsequently refused to hand over their weapons to the IPKF.

The result was that the LTTE now found itself engaged in military conflict with the Indian Army, and launched their first attack on an Indian army rations truck on October 8, killing five Indian para-commandos who were on board by strapping burning tires around their necks. The government of India then decided that the IPKF should disarm the LTTE by force, and the Indian Army launched number of assaults on the LTTE, including a month-long campaign dubbed *Operation Pawan* to win control of the Jaffna peninsula from the LTTE. When the IPKF engaged the LTTE, the then president of Sri Lanka, Ranasinghe Premadasa, began supporting LTTE and funded LTTE with arms. During the warfare with the ltte IPKF was also alleged for human rights violation against the civilians. Notably, IPKF was alleged to have perpetrated Jaffna teaching hospital massacre which was the killing of over 70 civilians including patients, doctors and nurses. The ruthlessness of this campaign, and the Indian army's subsequent anti-LTTE operations made it extremely unpopular amongst many Tamils in Sri Lanka. The conflict between the LTTE and the Indian Army left over 1,000 Indian soldiers dead.

The Indo-Sri Lankan Accord, which had been unpopular amongst Sri Lankans for giving India a major influence, now became a source of nationalist anger and resentment as the IPKF was drawn fully into the conflict. Sri Lankans protested the presence of the IPKF, and the newly-elected Sri Lankan president Ranasinghe Premadasa demanded its withdrawal, which was completed by March 1990.. on May 21, 1992, Rajiv Gandhi was assassinated and the LTTE was alleged to be the perpetrator. As a result India declared the LTTE to be a terrorist outfit in 1992. Bilateral relations improved in the 1990s and India supported the peace process but has resisted calls to get involved again. India has also been wary of and criticised the extensive military involvement of Pakistan in the conflict, accusing the latter of supplying lethal weaponry and encouraging Sri Lanka to pursue military action rather than peaceful negotiations to end the civil war.

INDIA-BANGLADESH RELATIONS

Indo-Bangladeshi relations are the ties between India and Bangladesh. Both states are part of the Indian subcontinent and have had a long common cultural, economic and political history. The people of the two countries are indistinguishable to most outsiders. The cultures of the two countries are similar; in particular India's West Bengal state and Bangladesh are both Bengali speaking.

At the outset India's relations with Bangladesh could not have been stronger because of India's unalloyed support for independence and opposition against Pakistan at the time. During the civil war, many refugees fled to India. India also intervened militarily and may have helped bring international attention to the issue through Indira Gandhi's visit to Washington, D.C. Afterwards India furnished relief and reconstruction aid. India extended recognition to Bangladesh prior to the end of the war in 1971 (the second country to do so after Bhutan) and subsequently lobbied others to follow suit.

During the Partition of India after independence in 1947, the Bengal region was divided into two: East Bengal (present-day Bangladesh) and West Bengal. East Bengal was made a part of the Islamic Republic of Pakistan due to the fact that both regions had an overwhelmingly large Muslim population, more than 85%. In 1955, the government of Pakistan changed its name from East Bengal to East Pakistan.

There were some confrontations between the two regions though. Firstly, in 1948, Jinnah declared that only Urdu would the official language of the entire nation, though more than 95% of the East Bengali population spoke Bengali. And when protests broke out in Bangladesh on February 21, 1952, Pakistani police fired on the protesters, killing hundreds. Secondly, East Bengal/East Pakistan was allotted only a small amount of revenue for its development out of the Pakistani national budget. Therefore, a separatist movement started to grow in the isolated province. When the main separatist party the Awami League, headed by Bangabandhu Shaikh Mujibur Rehman, won 167 of 169 seats up for grabs in the 1970 elections and got the right to form the government, the Pakistan president under Yahya Khan refused to recognize the election results and arrested Bangabandhu Shaikh Mujibur Rehman. This led to widespread protests in East Pakistan and in 1971, the Liberation War in the self-declared (By the Great Leader Bangabandhu Shaikh Mujibur Rahman on 26th.March 1971) state of Bangladesh started.

India under Indira Gandhi fully supported the cause of the Bangladeshis and its troops and equipment were used to fight the Pakistani forces. It also gave full support to the main Bangladeshi guerilla force, the Mukti Bahini. Finally, on 26 March, 1971, Bangladesh emerged as an independent state. Since then, there have been several issues of agreement as well as of dispute.

AREAS OF AGREEMENT

1. India played a central role in the independence of Bangladesh. 19,000 Indian soldiers died for the cause of an independent Bangladesh. India sheltered over 10 million refugees who were fleeing the atrocities of the occupying West Pakistan Army. India and its ally Bhutan were the first countries to recognize Bangladesh as an independent nation. Bangladeshis have some awareness of their obligation and gratitude towards India.
2. Bangladesh was faced with an economic crisis after independence. Its population was the 8th largest in the world at the time. India gave large amounts of aid to

Bangladesh. In recent years India provides co-operation and assistance during annual natural calamities. India is a supplier of staple foods such as rice and live animals which helps keep their prices affordable for the masses of Bangladesh.

3. Bangabandhu Shaikh Mujibur Rehman's first foreign visit as PM and the Founding Father of this newly born nation was to India and it was then decided Indo-Bangladesh relations would be guided by principles of democracy, socialism, nonalignment and opposition to colonialism and racism. Indira Gandhi too visited Bangladesh in 1972 and assured that India would never interfere in the internal affairs of the country.
4. In 1972, both the countries signed a 'Treaty of Friendship and Peace'. An Indo-Bangladesh Trade Pact was also signed.
5. The main opposition Awami League is generally considered to be friendly towards India.
6. Moderate Bangladeshis and those who are strong Bengali nationalists, including some artists, activits and students have a friendly disposition towards India. Bangladeshi Hindus and Buddhists have an attachment towards India which gave birth of their religions.

AREAS OF CONTENTION

1. A major bone of contention has been the construction of the Farakkha Barrage by India to increase water supply in the river Hoogly. Bangladesh insists that it does not receive a fair share of the Ganga waters, and on the other hand, it gets flooded in the monsoons when India releases excess.
2. There have also been disputes regarding the transfer of Teen Bigha Corridor to Bangladesh. There is some area of Bangladesh in West Bengal which is surrounded by India. This area is very near to Bangladesh and thus India leased three bigha land to Bangladesh to connect this land with mainland Bangladesh. There is dispute regarding this. However, this Corridor leased indefinitely to Bangladesh on 26 June, 1992.
3. A broad spectrum of India's public opinion is concerned about the perceived demographic challenge from Bangladesh. The right-wing Hindu parties such as the Bharatiya Janata Party have made a major election issue out of the reported migraton of Muslim Bangladeshis to India. While no reliable figures exist, the Bangladeshi Muslim population in India is generally estimated at between 15 million and 20 million and growing. Border states of India such as West Bengal and Assam are now over 25% Muslim, significantly higher than 1950 levels. With Bangladesh's population continuing to grow rapidly and doomsday global warming scenarios predicting half of Bangladesh will be under water by 2100, there are fears in India that tens of millions of Bangladeshis will migrate into India dramatically altering the balance of religious populations.

4. Indian border force's killing of people while crossing the border has been the topic of disputes. In August 2008, Indian Border Security Force officials admitted that they killed 59 people who were trying to cross the border between India and Bangladesh, in a 6 month long period.

There are also small pieces of land along the border region that Bangladesh is diplomatically trying to reclaim. Padua, part of Sylhet Division before 1971, has been under Indian control since the war in 1971. This small strip of land was re-occupied by the BDR in 2001, but later given back to India after Bangladesh government decided to solve the problem through diplomatic negotiations. South Talpatty island (called New Moor by India), administered under Satkhira district of Bangladesh, is still under Indian military occupation, though the Bangladesh government sent satellite images to the Indian government proving the island to be within Bangladeshi territory.

In recent years India has increasingly complained that Bangladesh does not secure its border properly. It fears an increasing flow of economically depressed Bangladeshis and it accuses Bangladesh of harboring Indian separatist groups like ULFA and alleged terrorist groups. The Bangladesh government has consistently denied these accusations. India estimates that over 20 million Bangladeshis are living illegally in India. One Bangladeshi official responded that "there is not a single Bangladeshi migrant in India". Since 2002, India has been constructing an India - Bangladesh Fence along much of the 2500 mile border.

But recent relations are not without bright spots. In May 2007 they announced that for the first time since the 1965 Indo-Pak War, rail service between Kolkata and Dhaka will be restored, a lapse of 42 years. Moreover in October 2007 some cooperation was announced on the border issues mentioned above. These signs of cooperation coincide for the moment at least with a change in Bangladeshi leadership that is expected to last until the end of 2008.

INDIA-NEPAL RELATIONS

Nepal, with an area of 1,47,181 sq. km., is a land-locked country, which is situated between the two Asian super powers, India in the east, west and south and China in the north. The country is situated in the central Himalayan region between the Indo-Gangetic plain and Tibetan plateau. Topographically the country is characterised by three ecological zones - the Tarai, the hills and the mountain. Its cultural landscape is diverse: consisting of more than 60 ethnic groups, speaking as many as 60 dialects, more than six creeds co-exist in this narrow buffer state. Hinduism and Buddhism overlap and mingle with tribal tradition.

India and Nepal share many common social, political, economic predicament besides a long 1,750 km border which has made communication easier and possible. This, in turn, has informed each other's history, culture, tradition, political, economic and strategic relations. The border between India and Nepal is open and the flow of people is allowed without any restriction. In sharp contrast, it is not very easy for a common man in one

SAARC country to travel to another without undergoing the cumbersome formalities of documentation. The only exception to such requirements is for travel between India and Nepal for nationals of either country, in accordance with the Treaty of Peace and Friendship of 1950. The advantage of an open border is felt by people living on both sides. At the same time the use of the open border is also a cause of concern when misused by criminals, smugglers and other subversive elements against Indian security interest. Article VII of the Treaty of Peace and Friendship grants citizens of both the countries to move, reside and own property and participate in trade and commerce in each other's territory. Both Nepal and India have accused each other of misusing this provision and exploiting the open border.

Relations between India and Nepal are close yet fraught with difficulties stemming from geography, economics, the problems inherent in big power-small power relations, and common ethnic and linguistic identities that overlap the two countries' borders. New Delhi and Kathmandu initiated their intertwined relationship with the 1950 Indo-Nepal Treaty of Peace and Friendshipý and accompanying letters that defined security relations between the two countries, and an agreement governing both bilateral trade and trade transiting Indian soil. The 1950 treaty and letters stated that "neither government shall tolerate any threat to the security of the other by a foreign aggressor" and obligated both sides "to inform each other of any serious friction or misunderstanding with any neighboring state likely to cause any breach in the friendly relations subsisting between the two governments." These accords cemented a "special relationship" between India and Nepal that granted Nepal preferential economic treatment and provided Nepalese in India the same economic and educational opportunities as Indian citizens.

1950- 1970

In the 1950s, Nepal welcomed close relations with India, but as the number of Nepalese living and working in India increased and the involvement of India in Nepal's economy deepened in the 1960s and after, so too did Nepalese discomfort with the special relationship. Tensions came to a head in the mid-1970s, when Nepal pressed for substantial amendments in its favor in the trade and transit treaty and openly criticized India's 1975 annexation of Sikkim as an Indian state. In 1975 King Birendra Bir Bikram Shah Dev proposed that Nepal be recognized internationally as a zone of peace; he received support from China and Pakistan. In New Delhi's view, if the king's proposal did not contradict the 1950 treaty and was merely an extension of nonalignment, it was unnecessary; if it was a repudiation of the special relationship, it represented a possible threat to India's security and could not be endorsed. In 1984 Nepal repeated the proposal, but there was no reaction from India. Nepal continually promoted the proposal in international forums, with Chinese support; by 1990 it had won the support of 112 countries.

1970- 1980

In 1978 India agreed to separate trade and transit treaties, satisfying a long-term Nepalese demand. In 1988, when the two treaties were up for renewal, Nepal's refusal to accommodate India's wishes on the transit treaty caused India to call for a single trade and transit treaty. Thereafter, Nepal took a hard-line position that led to a serious crisis in India-Nepal relations. After two extensions, the two treaties expired on March 23, 1989, resulting in a virtual Indian economic blockade of Nepal that lasted until late April 1990. Although economic issues were a major factor in the two countries' confrontation, Indian dissatisfaction with Nepal's 1988 acquisition of Chinese weaponry played an important role. New Delhi perceived the arms purchase as an indication of Kathmandu's intent to build a military relationship with Beijing, in violation of the 1950 treaty and letters exchanged in 1959 and 1965, which included Nepal in India's security zone and precluded arms purchases without India's approval. India linked security with economic relations and insisted on reviewing India-Nepal relations as a whole. Nepal had to back down after worsening economic conditions led to a change in Nepal's political system, in which the king was forced to institute a parliamentary democracy. The new government sought quick restoration of amicable relations with India.

1990s

The special security relationship between New Delhi and Kathmandu was reestablished during the June 1990 New Delhi meeting of Nepal's prime minister Krishna Prasad Bhattarai and Indian prime minister V.P. Singh. During the December 1991 visit to India by Nepalese prime minister Girija Prasad Koirala, the two countries signed new, separate trade and transit treaties and other economic agreements designed to accord Nepal additional economic benefits.

Indian-Nepali relations appeared to be undergoing still more reassessment when Nepal's prime minister Man Mohan Adhikary visited New Delhi in April 1995 and insisted on a major review of the 1950 peace and friendship treaty. In the face of benign statements by his Indian hosts relating to the treaty, Adhikary sought greater economic independence for his landlocked nation while simultaneously striving to improve ties with China.

INDIA-BHUTAN RELATIONS

In a region characterised till not so long ago by the familiar trend of mistrust and suspicion primarily directed towards India, there has been one exception—the Indo-Bhutan relations. Both countries have been able to strike the right note and sustain their friendship. The treaty of 1949 between India and Bhutan is said to be central to the two countries' relations. However, this cordiality has not come about by freezing relations as they were in 1949. If anything, Bhutan of today has changed in all respects, including its economy and international stature since 1949. The relationship has, thus, been one of dynamism and change.

What are the factors which link the two countries? Are Indo-Bhutan relations really free of tensions? Is the "perpetual peace and friendship" phrase used in the 1949 treaty to describe Indo-Bhutan relations really true for all time to come? Is it a relationship where India as the big power, puts pressure on Bhutan? Does the relationship serve only Indian interests or is it equally beneficial to Bhutan? What are the challenges that the relationship will face in the future in the context of the changing domestic, regional and international environment? Which factors, in spite of the challenges, will keep the two countries together in the face of the choices that they have? This essay attempts to answer these questions to understand the unique relationship that the two countries share.

THE TREATY OF 1949 AND ITS WORKING

The Treaty of 1949 provides the basic framework for conducting relations between the two countries. This section examines the Treaty in terms of its provisions and working.

PROVISIONS OF THE TREATY

The Treaty of 1949 has ten Articles. The very first Article tries to perpetuate Indo-Bhutanese friendship for all time to come by stating, "There shall be perpetual peace and friendship between the Government of India and the Government of Bhutan." However, the most important provision in the treaty is its Article 2, according to which, "The Government of India undertakes to exercise no interference in the internal administration of Bhutan. On its part, the Government of Bhutan agrees to be guided by the advice of the Government of India in regard to its external relations."

The point that has provoked some amount of critcism or controversy pertains to the second part of this Article since it tries to qualify Bhutan's external relations. Other Articles of the treaty deal with the annual payment of Rs. 5 lakh by the Government of India to the Government of Bhutan in continuance of the compensation which was paid by British India. Independent India however, has increased the amount to Rs 5 lakh from Rs 1 lakh earmarked earlier. To mark the friendship between the two countries, India agreed to return to the Government of Bhutan about 32 square miles of territory in the area known as Devangiri and the same was spelt out in the treaty. The treaty also establishes a free trade regime between India and Bhutan. Further, the citizens of both countries residing in each other's territory will be treated on par with own citizens.

The treaty also has provisions for extradition of Indian citizens in Bhutan and of Bhutanese citizens in India when required, and the procedure for the same has been spelt out. The mechanism for settling disputes arising out of differences in interpretation or application of the treaty is also mentioned. It is also stated that the treaty shall continue in perpetuity unless terminated or modified by mutual consent. Another important article is Article 6 of the treaty which refers to Bhutan importing arms and ammunition, machinery, warlike material or stores for the strength and welfare of its country. The clause is qualified by stating that such imports shall be undertaken with the assistance and approval of the Government of India from or through India into Bhutan. The Government of Bhutan, according to the treaty, agrees that there shall be no export of such arms and ammunition, etc. across the frontier of Bhutan either by the Government of Bhutan or by private individuals.

HISTORICAL PERSPECTIVE TO THE PROVISIONS OF THE TREATY

Reading and interpreting the treaty of 1949 between India and Bhutan in isolation to the relations and treaties which existed between Bhutan and British India will give an incomplete picture. In this context, the relevant provisions of two important treaties concluded between British India and Bhutan—the Treaty of Sinchula, 1865, and the Treaty of Punakha, 1910 are looked into.

Article 1 of the Treaty of Sinchula reads, "There shall henceforth be perpetual peace and friendship between the British Government and the Government of Bhutoon." Article 4 goes into details of the reasons for the compensation paid by the British Government to Bhutan. It is in continuance of this Article that India, as spelt out in Article 3 of the 1949 Treaty, till date makes an annual payment of Rs. 5 lakh. Article 6 of the 1865 treaty spells out details on surrender of Bhutanese subjects accused of any crime and taking refuge in British dominions. The various crimes are then mentioned. It is the same for British subjects accused of crimes and taking refuge in Bhutan. Article 9 of the treaty refers to provisions of free trade and commerce between the two governments. Article 8 is very important and it refers to the British government's arbitration in matters of differences which Bhutan might have with the Rajahs of Sikkim and Cooch Behar, and that the British government's decision would be abided by. Article 2 of the 1949 Treaty should be read in the background of Article 8 of the Treaty of 1865.

The Treaty of Punakha of 1910 has only two Articles. One deals with increasing the amount of the annual allowance paid to the Government of Bhutan by the British Government. The other deals with revising Article 8 of the 1865 Treaty. The revised Article reads, "The British Government undertakes to exercise no interference in the internal administration of Bhutan. On its part, the Bhutanese Government agrees to be guided by the advice of the British Government in regard to its external relations. In the event of disputes with, or causes of complaint against, the Maharajas of Sikkim and Cooch Behar, such matters will be referred for arbitration to the British government which will settle them in such manner as justice may require and insist upon the observance of its decisions by the Maharaja named." Article 2 of the 1949 Treaty should be read along with this provision of the 1910 Treaty. It throws light on the continuity of arrangements as existed between Bhutan and British India. It is thus important to note that all the provisions of the 1949 Treaty were not being negotiated for the first time.

At this stage, it is important to mention the circumstances under which the British sought to include Article 8 in the treaty of 1910 by which Bhutan agreed to be guided by the advice of the British government in regard to its external relations. The 1865 Treaty enabled the British government to negotiate the disputes of Bhutan with regard to Sikkim and Cooch Behar. However, with the Chinese forward policy towards Tibet and other Himalayan states, the British became concerned. The Chinese representative in Lhasa sought to liken the union of China, Tibet, Nepal, Bhutan and Sikkim to the blending of the five principal colours which would produce an excellent political model like a beautiful design. The British realised that it was essential to prevent China from encroaching on Bhutan if they wanted peace on the frontier.

The British were keen on maintaining Nepal, Bhutan and Sikkim as buffer states. Bhutan however, remained vulnerable to Chinese influence in as much as China claimed suzerainty over Bhutan. It was in such circumstances that it was proposed that in view of the great importance of the British interests at stake, it was necessary for the Government of India to persuade Bhutan to place its foreign relations under British control. For, going by the clauses of the treaty of 1865, the British could not prevent Bhutan from receiving Chinese agents. In return, it was suggested that the British should abstain from interfering in the internal administration of the country. The Treaty of 1910, thus, was an attempt by the British to checkmate China's ambition to either impose its authority on, or interfere in, Bhutan. Through this, Bhutan was maintained as a buffer state. The clause was thus prompted by the circumstances and postures advocated by China.

It is appropriate to note here that the British did not want to control Bhutan. One of the very first British missions to Bhutan advised against it in terms of the inhospitable terrain under which it would be difficult to hold the conquest. The British aim was primarily to find a route to trade with Tibet through Bhutan. Later, there was some controversy over the possession of the fertile and economically valuable duars of Assam and Bengal which was settled through the 1865 Treaty. Most important, even after the 1910 Treaty was signed, (following which Bhutan's external relations were placed under British India) the British Indian government maintained that there was no departure in its policy of non interference in the states bordering the frontiers of India and the obligations would not go beyond what was stated in the letter of the treaty.

WORKING OF THE TREATY OF 1949

The major provision which has to be examined is Article 2 of the treaty of 1949. When the controversy regarding Sino-Bhutan boundary arose, Nehru wrote to the Chinese, "Under the treaty relationship with Bhutan, the government of India are the only competent authority to take matters concerning Bhutan's external relations, and, infact, we have taken up with your government a number of matters on behalf of the Bhutan government." However since 1984, the government of India has not objected to Bhutan and China having direct bilateral negotiations regarding the border dispute on the northern side of the border. More than ten rounds have been held so far and their differences seem to have narrowed down. One of the factors enabling this was the move towards normalisation of relations between India and China.

Similarly, as Bhutan expands its relations with the outside world, it is interesting to note that the strict implementation of the 1949 Treaty does not take place. In 1971, Bhutan was the second country after India to recognise Bangladesh. The decision was in the interest of the Indian government. However, the important point is not the issue of recognition of Bangladesh by Bhutan but the fact that Bhutan took an independent foreign policy decision—which it could do again on any other issue.

One of the bilateral foreign policy problems presently facing Bhutan is its negotiations with the Nepalese government on the refugee issue. Bhutan's interactions with Nepal surely come under the realm of Bhutan's external relations. India's position, in spite of all that is written in the 1949 Treaty, has been that it will not interfere in the bilateral matter of the two countries.

It is not being indicated that India should go in for strict implementation of the Article 2 of the 1949 Treaty and thereby restrict the space Bhutan has to independently conduct its foreign relations. In the present circumstances neither is this feasible nor desirable. The changing regional and international environment and Bhutan's own desire to assert its independent sovereign status have resulted in not only a flexible interpretation of Article 2 of the Treaty of 1949 but also, in India assisting Bhutan to have an independent identity in the international forum. In fact over time, the treaty has been amended in spirit though not in letter. An important question, which follows, is whether this duality will stand against India's security interests. It will not be unwise to conclude that if a situation emerges in the near future whereby China makes moves with reference to Bhutan which are inimical to India's security, the position of India will not be that it is a bilateral issue between China and Bhutan. Would it be possible for India to then selectively apply Article 2 of the treaty with reference to a particular country or to a particular situation?

It is important to emphasise that the aim of Article 2 of the Treaty is not to bind Bhutan but to ensure India's security interests. At present India and Bhutan share a cordial relationship and the Bhutanese presently do not have any complaints over the provisions of the treaty. However, there have been occasions when there was controversy over its provisions, especially regarding the interpretation of the word 'guidance'. Thus, in a situation where Article 2 is not strictly implemented, it is being suggested that India should seek an assurance that issues concerning security of India will be respected by Bhutan. This will ensure that future changes in either the regional or international environment will not adversely affect India's security interests.

BHUTAN'S INTERESTS

For Bhutan, its relations with India have been beneficial on three specific fronts: the domestic, international and economic.

DOMESTIC AFFAIRS: NON INTERFERENCE BY INDIA

Even in the period of British India, there was no interference by it in the internal political struggle and civil war that was taking place in Bhutan. The monarchy as we know it today was established only in 1907. British India, by recognising it, gave additional legitimacy to the monarchy and contributed to stability. Later, in 1910, the Treaty of

Punakha, by incorporating the clause that there would be no interference in the internal affairs of Bhutan, ensured the primacy of the new regime. This continued after the withdrawal of the British from India. With a democratic India as its neighbour, it was feared that monarchy in Bhutan could face problems. However, this was not to be. Presently, even as Bhutan is witnessing a movement for change and democracy from certain quarters, India has continued to adhere to the clause of non interference in its internal affairs. It seems to believe that whatever changes take place, should be from within and not from outside.

In the past Bhutan had fears that following Sikkim's incorporation into India, it too would be affected. But India assured it that its territorial integrity would be respected. Bhutan also feared that like in Sikkim where the minorities were overtaken by the Nepali population, in Bhutan too the Nepalese would overtake the locals. Bhutan's problems at present revolve around the concept of "Greater Nepal." To this is linked the problem of refugees from southern Bhutan who are of Nepalese origin. There are a large number of Nepalese in India and the movement for Gorkhaland and the consequent autonomous council have made Bhutan concerned about its people of Nepalese origin and their intentions. India's official position of non-interference has ensured Bhutan a free hand to deal with its centrifugal tendencies in a manner as it feels is right.

INTERNATIONAL RELATIONS: COMING OUT OF ISOLATION

Bhutan has followed a policy of isolation from the beginning—it did not trust the British too. Following the threat from China, it was the aim of the British that Bhutan should come out of its isolation. It was slightly successful but the consequent World War II and later the British withdrawal in 1947 sent it into isolation again. To begin with, Bhutan was suspicious of independent India's intentions after the Chinese occupation of Tibet in 1950. However, following the Chinese action of 1958-59 it slowly realised that it needed to come out of isolation for its own survival. During this time when its territorial integrity was in danger, India ensured it security though there was no provision in the treaty of 1949 for the defence of Bhutan by India. Since then, Bhutan has tried to assert its sovereign existence at every forum.

India has made it clear that Bhutan's quest for an international role does not contradict with the provision of Article 2 of the 1949 Treaty. Its international journey began with becoming a member of the Colombo Plan in 1963. Bhutan's membership of the Colombo Plan was sponsored by India. Bhutan said that its admission to the Colombo Plan had considerable bearing on its sovereign and modern status and registered its first entry into a regional group of sovereign states. As a result of its membership, Bhutan received technical assistance from Japan, Australia, India, Canada , New Zealand and England. Later, in 1969, Bhutan's entry into the Universal Postal Union was sponsored by India. In 1971, Bhutan was admitted to the United Nations with the full assistance of India. In 1972 Bhutan became a member of Economic and Social Council for Asia and Pacific (ESCAP). The process thus continued and in 1985, Bhutan became a member of the

South Asian Association for Regional Cooperation (SAARC), providing it another forum to expand and conduct its foreign relations and this time more effectively since SAARC is a grouping of only seven countries.

After Bhutan became a member of the UN, it was opined by many that India had renounced its right to look after Bhutan's foreign relations which it had been enjoined to do under the Treaty of 1949. Surely India would have been aware that an independent international role and strict implementation of the 1949 Treaty would be contradictory. However, an independent Bhutan recognised by the international community ensured that its territorial integrity could not be easily violated and that Bhutan remained a buffer state. Further, in the changing regional and international context had India not taken into consideration the aspirations of Bhutan, some other country would have. Such a move would have been detrimental to India's long term interests. Presently, Bhutan has diplomatic and non diplomatic relations with many countries.

LOOKING AHEAD: POSSIBLE FUTURE SCENARIOS

In the light of the above analysis, some of the possible future scenarios need to be considered so that appropriate policies may be formulated by India.

In a first scenario, it is possible that the present cordial relations continue and eventhough Bhutan expands its interactions with the external world it remains equally sensitive to India's security concerns and to that extent, follows a restrictive policy. However, in the light of recent developments (the challenge arising out of camps set up in Bhutan by insurgents from north eastern parts of India as has already been discussed in the previous section), it is possible that non state actors, either from India or Bhutan or any third country, can establish camps in Bhutan given the geophysical terrain. With the access they have to modern arms and equipment, it is probable that they could undertake activities which might pose a grave danger to India's security.

In another possibility, it could be that with the spread of education and economic development, democratic changes take place in Bhutan whereby people become assertive of their rights and of the place of their country in the international arena. Though they presently acknowledge India's contribution to Bhutan in the economic and other spheres, it is possible that they might develop close friendly relations with China or other countries which may have implications for India's security.

Irrespective of which of the above scenario emerges in the future, there are two measures, which are necessary for India to take. First, it should deepen the close economic cooperation already taking place and linking the development of north east India and Bhutan. Secondly, it should arrive at an understanding with Bhutan that while Bhutan conducts its foreign relations, it should not impinge on India's security interests. This would remove the ambiguity, which presently marks the relations between the two countries with reference to Article 2 of the Treaty of 1949 and equip India to face the future challenges.

CONCLUSION

Proximity links both India and Bhutan as it does two neighbouring countries anywhere in the world. However the geo-strategic position of Bhutan has transformed the relation into one of vital importance to both the countries. There is no doubt that the security imperatives are at the core of the close relationship, not only for India but Bhutan too in terms of its security interests and territorial integrity.

India being the big power, had two choices: it could either have thrust its security concerns on Bhutan by force or it could have worked towards making Bhutan understand and appreciate India's security concerns and how its own (i.e. Bhutan's) security too is linked with India. India chose the second route. It, however, did not allow the relationship to be limited to a single point security agenda. It first expanded it to include the economic agenda and secondly, helped Bhutan find its rightful place in the international comity of nations. The relationship has its share of tensions revolving around Article 2 of the Treaty of 1949. It has been interpreted by some, including those in Bhutan, as limiting the sovereignty of Bhutan.

With time this criticism has, however, come down seeing the manner in which the treaty has been implemented. India wholeheartedly assisted Bhutan in getting membership of the UNO. Bhutan itself follows a restrictive policy as regards its relations with China and has come to appreciate the immense benefits of close ties with India. The above analysis has shown that Indo-Bhutan relations have not been static and have served the mutual interests of both countries. One can thus make the following observations:

The clauses in the 1949 Treaty do not reflect India's desire to dominate Bhutan but the concerns of India relate to the security not only of itself but of Bhutan too. India has not stuck to the strict implementation of the clauses and in practice there is a lot of flexibility.

Bhutan has gained immensely from the special relations it has had with India in all aspects of its development as a nation. It has grown in international stature and its sovereignty is fully recognised. Economically, India has helped in its all round development. Further, India has adhered to the clause that it will not interfere in the internal affairs of Bhutan.

While security concerns dominate the relationship, it is important to note that presently the security concerns facing the two countries emanate from activities within their borders and not due to the activities of a third country. The insurgents in India taking refuge in Bhutan and their possible linkages with the dissidents in Bhutan is a matter of great concern to both the countries.

The incorporation of a free trade regime in the Treaty of 1949 was not prompted by the Indian desire to ensure compliance of its security concerns by Bhutan. In fact, it was a continuation of the arrangements that existed during the British period

It is necessary to project the immense benefits which Bhutan has had from its association with India. Generally, India has to bear the brunt of being termed hegemonic and accused of reducing the freedom of, and interfering in, the other country's activities. It is necessary that the record be set straight. Historical circumstances guided the development of Indo-Bhutan relationship along unique lines. Geographically juxtaposed into a close proximity, the two countries have sought and obtained what they have needed from one another.

INDIA-MALDIVES RELATIONS

Bilateral relations between the Republic of India and the Republic of Maldives have been friendly and close in strategic, economic and military cooperation. India contributed to maintaining security on the island nation and has forged an alliance with respect to its strategic interests in the Indian Ocean.

The Maldives is located south of India's Lakshadweep Islands in the Indian Ocean and approximately 700 kilometres from Sri Lanka. Both nations established diplomatic relations after the independence of Maldives from British rule in 1966. Since then, India and Maldives have developed close strategic, military, economic and cultural relations. India has supported Maldives' policy of keeping regional issues and struggles away from itself, and the latter has seen friendship with India as a source of aid as well as a counter-balance to Sri Lanka, which is in proximity to the island nation and its largest trading partner.

DEVELOPMENT OF BILATERAL RELATIONS

India and Maldives officially and amicably decided their maritime boundary in 1976, although a minor diplomatic incident occurred in 1982 when the brother of the President of Maldives Maumoon Abdul Gayoom declared that the neighbouring Minicoy Island that belonged to India were a part of Maldives; Maldivies quickly and officially denied that it was laying claim to the island. India and Maldives signed a comprehensive trade agreement in 1981. Both nations are founding members of the South Asian Association for Regional Cooperation (SAARC), the South Asian Economic Union and signatories to the South Asia Free Trade Agreement. Indian and Maldivian leaders have maintained high-level contacts and consultations on regional issues.

OPERATION CACTUS

In November 1988 speedboats carrying 80 armed militants of the People's Liberation Organisation of Tamil Eelam landed in Maldives and along with allies who had infiltrated the country, began taking over the government. The plot, planned in Sri Lanka by the Tamil nationalist group was believed to be an attempt by a Maldivian businessman and politician opposed to the regime of the President of Maldives Maumoon Abdul Gayoom to gain control while the PLOTE sought a safe haven and base for its activities.

The militants took control of the airport in Male, the national capital, but failed to capture the President of Maldives Maumoon Abdul Gayoom, who had fled and asked for military aid from India on November 3. The then-Indian Prime Minister Rajiv Gandhi ordered 1,600 troops to aid the Maldivian government. In a military operation codenamed "Operation Cactus," Indian forces arrived within 12 hours of the request for aid being made, squashed the coup attempt and achieved full control of the country within hours. 19 PLOTE militants were killed and 1 Indian soldier wounded.

India's intervention was endorsed by other nations such as the United States, Soviet Union, Great Britain and its neighbours Nepal and Bangladesh. Its speedy and decisive victory and the restoration of the Maldivian government brought both nations even closer in friendship and cooperation. In wake of internal security crises and tensions with Sri Lanka, Maldives saw its relationship with India as a source of future security.

INDIA-AFGHANISTAN RELATIONS

Bilateral relations between the Republic of India and the Islamic Republic of Afghanistan have been traditionally strong and friendly. While India was the only South Asian country to recognise the Soviet-backed Democratic Republic of Afghanistan in the 1980s, its relations were diminished during the Afghan civil wars and the rule of the Islamist Taliban in the 1990s. India aided the overthrow of the Taliban and became the largest regional provider of humanitarian and reconstruction aid.

Afghanistan bordered British India's Northwest Frontier Province (NWFP), which was home to a significant Pashtun population that participated extensively in the Indian independence movement. Although the NWFP became a part of Pakistan in 1947, India and Afghanistan maintained significant cultural and economic links. Films and music of India are widely popular in Afghanistan and Afghan products such as carpets, nuts and fruit are exported to India. For most of their independent history, both nations have enjoyed traditionally friendly relations and have cooperated over respective conflicts with Pakistan. Since April 2007, Afghanistan is eighth member of SAARC after India endorsed Afghan full membership.

CIVIL WARS AND TALIBAN

India was the only South Asian nation to recognise the Soviet-backed Democratic Republic of Afghanistan and the Soviet Union's military presence in Afghanistan, and provided humanitarian aid to the country. Following the withdrawal of the Soviet armed forces from Afghanistan in 1989, India and the international community supported the coalition government that took control, but relations and contacts ended with the outbreak of another civil war, which brought to power the Taliban, an Islamist militia supported by Pakistan.

The Taliban regime was recognised only by Saudi Arabia, Pakistan and the United Arab Emirates (UAE). The rise of Islamism in Afghanistan and the proliferation of Afghan mujahideen in the militancy in Indian-administered Kashmir turned the Taliban and Afghanistan into a security threat for India. The destruction of the Bamiyan Buddha monuments by the Taliban led to outrage and angry protests by India, the birthplace of Buddhism. In 1999, the Indian Airlines Flight 814 hijacked by Muslim militants landed and stayed in Kandahar in Afghanistan and the Taliban and Pakistan's Inter-Services Intelligence (ISI) were suspected of supporting them. India became one of the key supporters of the anti-Taliban Northern Alliance.

POST-2001

During the U.S.-led invasion of Afghanistan in 2001, India offered intelligence and other forms of support for the Coalition forces. After the overthrow of the Taliban, India established diplomatic relations with the newly-established democratic government, provided aid and participated in the reconstruction efforts. India has provided USD 650-750 million in humanitarian and economic aid, making it the largest regional provider of aid for Afghanistan. The Indian Army's Border Roads Organisation is constructing a major road in the remote Afghan province of Nimroz. India's support and collaboration extends to rebuilding of air links, power plants and investing in health and education sectors as well as helping to train Afghan civil servants, diplomats and police. India also seeks the development of supply lines of electricity, oil and natural gas.

Both nations also developed strategic and military cooperation against Islamic militants. Owing to the killing of an Indian national by Taliban militants in November 2005, India deployed 200 soldiers of the Indo-Tibetan Border Police (ITBP) to provide security for Indian nationals and the projects supported by India. Afghanistan strengthened its ties with India in wake of persisting tensions and problems with Pakistan, which was suspected of continuing to shelter and support the Taliban. India pursues a policy of close cooperation in order to bolster its standing as a regional power and contain its rival Pakistan, which it maintains is supporting Islamic militants in Kashmir and other parts of India.

On July 7, 2008 the Indian embassy in Kabul was attacked by a suicide car bomb - the deadliest attack in Kabul since the fall of the Taliban in 2001. The bombing killed 58 people and wounded 141. Senior Indian Army officer Brigadier Ravi Datt Mehta was entering the embassy gates in a car along with V. Venkateswara Rao when the attack took place. Both were killed in the blast.

During the 15th SAARC summit in Colombo. India pledged another USD $450 million along with $750 million already pledged for ongoing and forthcoming projects.

POLITICAL INTERACTION AND EXCHANGE OF HIGH LEVEL VISITS

Since November 2001, regular exchange of high level visits provided impetus to bilateral relations. So far, President Karzai visited India five times (i) as Chairman of the Afghan Interim Administration to India, February 26-27, 2002 and was accompanied by 13 Ministers. During the visit, Indian PM announced a grant of US $ 10 million for immediate use by the Afghan government, (ii) as President of Transitional Islamic State of Afghanistan accompanied by three Ministers to India (March 5-8, 2003). During this visit, Himachal Pradesh University conferred honorary doctorate on President Karzai. PM announced a financial commitment of US$'70 million for the construction of Zaranj-Delaram road in Afghanistan. Both sides also signed a Preferential Trade Agreement and (iii) President Hamid Karzai paid a working visit to India accompanied by 8 Ministers from February 23-25, 2005. Two MOUs on cooperation in the fields of Civil Aviation and Media & Information were signed and (iv) State visit from April 9-13, 2006. During the State visit, both countries signed three MOUs. (v) President Karzai led a large delegation to attend Second RECC on Afghanistan on November 15-19, 2006 in New Delhi. President Karzai has been invited to attend the SAARC Summit in April 2007. Such visits reflect the intensity and inherent strength in the bilateral relationship.

PRESIDENT KARZAI'S VISIT TO INDIA, APRIL 9-13, 2006

President Hamid Karzai's fourth visit to India was a State visit from April 9-13, 2006. His delegation included six abinet Ministers (Commerce Minister Arsala, Foreign Minister Dr. Abdullah, Defence Minister Wardak, Finance Minister Dr. Ahady, Rural Development Minister Atmar & Information, Culture & Tourism Minister Dr. Raheen), other senior officials, Deputy Ministers, nine members of the Parliament and six senior religious leaders and 35-member business delegation. President Karzai had meetings with President, Vice President and substantive discussions with PM. Minister for Panchayati Raj Mr. Mani Shankar Aiyar and Chairperson of UPA Sonia Gandhi also called on President Karzai. Three agreements - MOU on Cooperation in the Field of Standardization, MoU on Cooperation in the Field of Rural Development and MOU on Cooperation in the Field of Education- were signed during the visit.

The Joint Statement issued at the end of the visit identified the following main points:

a) An additional pledge of US $ 50 million of assistance taking India's total assistance package to US $ 650 million.

b) Agreement in principle to conclude an EXIM Bank Line of Credit of US $ 50 million to encourage bilateral business-to-business relations.

c) Establishment of a Joint Committee at the level of Commerce Ministers, to review the bilateral commercial relations in the context of the bilateral Presidential Trade Agreement signed in March 2003.

Afghan Foreign Minister Dr. Rangin Dafdar Spanta made his maiden official visit to India on June 29 - July 1, 2006 after assuming charge. During the visit, he had meetings with Prime Minister, Minister of State for External Affairs, Shri Anand Sharma, Foreign Secretary and other senior government officials. He also had interaction with academicians, journalists, writers and diplomats etc. at a discussion on "Afghanistan: Foreign Policy, Regional Relations and Future Perspectives" at the Indian Council of World Affairs.

Some of the other significant visit to India from Afghan side in the last 2 years including the visit of Dr. Abdullah Abdullah, the then Afghan Foreign Minister, on July 3-4, 2005. Health Minister Dr. Sayed Mohammad Amin Fatemi visited India with a delegation and attended Conference on Telemedicines in Bangalore, March 17-19, 2005.

Afghan Minister of Rural Rehabilitation and Development, Mohammad Hanif Atmar, visited India from October 1-6, 2005. Afghan Minister of State for Parliamentary Affairs, Farooq Wardak, accompanied by three senior officials, visited India from May 16-14, 2006.

From the Indian side, the then EAM Jaswant Singh visited Kabul on December 22, 2001 to attend inauguration of Interim Authority under the chairmanship of President Hamid Karzai. The then EAM Yashwant Sinha, in his visit from August 10-12, 2002, announced reconstruction assistance of US $ 4 million each for Indira Gandhi hospital and Habibia School. He also visited Herat, Mazar-e-Sharif and Kandahar. During his visit on February 15, 2005, EAM Natwar Singh handed over Surgical Block of Indira Gandhi Institute of Child Health (IGICH) and 50 trucks to Afghan National Army (ANA). He also announced setting up of a diagnostic center with Indian assistance in IGICH.

PM'S VISIT TO AFGHANISTAN, AUGUST 22-29, 2005

At the invitation of the President of Afghanistan, Prime Minister Dr. Manmohan Singh paid a state visit to Afghanistan from August 22-29, 2005. The high-level delegation included Minister of External Affairs, National Security Adviser, Member of Parliament Rahul Gandhi, Foreign Secretary and other senior officials. PM Dr. Manmohan Singh and President Hamid Karzai reaffirmed their common interest in reinvigorating the past ties and developing a new partnership for the 21st century.

The Prime Minister reiterated India's continued commitment to the reconstruction and economic development of Afghanistan and pledged an additional US $ 50 million assistance, taking the total pledged assistance to $ 650 millions. During the visit, three important MOUs/Agreements, i) MOU on Small Developmental Projects, ii) Agreement on Cooperation in the field of Healthcare and Medicinal Science, and iii) MOU on Cooperation in the field of Agricultural Research & Education were signed. MOS (EA), Shri E. Ahmad led India's delegation to attend the 'Regional Economic Cooperation Conference' held at Kabul from December 2-4, 2005. MOS for Tourism Smt. Renuka Chowdhury led a delegation to Kabul from December 6-8, 2005 and signed an MOU for Cooperation in the field of Tourism.

EXTERNAL AFFAIRS MINISTER (EAM)'S VISIT TO AFGHANISTAN (JANUARY 23-24, 2007) [H]

External Affairs Minister, Pranab Mukherjee, accompanied by Foreign Secretary and other senior officials visited Kabul on January 23-24, 2007. During the visit, Minister Mukherjee handed over the formal invitation to President Karzai to the 14th SAARC

Summit Meeting to be held in New Delhi on April 3-4, 2007. Afghanistan will formally become a member of SAARC during the New Delhi Summit in April 2007. Minister Mukherjee also had delegation level talks with Foreign Minister of Afghanistan Dr Rangin Dadfar Spanta. The two Foreign Ministers witnessed the signing of a MOU among India, Afghanistan and UNDP on Capacity Building in Public Administration.

Under this MoU, India will be send 30 civil servants to Afghanistan for a period of one year to capacity building of Afghan Ministries and Departments. Minister Mukherjee also announced an additional aid assistance of US$ 100 million towards Afghanistan's reconstruction. With this, India's total pledge to Afghanistan is US$ 750 million. Minister Mukherjee also handed over the Polyclinic Block of the Indira Gandhi Institute for Child Health Care and a consignment of medicines from India to Afghan authorities. Minister Mukherjee unveiled a plaque naming the road adjacent to Indira Gandhi Institute for Child Health Care (IGICH) as "Indira Gandhi street" in memory of former Prime Minister of India Indira Gandhi.

INDIAN COMMUNITY

There are approximately 3500 to 4000 Indian Nationals in Afghanistan. Many of them are working in various Government of India assistance projects in Afghanistan. Indian nationals are also working in different capacities with Government of Afghanistan, International Agencies operating in Afghanistan and in the private sector. In addition, around 3,000 persons belonging to Sikh and Hindu religions permanently live in Afghanistan, spread over various provinces like Kabul, Ghazni, Khost, Kandahar, Helmand, Jalalabad and Parwan. All these persons are Afghan nationals and are treated as Afghan Sikhs and Hindus.

Chapter 10

India and South Asia: Economic Relations

INDIA-PAKISTAN ECONOMIC RELATIONS

GRANTING THE MFN STATUS TO INDIA

They generally give what they project as the pending dispute over the future of Jammu & Kashmir (J&K) as the reason. They say that unless and until the Kashmir dispute is resolved, there cannot be a normalisation of the economic relations. But, the real reasons are more economic than political. At the time of its birth in 1947, Pakistan's was essentially a three-commodity and one-port economy. It continues to be so. There has been no major diversification of the economy. Textiles, leather goods and sports goods still account for over 75 per cent of its exports and over two-thirds of its tax revenue. Karachi is the only major port available for international trade and will continue to be so until the Gwadar port in Balochistan, now under construction with Chinese assistance, gets going.

The Pakistani textile industry is export-dependent. The quality and the cost of its production are determined by the external and not the internal market. As against this, the Indian textile industry is not export-dependent to that extent and domestic demand plays a more important role in determining the quality and the cost of its production. It is said that, consequently, Pakistani textiles are of a much better quality than Indian textiles, but much more expensive and hence not easily affordable by the poorer sections of the Pakistani society. Many of the Indian textiles, though poorer in quality, are within the reach of the poor people. Hence, the Pakistani textile magnates have always been worried that if the Pakistani market is thrown open to Indian industries, the cheaper Indian textiles could flood their market affecting them. In Pakistan, while the feudal landlords continue to wield considerable political power and generally align themselves with the military, the textile magnates and traders wield considerable economic power by virtue of the fact that they constitute the largest single group of tax-payers.

When she was the Prime Minister between 1993 and 1996, Mrs.Benazir Bhutto had set up a working group to examine the implications of Pakistan granting the MFN status to India. The group had strongly advised against it till its economy was diversified to the same extent as that of India, thereby reducing its dependence on textile exports. It recommended a crash programme to diversify the economy. It drew the attention of the Government to what it described as the economic plight of Bangladesh because of India's alleged economic hegemony there and warned that Pakistan could become another economic Bangladesh if it prematurely opened its market to India.

At a meeting convened by her to discuss this report, officials of her Foreign Office advised that she should link the refusal to grant the MFN status to the continuing Kashmir dispute and should not give the economic reasons, though they were valid. She accepted their advice. The Nawaz Sharif and the Pervez Musharraf Governments have also been following this advice.

The Benazir Bhutto and the Nawaz Sharif Governments did not take any steps to diversify the economy and reduce the dependence on textile exports. One of the first acts of Musharraf after seizing power in October,1999, was to give a push to the diversification programme with Chinese assistance, with emphasis on information technology (software), development of its untapped mineral resources etc. The programme has made some headway, but it will take some more years before Pakistan feels confident that it will have a level playing field if it normalises economic relations with India.

Another reason for Pakistan's reluctance is the fear that it could find it difficult to resist Indian pressure to allow India and Afghanistan to use the land route for their bilateral trade, by granting India transit rights. Presently, while the Government of Pakistan is prepared to concede transit rights to Afghanistan for its exports to India, it is not prepared to grant transit rights to India for its exports to Afghanistan. There are two reasons for it.

Firstly, even while accusing India of exercising economic hegemony over its smaller neighbours, Pakistan wants to exercise economic hegemony over Afghanistan and does not want India as a competitor there.

Secondly, Afghanistan's transit trade through Pakistan is a lucrative source of revenue for the Karachi port through which most of Afghanistan's external trade passes and for the Pakistani road transport companies, many of which are owned by the Pakistan army and retired Pakistani Army officers. For example, it is said that Lt.Gen.(retd) Hamid Gul, former Director-General of the Inter-Services Intelligence (ISI), has minted millions since his retirement by handling part of Afghanistan's transit trade. There are many others who have similarly profited. They are worried that if a two-way transit trade between India and Afghanistan is allowed, Kabul might start using the Mumbai port for part of its external trade, thereby affecting their profits. They are, therefore, in the forefront of those opposing the normalisation of economic relations with India. Instead of admitting the real reason, they cite the so-called Kashmir dispute as the reason.

PRESENT STATE OF TRADE BETWEEN INDIA AND PAKISTAN

Pakistan has a restricted approved list of commodities in respect of which it allows bilateral trade. The total value of this legitimate trade is estimated at US $ 400 million. There is a much larger bilateral trade estimated at over US $ one billion either through trans-border smuggling or through third countries such as Singapore and the United Arab Emirates. Goods smuggled across the border include items such as cheap textiles, audio and video cassettes, pan leaves etc. Third country exports to Pakistan are mainly in respect of machinery and spare parts, particularly for their textile industry and even for Government-owned port installations. Before 9/11, the Government itself turned a blind eye to or even encouraged third-country imports of Indian machinery and spare parts because of Pakistan's precarious foreign exchange reserves. Pakistani industrialists could not afford to import them from the West or Japan or South Korea. After 9/11, Pakistan's foreign exchange reserves have increased nearly seven-fold and, consequently, the same dependence on third-country imports from India is not there.

POSITION REGARDING THE GAS PIPELINE FROM IRAN TO INDIA VIA PAKISTAN

The proposal for a gas pipeline was first mooted by Iran when Benazir Bhutto was the Prime Minister between 1993 and 1996. It was taken up with the Nawaz Sharif Government also. At that time, the Inter-Services Intelligence (ISI) had advised them that they should not agree to the extension of the pipeline to India since the availability of gas from Iran could strengthen India's economic and industrial capability. Benazir and Nawaz told Iran that while the pipeline could connect Iran and Pakistan, it could not be extended to India. A few months after seizing power in October, 1999, Musharraf had been to Teheran on his first visit. The Iranian authorities urged him to re-consider the decision of his predecessors and allow the extension of the pipeline to India. On his return to Islamabad, he ordered a re-examination of the case and lifted Pakistan's objection to its extension to India.

In reply to criticism by the Islamic fundamentalist parties, he said that while Pakistan would continue to reject proposals for the normalisation of the economic relations with India, it would treat the pipeline issue as a stand-alone issue without linking it to the Kashmir dispute. He justified his decision on the following grounds. First, Pakistan would need additional energy for diversifying its industrial capability and for stepping up production. Second, a gas pipeline required huge investment and no foreign company would be prepared to make that kind of investment for selling gas in Pakistan alone which would not bring adequate returns on the investment. Only its extension to India would make it profitable for the investors. Third, at a time when Pakistan's economy was in a state of collapse, it badly needed the US $ 800 million per annum offered by Iran as transit fee for the gas.

The project did not take off due to India's security concerns which arose from the following factors. First, the pipeline would have to pass through the Sunni majority areas of Balochistan where there is considerable anti-Teheran and anti-Islamabad feelings. Balochistan itself is an important source of gas. The gas pipelines connecting Balochistan with industries and towns in Punjab are already subject to frequent attacks by Baloch nationalist groups fighting for the independence of Balochistan. Second, the Islamic fundamentalist and jihadi organisations, which are opposed to the extension of the pipeline to India till the Kashmir issue is resolved, might disrupt the gas supply through sabotage even if the Baloch nationalists do not do so to express their anger against Islamabad.

Another security-related aspect is the possibility of the Government of Pakistan itself stopping the supplies in the event of a military conflict with India. Pakistani authorities counter this by pointing out that whenever there was any conflict or danger of a conflict, it was India, which tried to punish Pakistan economically and not vice versa. In this connection, they refer to India's suspension of the overflight rights of its airlines in 1971 and 2002. They also refer to the demand by Indian hawks in 2002 for the suspension of the Indus Waters Treaty in order to deprive the Pakistani farmers of water.

While there were no direct talks between India and Pakistan on the security issue, in its discussions with Teheran, Islamabad was repeatedly holding out the assurance that it would ensure the security of the supplies to India. One of the suggestions reportedly under consideration was that if there was any sabotage of the pipeline in Pakistani territory, Iran would shut off the supply to Pakistan too till the damaged pipeline was repaired. This would ensure that Pakistan took effective measures for the security of the pipeline and that if , despite these measures, there was a disruption of the supplies, stoppage of supplies to its own consumers would make it repair the damage fast.

As a result of the post-9/11 improvement in the Pakistani economy and the seven-fold increase in its foreign exchange reserves, it is no longer as dependent on the transit fee as it was in the past for preventing an economic break-down. Despite this, it is as keen as it was in the past for an early implementation of the project without linking it to the Kashmir issue because its expanding economy badly needs additional energy supplies. The pipelines for bringing gas and oil from Turkmenistan, which have been under discussion since 1994, are unlikely to materialise in the near future till the security situation improves in Afghanistan. Even in respect of oil and gas from Turkmenistan, foreign investors are not prepared to invest heavily unless there is a possibility of the pipelines being extended to India.

There has recently been a change in the policy of the Government of India of not discussing the issue directly with Pakistan. Negotiations are already on on this subject. The statements made by Mr.Shaukat Aziz, the Pakistani Prime Minister, during his visit to New Delhi on November 23 and 24, 2004, underline Pakistan's continuing keenness to go ahead with this project despite the lack of progress in the talks on Kashmir. Mr.Aziz has described the pipeline project as an important confidence-building measure.

According to media reports, the Government of India is now trying to link progress on this issue to Pakistan's granting the MFN status to India. Mr.Aziz has warned that if there is continued delay, Pakistan might be constrained to go ahead with the project on its own in order to meet its pressing requirements. He has also pointed out that to meet Pakistani requirements only, a pipeline with a smaller diameter would be sufficient. Once such a pipeline has been laid, according to him, there would be no possibility of extending it to India, which would require a larger diameter.

An unknown and inadequately discussed aspect of the pipeline issue is the likely attitude of the USA. The economic sanctions imposed by the USA against Iran in 1979 continue and there is no prospect of an improvement in the US-Iran relations in the near future. On the contrary, relations have further worsened because of US suspicions of Iran embarking on a clandestine military nuclear project. If Iran continues to resist US demands for abandoning this project, there is a possibility of the US engineering multilateral economic sanctions against it through the UN Security Council.

The present US sanctions against Iran prevent not only US companies from having normal business relations with Iran, but also foreign companies which use American licenses, patents, equipment and spare parts. Though there are no sanctions of the European Union against Iran, there were reported instances in the past of the US pressurising European companies not to supply to Iran equipment and technologies which, in the US perception, would be of strategic significance.

Neither Iran nor Pakistan nor India would have the kind of money, equipment and technology required for laying the pipeline. Iran will have to raise money abroad to make the project a reality. At present, multilateral institutions such as the Asian Development Bank seem to be inclined to financially support the project, but unless and until there is an improvement in the USA's relations with Iran and it gives satisfaction to Washington DC on the nuclear issue, it is doubtful whether the US would let the project go through. The fact that the US has not come in the way of an Australian company doing a feasibility study of the project does not necessarily mean that it would not try to stand inn the way of the project.

INDIA-SRI LANKA ECONOMIC RELATIONS

India and Sri Lanka are member nations of several regional and multilateral organisations such as the South Asian Association for Regional Cooperation (SAARC), South Asia Co-operative Environment Programme, South Asian Economic Union and BIMSTEC, working to enhance cultural and commercial ties. Since a bilateral free trade agreement was signed and came into effect in 2000, Indo-Sri Lankan trade rose 128% by 2004 and quadrupled by 2006, reaching USD 2.6 billion. Between 2000 and 2004, India's exports to Sri Lanka in the last four years increased by 113%, from USD 618 million to $1,319 million while Sri Lankan exports to India increased by 342%, from $44 million to USD $194 million. Indian exports account for 14% of Sri Lanka's global imports. India is also the fifth largest export destination for Sri Lankan goods, accounting for 3.6% of its exports. Both nations are also signatories of the South Asia Free Trade Agreement (SAFTA).

Negotiations are also underway to expand the free trade agreement to forge stronger commercial relations and increase corporate investment and ventures in various industries.

India's National Thermal Power Corp (NTPC) is also scheduled to build a 500 MW thermal power plant in Sampoor (Sampur). The NTPC claims that the this plan will take the Indo-Sri Lankan relationship to new level.

FISHERMEN ISSUE

There have been several incidents of firing on Indian fishermen fishing in Palk Bay.Indian Government has always taken up the issue of safety of Indian fishermen on a priority basis with the Government of Sri Lanka. Presently there is no bona fide Indian fisherman in the Sri Lankan custody. A Joint Working Group (JWG) has been constituted to deal with the issues related to Indian fishermen straying in Sri Lankan territorial waters, work out modalities for prevention of use of force against them and the early release of confiscated boats and explore possibilities of working towards bilateral arrangements for licensed fishing. The JWG last met in Jan 2006.

DEVELOPMENT COOPERATION

India is active in a number of areas of development activity in Sri Lanka. About one-sixth of the total development credit granted by GOI is made available to Sri Lanka.

Lines of credit: In the recent past three lines of credit were extended to Sri Lanka: US$ 100 million for capital goods, consumer durables, consultancy services and food items, US$ 31 million for supply of 300,000 MT of wheat and US$ 150 million for purchase of petroleum products. All of these lines of credit have been fully utilized. Another line of credit of US$ 100 million is now being made available for rehabilitation of the Colombo-Matara railway.

A number of development projects are implemented under 'Aid to Sri Lanka' funds. In 2006-07, the budget for 'Aid to Sri Lanka' was Rs 28.2 Crs.

Small Development Projects: A MoU on Cooperation in Small Development Projects has been signed. Projects for providing fishing equipments to the fishermen in the East of Sri Lanka and solar energy aided computer education in 25 rural schools in Eastern Sri Lanka are under consideration.

Health Projects: We have supplied medical equipments to hospitals at Hambantota and Point Pedro, supplied 4 state of the art ambulances to the Central Province, implemented a cataract eye surgery programme for 1500 people in the Central Province and implemented a project of renovation of OT at Dickoya hospital and supplying equipment to it.

The projects under consideration are: Construction of a 150-bed hospital at Dickoya, upgradation of the hospital at Trincomalee and a US$ 7.5 million grant for setting up a Cancer Hospital in Colombo.

Education Projects: Upgradation of the educational infrastructure of the schools in the Central province including teachers' training, setting up of 10 computer labs, setting up of 20 e-libraries (Nenasalas), Mahatma Gandhi scholarship scheme for +2 students and setting up of a vocational training centre in Puttalam. India also contributes to the Ceylon Workers Education Trust that gives scholarships to the children of estate workers.

Training: A training programme for 465 Sri Lankan Police officers has been commenced in Dec 2005. Another 400 Sri Lankan Police personnel are being trained for the course of 'Maintenance of Public Order'.

INDIA AND BANGLADESH: ECONOMIC RELATIONS

The political relationship between India and Bangladesh may not be very encouraging, but the economic relationship recently has improved in favour of Bangladesh. For a long time India's eastern neighbour has been complaining about the growing imbalance in trade. However, the latest data released by Bangladesh have indicated that there has been a significant change in this relationship.

There has been a massive increase in the exports of Bangladesh to India. It has risen by 68 percent, amounting to $241.96 million in fiscal 2005-06. In the preceding year, they stood at $143.66 million only. This increase in exports has largely been to northeastern states. On the other hand, according to the statistics provided by Export Promotion Bureau (EPB) of Bangladesh imports from India have dropped by around 8 percent, totaling $1,868 million in the last financial year from $2,025.78 million in FY 2004-05. As a result of this rise in exports and decline in imports the trade deficit of Bangladesh with India narrowed by around 14 percent in the last financial year.

The trade deficit of Bangladesh with India had ballooned to a record $2,003 million in 2003-04. However, it came down to $1,882 million in the following year and $1,626 million in FY 05-06.

According to vice-chairman of Export Promotion Bureau (EPB), Mir Sahabuddin Mohammad exports to the northeastern states of India have increased substantially in the last financial year. This rise is because of change of policy of government of India which has facilitated the work of businessmen. Earlier the banks in the northeastern India could not open letters of credit (L/Cs) for imports from Bangladesh, discouraging potential importers. But now they can open L/Cs, which has facilitated the trade between the two countries. Though Bangladesh has a trade deficit with India, it is surplus with the northeastern states.

Bangladesh has also made sustained effort to increase its exports to India. EPB had organised several exhibitions in India and received a good response from the Indian importers and buyers. Bangladeshi officials say that there are demands for Bangladeshi products including toiletries, cosmetics, melamine, fish, leather and ceramics in these Indian states.

Despite this jump in exports, Bangladeshi exporters are still complaining that some non-tariff barriers like mandatory testing required by India, inadequate banking facilities and poor infrastructure at the land ports are hindering Bangladesh's export growth to India. They also claim that India deliberately tries to stall import from Bangladesh, as its land customs officials are not informed about the preferential market access given to Dhaka by New Delhi.

Bangladesh has earlier not been able to export to India because it had a very small export basket. Besides, its products were not very competitive internationally. As a result they have not been able to penetrate into Indian economy that is increasingly getting globalised.

Still, India has been trying to help Bangladesh and is willing to relax restrictions for Bangladesh even in the area of restricted categories like readymade garments for which Bangladesh has been insisting.

SHARING OF WATER RESOURCES

Regarding sharing of water resources, the two sides decided to leave it up to the upcoming meeting of the water-resources secretaries at the Joint Committee of Experts (JCE) to sort out details on common river water sharing, minor irrigation and drinking water schemes, flood-mitigation cooperation, and dredging and river bank protection work. The two foreign secretaries hoped to hold a Joint Rivers Commission meeting at the earliest after the JCE meeting.

EMPHASIS ON INCREASED CONNECTIVITY

The two sides also stressed the need for greater land and train links. India agreed to send a team in the first week of July to coordinate outstanding logistical issues to start the long-awaited Dhaka-Kolkata rail-link. Menon observed that "there is a tremendous positive response" from the two countries towards the restoration of missing links. The chief advisor of Bangladesh caretaker government was also of the view that passenger and goods train service between the two countries will help peoples of both the countries.

PROBLEM OF INFRASTRUCTURE

The trade between India and Bangladesh also suffers because of poor infrastructural facilities. The reason behind this under development of infrastructure has been the reluctance of Bangladesh to provide trans-shipment facilities to India. This has discouraged both sides from constructing proper road and rails links.

The infrastructural bottleneck was also highlighted by the multilateral donor agency World Bank. The donor agency feels that an inter-country railway link between Bangladesh and India would accelerate economic growth of the two countries. Speaking at a press conference in Dhaka on July 3, 2006 World Bank Country Director Christine I Wallich said, "When I first came to Bangladesh, I had visited some border areas and found the possibility of such a railway linkage."

The issue of infrastructure was also raised by Indian High Commissioner Veena Sikri when Bangladesh Commerce Minister Hafiz Uddin Ahmad tried to highlight the issue of trade gap while inaugurating the Indian Cotton Yarn and Fabric Show 2006 at a hotel in Dhaka on July 9. Sikri suggested that Bangladesh develop its Mangla port and link it with Haldia port in West Bengal to accelerate trade and reduce the trade gap between the two countries. She stressed the need for increased direct transport links with Bangladesh, which in turn has invited India to invest more in its fabric and yarn sector. Noting that Bangladesh remained India's third largest export destination for fabric and the second largest for yarn, Sikri said that increase in trade and the bridging of the deficit would depend on how fast Bangladesh improved its infrastructure.

The issue of infrastructural bottleneck was discussed at the fourth meeting of the Indo-Bangladesh Joint Working Group (JWG) on trade which was held in Agartala on July 5 and 6 this year. MVPC Sastri, joint secretary in the commerce ministry, headed the Indian delegation while additional secretary in the commerce ministry Elias Ahmed led the Bangladesh team. Senior officials of the commerce and industries departments of the five bordering states - West Bengal, Assam, Meghalaya, Mizoram and Tripura - also participated in the meeting, being held in the northeastern state for the first time.

In this meeting India and Bangladesh have decided to modernise and upgrade existing infrastructure, including roads, to boost their bilateral trade. After the meeting Sastry said, 'We have decided to modernise and upgrade our existing infrastructure including road connectivity to further boost the trade between the two countries - especially between the northeastern states of India and Bangladesh.'

In this meeting once again the issue of huge bilateral trade gap existing between the two nations was discussed. Sastry, who led the 16-member Indian team said, 'The northeastern states of India have huge resources and raw materials and these can be exported to Bangladesh. After due processing, the finished products can be made available to the people of the region at much cheaper rates.'

It was also decided that the custom officials of both the countries will soon meet and review the performance of 176 land custom stations in the five states along the India-Bangladesh border. Some of the stations will be further strengthened and some of them will be redeployed. Earlier, India had allocated Rs.2 billion for the development of five trade centres at Sutarkandhi and Karimganj in Assam, Demagiri in Mizoram, Dawki in Meghalaya and Moreh in Manipur.

Recently Tripura Chief Minister Manik Sarakar also highlighted that business in India's northeast would get a major boost if the region is allowed to use Bangladeshi ports for speedier transportation of goods. Speaking to media on September 14 he said, "Business between India's northeast and Southeast Asia would grow if we are allowed to use the Bangladeshi ports of Chittagong and Ashuganj for ferrying goods and other raw materials." Chittagong port is just 75 km from south Tripura's border town of Sabroom, while the Ashuganj port is 25 km from state capital Agartala. It is believed that Bangladesh would benefit immensely if India was allowed to access its ports. According to Sarkar the northeastern market is estimated to be about Rs.200 billion and this could help Bangladesh ease its trade deficit with India.

Unfortunately, an attitude of cooperation has not been seen from the side of Bangladesh. The country has negative trade balance with most countries and uses remittances from expatriate Bangladeshis to finance its imports. But Bangladesh appears to be obsessed with the trade gap, which it has with India. As a result, in recent times the country has been following policies which discourage import from India. No wonder, the latest data show that the Bangladesh import from India has declined.

In the past, India has been the largest trading partner of Bangladesh. That is no longer the situation. Sometime back data released from Bangladesh indicated that China has replaced India as its largest trading partner. There is no denying the fact that Chinese economy has been growing and making its presence felt in the world, the increase in Sino-Bangladesh trade is also because of a conscious policy followed by both these countries. There is nothing wrong if Bangladesh tries to increase its trade with China. What is problematic is its attempt to restrict economic relationship with India, which is showing in the latest data of imports.

Bangladesh thinks that its negative trade balance with India is because of the tariff and para-tariff barriers, which is not true. Even if India reduces its duties to 0-5 percent which it has agreed to do under SAFTA, a yawning trade gap would remain. Bangladesh must realize that if it wants to reduce this gap it would have to come up with more products of quality which are internationally competitive.

India knows the limitation of Bangladesh. Hence to help the country on this count, India's leading business house, Tata group suggested a three billion dollar investment proposal. Had this proposal been accepted by Bangladesh it would have drastically changed the complexion of bilateral trade. Unfortunately Bangladesh does not want to take any policy decision which is viewed as pro-India in an election year. Though sound economics demanded this, political considerations are keeping the proposal in abeyance. There is almost no hope that the Bangladesh government would approve a $3-billion investment by the Tata group before the formation of next government. Alan Rosling, executive director of Tata Sons said, "If we can't make progress, we will cut back our commitments in these projects and reallocate our resources." He also felt that the priority for the group might change in next six months. Hence the opportunity for Bangladesh is now.

Officials in Bangladesh are however, hopeful that the Tata group would stay on course until after the polls. Mahmudur Rahman, energy adviser to the Bangladesh government is optimistic that Tata will eventually show their patience for six more months after doing "all the hard work covering nearly two years."

The investment by the Tata group would have exceeded all the foreign investment Bangladesh has received since 1972. It could have boosted Bangladesh's GDP by 1.9

percent annually, and benefit its balance of payments by as much as $18 billion, besides creating jobs for 24,000 people. The coal project could have added to the energy supply of Bangladesh, where just 30 percent of its 140 million people have access to electricity.

A pullout by the Tatas would be a further setback to the country's creaky power infrastructure and its ability to attract critical foreign investment. A section in both India and Bangladesh believes that the proposal of Tatas might become a reality after the next government is formed in Bangladesh. But if that does not happen, it would seriously hurt the economic interests of Bangladesh.

CONCLUSION

The huge trade gap existing between India and Bangladesh has more to do with the differing nature of economies of both countries. It is not because of any hostile or restrictive policy followed by India. Bangladesh is dependent on India even for the import of its essentials. When India restricted export of these items because of growing domestic demand, prices of these commodities shot up in Bangladesh. Besides, India is exporting a number of other items. On the other hand, Bangladesh has very few items to offer. Hence a huge trade gap is bound to exist. Bangladesh could have bridged this gap by providing trans-shipment facility to India.

Unfortunately, the country does not want to do that as any policy which is pro-India is perceived as anti-national by many in Bangladesh. India has also tried to encourage investment in Bangladesh so that the number of products exported from that country can be increased. But even in that case, Bangladesh has shown little interest. The recent increase in Bangladeshi export to northeastern India is because of favourable policy followed by this country. India wants to deepen the economic relationship between Bangladesh and northeastern India which will be beneficial for both of them. A lot will depend on the attitude of the government formed after the next elections in Bangladesh.

ECONOMIC RELATIONS BETWEEN INDIA AND NEPAL

India has made tremendous progress in IT sector in recent years and has developed outsourcing market for the US and some ountries of western Europe. Nepal could also benefit from such development. Nepal could also be an attractive destination for FDI from India. It is already the largest investor in Nepal. Indian investors have identified such advantages offered by Nepal such as attractive incentives, Government's positive attitude towards investors, low cost locations, cheap labour cost, easily trainable workforce as some of the factors which will make it attractive to Indian investors. Indian investment in Nepal is 36% of FDI and includes such sectors as tourism, consumer durables, garments and carpets. Such Indian companies as Dabur, Colgate and Hindustan Lever have set up factories in Nepal with the objective to export their finished products to India.

Tourism and hydropower development are two sectors in which Nepal enjoys comparative advantage and could be attractive for Indian investors. Nepal is an attractive destination for Indian tourists who visit the country for pilgrimage and sightseeing. An increasing number of young Indians are also visiting the country for honeymoon and adventure tourism. It could also attract more tourists during summer in order to get away from the heat of the Indian plains during summer. Lack of adequate number of airline seats had been a major impediment. However, such private airlines from India as Air Sahara and Jet Air have started flying to Nepal in 2004 and some private Nepalese airlines such as Cosmic Air might soon start flying to some Indian cities. There are also prospects of developing health tourism. There is scope for co-operation in hotel management between India and Nepal.

Nepal is one of the countries selected by China for sending tourists. There are already Chinese tourists visiting Nepal. There are prospects that a large number of Chinese tourists would be visiting Nepal and India to such places as Lumbini, Bodhgaya, Sarnath and Kushinagar for pilgrimage tourism as they have more disposable income due to economic development. There are already many Indians visiting Manasarovar via Nepal for pilgrimage.

Nepal has one of the highest potential for development of hydroelectric power as variation in altitude and adequate amount of water are present to an extraordinary degree. It is estimated that Nepal enjoys a power generating capacity of 83,000 MW. Demand for consumption of electric power in North India has increased dramatically in recent years. There are prospects for co-operation between Nepal and India in this sector. Bilateral and multilateral donor agencies are interested in funding hydroelectric power development projects in Nepal when they are assured that there exists a market in India. There has been some apprehension in Nepal that India is unwilling to be dependent upon such a vital source of energy outside its own borders. Nepal's experience in utilizing water resources in co-operation with India has not always been encouraging. Kosi Project was the first major river project. It was primarily a flood control project that benefited Bihar and there was very small amount of power produced that could benefit Nepal in view of size of project. Similarly, Gandak Project utilizing another major river of Nepal was primarily for irrigation that benefited UP and Bihar in India and gave some benefits to Nepal as well.

INDIA BHUTAN ECONOMIC RELATIONS

BHUTAN'S ECONOMIC CONCERNS AND INDIA

Bhutan is not only a landlocked country but also extremely backward. Having decided to come out of isolationism, India helped it by completely financing the first two five-year plans. Presently, the Indian government is involved in many projects, which include hydropower plants, cement plants, roads, etc. 40 per cent of the external revenue that Bhutan gets is presently from the sale of electricity to India. In this sense, Bhutan has benefited immensely from assistance by India. Most important, of the total aid given by India to other developing countries in 1996-97, the share of Bhutan was 52 per cent, which amounts to Rs. 181 crore. There is a free trade regime between India and Bhutan not requiring even customs posts on the Indian side of the border. Being a landlocked country, India provides it with about 13 transit routes. Presently, Bhutan is very keen on sub-regional cooperation through the growth quadrangle which encompasses Bangladesh, Nepal and the north eastern parts of India. It is emphasising on the economic content in its relations with the SAARC member countries.

THE CHINA FACTOR

The China factor has been very important in defining the nature of relationship between India and Bhutan. In fact, it is this which gives Bhutan the geostrategic importance with respect to Indian interests. It is interesting to note that to begin with, the British were primarily interested in Bhutan for facilitating a trade route to access Tibet, that is to say, the aims were purely economic in nature. It was only later when China started laying claims to the territory of Bhutan that the clause enabling British India to guide the foreign relations of Bhutan was incorporated in the Treaty of 1910. Later, independent India too included this clause in the Treaty of 1949. The Chinese occupation of Tibet and later the uprisings in Tibet following the Chinese action there, made Bhutan think seriously about coming out of its isolationist policy. This later led to the close involvement of India in Bhutan's economic development. In 1958, China had not only claimed Indian territory, its maps also showed 200 sq miles of Bhutanese territory as part of Tibet. It was at this defining moment that Nehru said in the Parliament that any attack on Bhutan would be considered an attack on India. Later, India's defeat against China in the 1962 War, made Bhutan skeptical about the capability of India to look after its defence. But confidence was restored following the Indian victory in 1971. The process of normalisation of relations between India and China, made it possible for Bhutan to have direct bilateral talks with China on the boundary question, thus, providing Bhutan an extra space to conduct its foreign policy.

It is seen that the attitude of China towards Tibet has played a major role in shaping Bhutan's attitude towards India. Bhutan has many historical links with Tibet. The experience of the Tibetan refugees has made it apprehensive of developing close ties with China. In fact, the desire of Bhutan to gain recognition in the international arena has a lot to do with the attitude of China. The fear that Bhutan will go into China's fold seems unlikely with regard to the current state of beneficial relations Bhutan has with India and its past experience with China. Bhutan's experience with China has not been all smooth sailing and, in fact Bhutan itself follows a restrictive policy with regard to its interaction with China. The then Foreign Minister Tsering said in an interview that Bhutan had "correct relations" with Beijing. He added that there was not much trade or economic interaction. Bhutan was conducting negotiations with China on the 500-km-long border and the area under dispute was small, according to the minister.

INDIA'S INTERESTS

Bhutan has immense security imperatives for India. A stable, independent Bhutan is essential for it to be an effective buffer state. India does not have any imperial or colonial agenda while dealing with Bhutan. Prime Minister Nehru said in 1958 in the most categorical terms that though Bhutan is a small country, it should remain independent in choosing its own way of life. This policy enunciated by Nehru was continued by the succeeding governments in India, which has played an active role in Bhutan getting the international recognition that it deserves. While initially the economic aid given by India can be said to have been influenced by security concerns in enabling Bhutan to have the essential infrastructure, in later years this has not been so. It presently follows a policy of mutual benefit from the projects which are being undertaken in Bhutan.

The market for these projects will be India and in this manner it also ensures the development of the north-east part of India. While Bhutan is a small country and its wants are limited, with time they are sure to grow. Any amount of Indian aid would then not be able to meet the required needs. However, through the approach being presently followed, India ensures the sustainable development of Bhutan. The 336MW Chukha Hydel project ensures power supply to parts of West Bengal and Assam. This one project provides nearly 40 per cent of Bhutan's national revenue. The 1020MW Tala project is under way and once it is commissioned, the revenue Bhutan can earn will be substantial. On the Indian side, with such projects the power shortage problem will be partially resolved.

The goodwill India is able to generate through its activities are likely to ensure that whatever changes might come in the future in the political structures in Bhutan, the attitude towards it will not change. Bhutan will see it in its own interest to be friendly with India for it is beneficial to it economically and in the international arena.

India's major concerns with Bhutan presently are those relating to the disturbed situation in the north-east. It is reported that insurgents have established camps in the border areas of Bhutan, and without Bhutan's help, it will not be possible to combat the insurgency. India and Bhutan have concluded an extradition agreement in 1996. Though the 1949 Treaty mentions extradition, the present agreement is aimed at simplifying the procedure and making it more effective to deal with cross border terrorism and organised crime. Bhutan is not in any way assisting these insurgents, but its police forces are limited to meet such contingencies. Important questions thus arise about implementation of the extradition treaty.

India is spending crores of rupees on combating insurgency in the North East. By setting camps in Bhutan, these insurgents are able to escape from the Indian authorities. In days to come the problem may assume serious dimensions. There is also the danger that if Bhutan were to take stern action against them, then the militants would disturb the peace and harmony there. There are as yet no confirmed reports that the two governments have taken a joint action or conducted joint raids against the hideouts of these insurgents, but both are closely cooperating and this issue remains on the top of the agenda.

ECONOMIC RELATIONS BETWEEN INDIA AND MALDIVES

Since the success of Operation Cactus, the relations between India and Maldives have expanded significantly. India has provided extensive economic aid and has participated in bilateral programs for the development of infrastructure, health, civil aviation, telecommunications and labour resources. It established the Indira Gandhi Memorial Hospital in Male, the capital of Maldives, expanded telecommunications and air links and increased scholarships for Maldivian students. While India's exports to Maldives during 2006 were worth Rs. 384 crores, imports were worth less than Rs. 6 crores. The State Bank of India has contributed more than USD 500 million to aid the economic expansion of Maldives. India and Maldives have announced plans to jointly work to expand fisheries and tuna processing.

INDIA-AFGHANISTAN ECONOMIC RELATIONS

After nearly three decades of civil war, since the fall of Taliban regime, Afghanistan resumed efforts to bring back its derailed economy on track. In pursuance of these efforts, a Preferential Trade Agreement was signed between India and Afghanistan in March 2003. According to this agreement, custom duty on various Afghan exportable items was waived/reduced by India to encourage bilateral trade. With Afghanistan set to join as a full fledged member of SAARC in April 2007, the trade and commerce is expected to improve further.

At present Afghanistan in the process of building up an institutionalized system of updated database for imports and exports to and from India. India's bilateral trade with Afghanistan has remained around US $ 200 millions in last four years. However, substantial trade of Indian items is carried via UAE, which does not get reflected in trade statistics of India and Afghanistan. Principal exports items from India are tea, tyres & tubes, pharmaceutical products. In turn, Afghanistan's principal export items to India are dry and fresh fruits, medicinal herbs and asafoetida (hing).

As per official figures, in 2005 Afghanistan's total merchandises exports were around US$ 384 millions, which excludes contraband trade and re-exports. During the same period, Afghanistan's total merchandise imports were US$ 2471 million (Some of which were re-exported). The import figures do not include smuggling and duty free donor imports. According to Afghan official data, during 2005, India's exports to Afghanistan were about US $136.75 million and India's imports from Afghanistan was about US $58.58 million. The trade between India and Afghanistan in last five years was given in tabular form.

For Afghanistan, the main regional players in terms of cross border trade have been Pakistan and Iran. Jalalabad and Herat have emerged as hubs of trade, with most of Afghanistan's external trade by land passing through these two cities. Being dominantly agro-based economy, Afghan principal export items are mostly agro and horticulture produces. Export of these products picks up after the month of August every year.

As per the official figures, the trade between India and Afghanistan as % of Afghanistan's total trade was marginal during the period 2002-2004. Lack of transit through Pakistan, security risks and absence of direct road, rail and sea routes between the two countries are some of the key factors for the low volume of Indo-Afghan trade. At present, more than 60 Indian Companies have registered with the Afghan Investment Support Agency (AISA). AISA has MOU with CII and FICCI and Road shows in India are on the anvil to promote Indian investment in Afghanistan. Afghanistan International Chamber of Commerce (AICC) has a MOU with CII to promote business links between two countries.

INDIA'S ASSISTANCE PROGRAMME IN AFGHANISTAN

India has, till date, pledged US $ 750 million towards the economic reconstruction efforts in Afghanistan. This is a substantial amount for a non-traditional donor like India. India has taken projects in varied sectors including humanitarian, infrastructure, health, rural development, etc. Over the last four years, US$ 270 million has already been utilised, and the highest expenditure was in the last financial year 2005-06 of US$ 85 million. Some of the major projects are as under:

(i) India has committed food assistance of 1 million tonnes of wheat (equivalent to US$ 100 million) to Afghanistan. A part of this assistance is being converted into high protein biscuits for School Feeding Programme in Afghanistan and supplied through World Food Programme (WFP). More than 41,800 tonnes of biscuits were supplied in four tranches till August 2006. Under the programme, around 1 million Afghan school children are receiving a package of 100 grams of biscuits every day.

(ii) India is constructing 220kV Double Circuit Transmission Line from Pul-e-Khumri to Kabul and a 220/110/20 kV Sub-station at Kabul in Afghanistan. Power Grid Corporation of India is executing the project at an estimated cost of US $ 111 million (=Rs. 478.72 crores). The project work commenced in October 2005 and would be completed by February 2009.

(iii) India is re-constructing the Zaranj - Delaram road at an estimated cost of Rs.377.47 crores (approx. US$ 84 million). Border Roads Organization is executing the 218 km road in southwestern Afghanistan, which will provide an additional outlet to Afghanistan to sea via Iran. Work on the project has commenced and would be completed by end 2008.

(iv) India is reconstructing the Salma Dam Power Project in Herat province at an estimated cost of US $ 109.3 million (=Rs. 487 crores). Water and Power Consultancy Services (India) Ltd. (WAPCOS) is executing the project, which will provide 42 MW of power to Herat province. The main civil work has begun in March 2006 and the project is expected to be completed by January 2009.

(v) India had announced at the Tokyo Conference in January 2002, an assistance of US$ 100 million for Afghanistan's reconstruction. The entire amount has been operationalised on various projects/programmes till date.

(vi) India will also be constructing Afghanistan's new Parliament building at an estimated cost of US $ 75 million. The actual construction work will commence in July 2007 and will be completed by June 2010.

(vii) Since March 2006, ICCR is implementing the award of scholarship to 500 Afghan students for university education in India. More than 405 students have already joined various Universities.

(viii) Technical Cooperation Division is also implementing 500 short-term training programmes for Afghan trainees from March 2006 onwards. Out of this, 376 (220 have retuned after completion of the training and 156 are still undergoing training in India) slots have been utilised. The remaining slots will be filled during January to March 2007.

India has undertaken, in partnership with the Afghan government, projects in a wide range of sectors, including hydro-electricity, road construction, agriculture, industry, telecommunications, information & broadcasting, education and health. Some of the other important projects undertaken under our financial assistance include:

- Supply of 400 buses to the public transport system
- Supply of 3 Airbus aircraft to Ariana Airlines
- Operation of Indian Medical Missions in Kabul, Mazar-e-Sharif, Herat, Jalalabad and Kandahar. The 15 doctors in the 5 IMMs, on an average, treat more than 3.5 lakhs patient every year since 2003.
- Rehabilitation of Habibia School
- Reconstruction of Indira Gandhi Institute for Child Health
- Setting up of a common facility and tool room centre at Industrial Park in Kabul.
- Emergency restoration of basic telecommunication network in 11 provincial capitals
- Construction of 5000 MT capacity cold storage in Kandahar
- Supply of power transmission line equipment and substations in Faryab province
- Supply of 105 utility vehicles/ equipments (water tankers, rear drop tippers,

dump trucks, bulldozers, motor graders and garbage tippers) to the Kabul Municipality.

- Supply of 200 mini buses
- Revamping/restoration of information set up, including restoration/ augmentation of TV hardware in Jalalabad and Niagara Province.
- Institutional capacity building and training of more than 1300 Afghans in different fields in various training institutes in India
- Supply of 300 vehicles to the Afghan National Army
- Setting up of Computer Training Centre at Kabul, Herat, Kandahar, Pul-e-Khumri and Jalalabad
- Donation of educational kits to Habibia School in Kabul, Laboratory equipments and sports goods for schools in Nimroz Province, books to Kandahar and Khost universities, and training of teachers.
- Supply of 105 vehicles to Kabul Municipality by Eicher, Tata and BEML
- Construction of 32 deep wells in Herat province and additional 18 are being drilled
- Supply of 67 tons of vegetable seeds to the Ministry of Agriculture
- Solar electrification of Teachers Training Centre at Signan, Badakhshan province
- Restoration/ augmentation of TV hardware in Jalalabad and Nangarhar Province including setting up of a TV studio, a TV transmitter, a Mobile TV satellite uplink and five TV relay centres
- Supply of 20000 Desk-cum-Benches for schools in Afghanistan through Ministry of Education
- Supply of equipment for digitizing of negatives at Bhaktar News Agency
- Supply of 1000 Sewing machines

Some of the projects, which are new, ongoing or will be completed in the near future include:

- Rehabilitation of Amir Ghazi, Quargah Reservoir Dam
- Multidisciplinary projects to wean away poppy cultivators in Nangarhar province
- Adoption of 100 villages for solar lighting
- Expansion of TV coverage to 22 provinces in Afghanistan
- Construction of additional cold storage facilities in Afghanistan
- Supply of 30000 Desk-cum-Benches to schools in Nangarhar province
- Setting up of a Centre for Skill Building Initiative in Kabul

- Setting up of five Toilet complexes in Afghanistan by Sulabh International
- Supply of 10 Ambulances
- Technical assistance to the Women's Vocational Training Centre in Bagh-e-Zanana, Kabul
- Setting up of 11 multipurpose Community Tele-centre
- Supply of equipment to Kabul Times Newspaper
- Contribution for Border Management of Afghan Police
- Annual contribution of US $ 200,000 for five years to Afghan Reconstruction Trust Fund

SCHOLARSHIPS TO AFGHAN NATIONALS

India is providing annually 500 ICCR scholarships to Afghan students for University courses and 500 short-term ITEC scholarships to Afghan government officials for professional and specialized courses.

VISA REGULATIONS

Indian nationals require visa to travel to Afghanistan. The visa can be obtained from Afghan Embassies without any visa fee.

AIRLINKS WITH INDIA

Indian Airlines, Ariana Afghan Airlines and Kam Air operate commercial flights on Delhi-Kabul-Delhi sector. Indian Airlines operate four times a week, Ariana Afghan Airlines twice a week and Kam Air three times a week.

BIBLIOGRAPHY

Abu-l-Fazl (1972-1973) *The Akbar Nama*, 3 volumes tr. Delhi: H. Beveridge.

Agoncillo, Teodoro A. and Milagros C. Guerrero (1977) *History of the Filipino People*, Quezon City.

Andaya, Barbara Watson and Leonard Y. Andaya (2001) *A History of Malaysia* Honolulu.

Andaya, Leonard Y. (1975) *The Kingdom of Johor 1641-1728*, Kuala Lumpur.

Gregory L. Possehl (ed.) (1979) *Ancient Cities of the Indus*, Durham.

Apte, V. M. (1954) *Social and Religious Life in the Grihya Sutras*, Bombay.

Arnold, Edwin (1969) *The Light of Asia*, Wheaton.

Barwise, J. M. and N. J. White (2002) *A Traveller's History of Southeast Asia*, New York.

Nicholas, Tarling (ed.) (1992) *The Cambridge History of Southeast Asia*, 2 vols. Cambridge.

Chakrabongse, Chula (1967) Lords *of Life: A History of the Kings of Thailand*, London.

Chandler, David (1996) A *History of Cambodia*, Boulder.

Chandler, David P. *et al*, (1987) *In Search of Southeast Asia: A Modern History*. Honolulu.

Chapuis, Oscar (1995) *A History of Vietnam from Hong Bang to Tu Duc*, Westport.

Basham, A. L. (1954) *The Wonder That Was India*, New York.

Bhattacharji, Sukumari (1984) Literature *in the Vedic Age*, 2 vols. Calcutta.

Warren, H.C. (1896) *Buddhism in Translations* tr. New York.

Goddard, Dwight (ed.) (1938) A *Buddhist Bible*, Thetford.

Burgess, James (1913) *The Chronology of Modern India*, Edinburgh.

Rapson, E.J. (ed.) (1922) The *Cambridge History of India, vol. 1: Ancient India*, Cambridge.

Majumdar, R.C. (ed.) (1954) The Classical *Age*, Bombay.

Sastri Nilkantha, K.A. (ed.) (1957) A *Comprehensive History of India, vol. 2: The Mauryas & Satavahanas 325 B.C.-A.D.* Bombay.

Banerjee, A.C. and D.K. Ghosh (ed.) (1978) A *Comprehensive History of India, vol. 9: (1712-1772)*, New Delhi.

Datta, K.K. and V.A. Narain (ed.) (1985) A *Comprehensive History of India, vol. 11: (1818-1858)*, New Delhi.

Coomeraswamy, Ananda K. (1928) *Buddha and the Gospel of Buddhism*, London.

Chatterji, Suniti Kumar (ed.) (1958) The *Cultural Heritage of India, vol. 1: The Early Phases*, Calcutta.

Bhattacharyya, Haridas (ed.) (1956) The *Cultural Heritage of India, vol. 4: The Religions,* Calcutta.

Cunningham, Joseph Davey (1915) *A History of the Sikhs*, Delhi.

Dasgupta, Surendranath, (1922) *A History of Indian Philosophy*, vols.1 and 2. Delhi.

De Silva, Chandra Richard (1997) Sri *Lanka: A History*, New Delhi.

De Silva, K. M. (1981) *A History of Sri Lanka*, London.

Dunn, Ross E. (1986) *The Adventures of Ibn Battuta*,Berkeley.

Dutt, Romesh Chunder (1981) A *History of Civilization in Ancient India*, Calcutta.

Edwardes, Michael (1967) *British India 1772-1947*, New York.

Eliade, Mircea (1969) *Yoga Immortality and Freedom* tr. Princeton.

Geiger, Wilhelm (1960) *Culture of Ceylon in Medieval Times*, Wiesbaden.

Anderson, G.L. (ed.) (1966) The *Genius of the Oriental Theater*, New York.

Ghoshal, U. N. (1966) A *History of Indian Political Ideas*, London.

Ghosh, Manomohan (1968) *A History of Cambodia*, Calcutta.

Hall, D. G. E. (1981) *A History of South-East Asia*, New York.

James, Lawrence (1998) *Raj: The Making and Unmaking of British India*, New York.

Kautilya, *Arthasastra* (1915) tr. Mysore: R. Shamasastry.

John Bastin and Robin W. Winks (ed.) (1966) *Malaysia: Selected Historical Readings*, London.

Manich, M. L. (1970) *History of Anglo-Thai Relations*, Bangkok.

Manich, M. L. (1967) *History of Laos (including the history of Lannathai, Chiengmai)* Bangkok.

Manich, M. L. (1970) *History of Thailand & Cambodia*, Bangkok.

Marsden, William (1966) *The History of Sumatra*, New York.

Molina, Antonio M. (1960) *The Philippines Through the Centuries*, vol. 1, Manila.

Morga, Antonio de (1907) *History of the Philippines*, 2 volumes. Cleveland.

Moorhead, F. J. (1957) *A History of Malaya and Her Neighbors*, Volume 1. London.

Moorhead, F. J. (1963) *A History of Malaya*, Volume 2. Kuala Lumpur.

Myint-U, Thant (2001) *The Making of Modern Burma*, Cambridge.

Kennedy, J. (1970) *A History of Malaya*, London.

Koenig, William J. (1990) *The Burmese Polity, 1752-1819*, Ann Arbor.

Lieberman, Victor (2003) *Strange Parallels Southeast Asia in Global Context, c. 800-1830*. Cambridge.

Majumdar, R. C. *et al.* (1960) *An Advanced History of India*, London.

Malik, Hafeez (1980) *Sir Sayyid Ahmad Khan and Muslim Modernization in India and Pakistan*, New York.

Mill, James and Horace Hayman Wilson (1848) *The History of British India*, 9 volumes. London.

Moon, Penderel (1989) *The British Conquest and Dominion of India*, London.

Nguyen-Van-Thai and Nguyen-Van-Mung (1958) *A Short History of Vietnam*,Saigon.

Percival Spear, (ed.) (1958), The *Oxford History of India* Oxford.

Radhakrishnan, S. (1931) *Indian Philosophy*, vol. 2. London.

Rawson, Philip (1967) *The Art of Southeast Asia*, New York.

Reid, Anthony (1988) *Southeast Asia in the Age of Commerce 1450-1680, vol. 1: The Lands below the Winds*. New Haven.

Reid, Anthony (1993) *Southeast Asia in the Age of Commerce 1450-1680, vol. 2: Expansion and Crisis*, New Haven.

Ricklefs, M. C. (1993) *A History of Modern Indonesia since c. 1300*. Stanford.

Sanwal, B. D. (1965) *Nepal and the East India Company*, New York.

Sar Desai, D. R. (1997) *Southeast Asia: Past & Present*, Boulder.

Sastri Nilkantha, K.A. (ed.) (1967) Age of the Nandas and Mauryas, Delhi.

Marr David G. and A. C. Milner (ed.) (1986) *Southeast Asia in the 9th to 14th Centuries* Singapore.

Patricia Herbert and Anthony Milner (ed.) (1989) *Southeast Asia: Languages and Literatures*, Honolulu.

Shakabpa, Tsepon W. D. (1967) *Tibet: A Political History*, New Haven.

Smith, Vincent A., J. B. Harrison, and Percival Spear (1958) *The Oxford History of India*, Oxford.

Stein, R. A. (1972) *Tibetan Civilization* tr. J. E. S. Driver. Stanford.

Tate, D. J. M. (1971) *The Making of Modern South-east Asia, vol. 1: The European Conquest*, New York.

Taylor, Jean Gelman (2003) *Indonesia: Peoples and Histories*, New Haven.

Thapar, Romila (1978) *Ancient Indian Social History*, New Delhi.

Thapar, Romila (1966) *A History of India*, vol.1. Baltimore.

Vlekke, Bernard H. M. (1959) *Nusantara: A History of Indonesia*, Chicago.

Williams, Lea E. (1976) *Southeast Asia: A History*, New York.

Winstedt, Richard (1961) *A History of Classical Malay Literature*, Kuala Lumpur.

Wood, W. A. R. (1933) *A History of Siam from the Earliest Times to the Year A.D. 1781*, Bangkok.

Wyatt, David K.(2003) *Thailand: A Short History*, New Haven.

Walker, Benjamin (1968) *The Hindu World*, 2 vols. New York.

Lin Yutang (ed.) (1942) The *Wisdom of China and India*, New York.

Woodruff, Philip (1953) *The Men Who Ruled India, vol. 1: The Founders*. London.

Woodruff, Philip (1954) *The Men Who Ruled India, vol. 2: The Guardians*. New York.

Zuñiga, Joaquin Martinez de (1966) *An Historical View of the Philippine Islands* tr. John Maver, Manila.

INDEX